*It's starting!

This is my third series to be collected into graphic novels. Forgive me if this sounds reckless, but the thing I prioritize most when drawing manga is creating something that I can enjoy. This one might not remain popular, but for now, I'll just be happy if everyone finds it as fun as I do.

KOHEI HORIKOSHI

1

SHONEN JUMP Manga Edition

STORY & ART **KOHEI HORIKOSHI**

TRANSLATION & ENGLISH ADAPTATION **Caleb Cook**
TOUCH-UP ART & LETTERING **John Hunt**
DESIGNER **Shawn Carrico**
EDITOR **Mike Montesa**

BOKU NO HERO ACADEMIA © 2014 by Kohei Horikoshi
All rights reserved.
First published in Japan in 2014 by SHUEISHA Inc., Tokyo.
English translation rights arranged by SHUEISHA Inc.

Printed in the U.S.A.

Published by VIZ Media, LLC
P.O. Box 77010
San Francisco, CA 94107

10 9 8
First printing, August 2015
Eighth printing, October 2018

VIZ MEDIA
viz.com

shonenjump.com

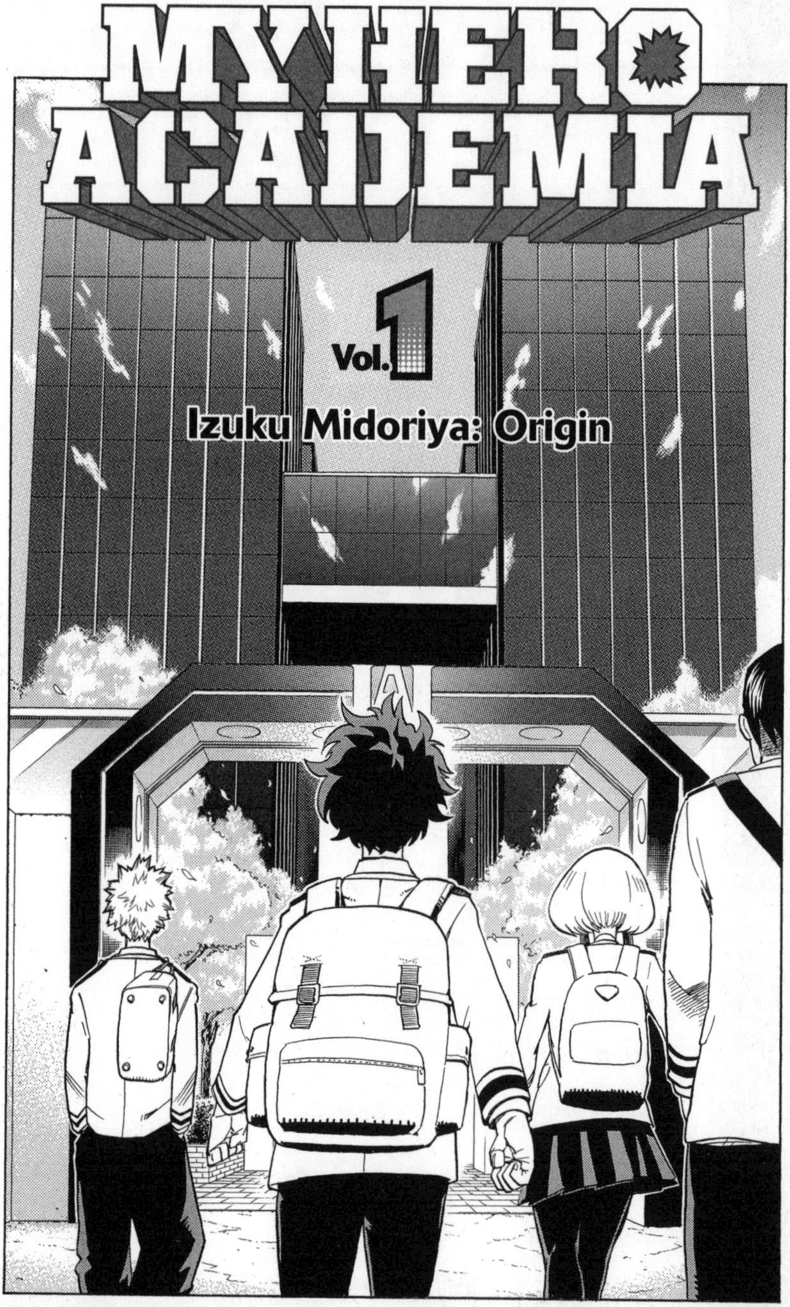
MY HERO ACADEMIA
Vol. 1
Izuku Midoriya: Origin

KOHEI HORIKOSHI

SHONENJUMP MANGA

MY HERO ACADEMIA

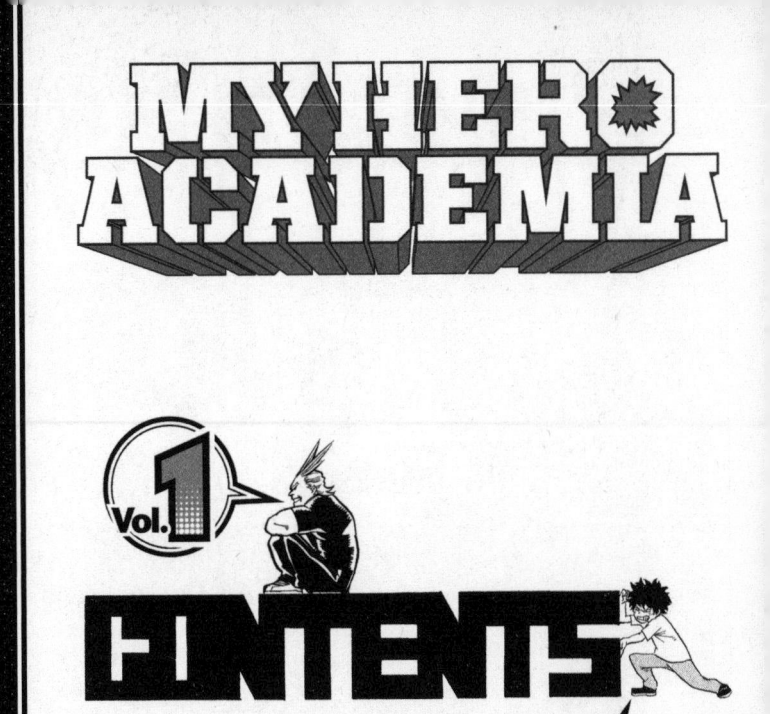

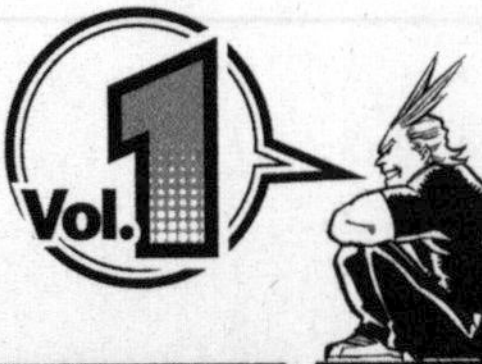
Vol.1

CONTENTS

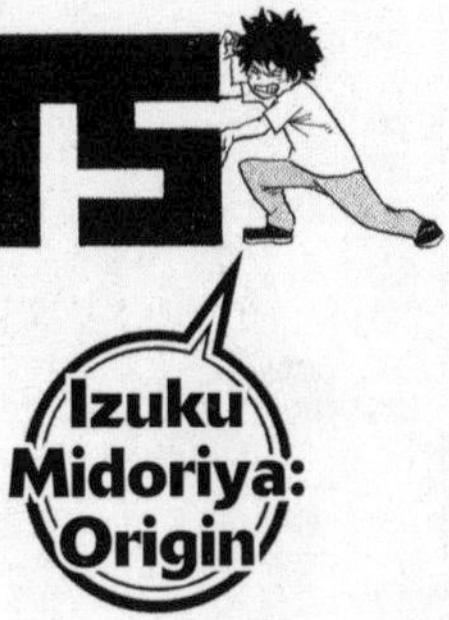
Izuku Midoriya: Origin

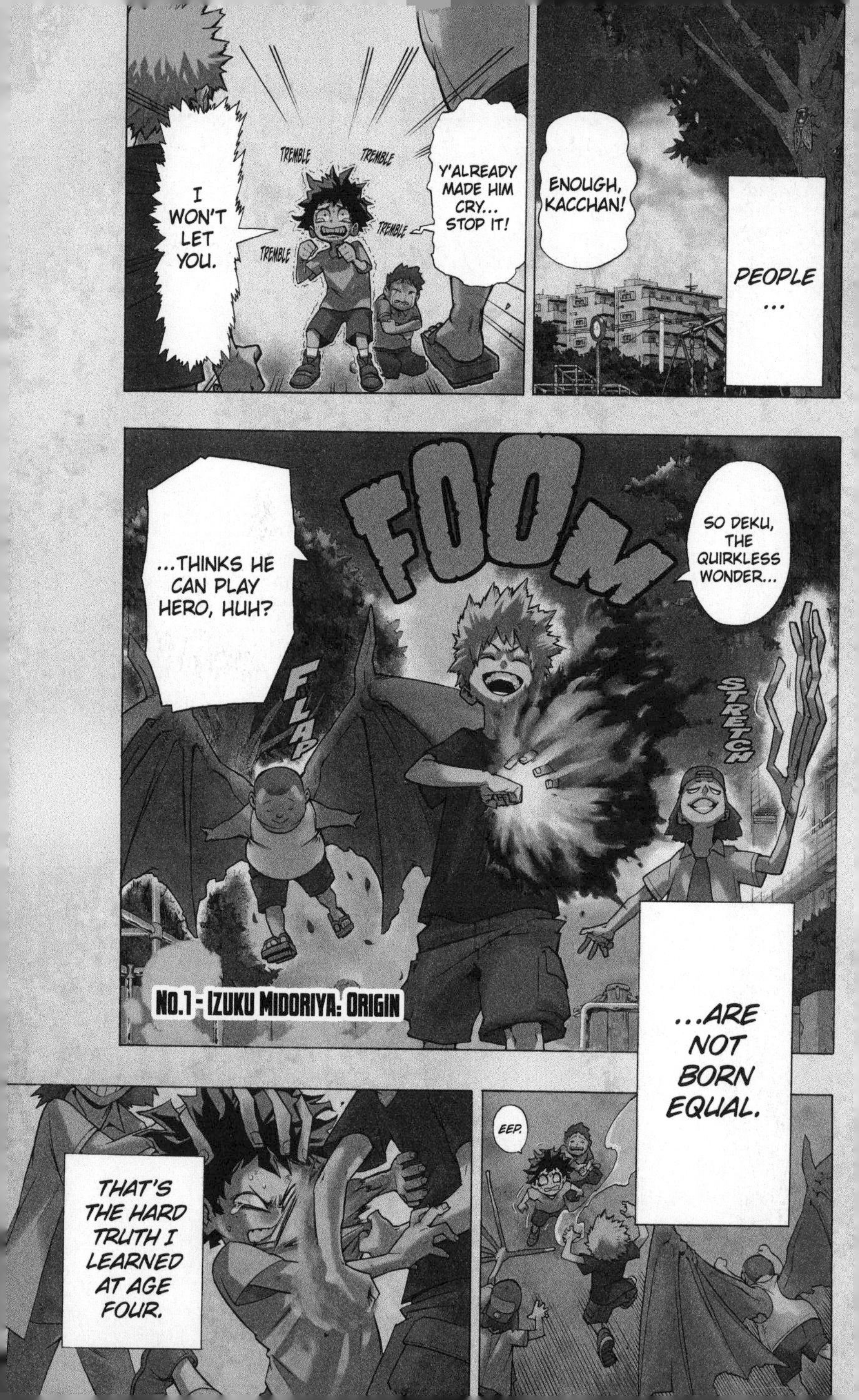
PEOPLE
...
ENOUGH, KACCHAN!
Y'ALREADY MADE HIM CRY... STOP IT!
TREMBLE
TREMBLE
TREMBLE
TREMBLE
I WON'T LET YOU.
SO DEKU, THE QUIRKLESS WONDER...
FOOM
...THINKS HE CAN PLAY HERO, HUH?
STRETCH
FLAP
NO.1 - IZUKU MIDORIYA: ORIGIN
...ARE NOT BORN EQUAL.
EEP.
THAT'S THE HARD TRUTH I LEARNED AT AGE FOUR.

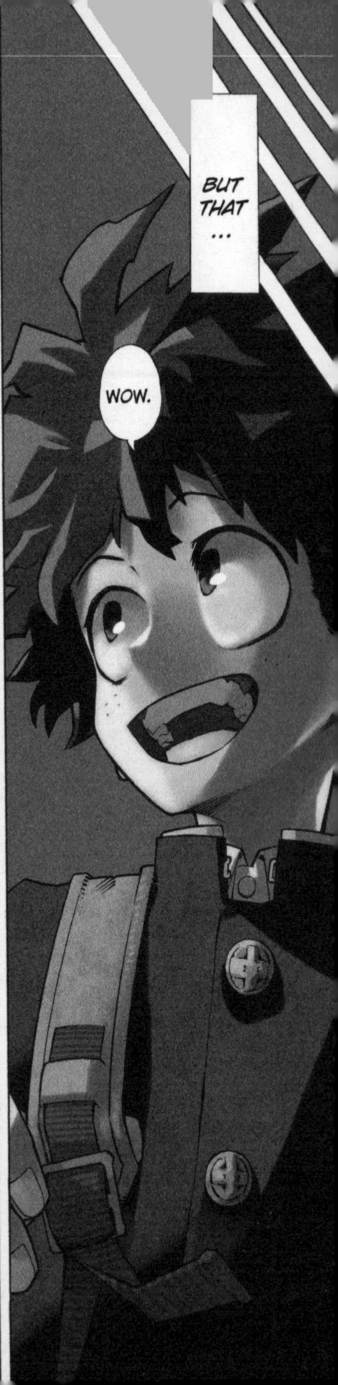
BUT THAT ...
WOW.
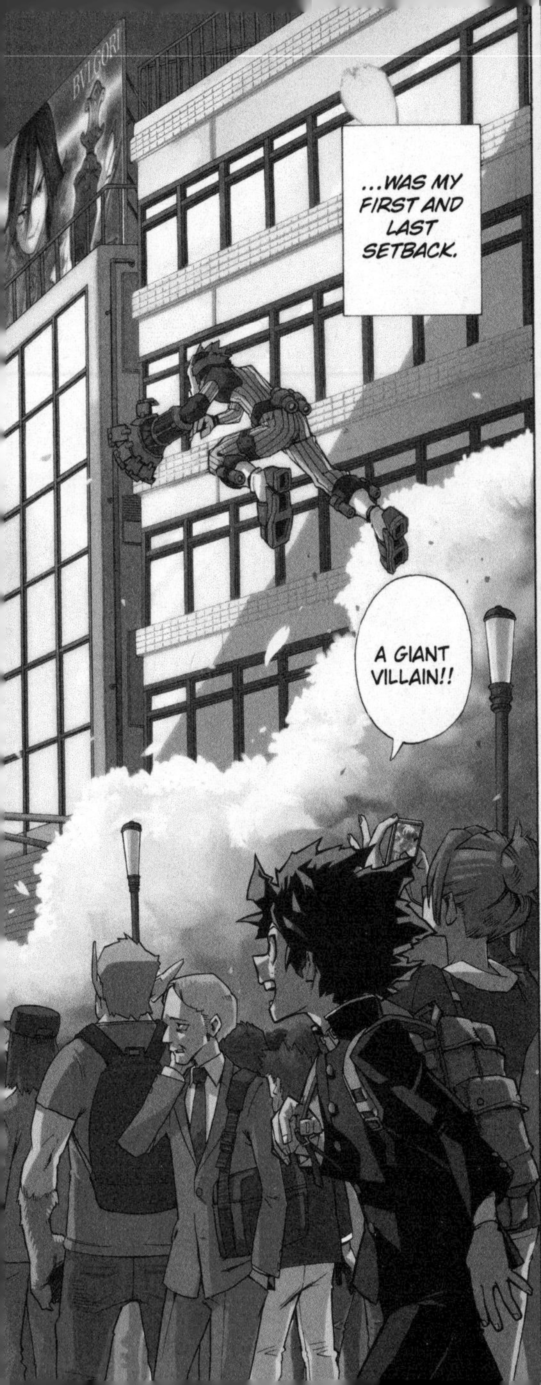
...WAS MY FIRST AND LAST SETBACK.
A GIANT VILLAIN!!
BVLGARI

NO.1 - IZUKU MIDORIYA: ORIGIN

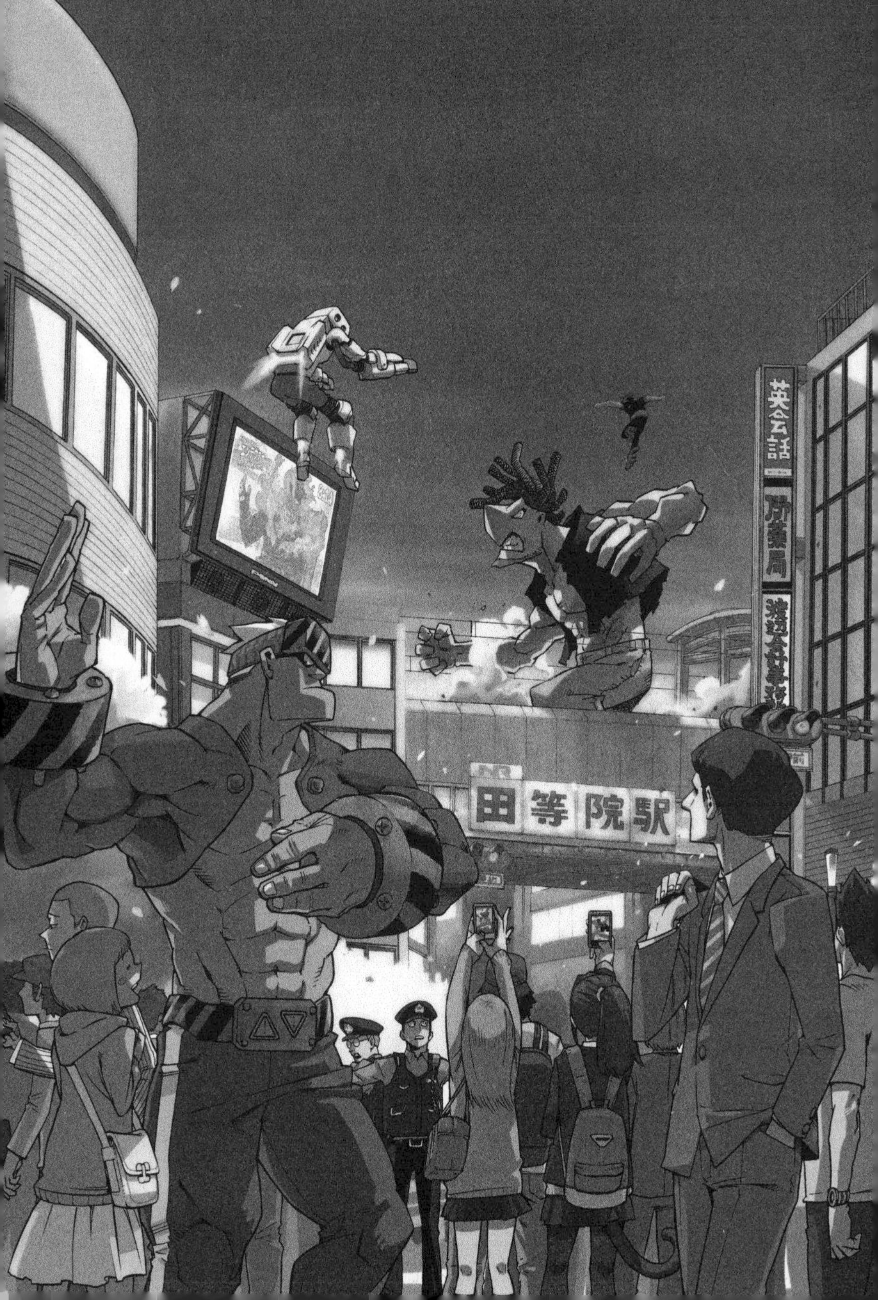
英会話
田等院駅

MY HERO ACADEMIA

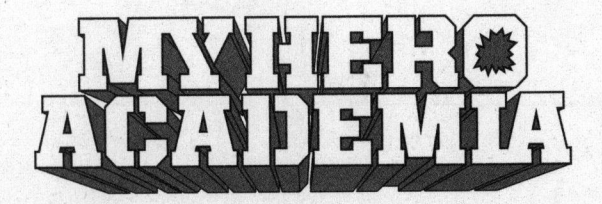

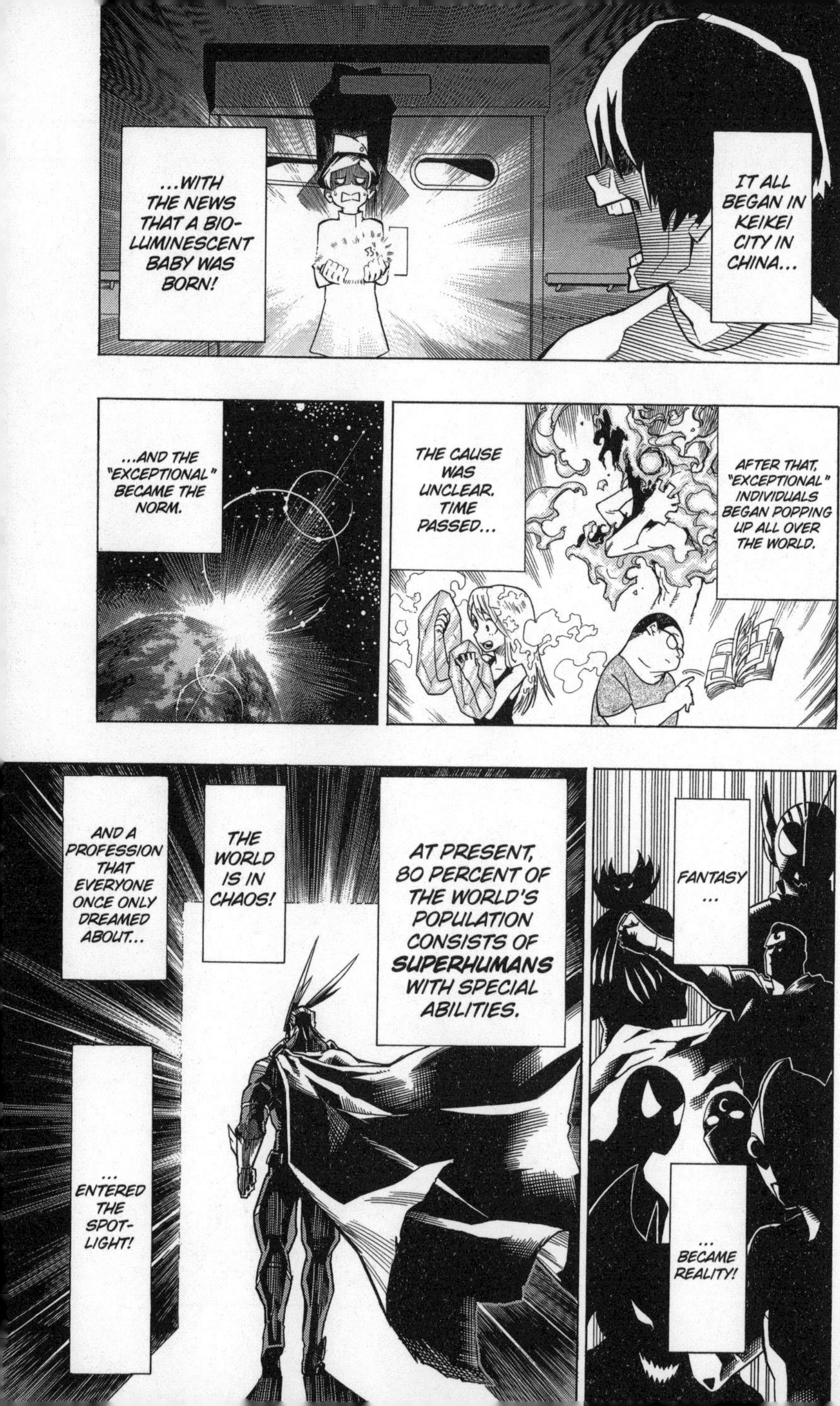
IT ALL BEGAN IN KEIKEI CITY IN CHINA...
...WITH THE NEWS THAT A BIO-LUMINESCENT BABY WAS BORN!
AFTER THAT, "EXCEPTIONAL" INDIVIDUALS BEGAN POPPING UP ALL OVER THE WORLD.
THE CAUSE WAS UNCLEAR. TIME PASSED...
...AND THE "EXCEPTIONAL" BECAME THE NORM.
FANTASY ...
... BECAME REALITY!
AT PRESENT, 80 PERCENT OF THE WORLD'S POPULATION CONSISTS OF **SUPERHUMANS** WITH SPECIAL ABILITIES.
THE WORLD IS IN CHAOS!
AND A PROFESSION THAT EVERYONE ONCE ONLY DREAMED ABOUT...
... ENTERED THE SPOT-LIGHT!

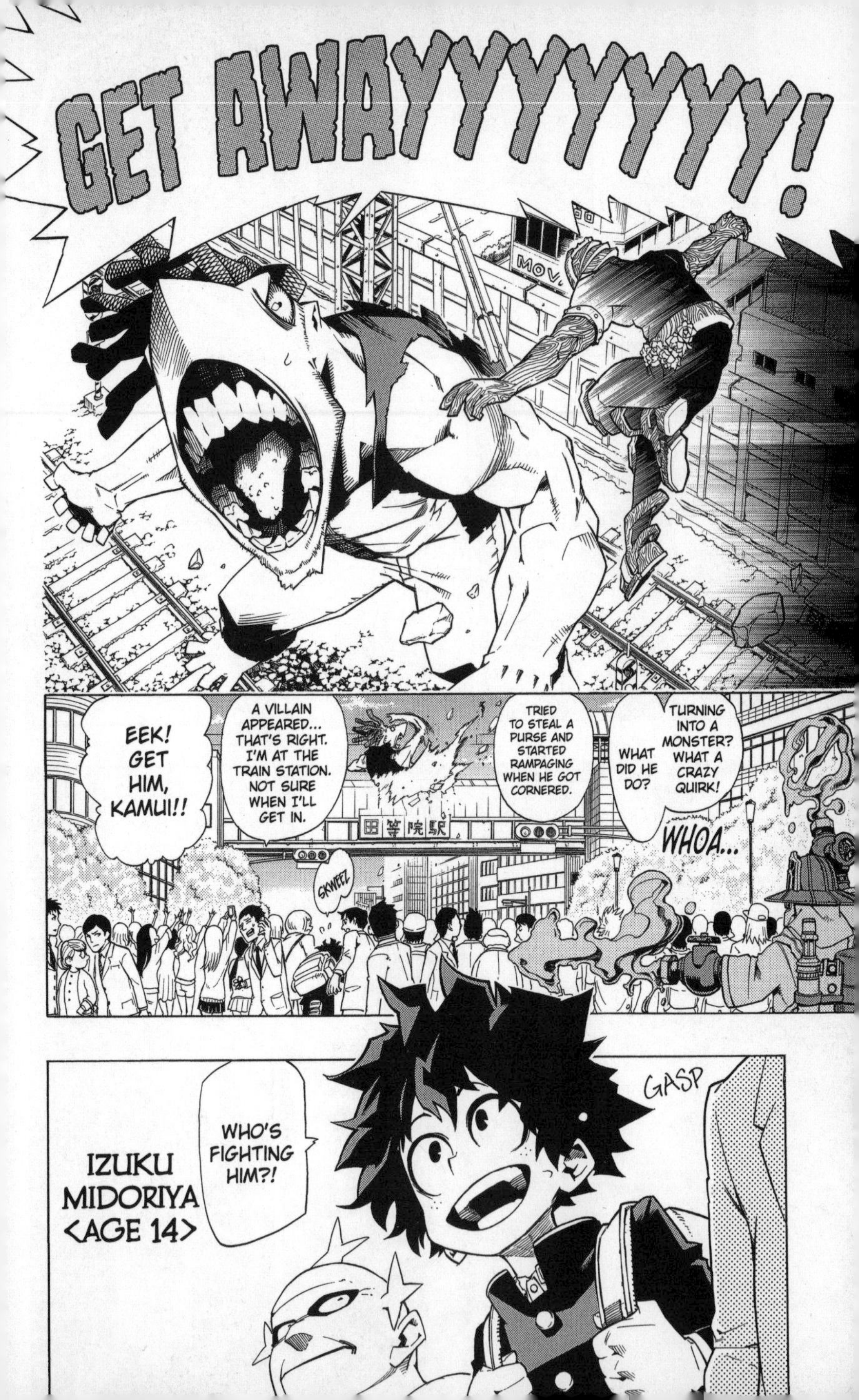
GET AWAYYYYYYY!
TURNING INTO A MONSTER? WHAT A CRAZY QUIRK!
WHAT DID HE DO?
WHOA...
TRIED TO STEAL A PURSE AND STARTED RAMPAGING WHEN HE GOT CORNERED.
A VILLAIN APPEARED... THAT'S RIGHT. I'M AT THE TRAIN STATION. NOT SURE WHEN I'LL GET IN.
EEK! GET HIM, KAMUI!!
田等院駅
SKWEEL
GASP
WHO'S FIGHTING HIM?!
IZUKU MIDORIYA <AGE 14>

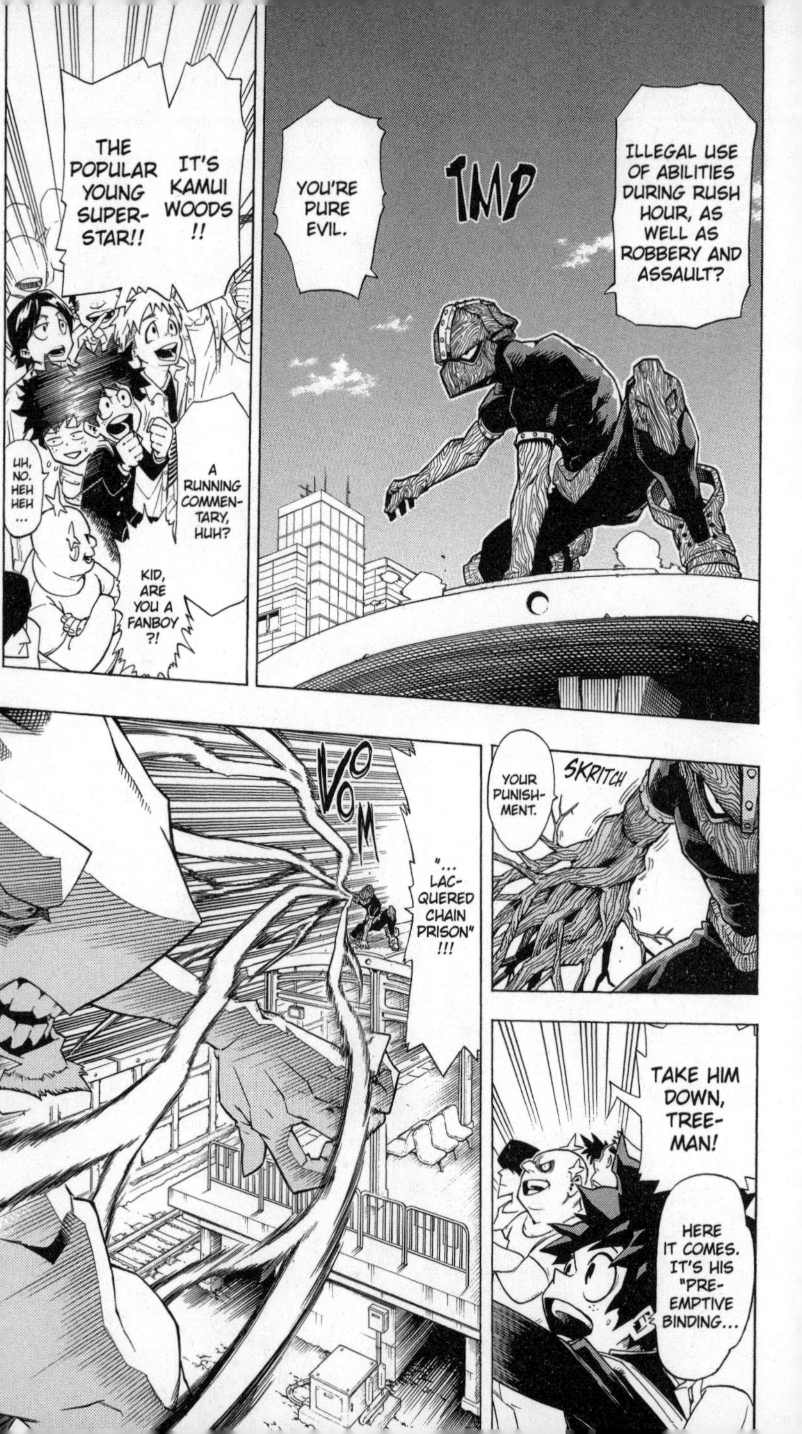
ILLEGAL USE OF ABILITIES DURING RUSH HOUR, AS WELL AS ROBBERY AND ASSAULT?
TMP
YOU'RE PURE EVIL.
IT'S KAMUI WOODS!!
THE POPULAR YOUNG SUPER-STAR!!
A RUNNING COMMEN-TARY, HUH?
KID, ARE YOU A FANBOY?!
UH, NO. HEH HEH...
SKRITCH
YOUR PUNISH-MENT.
TAKE HIM DOWN, TREE-MAN!
HERE IT COMES. IT'S HIS "PRE-EMPTIVE BINDING...
VOOM
"...LAC-QUERED CHAIN PRISON"!!!

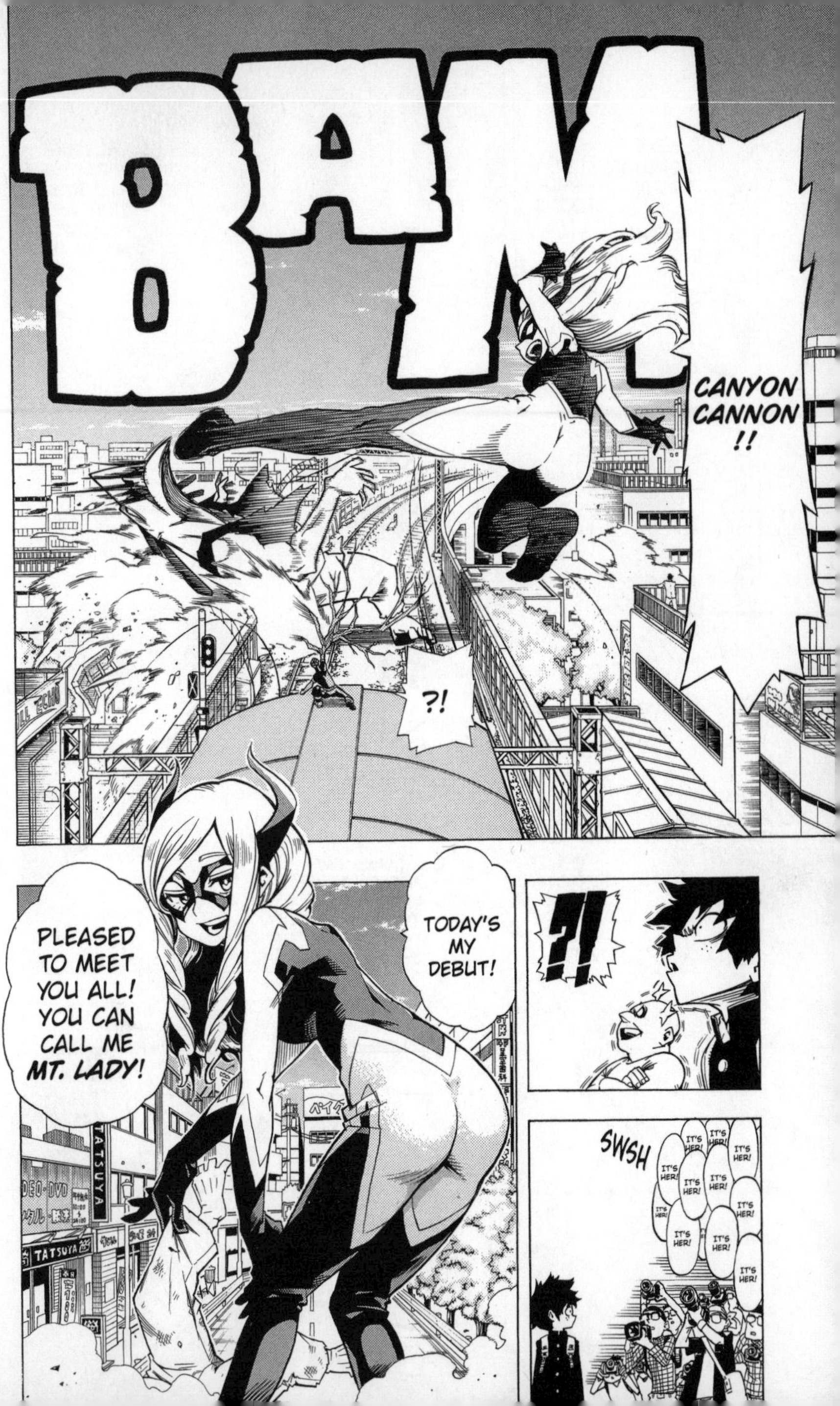
BAM
CANYON CANNON !!
?!
?!
SWSH
IT'S HER!
IT'S HER!
IT'S HER!
IT'S HER!
IT'S HER!
IT'S HER!
IT'S HER!
IT'S HER!
IT'S HER!
IT'S HER!
IT'S HER!
TODAY'S MY DEBUT!
PLEASED TO MEET YOU ALL! YOU CAN CALL ME MT. LADY!

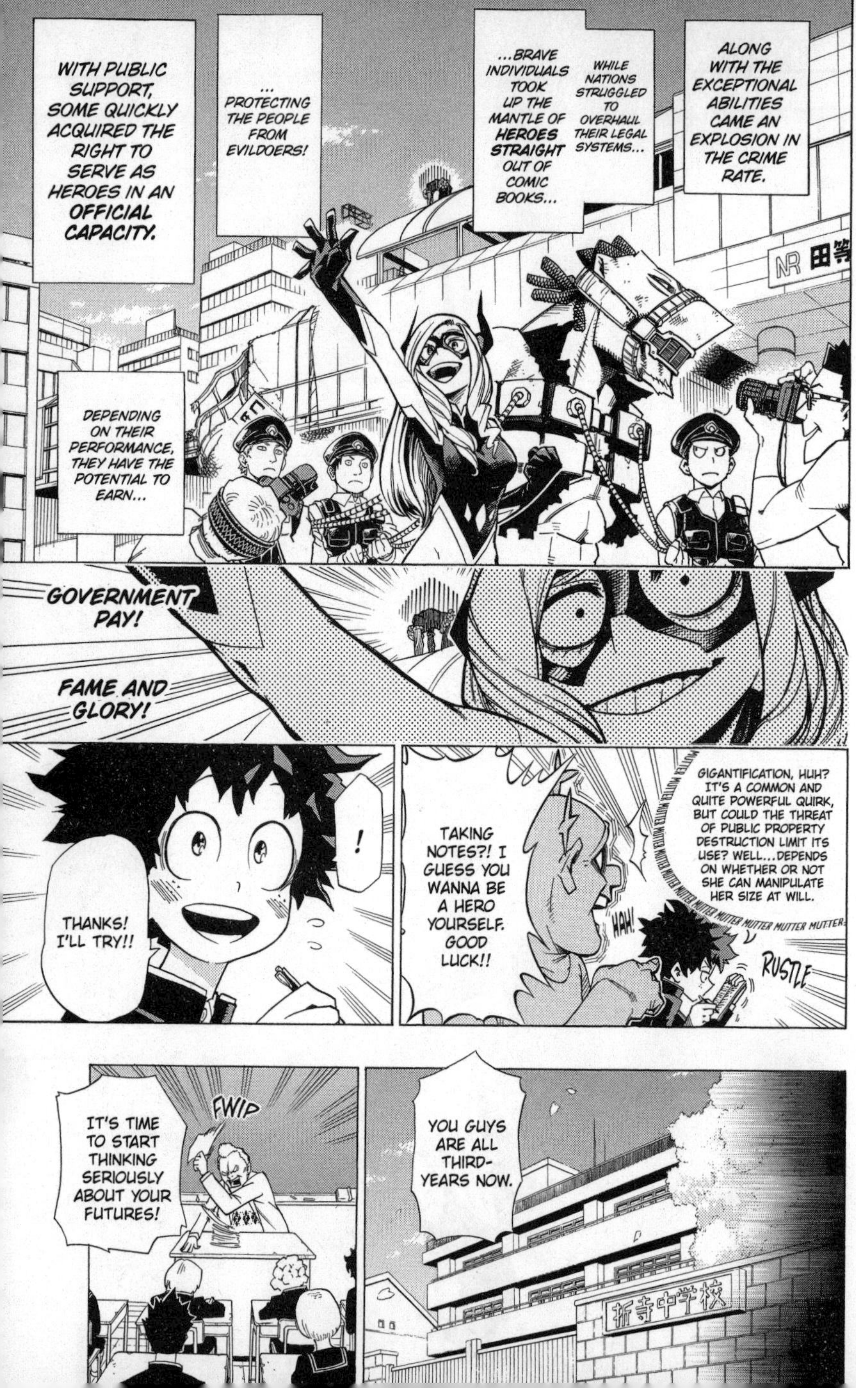
ALONG WITH THE EXCEPTIONAL ABILITIES CAME AN EXPLOSION IN THE CRIME RATE.
WHILE NATIONS STRUGGLED TO OVERHAUL THEIR LEGAL SYSTEMS...
...BRAVE INDIVIDUALS TOOK UP THE MANTLE OF HEROES STRAIGHT OUT OF COMIC BOOKS...
...PROTECTING THE PEOPLE FROM EVILDOERS!
WITH PUBLIC SUPPORT, SOME QUICKLY ACQUIRED THE RIGHT TO SERVE AS HEROES IN AN OFFICIAL CAPACITY.
DEPENDING ON THEIR PERFORMANCE, THEY HAVE THE POTENTIAL TO EARN...
GOVERNMENT PAY!
FAME AND GLORY!
GIGANTIFICATION, HUH? IT'S A COMMON AND QUITE POWERFUL QUIRK, BUT COULD THE THREAT OF PUBLIC PROPERTY DESTRUCTION LIMIT ITS USE? WELL...DEPENDS ON WHETHER OR NOT SHE CAN MANIPULATE HER SIZE AT WILL.
MUTTER MUTTER MUTTER MUTTER MUTTER MUTTER MUTTER MUTTER MUTTER MUTTER
TAKING NOTES?! I GUESS YOU WANNA BE A HERO YOURSELF. GOOD LUCK!!
HAH!
RUSTLE
!
THANKS! I'LL TRY!!
YOU GUYS ARE ALL THIRD-YEARS NOW.
折寺中学校
FWIP
IT'S TIME TO START THINKING SERIOUSLY ABOUT YOUR FUTURES!

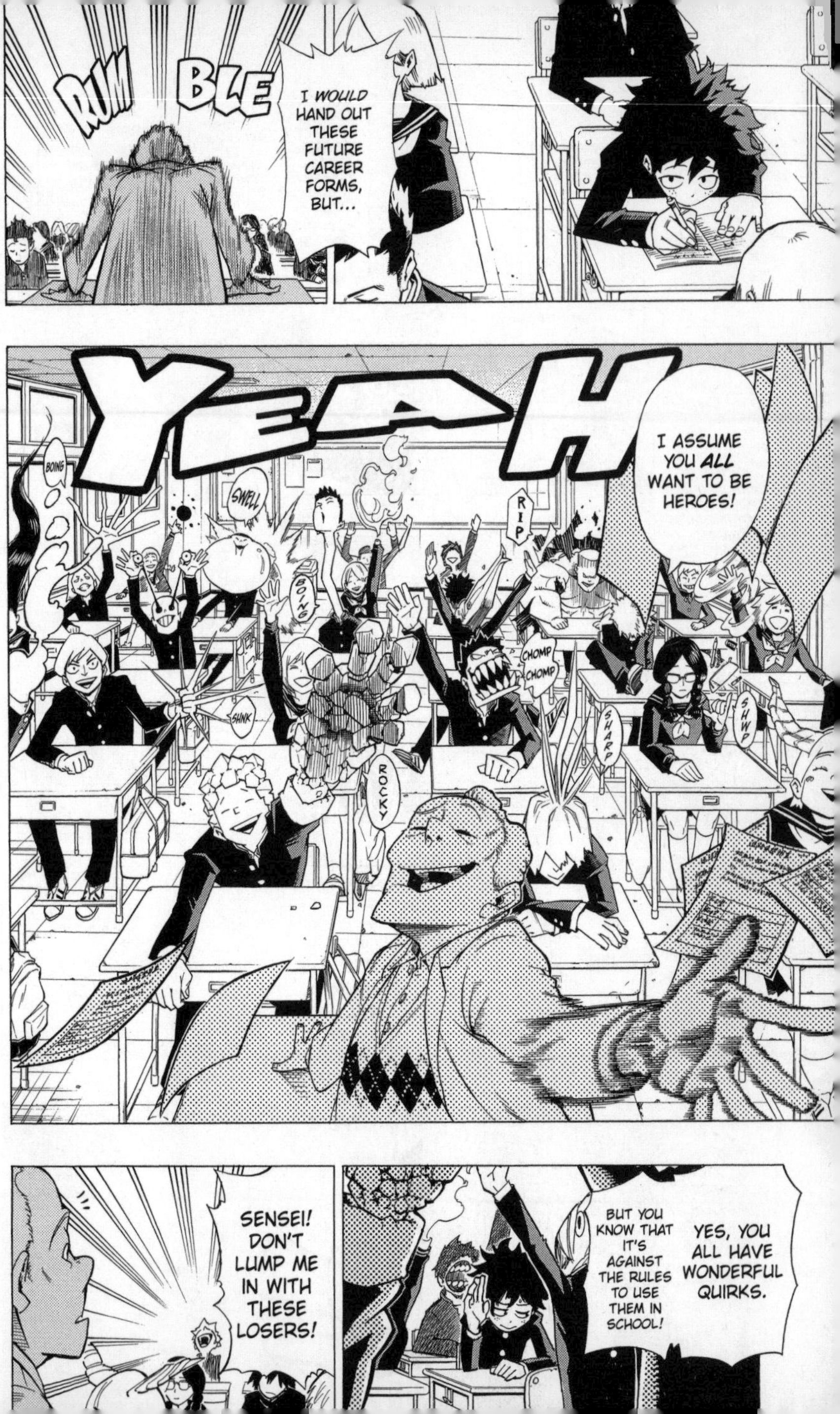
RUMBLE
I WOULD HAND OUT THESE FUTURE CAREER FORMS, BUT...
I ASSUME YOU ALL WANT TO BE HEROES!
YEAH
RIP
SWELL
BOING
BOING
CHOMP CHOMP
SHWP
SHARP
SHNK
ROCKY
YES, YOU ALL HAVE WONDERFUL QUIRKS.
BUT YOU KNOW THAT IT'S AGAINST THE RULES TO USE THEM IN SCHOOL!
SENSEI! DON'T LUMP ME IN WITH THESE LOSERS!

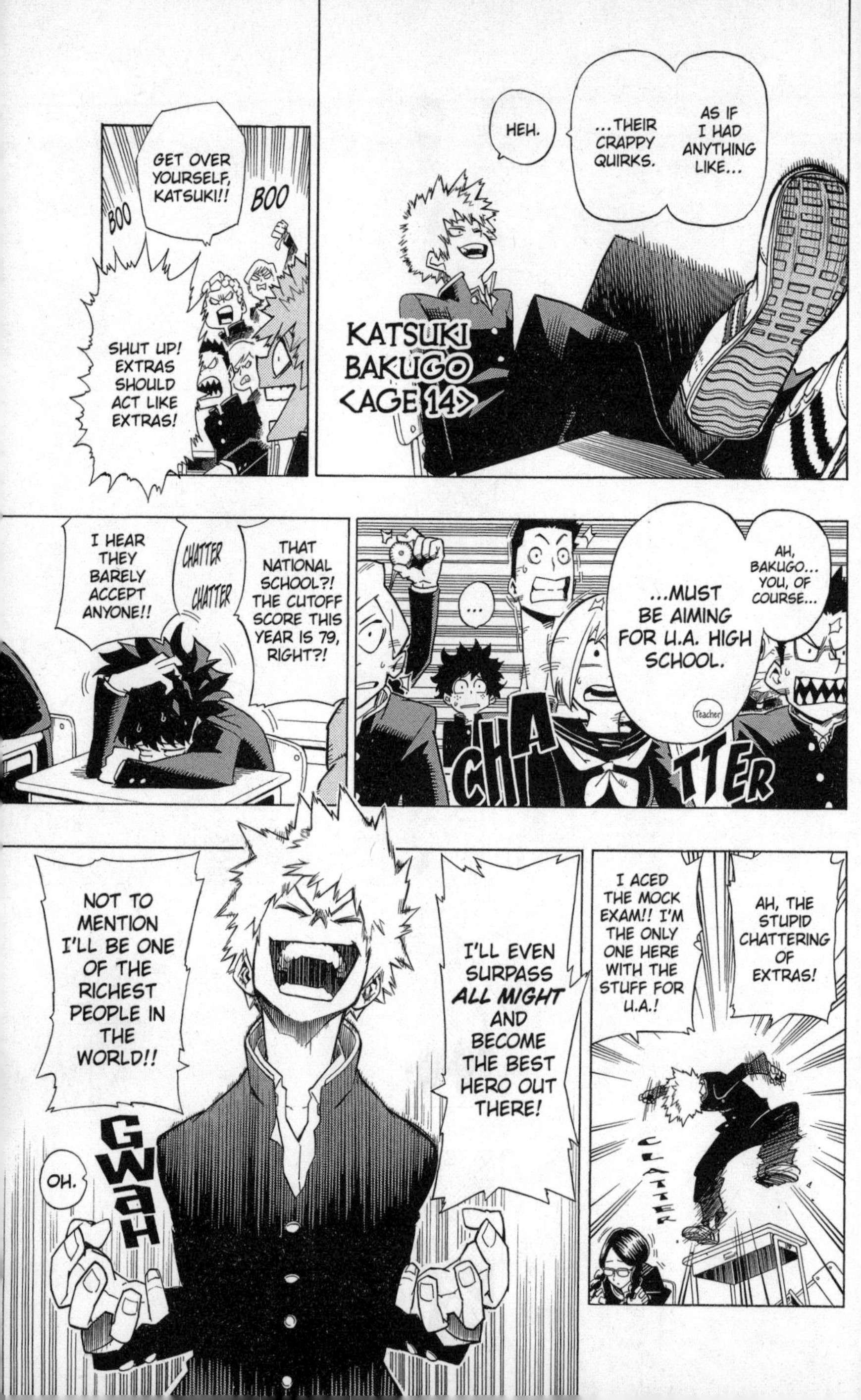
AS IF I HAD ANYTHING LIKE...
...THEIR CRAPPY QUIRKS.
HEH.
KATSUKI BAKUGO <AGE 14>
GET OVER YOURSELF, KATSUKI!!
BOO
BOO
SHUT UP! EXTRAS SHOULD ACT LIKE EXTRAS!
AH, BAKUGO... YOU, OF COURSE...
...MUST BE AIMING FOR U.A. HIGH SCHOOL.
Teacher
...
CHA TTER
THAT NATIONAL SCHOOL?! THE CUTOFF SCORE THIS YEAR IS 79, RIGHT?!
CHATTER
CHATTER
I HEAR THEY BARELY ACCEPT ANYONE!!
AH, THE STUPID CHATTERING OF EXTRAS!
I ACED THE MOCK EXAM!! I'M THE ONLY ONE HERE WITH THE STUFF FOR U.A.!
CLATTER
I'LL EVEN SURPASS ALL MIGHT AND BECOME THE BEST HERO OUT THERE!
NOT TO MENTION I'LL BE ONE OF THE RICHEST PEOPLE IN THE WORLD!!
GWAH
OH.

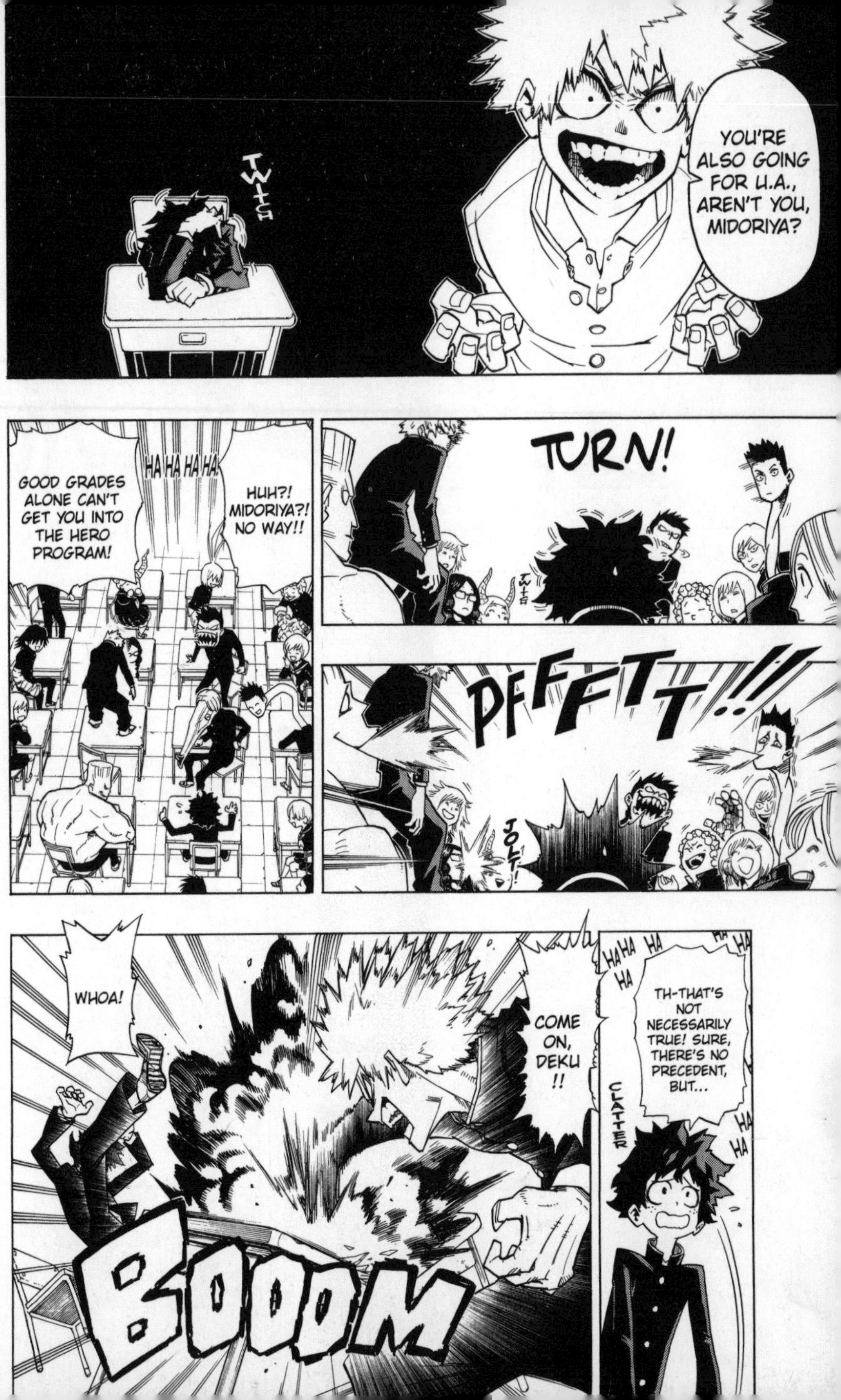
YOU'RE ALSO GOING FOR U.A., AREN'T YOU, MIDORIYA?
TWITCH
TURN!
TWITCH
PFFFTTT!!!
JOLT!
HUH?! MIDORIYA?! NO WAY!!
HA HA HA HA
GOOD GRADES ALONE CAN'T GET YOU INTO THE HERO PROGRAM!
HA HA HA HA HA HA
TH-THAT'S NOT NECESSARILY TRUE! SURE, THERE'S NO PRECEDENT, BUT...
CLATTER
COME ON, DEKU!!
WHOA!
BOOOM

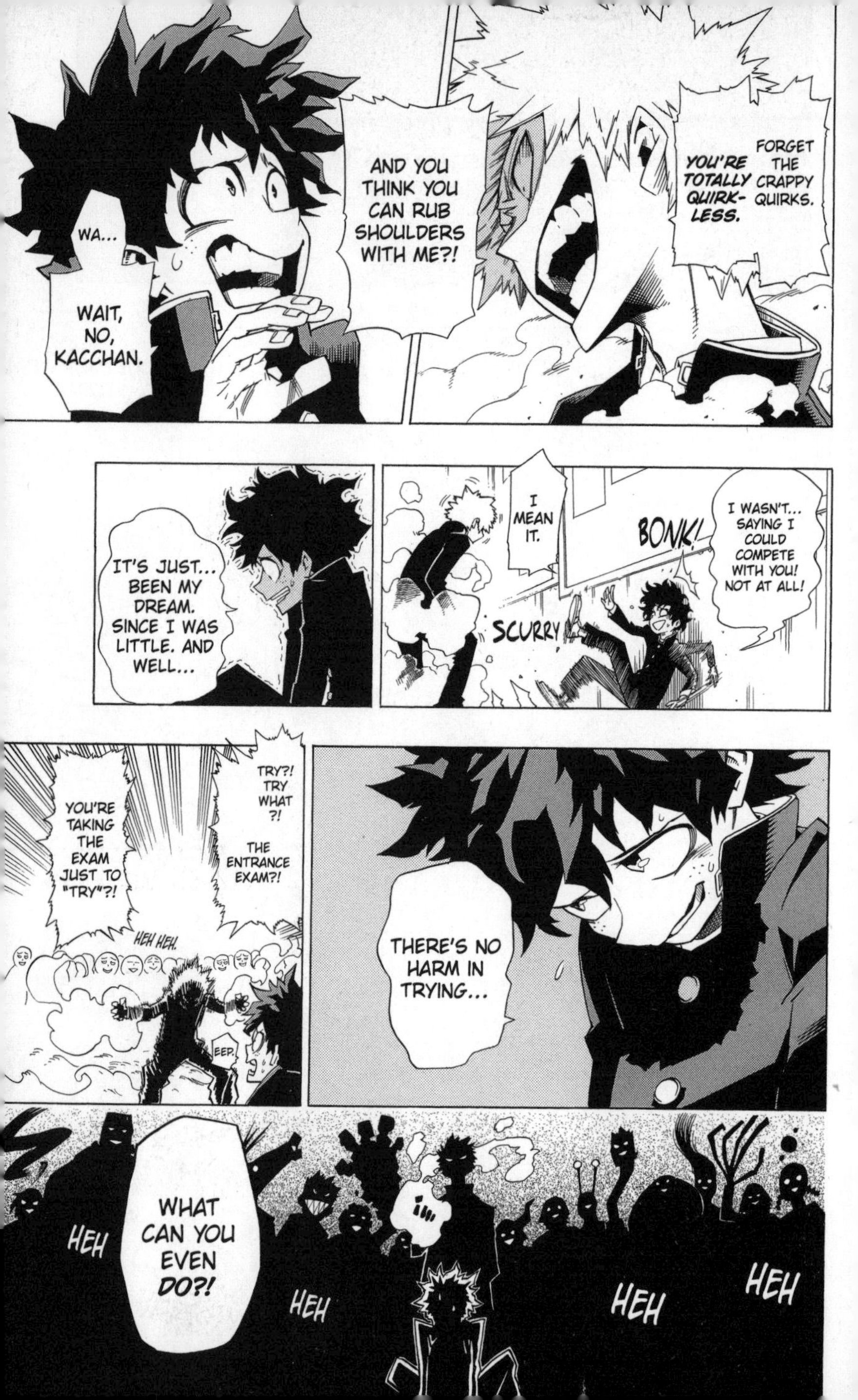
FORGET THE CRAPPY QUIRKS.
YOU'RE TOTALLY QUIRKLESS.
AND YOU THINK YOU CAN RUB SHOULDERS WITH ME?!
WA...
WAIT, NO, KACCHAN.
I WASN'T... SAYING I COULD COMPETE WITH YOU! NOT AT ALL!
BONK!
I MEAN IT.
SCURRY
IT'S JUST... BEEN MY DREAM. SINCE I WAS LITTLE. AND WELL...
THERE'S NO HARM IN TRYING...
TRY?! TRY WHAT?!
THE ENTRANCE EXAM?!
YOU'RE TAKING THE EXAM JUST TO "TRY"?!
HEH HEH.
EEP.
HEH
HEH
WHAT CAN YOU EVEN DO?!
HEH
HEH

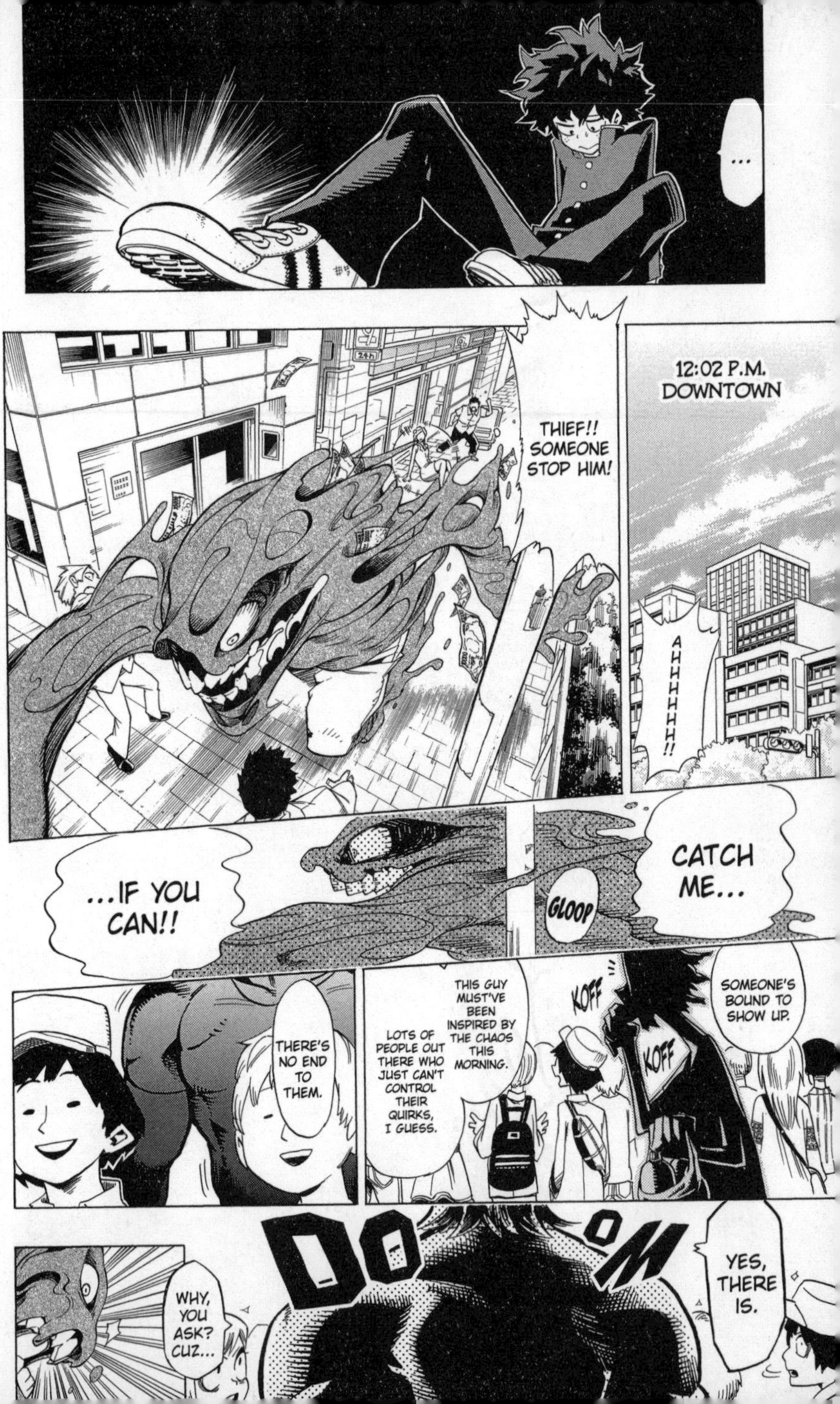
...
12:02 P.M.
DOWNTOWN
AHHHHHH!!
THIEF!! SOMEONE STOP HIM!
CATCH ME...
GLOOP
...IF YOU CAN!!
SOMEONE'S BOUND TO SHOW UP.
KOFF
KOFF
THIS GUY MUST'VE BEEN INSPIRED BY THE CHAOS THIS MORNING.
LOTS OF PEOPLE OUT THERE WHO JUST CAN'T CONTROL THEIR QUIRKS, I GUESS.
THERE'S NO END TO THEM.
YES, THERE IS.
DO-OM
WHY, YOU ASK? CUZ...

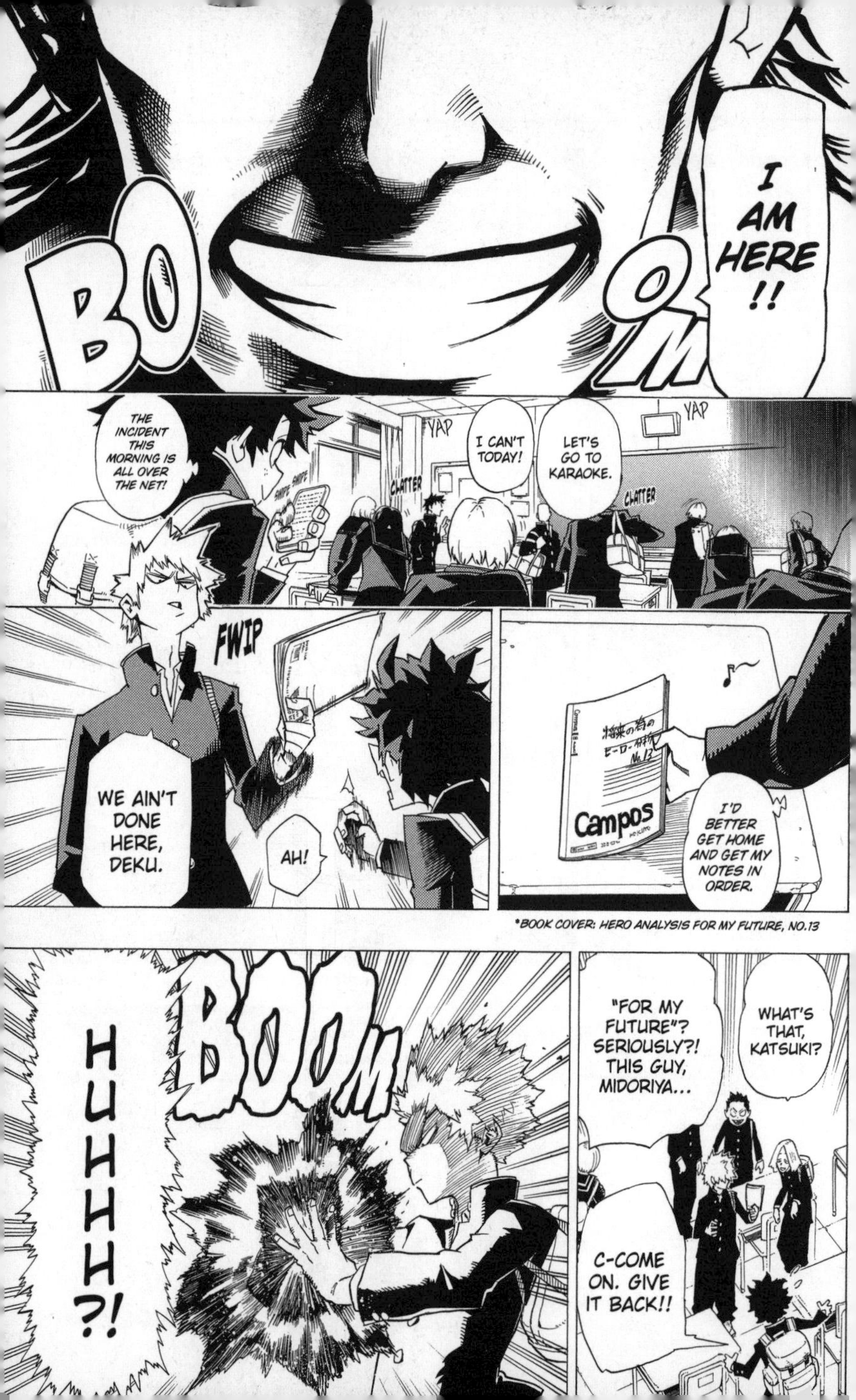
I AM HERE!!
BOOM
YAP
LET'S GO TO KARAOKE.
I CAN'T TODAY!
CLATTER
YAP
CLATTER
THE INCIDENT THIS MORNING IS ALL OVER THE NET!
SWIPE SWIPE
I'D BETTER GET HOME AND GET MY NOTES IN ORDER.
Campos
FWIP
WE AIN'T DONE HERE, DEKU.
AH!
WHAT'S THAT, KATSUKI?
"FOR MY FUTURE"? SERIOUSLY?! THIS GUY, MIDORIYA...
C-COME ON. GIVE IT BACK!!
BOOM
HUHHH?!

*BOOK COVER: HERO ANALYSIS FOR MY FUTURE, NO.13

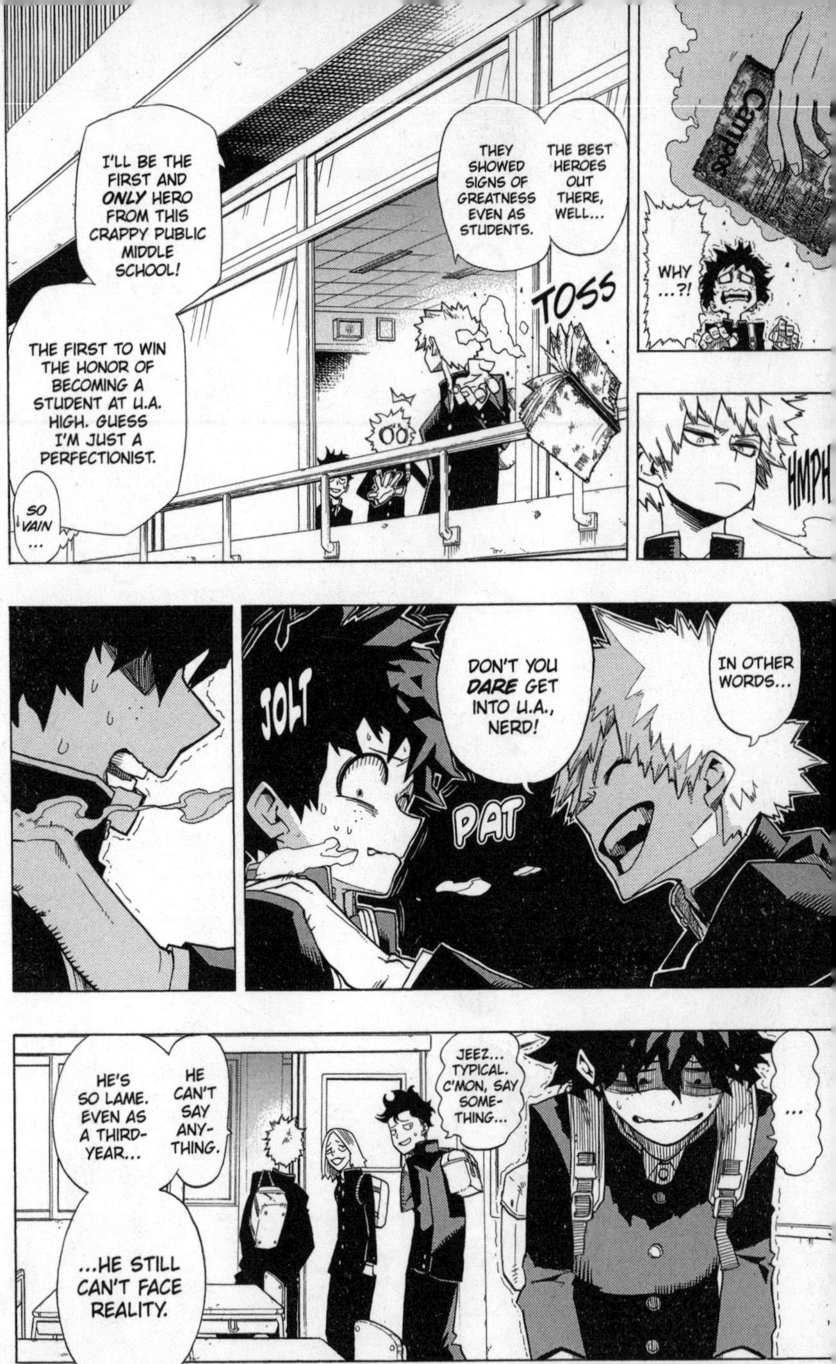
Campus
WHY ...?!
HMPH
THE BEST HEROES OUT THERE, WELL...
THEY SHOWED SIGNS OF GREATNESS EVEN AS STUDENTS.
TOSS
I'LL BE THE FIRST AND ONLY HERO FROM THIS CRAPPY PUBLIC MIDDLE SCHOOL!
THE FIRST TO WIN THE HONOR OF BECOMING A STUDENT AT U.A. HIGH. GUESS I'M JUST A PERFECTIONIST.
SO VAIN ...
IN OTHER WORDS...
DON'T YOU DARE GET INTO U.A., NERD!
PAT
JOLT
...
JEEZ... TYPICAL. C'MON, SAY SOME-THING...
HE CAN'T SAY ANY-THING.
HE'S SO LAME. EVEN AS A THIRD-YEAR...
...HE STILL CAN'T FACE REALITY.

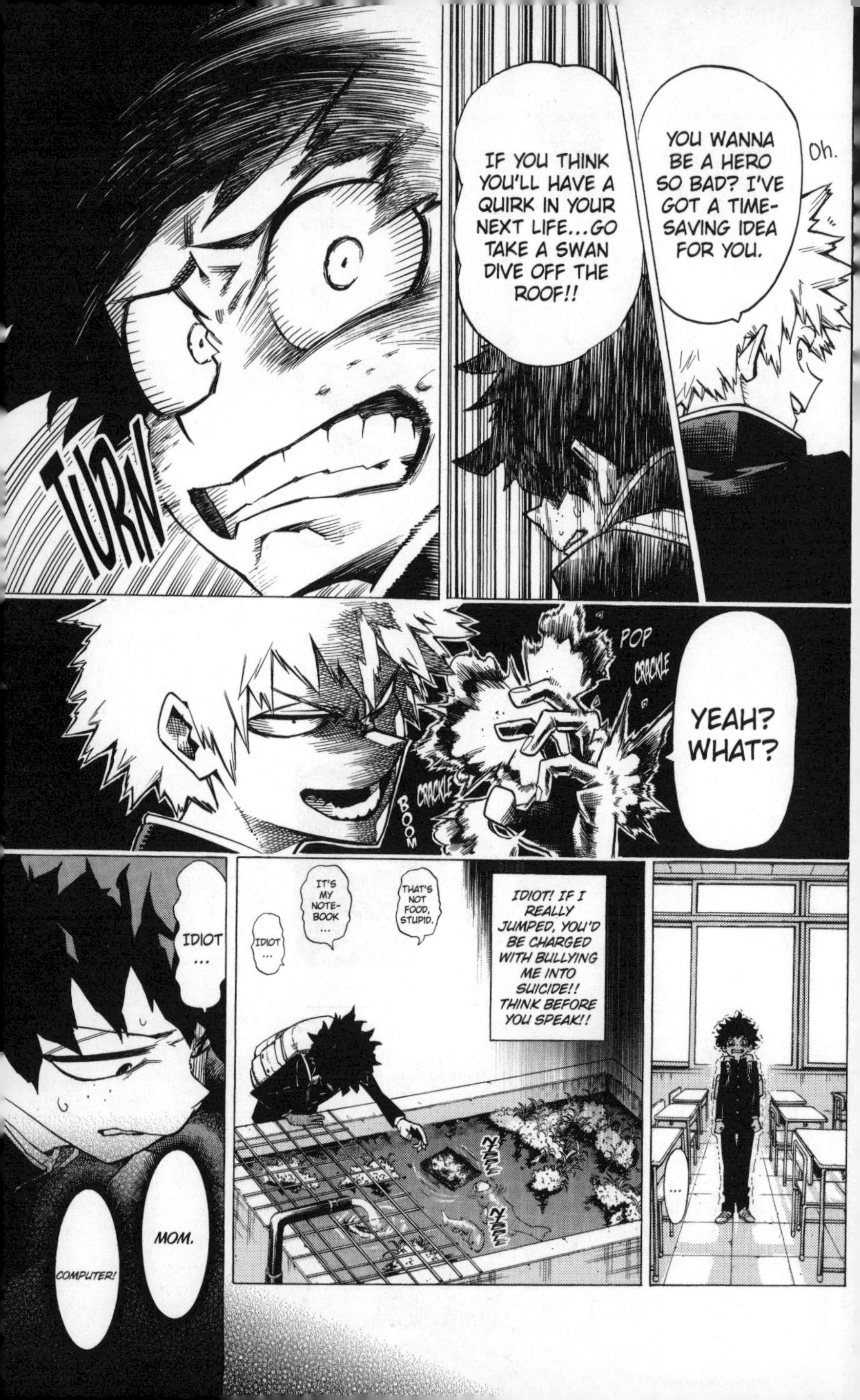
Oh.
YOU WANNA BE A HERO SO BAD? I'VE GOT A TIME-SAVING IDEA FOR YOU.
IF YOU THINK YOU'LL HAVE A QUIRK IN YOUR NEXT LIFE...GO TAKE A SWAN DIVE OFF THE ROOF!!
TURN
YEAH? WHAT?
POP
CRACKLE
CRACKLE
BOOM
IDIOT! IF I REALLY JUMPED, YOU'D BE CHARGED WITH BULLYING ME INTO SUICIDE!! THINK BEFORE YOU SPEAK!!
...
THAT'S NOT FOOD, STUPID.
IT'S MY NOTE-BOOK ...
IDIOT ...
IDIOT ...
MOM.
COMPUTER!

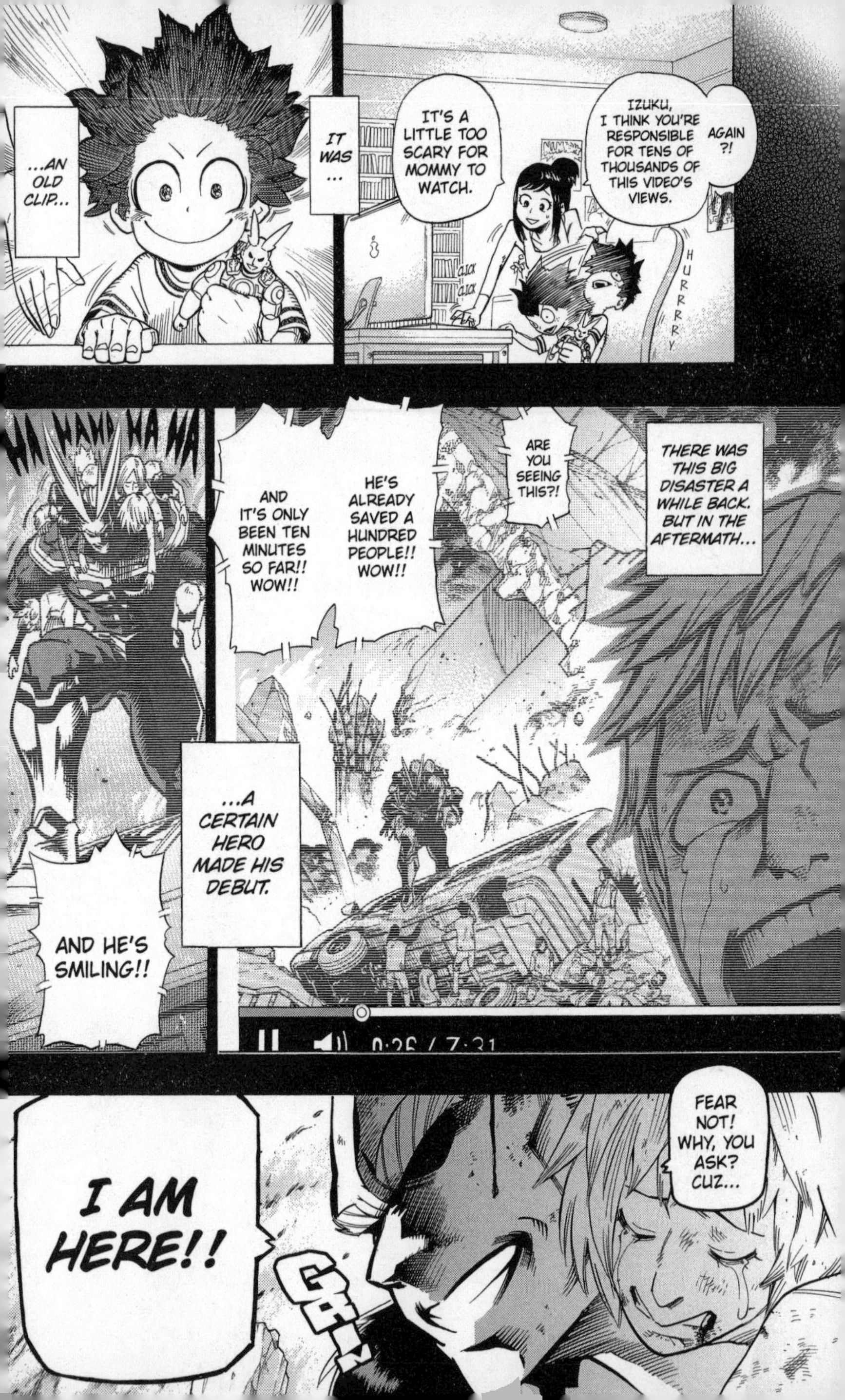
IZUKU, I THINK YOU'RE RESPONSIBLE FOR TENS OF THOUSANDS OF THIS VIDEO'S VIEWS.
AGAIN ?!
IT'S A LITTLE TOO SCARY FOR MOMMY TO WATCH.
HURRRRY
CLICK CLICK
IT WAS ...
...AN OLD CLIP...
THERE WAS THIS BIG DISASTER A WHILE BACK. BUT IN THE AFTERMATH...
ARE YOU SEEING THIS?!
HE'S ALREADY SAVED A HUNDRED PEOPLE!! WOW!!
AND IT'S ONLY BEEN TEN MINUTES SO FAR!! WOW!!
...A CERTAIN HERO MADE HIS DEBUT.
HA HA HA HA HA
AND HE'S SMILING!!
0:26 / 7:31
FEAR NOT! WHY, YOU ASK? CUZ...
GRIN
I AM HERE!!

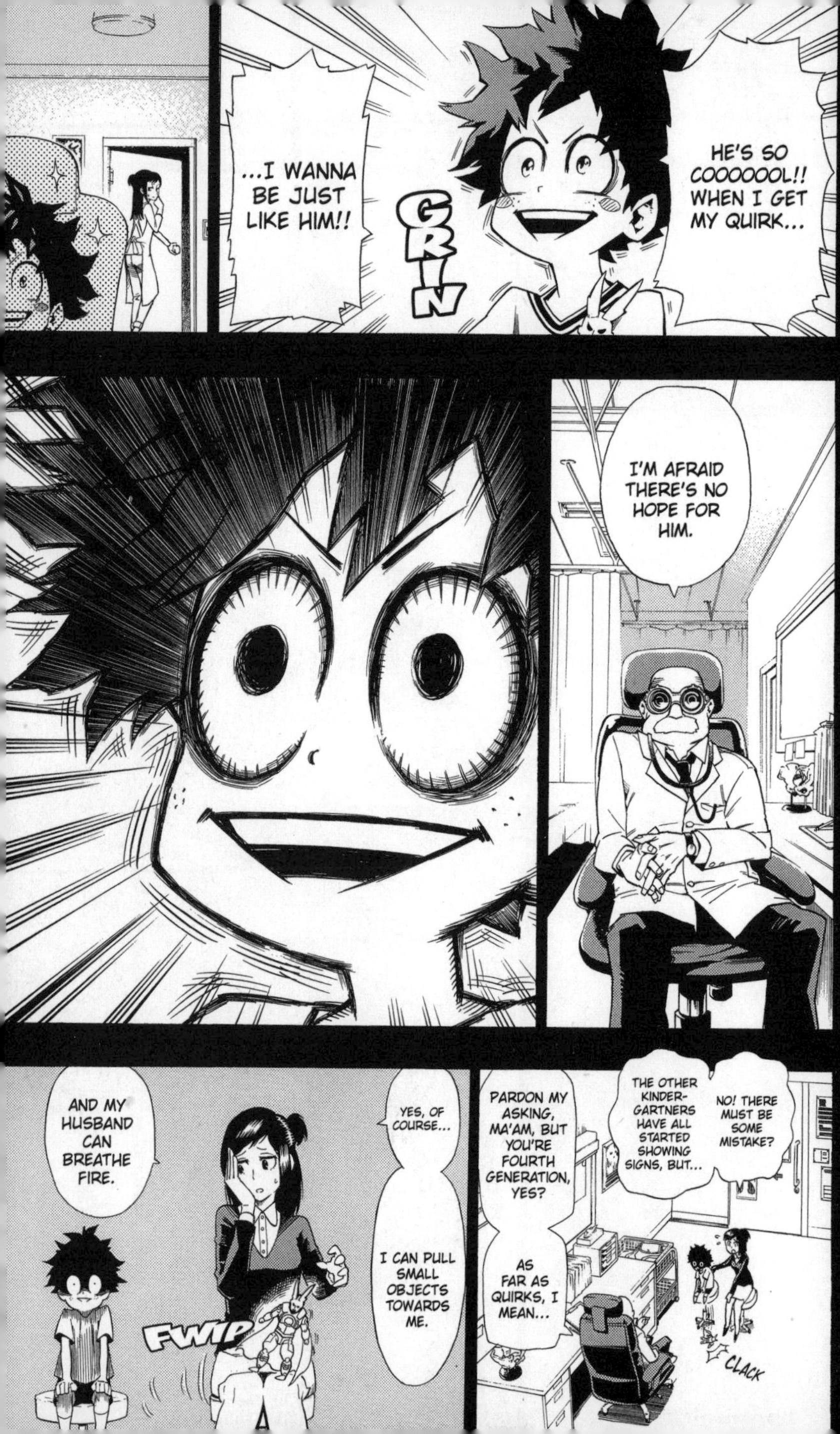
HE'S SO COOOOOOL!! WHEN I GET MY QUIRK...
GRIN
...I WANNA BE JUST LIKE HIM!!
I'M AFRAID THERE'S NO HOPE FOR HIM.
NO! THERE MUST BE SOME MISTAKE?
THE OTHER KINDER-GARTNERS HAVE ALL STARTED SHOWING SIGNS, BUT...
PARDON MY ASKING, MA'AM, BUT YOU'RE FOURTH GENERATION, YES?
AS FAR AS QUIRKS, I MEAN...
CLACK
YES, OF COURSE...
I CAN PULL SMALL OBJECTS TOWARDS ME.
AND MY HUSBAND CAN BREATHE FIRE.
FWIP

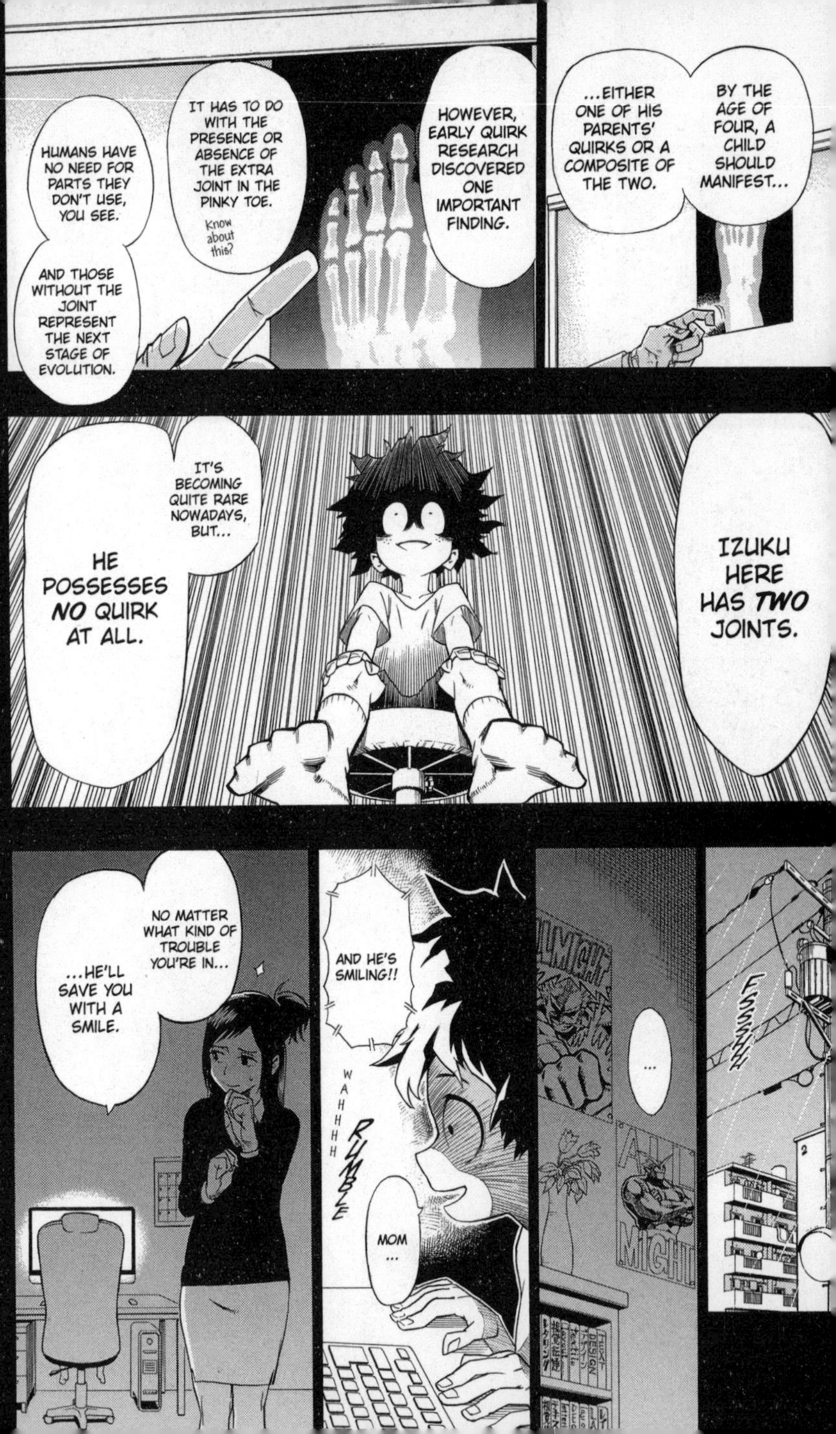
BY THE AGE OF FOUR, A CHILD SHOULD MANIFEST...
...EITHER ONE OF HIS PARENTS' QUIRKS OR A COMPOSITE OF THE TWO.
HOWEVER, EARLY QUIRK RESEARCH DISCOVERED ONE IMPORTANT FINDING.
IT HAS TO DO WITH THE PRESENCE OR ABSENCE OF THE EXTRA JOINT IN THE PINKY TOE.
Know about this?
HUMANS HAVE NO NEED FOR PARTS THEY DON'T USE, YOU SEE.
AND THOSE WITHOUT THE JOINT REPRESENT THE NEXT STAGE OF EVOLUTION.
IZUKU HERE HAS TWO JOINTS.
IT'S BECOMING QUITE RARE NOWADAYS, BUT...
HE POSSESSES NO QUIRK AT ALL.
FSSSHH
...
MOM ...
RUMBLE
WAHHHH
AND HE'S SMILING!!
NO MATTER WHAT KIND OF TROUBLE YOU'RE IN...
...HE'LL SAVE YOU WITH A SMILE.

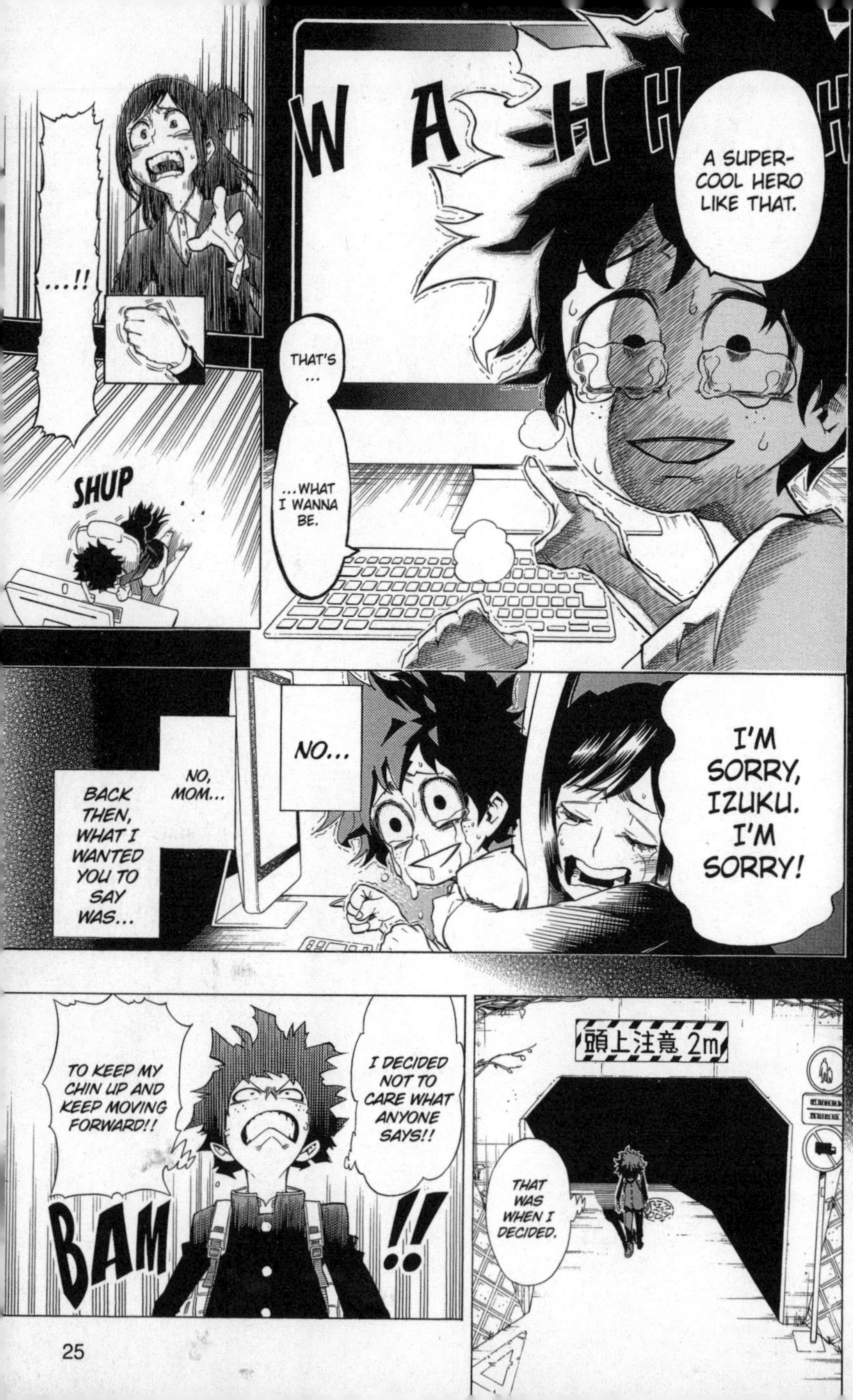
WAHHH
A SUPER-COOL HERO LIKE THAT.
THAT'S ...
...WHAT I WANNA BE.
...!!
SHUP
I'M SORRY, IZUKU. I'M SORRY!
NO...
NO, MOM...
BACK THEN, WHAT I WANTED YOU TO SAY WAS...
頭上注意 2m
THAT WAS WHEN I DECIDED.
I DECIDED NOT TO CARE WHAT ANYONE SAYS!!
TO KEEP MY CHIN UP AND KEEP MOVING FORWARD!!
BAM
!!

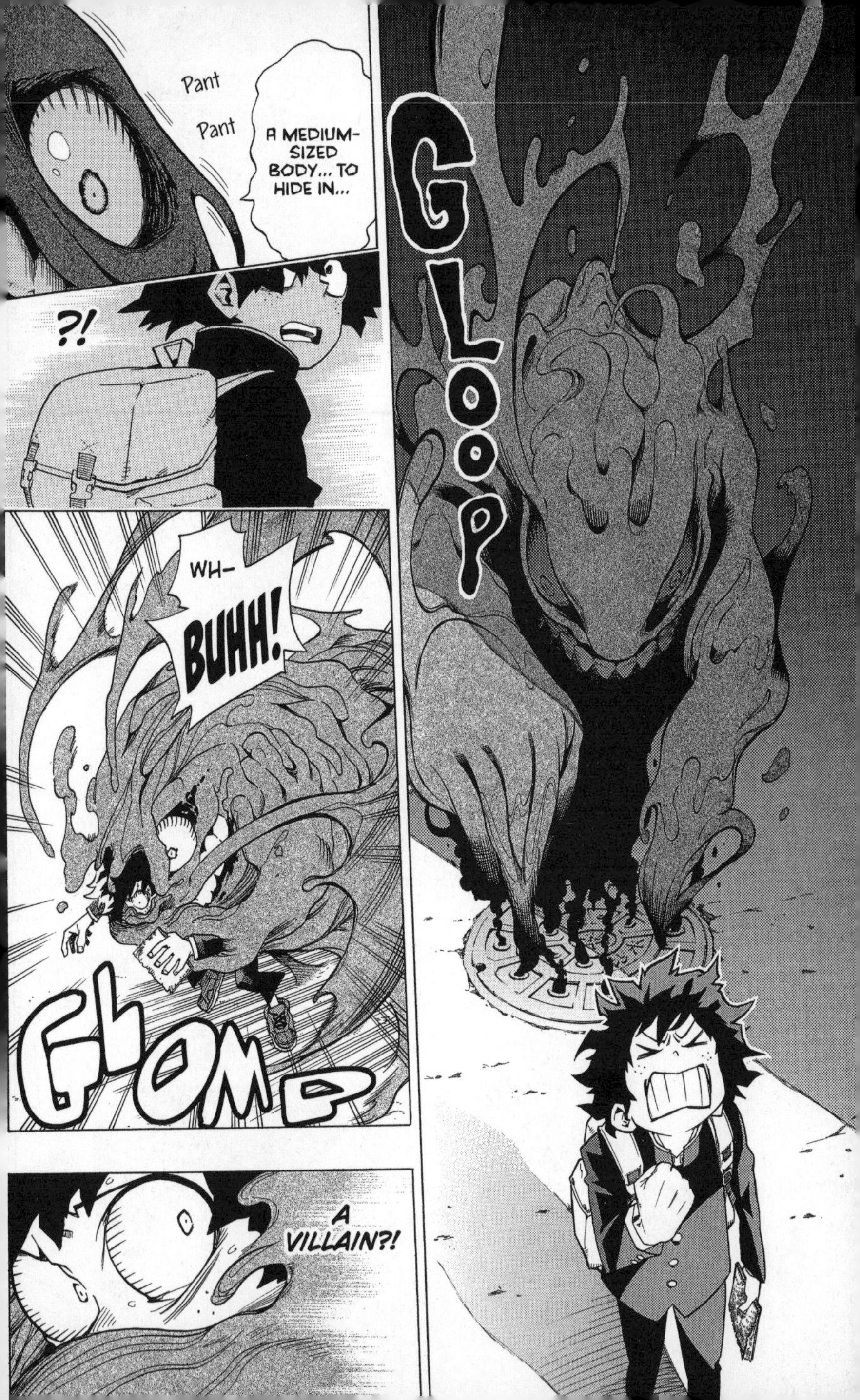
GLOOP
Pant
Pant
A MEDIUM-SIZED BODY... TO HIDE IN...
?!
WH-
BUHH!
GLOMP
A VILLAIN?!

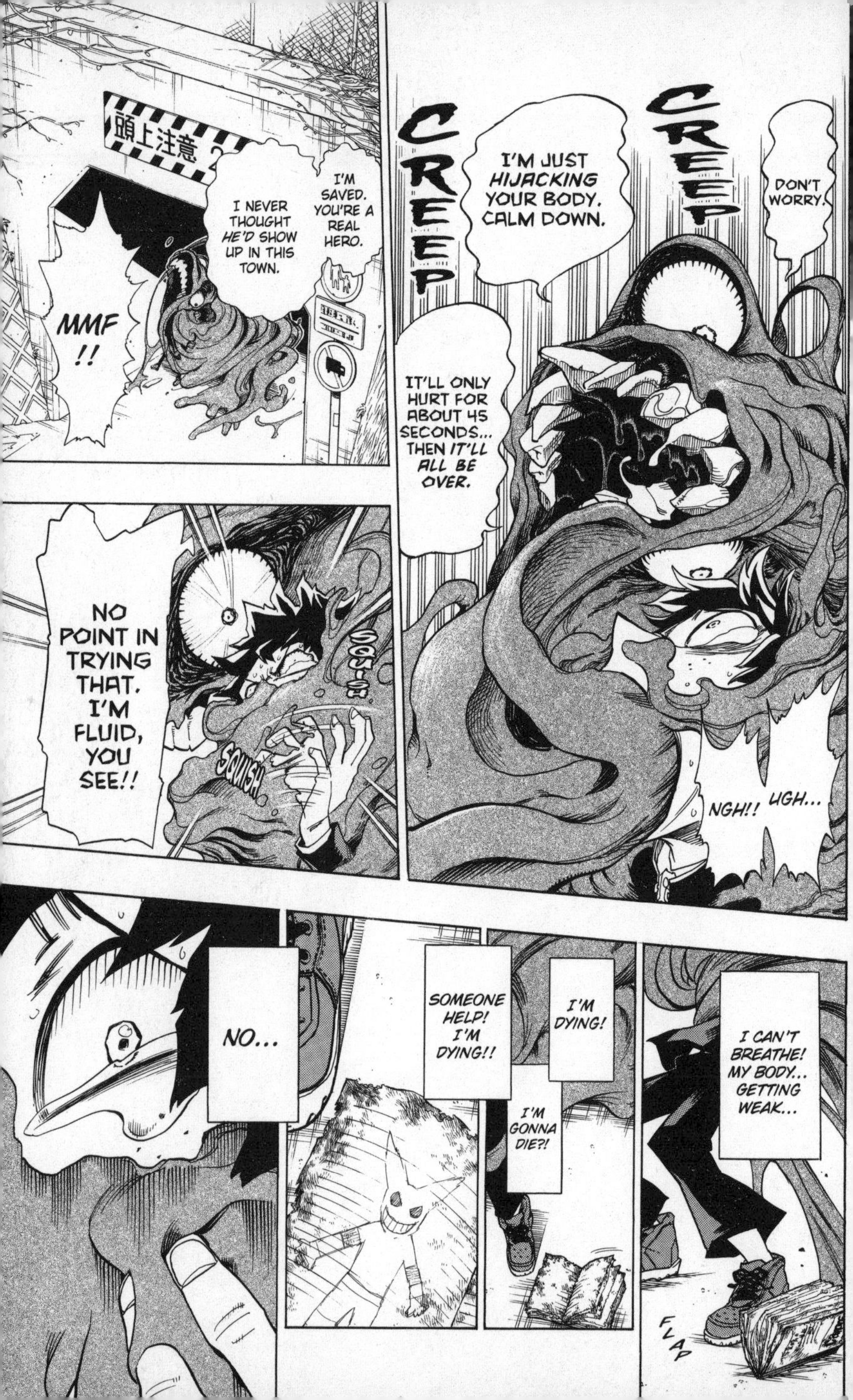
DON'T WORRY.
CREEP
I'M JUST HIJACKING YOUR BODY. CALM DOWN.
CREEP
IT'LL ONLY HURT FOR ABOUT 45 SECONDS... THEN IT'LL ALL BE OVER.
UGH...
NGH!!
I'M SAVED. YOU'RE A REAL HERO.
I NEVER THOUGHT HE'D SHOW UP IN THIS TOWN.
頭上注意
MMF !!
SQUISH
SQUISH
NO POINT IN TRYING THAT. I'M FLUID, YOU SEE!!
I CAN'T BREATHE! MY BODY... GETTING WEAK...
FLAP
I'M DYING!
I'M GONNA DIE?!
SOMEONE HELP! I'M DYING!!
NO...

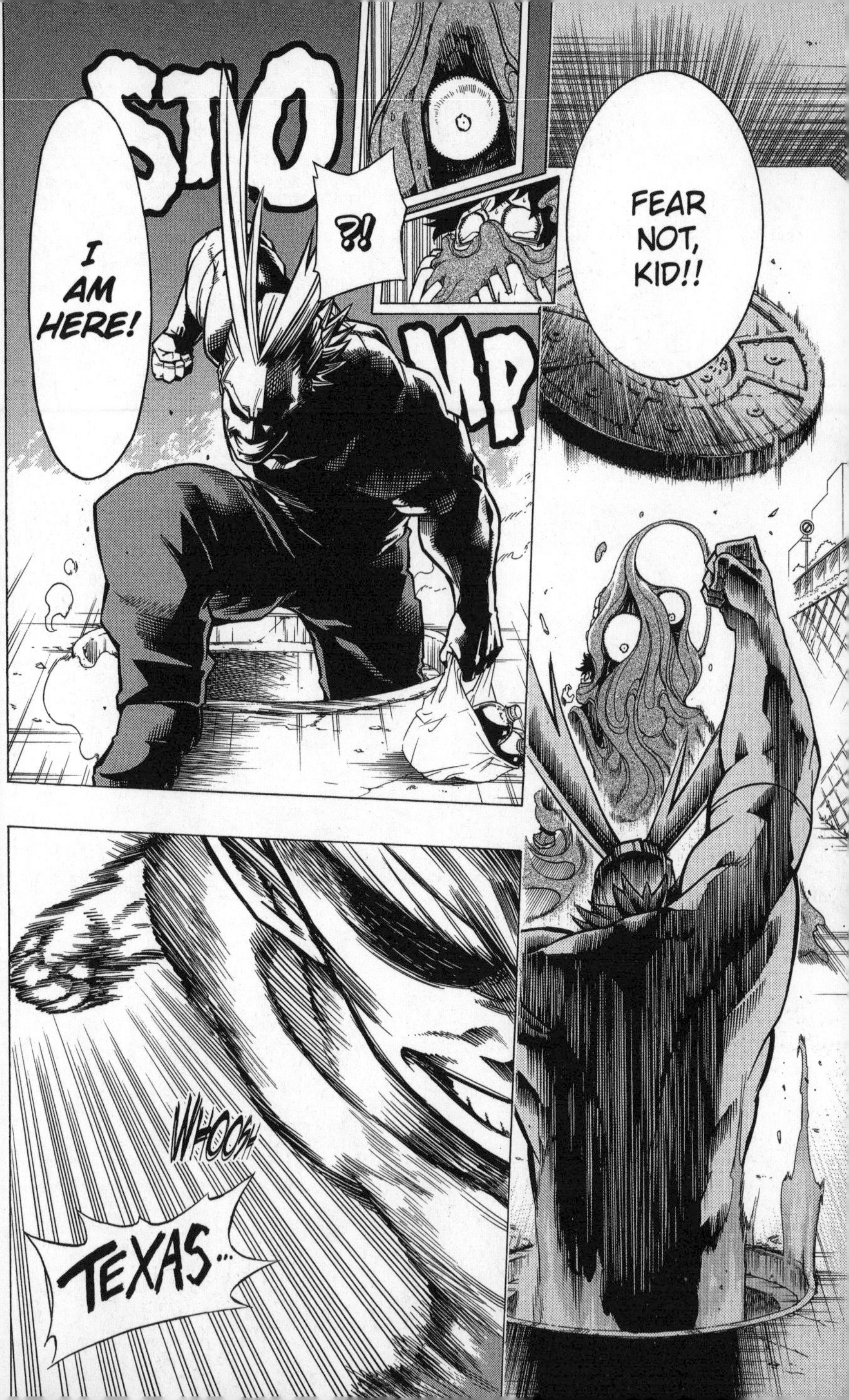
FEAR NOT, KID!!
?!
STO
MP
I AM HERE!
WHOOM
TEXAS...

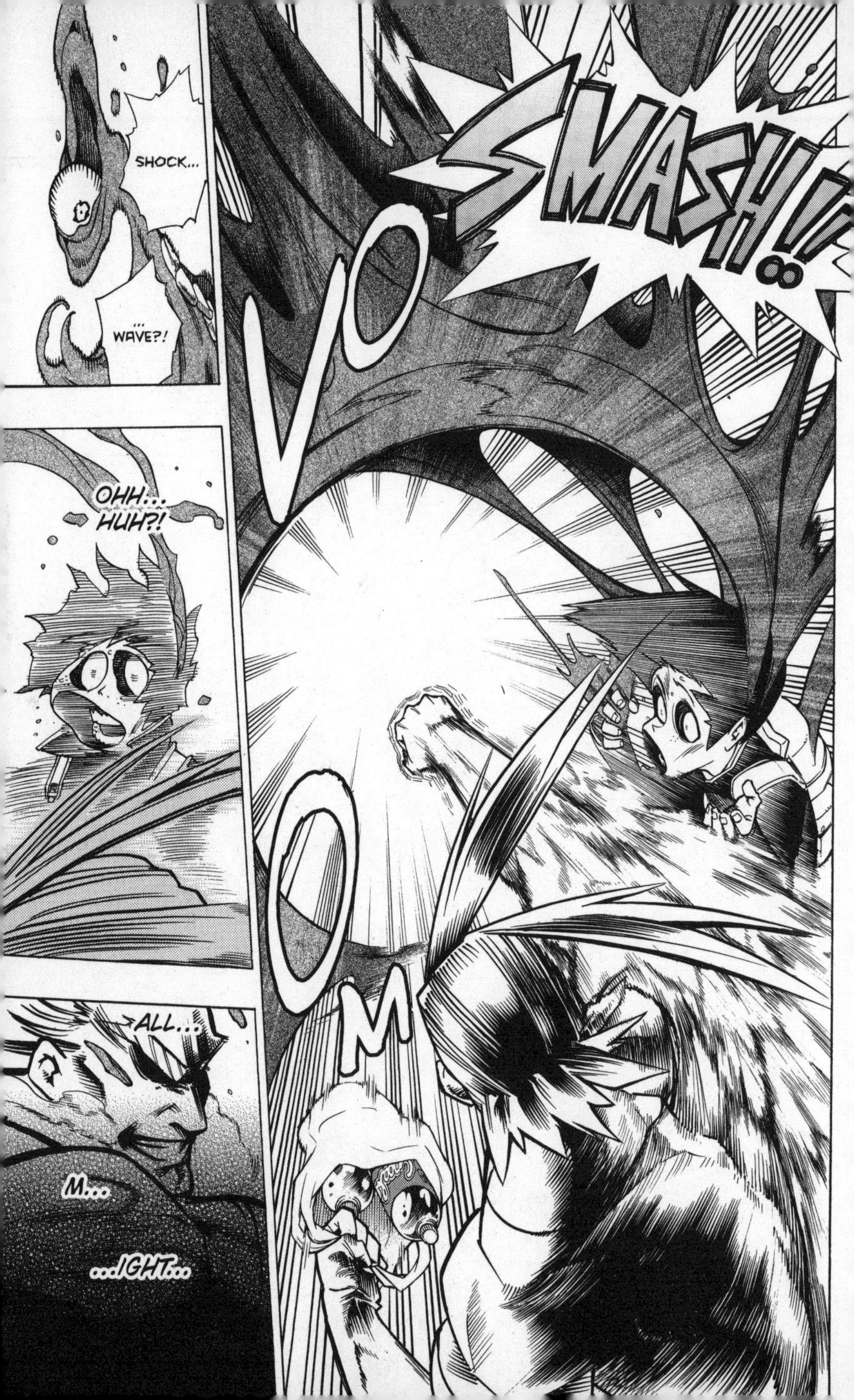
SMASH!!
VOOOM
SHOCK...
... WAVE?!
OHH... HUH?!
ALL...
M...
...IGHT...

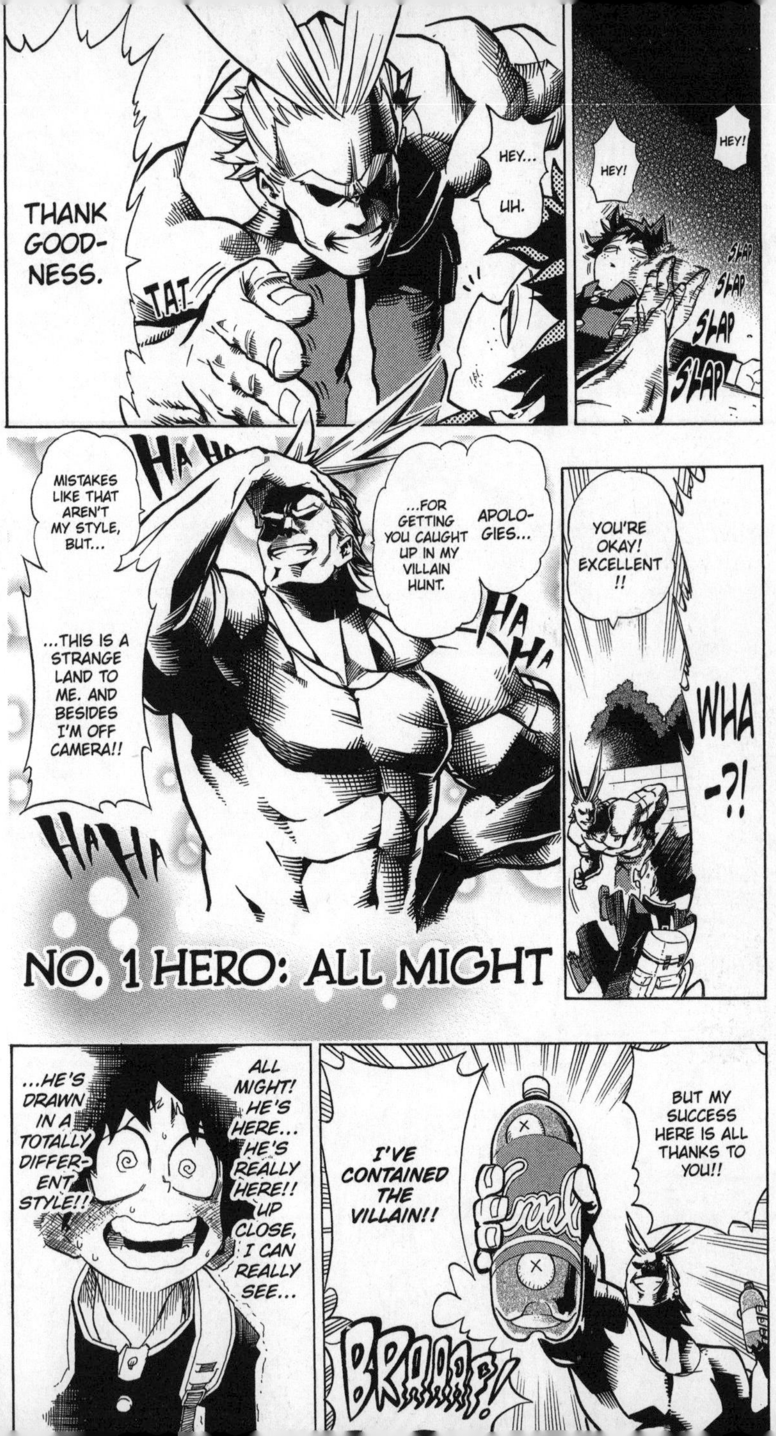
HEY!
HEY!
SLAP SLAP SLAP SLAP
HEY...
UH.
THANK GOODNESS.
TAT
YOU'RE OKAY! EXCELLENT!!
WHA-?!
APOLOGIES...
...FOR GETTING YOU CAUGHT UP IN MY VILLAIN HUNT.
HA HA
MISTAKES LIKE THAT AREN'T MY STYLE, BUT...
...THIS IS A STRANGE LAND TO ME. AND BESIDES I'M OFF CAMERA!!
HA HA
HA HA
NO. 1 HERO: ALL MIGHT
BUT MY SUCCESS HERE IS ALL THANKS TO YOU!!
I'VE CONTAINED THE VILLAIN!!
BROOOP?!
ALL MIGHT! HE'S HERE... HE'S REALLY HERE!! UP CLOSE, I CAN REALLY SEE...
...HE'S DRAWN IN A TOTALLY DIFFERENT STYLE!!

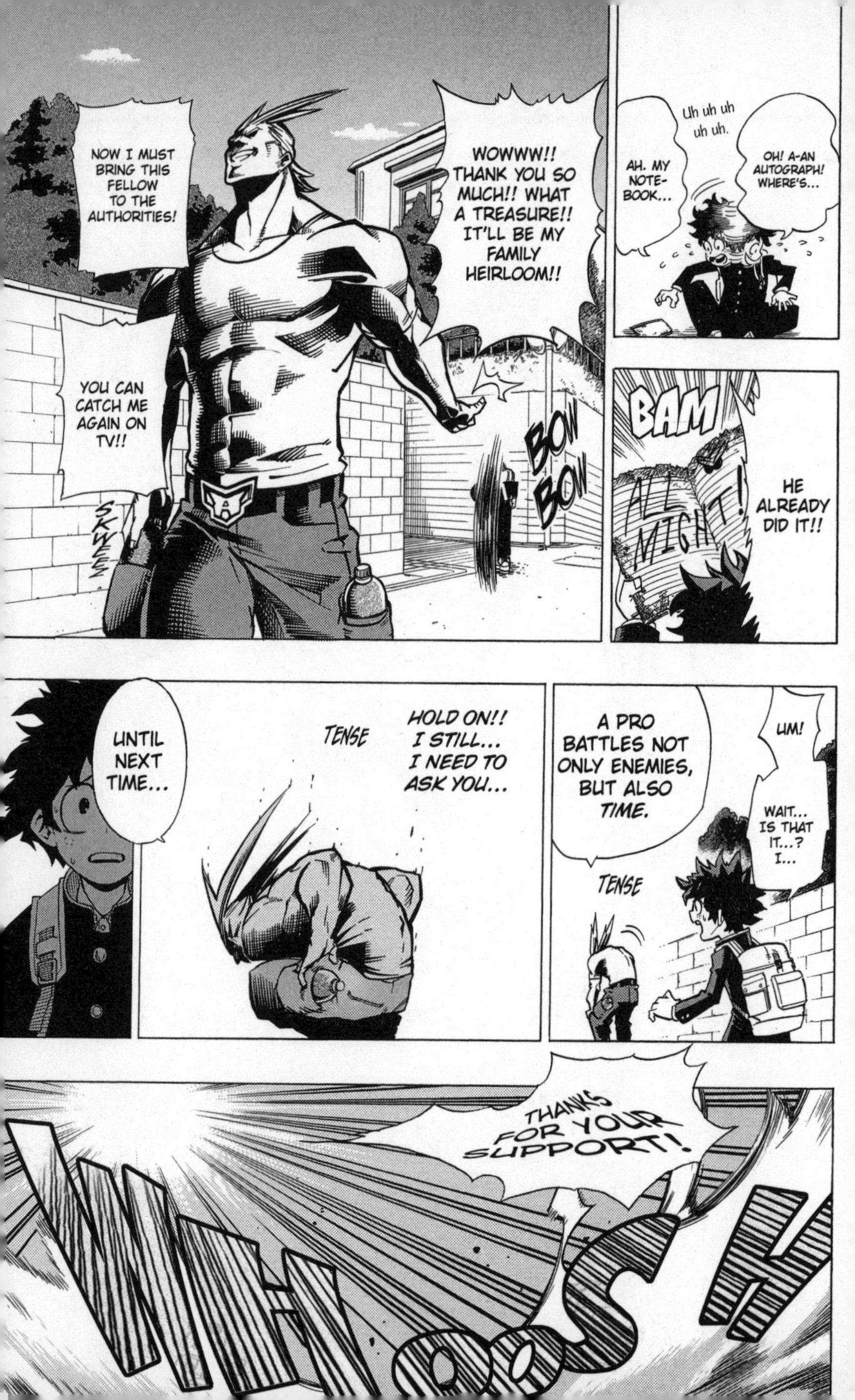
OH! A-AN AUTOGRAPH! WHERE'S...
Uh uh uh uh uh.
AH. MY NOTE-BOOK...
BAM
ALL MIGHT!
HE ALREADY DID IT!!
WOWWW!! THANK YOU SO MUCH!! WHAT A TREASURE!! IT'LL BE MY FAMILY HEIRLOOM!!
BOW BOW
NOW I MUST BRING THIS FELLOW TO THE AUTHORITIES!
YOU CAN CATCH ME AGAIN ON TV!!
SKWEEZ
UM!
WAIT... IS THAT IT...? I...
A PRO BATTLES NOT ONLY ENEMIES, BUT ALSO TIME.
TENSE
HOLD ON!! I STILL... I NEED TO ASK YOU...
TENSE
UNTIL NEXT TIME...
THANKS FOR YOUR SUPPORT!
WHOOSH

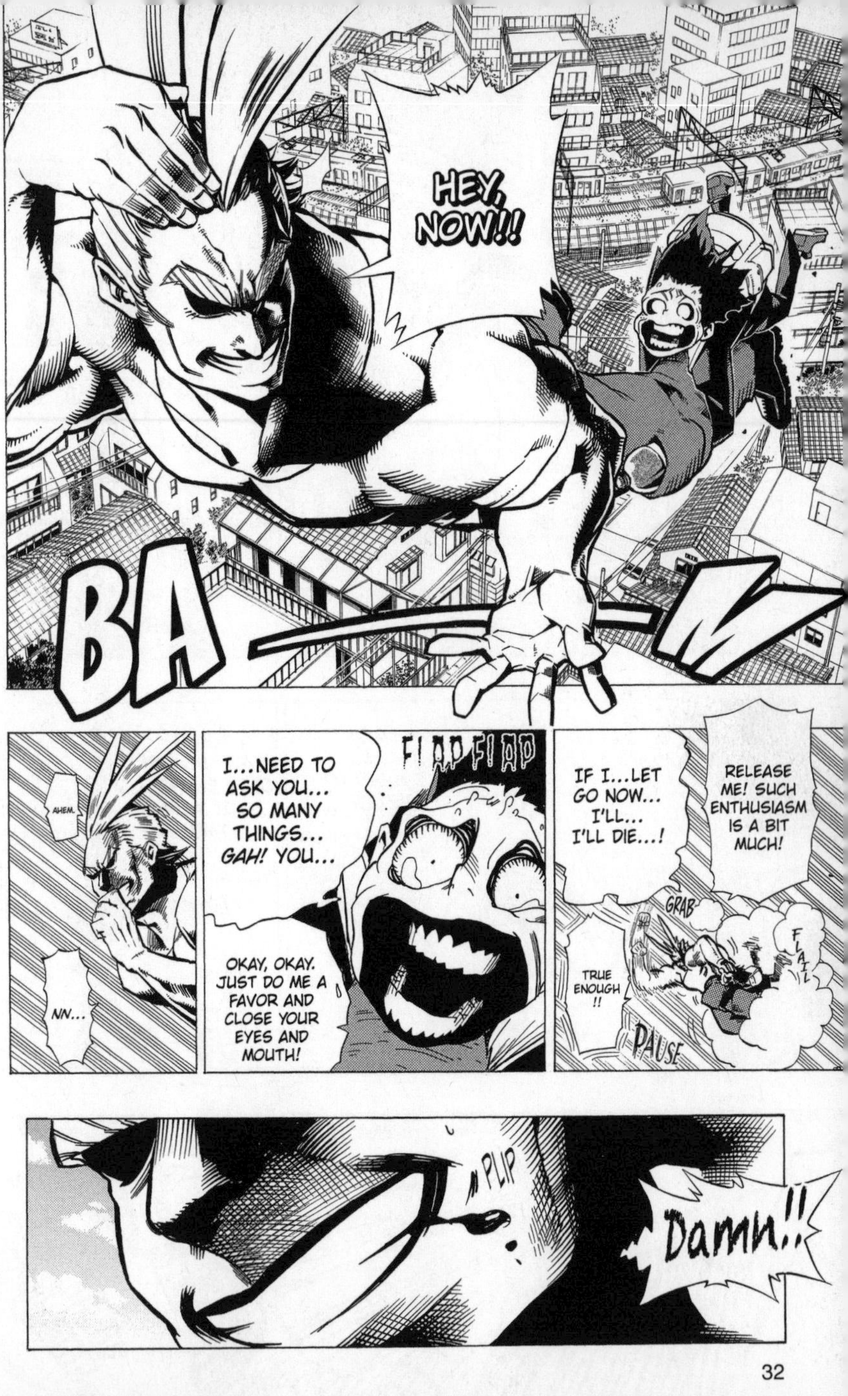
HEY, NOW!!
BA-M
RELEASE ME! SUCH ENTHUSIASM IS A BIT MUCH!
IF I...LET GO NOW... I'LL... I'LL DIE...!
GRAB
FLAIL
TRUE ENOUGH !!
PAUSE
FLAP FLAP
I...NEED TO ASK YOU... SO MANY THINGS... GAH! YOU...
OKAY, OKAY. JUST DO ME A FAVOR AND CLOSE YOUR EYES AND MOUTH!
AHEM.
NN...
Damn!!
PLIP

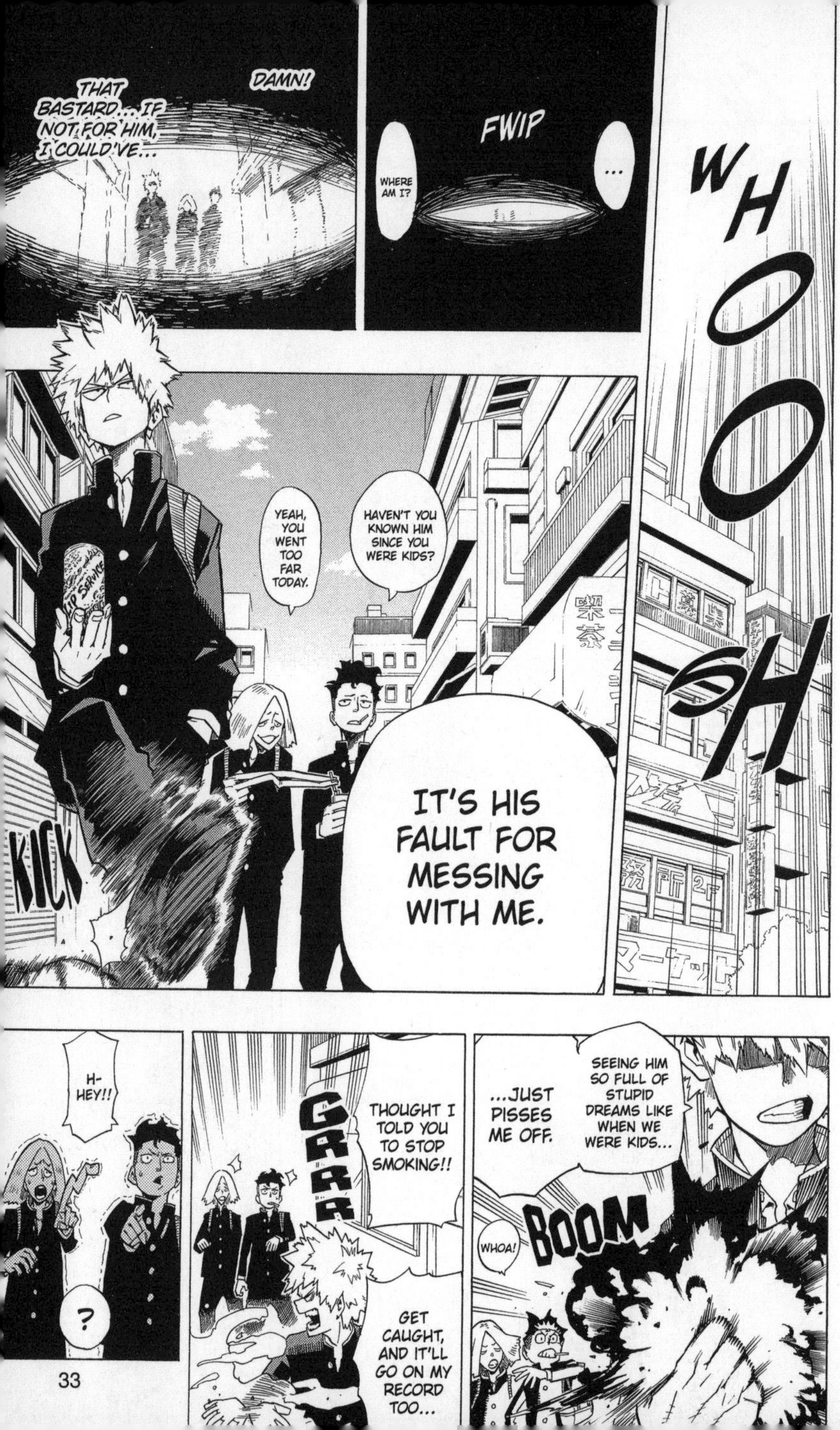

WHOOOSH
...
FWIP
WHERE AM I?
DAMN!
THAT BASTARD... IF NOT FOR HIM, I COULD'VE...
HAVEN'T YOU KNOWN HIM SINCE YOU WERE KIDS?
YEAH, YOU WENT TOO FAR TODAY.
IT'S HIS FAULT FOR MESSING WITH ME.
KICK
SEEING HIM SO FULL OF STUPID DREAMS LIKE WHEN WE WERE KIDS...
...JUST PISSES ME OFF.
BOOM
WHOA!
GRRR
THOUGHT I TOLD YOU TO STOP SMOKING!!
GET CAUGHT, AND IT'LL GO ON MY RECORD TOO...
H-HEY!!
?

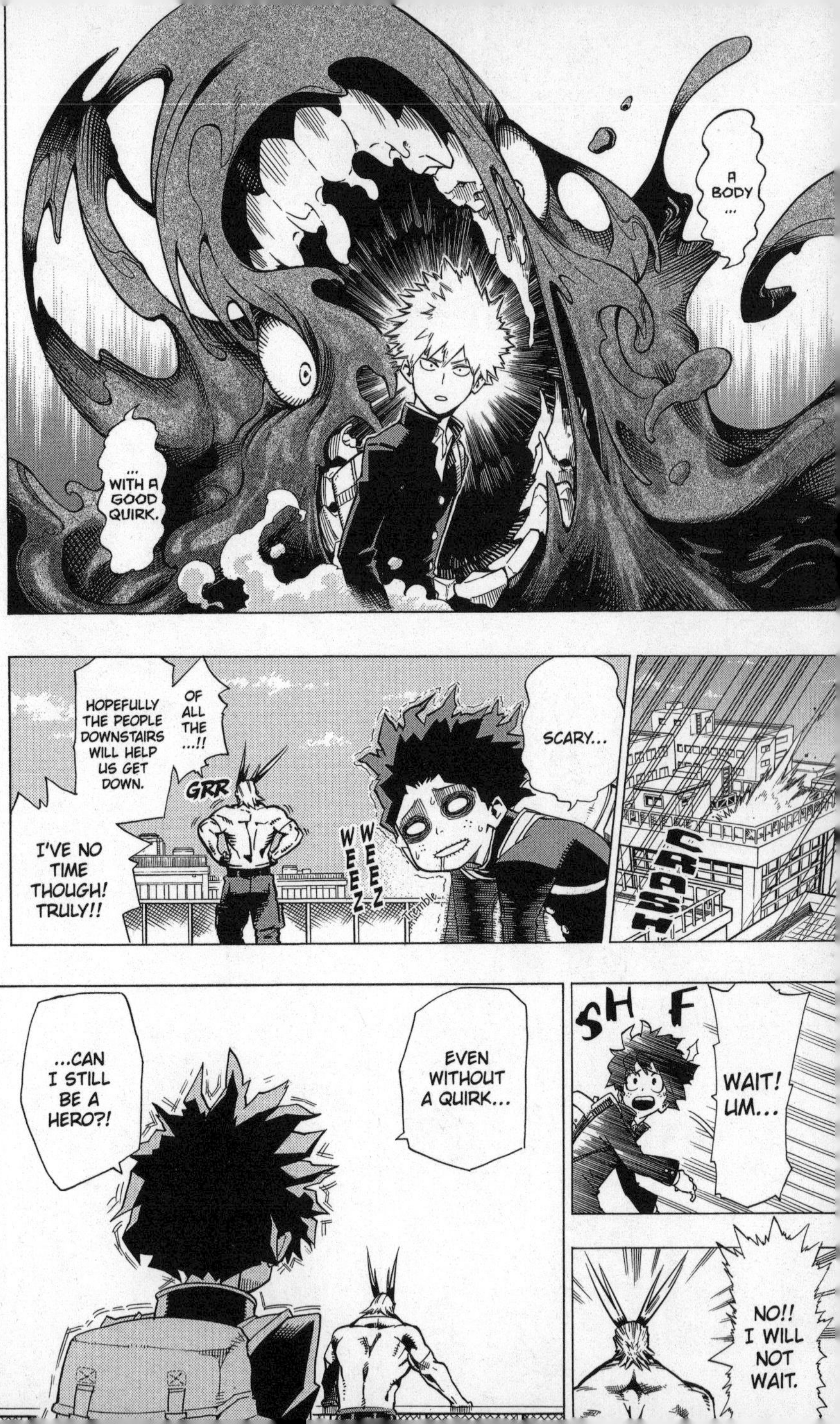
A BODY ...
... WITH A GOOD QUIRK.
CRASH
SCARY...
OF ALL THE ...!!
HOPEFULLY THE PEOPLE DOWNSTAIRS WILL HELP US GET DOWN.
GRR
I'VE NO TIME THOUGH! TRULY!!
WEEZ WEEZ
Tremble
SH F
WAIT! UM...
NO!! I WILL NOT WAIT.
EVEN WITHOUT A QUIRK...
...CAN I STILL BE A HERO?!

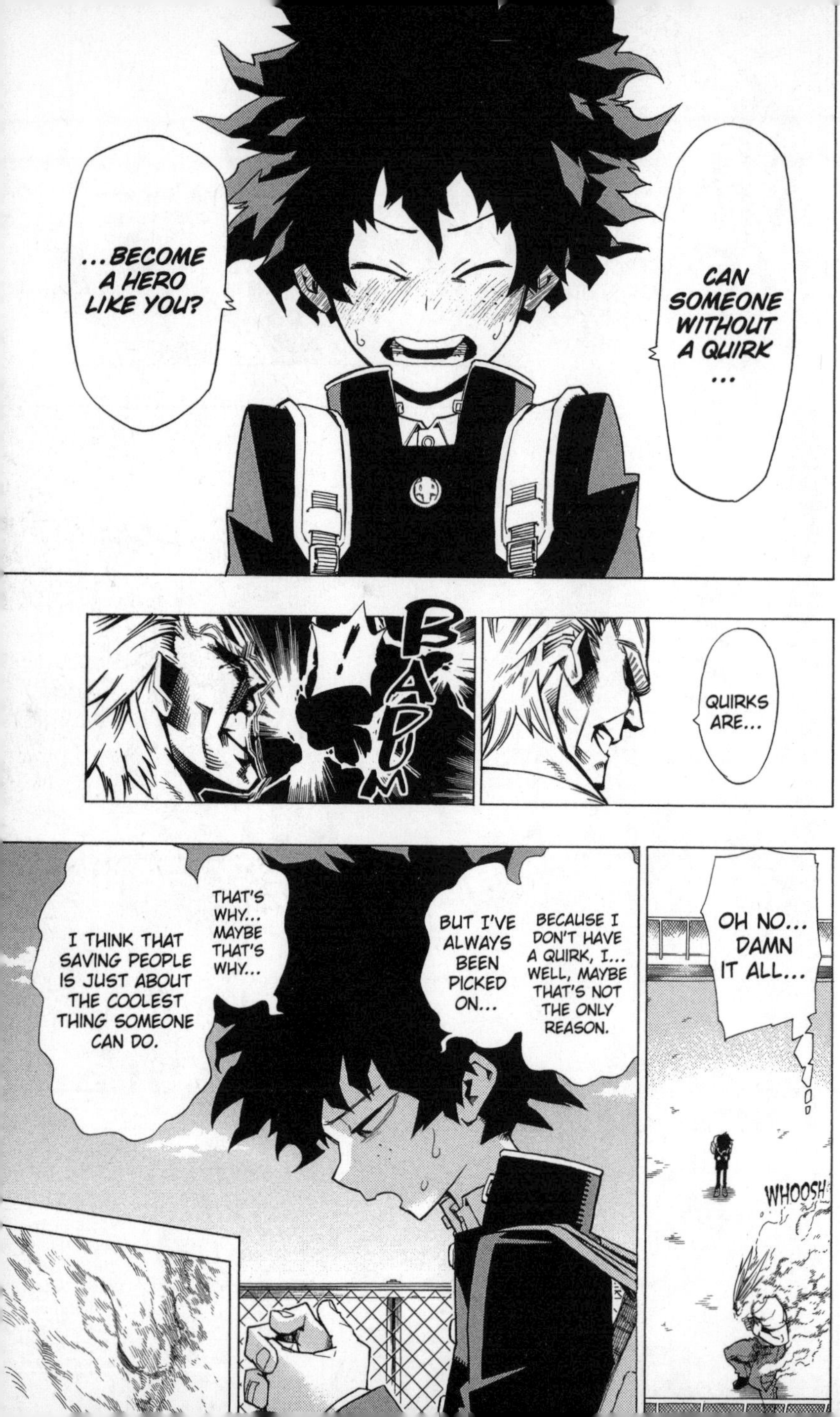
CAN SOMEONE WITHOUT A QUIRK ...
...BECOME A HERO LIKE YOU?
QUIRKS ARE...
BADUM
OH NO... DAMN IT ALL...
WHOOSH
BECAUSE I DON'T HAVE A QUIRK, I... WELL, MAYBE THAT'S NOT THE ONLY REASON.
BUT I'VE ALWAYS BEEN PICKED ON...
THAT'S WHY... MAYBE THAT'S WHY...
I THINK THAT SAVING PEOPLE IS JUST ABOUT THE COOLEST THING SOMEONE CAN DO.

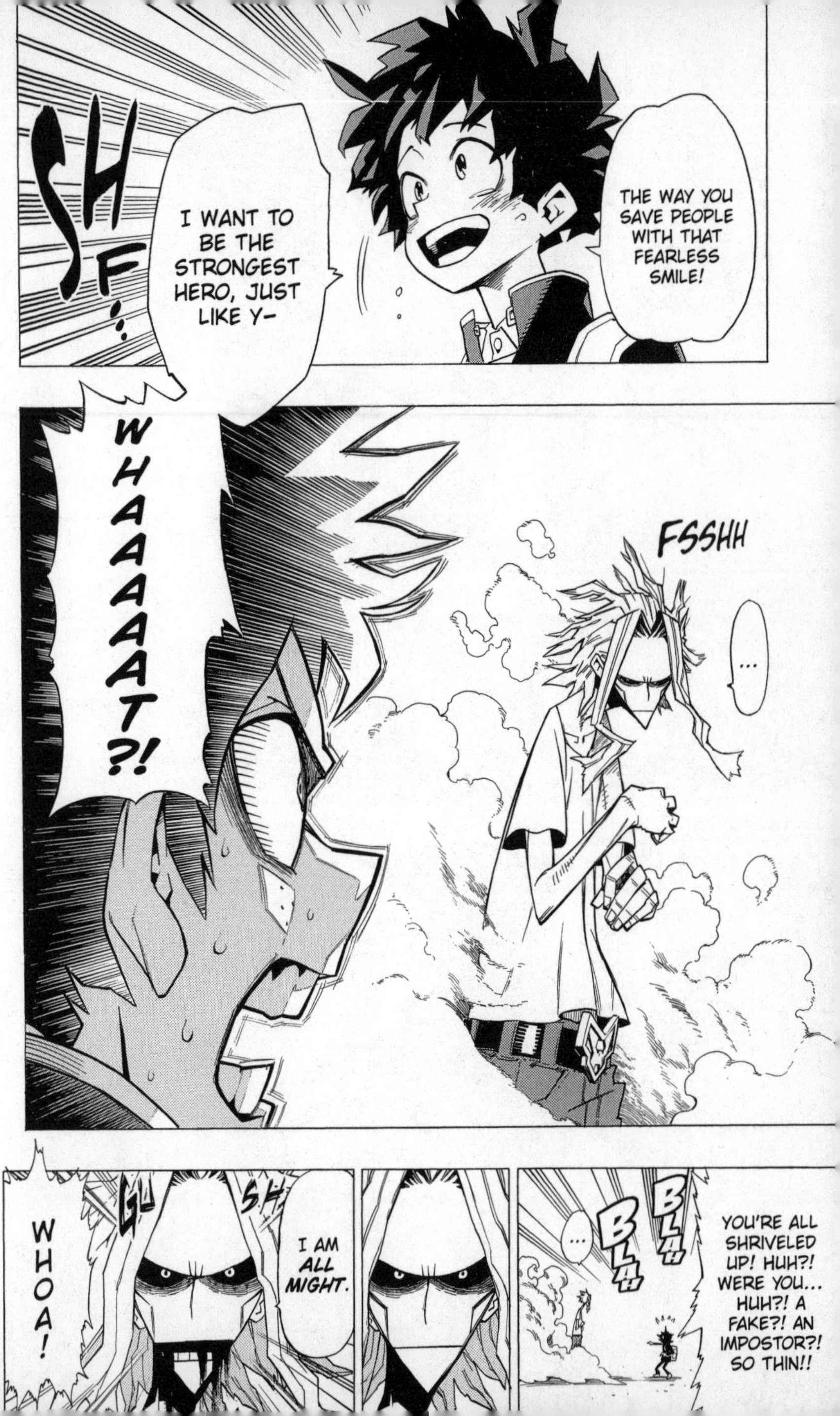
THE WAY YOU SAVE PEOPLE WITH THAT FEARLESS SMILE!
I WANT TO BE THE STRONGEST HERO, JUST LIKE Y-
SHF...
...
FSSHH
WHAAAAAAT?!
YOU'RE ALL SHRIVELED UP! HUH?! WERE YOU... HUH?! A FAKE?! AN IMPOSTOR?! SO THIN!!
BLAH
BLAH
...
I AM ALL MIGHT.
SH
GU
WHOA!

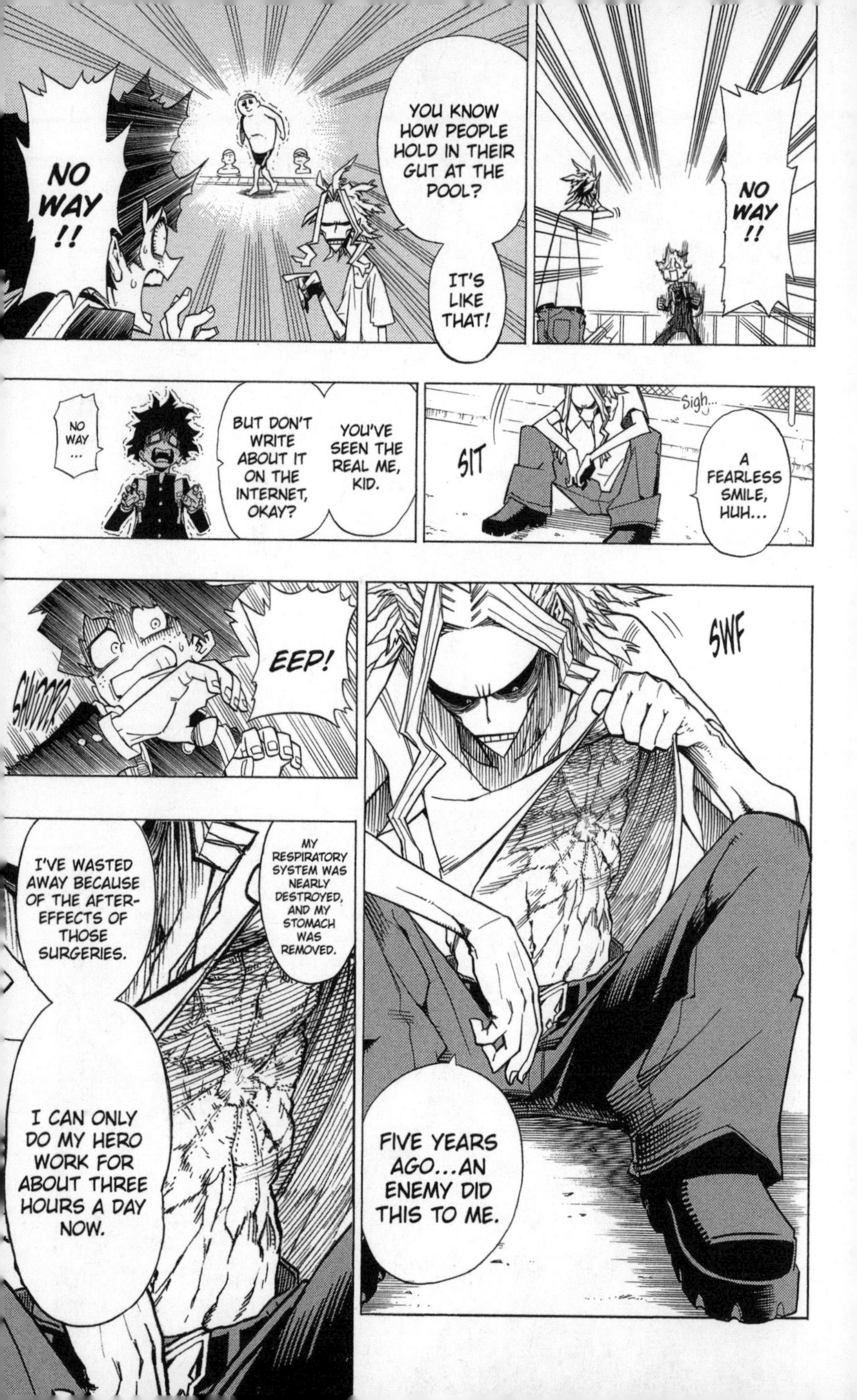
NO WAY !!
YOU KNOW HOW PEOPLE HOLD IN THEIR GUT AT THE POOL?
IT'S LIKE THAT!
NO WAY !!
Sigh...
A FEARLESS SMILE, HUH...
SIT
YOU'VE SEEN THE REAL ME, KID.
BUT DON'T WRITE ABOUT IT ON THE INTERNET, OKAY?
NO WAY ...
SWF
FIVE YEARS AGO...AN ENEMY DID THIS TO ME.
EEP!
SHOOOO
MY RESPIRATORY SYSTEM WAS NEARLY DESTROYED, AND MY STOMACH WAS REMOVED.
I'VE WASTED AWAY BECAUSE OF THE AFTER-EFFECTS OF THOSE SURGERIES.
I CAN ONLY DO MY HERO WORK FOR ABOUT THREE HOURS A DAY NOW.

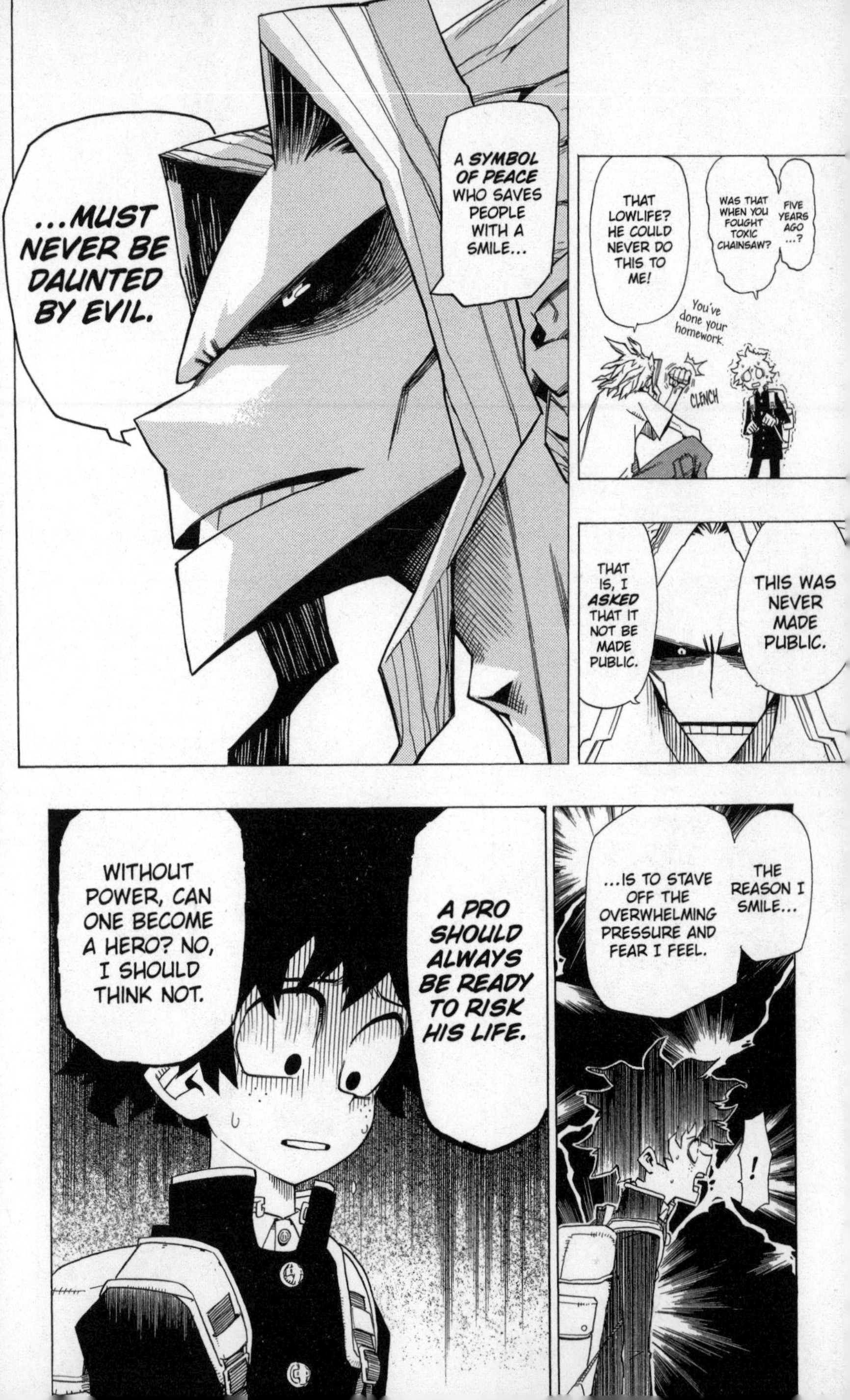

FIVE YEARS AGO ...?
WAS THAT WHEN YOU FOUGHT TOXIC CHAINSAW?
THAT LOWLIFE? HE COULD NEVER DO THIS TO ME!
You've done your homework.
CLENCH
THIS WAS NEVER MADE PUBLIC.
THAT IS, I *ASKED* THAT IT NOT BE MADE PUBLIC.
A *SYMBOL OF PEACE* WHO SAVES PEOPLE WITH A SMILE...
...MUST NEVER BE DAUNTED BY EVIL.
THE REASON I SMILE...
...IS TO STAVE OFF THE OVERWHELMING PRESSURE AND FEAR I FEEL.
!
A PRO SHOULD ALWAYS BE READY TO RISK HIS LIFE.
WITHOUT POWER, CAN ONE BECOME A HERO? NO, I SHOULD THINK NOT.

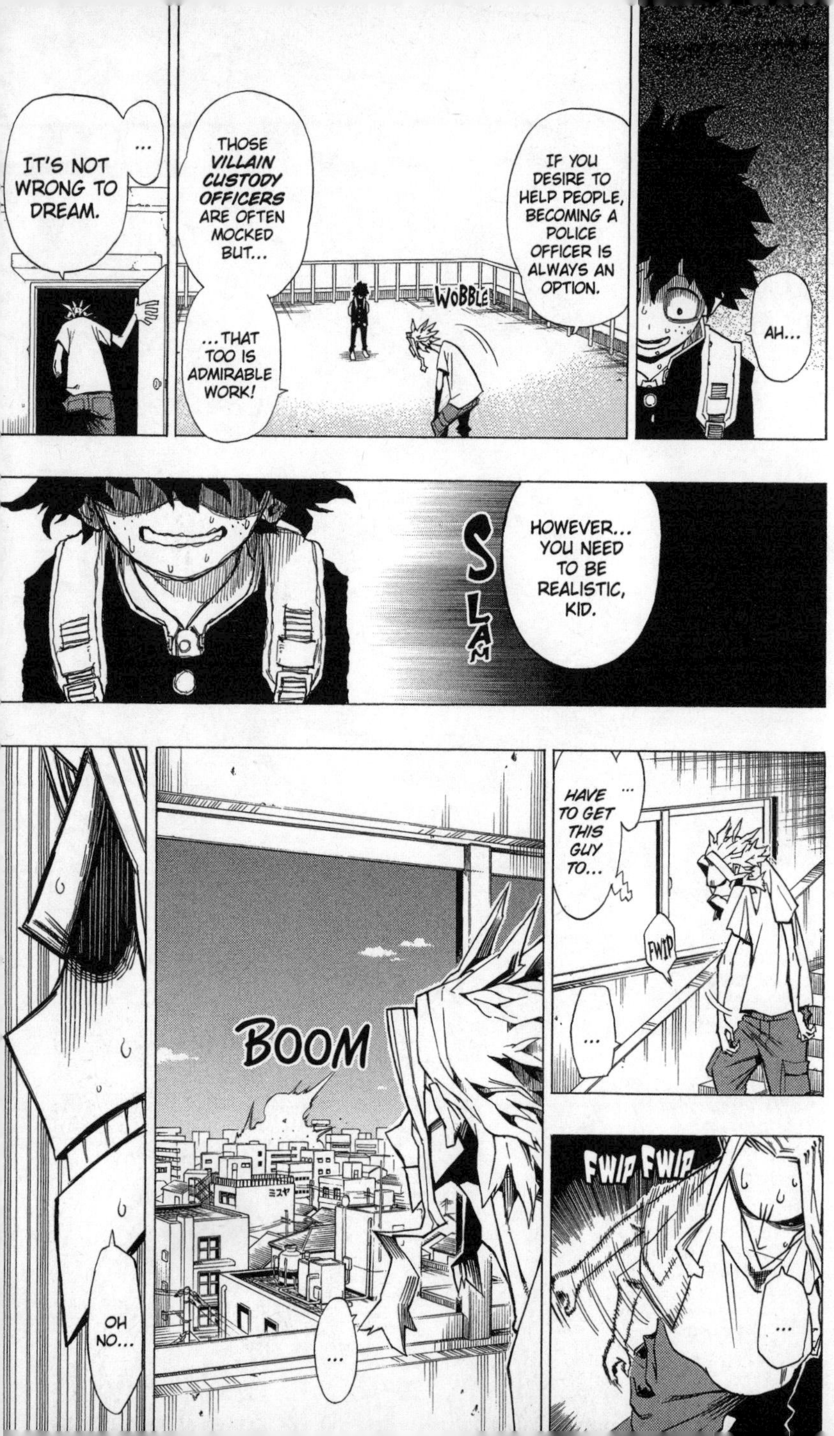
AH...
IF YOU DESIRE TO HELP PEOPLE, BECOMING A POLICE OFFICER IS ALWAYS AN OPTION.
WOBBLE
THOSE VILLAIN CUSTODY OFFICERS ARE OFTEN MOCKED BUT...
...THAT TOO IS ADMIRABLE WORK!
...
IT'S NOT WRONG TO DREAM.
HOWEVER... YOU NEED TO BE REALISTIC, KID.
SLAM
...
HAVE TO GET THIS GUY TO...
FWIP
...
FWIP FWIP
...
BOOM
...
OH NO...

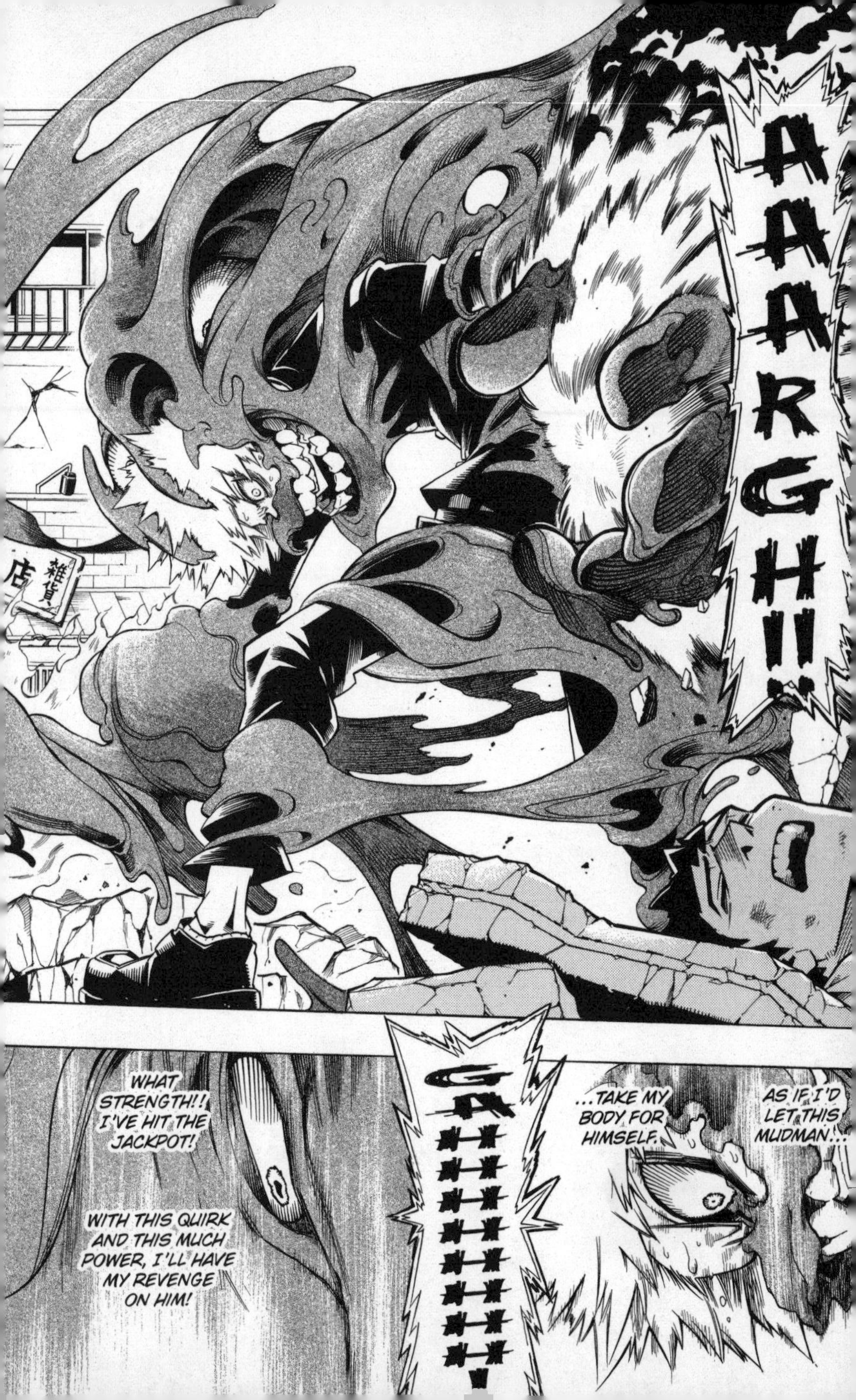
AAARGH!!
雑貨店
AS IF I'D LET THIS MUDMAN...
...TAKE MY BODY FOR HIMSELF.
GAHHHHHHHHHHH!
WHAT STRENGTH!! I'VE HIT THE JACKPOT!
WITH THIS QUIRK AND THIS MUCH POWER, I'LL HAVE MY REVENGE ON HIM!

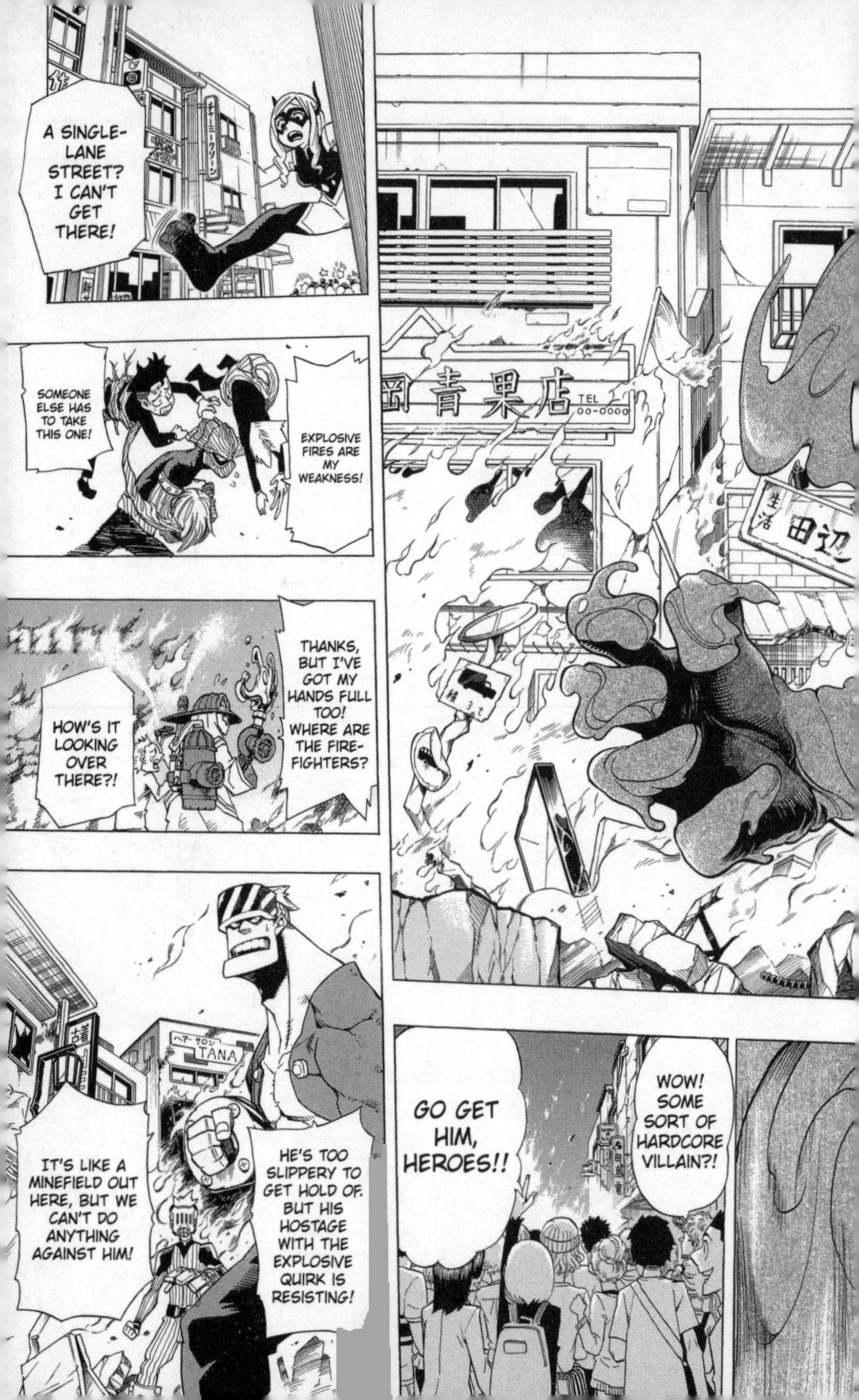
WOW! SOME SORT OF HARDCORE VILLAIN?!
GO GET HIM, HEROES!!
A SINGLE-LANE STREET? I CAN'T GET THERE!
EXPLOSIVE FIRES ARE MY WEAKNESS!
SOMEONE ELSE HAS TO TAKE THIS ONE!
THANKS, BUT I'VE GOT MY HANDS FULL TOO! WHERE ARE THE FIRE-FIGHTERS?
HOW'S IT LOOKING OVER THERE?!
HE'S TOO SLIPPERY TO GET HOLD OF. BUT HIS HOSTAGE WITH THE EXPLOSIVE QUIRK IS RESISTING!
IT'S LIKE A MINEFIELD OUT HERE, BUT WE CAN'T DO ANYTHING AGAINST HIM!

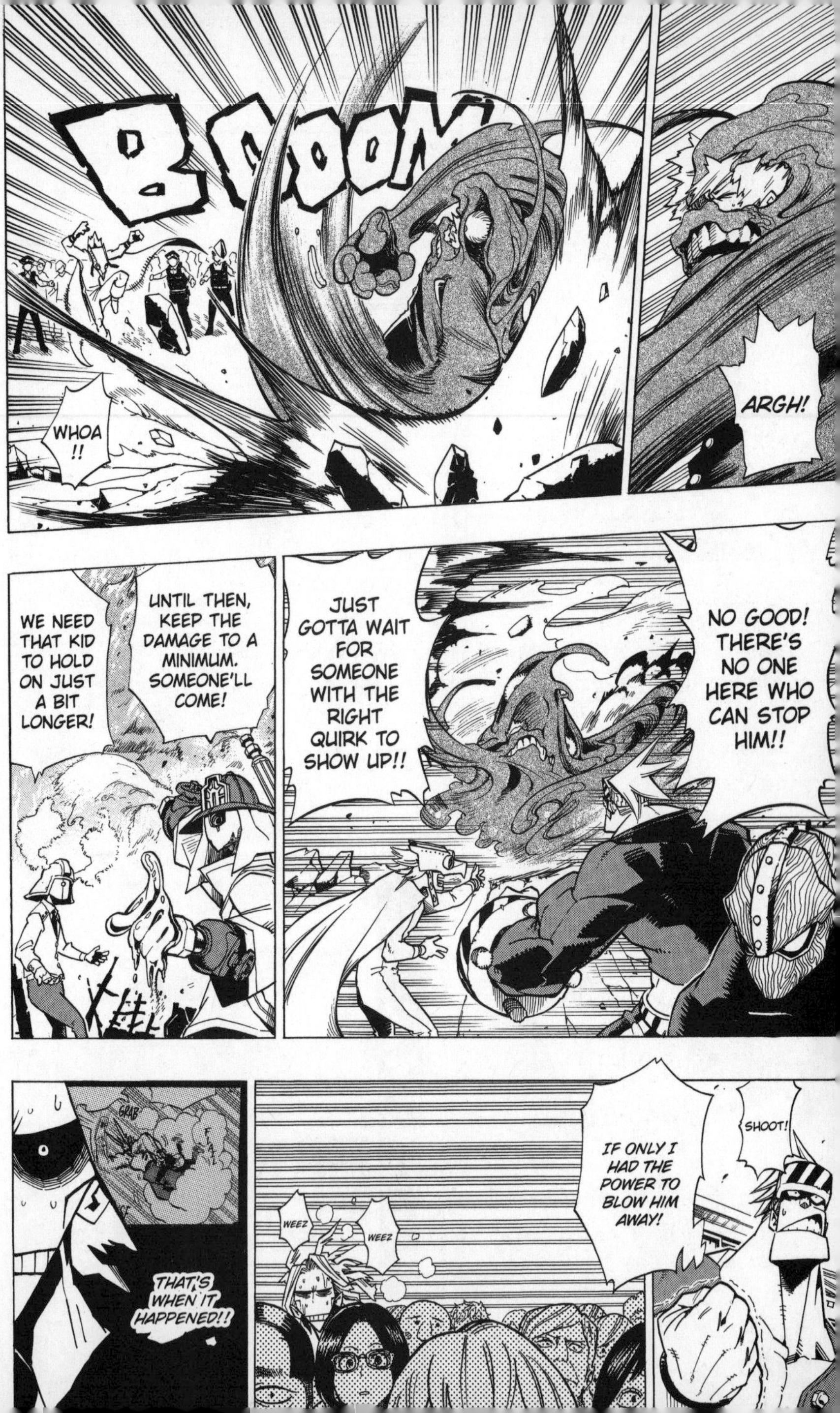
ARGH!
BOOOM
WHOA!!
NO GOOD! THERE'S NO ONE HERE WHO CAN STOP HIM!!
JUST GOTTA WAIT FOR SOMEONE WITH THE RIGHT QUIRK TO SHOW UP!!
UNTIL THEN, KEEP THE DAMAGE TO A MINIMUM. SOMEONE'LL COME!
WE NEED THAT KID TO HOLD ON JUST A BIT LONGER!
SHOOT!
IF ONLY I HAD THE POWER TO BLOW HIM AWAY!
WEEZ
WEEZ
GRAB
THAT'S WHEN IT HAPPENED!!

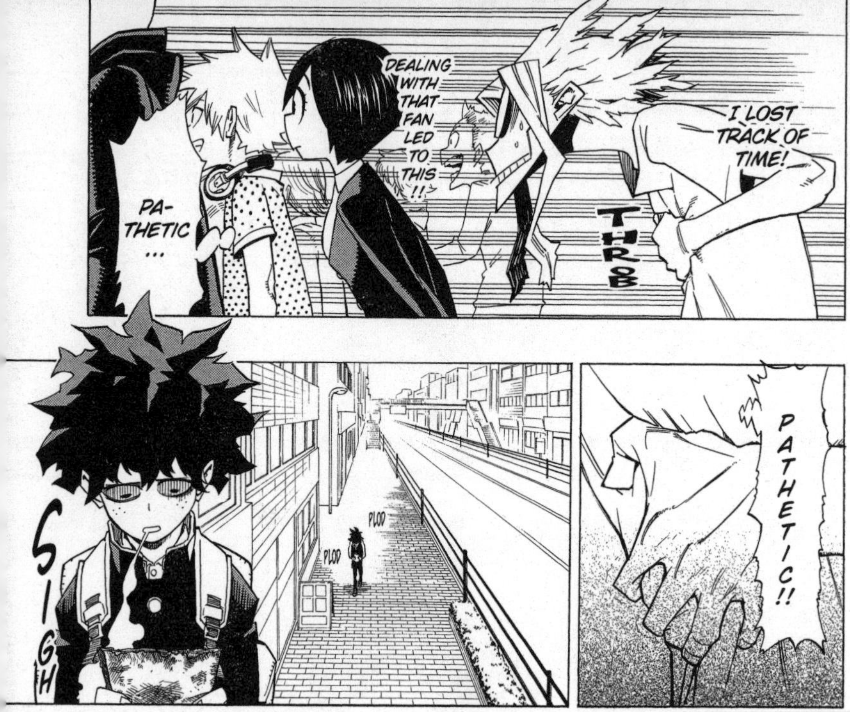
I LOST TRACK OF TIME!
THROB
DEALING WITH THAT FAN LED TO THIS!!
PA-THETIC...
PATHETIC!!
PLOD
PLOD
SIGH

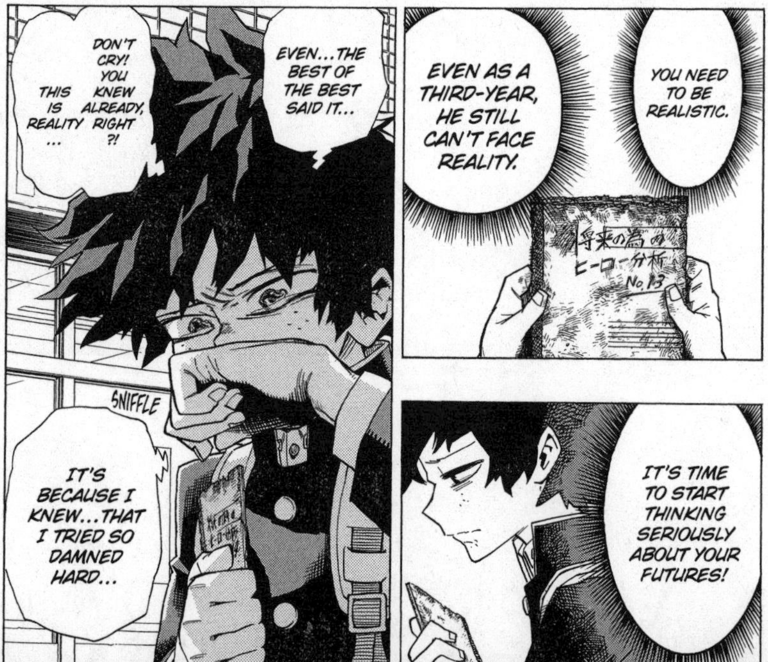
YOU NEED TO BE REALISTIC.
EVEN AS A THIRD-YEAR, HE STILL CAN'T FACE REALITY.
将来の為の
ヒーロー分析
No.13
IT'S TIME TO START THINKING SERIOUSLY ABOUT YOUR FUTURES!
DON'T CRY! YOU KNEW ALREADY, RIGHT?! THIS IS REALITY...
EVEN...THE BEST OF THE BEST SAID IT...
SNIFFLE
IT'S BECAUSE I KNEW...THAT I TRIED SO DAMNED HARD...

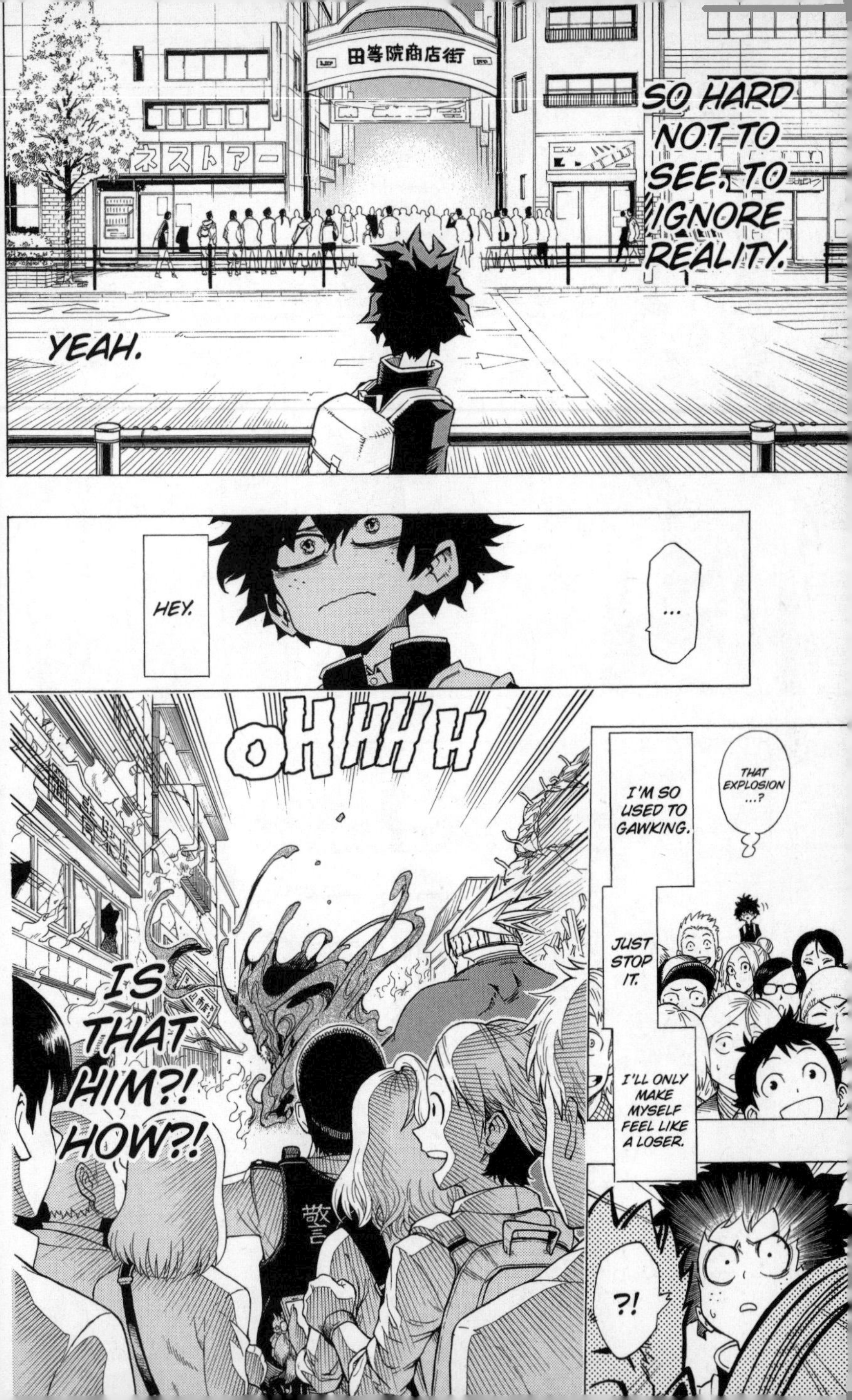
田等院商店街
SO HARD NOT TO SEE. TO IGNORE REALITY.
YEAH.
...
HEY.
THAT EXPLOSION ...?
I'M SO USED TO GAWKING.
JUST STOP IT.
I'LL ONLY MAKE MYSELF FEEL LIKE A LOSER.
?!
OHHHH
IS THAT HIM?! HOW?!

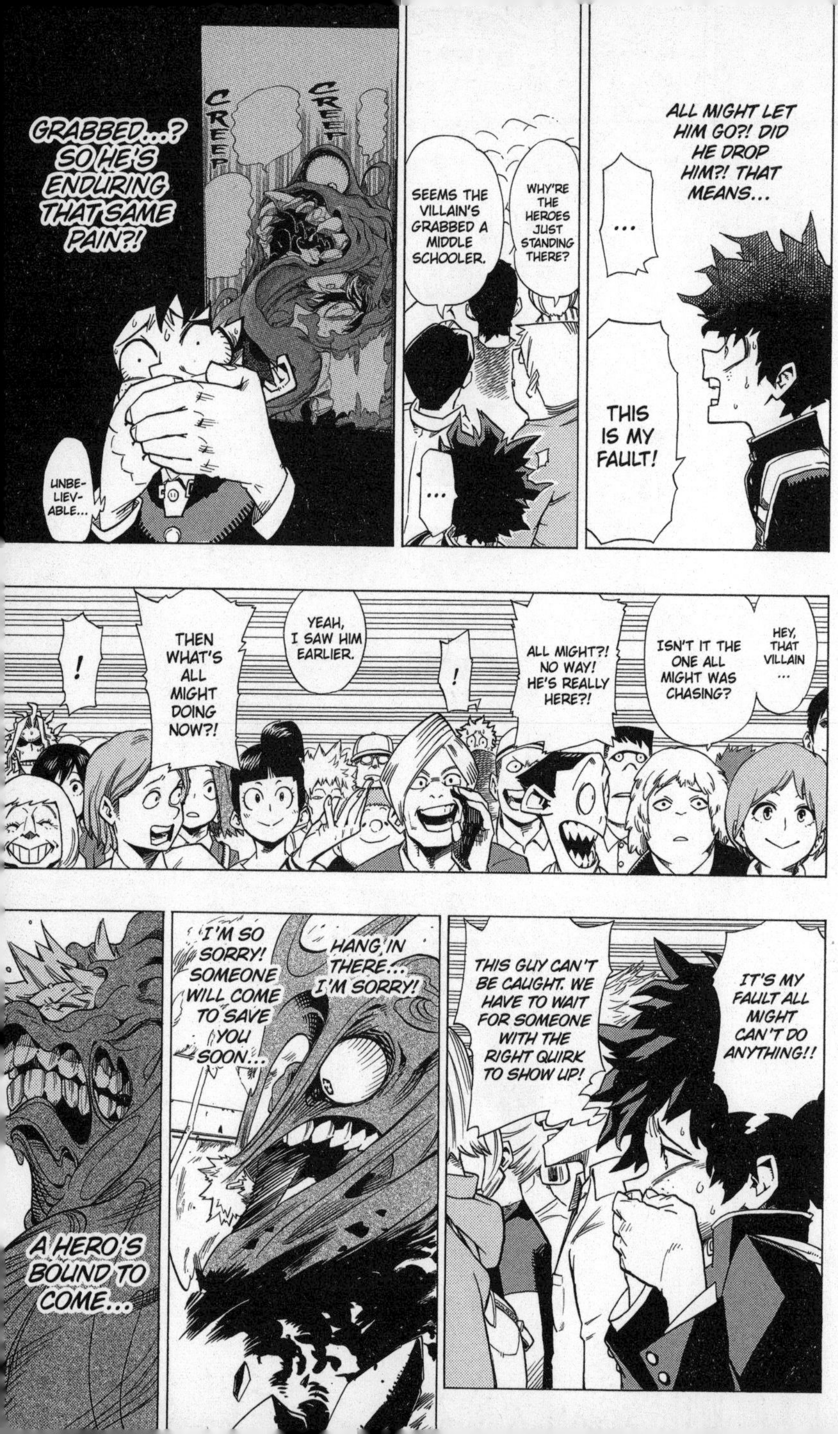
ALL MIGHT LET HIM GO?! DID HE DROP HIM?! THAT MEANS...
...
THIS IS MY FAULT!
SEEMS THE VILLAIN'S GRABBED A MIDDLE SCHOOLER.
WHY'RE THE HEROES JUST STANDING THERE?
...
GRABBED...? SO HE'S ENDURING THAT SAME PAIN?!
CREEP
CREEP
UNBE-LIEV-ABLE...
HEY, THAT VILLAIN ...
ISN'T IT THE ONE ALL MIGHT WAS CHASING?
ALL MIGHT?! NO WAY! HE'S REALLY HERE?!
!
YEAH, I SAW HIM EARLIER.
THEN WHAT'S ALL MIGHT DOING NOW?!
!
IT'S MY FAULT ALL MIGHT CAN'T DO ANYTHING!!
THIS GUY CAN'T BE CAUGHT. WE HAVE TO WAIT FOR SOMEONE WITH THE RIGHT QUIRK TO SHOW UP!
HANG IN THERE... I'M SORRY!
I'M SO SORRY! SOMEONE WILL COME TO SAVE YOU SOON...
A HERO'S BOUND TO COME...

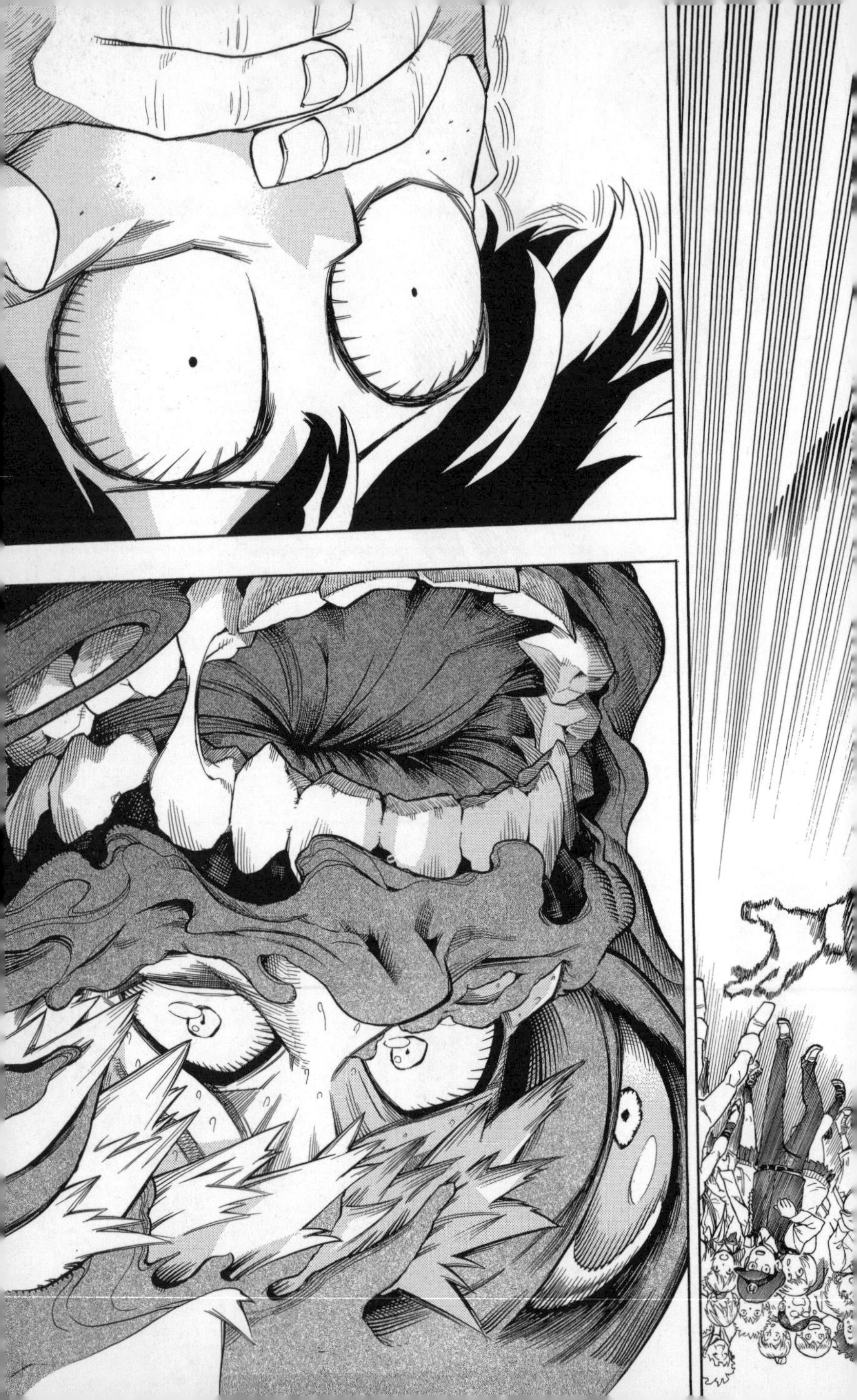

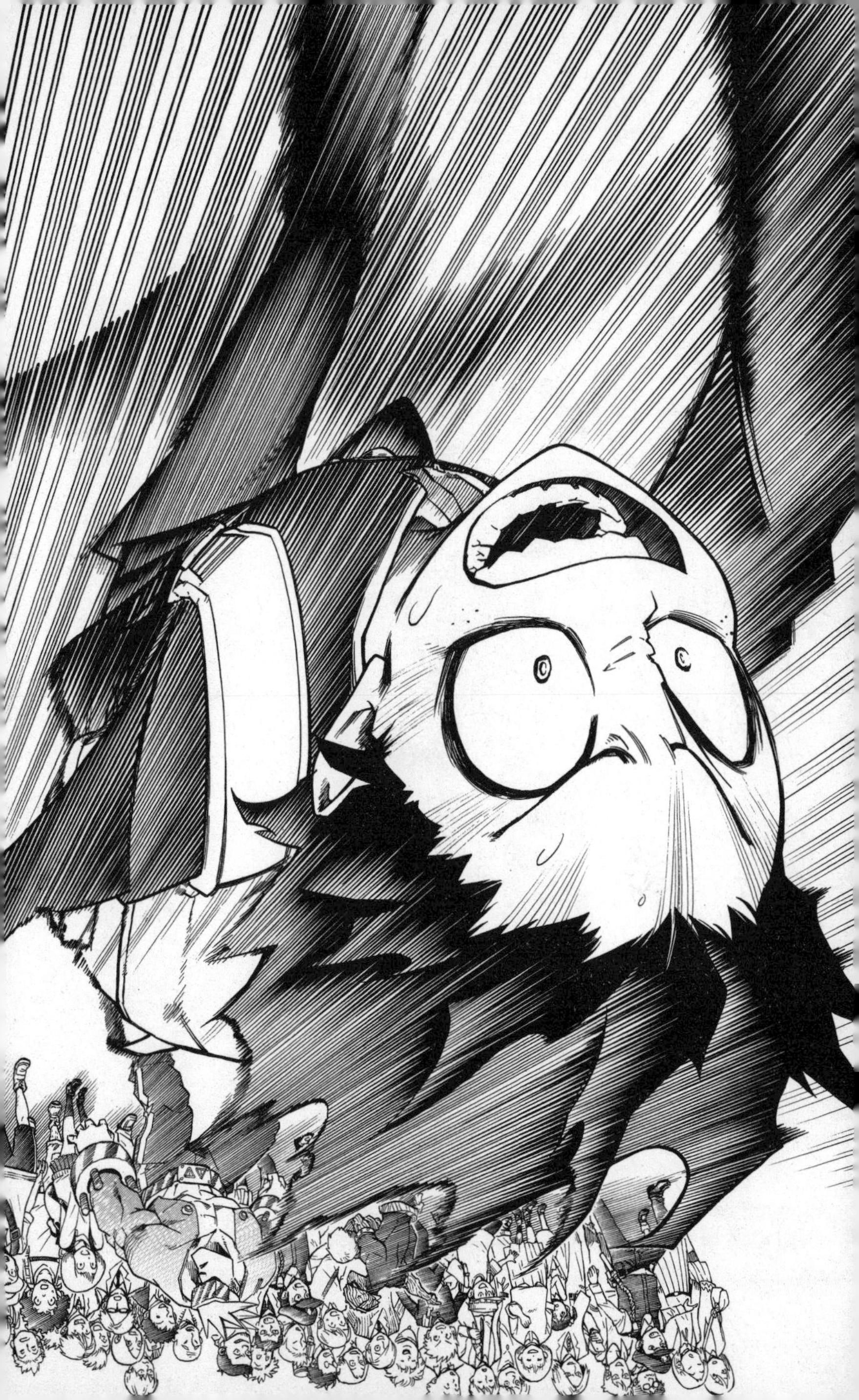

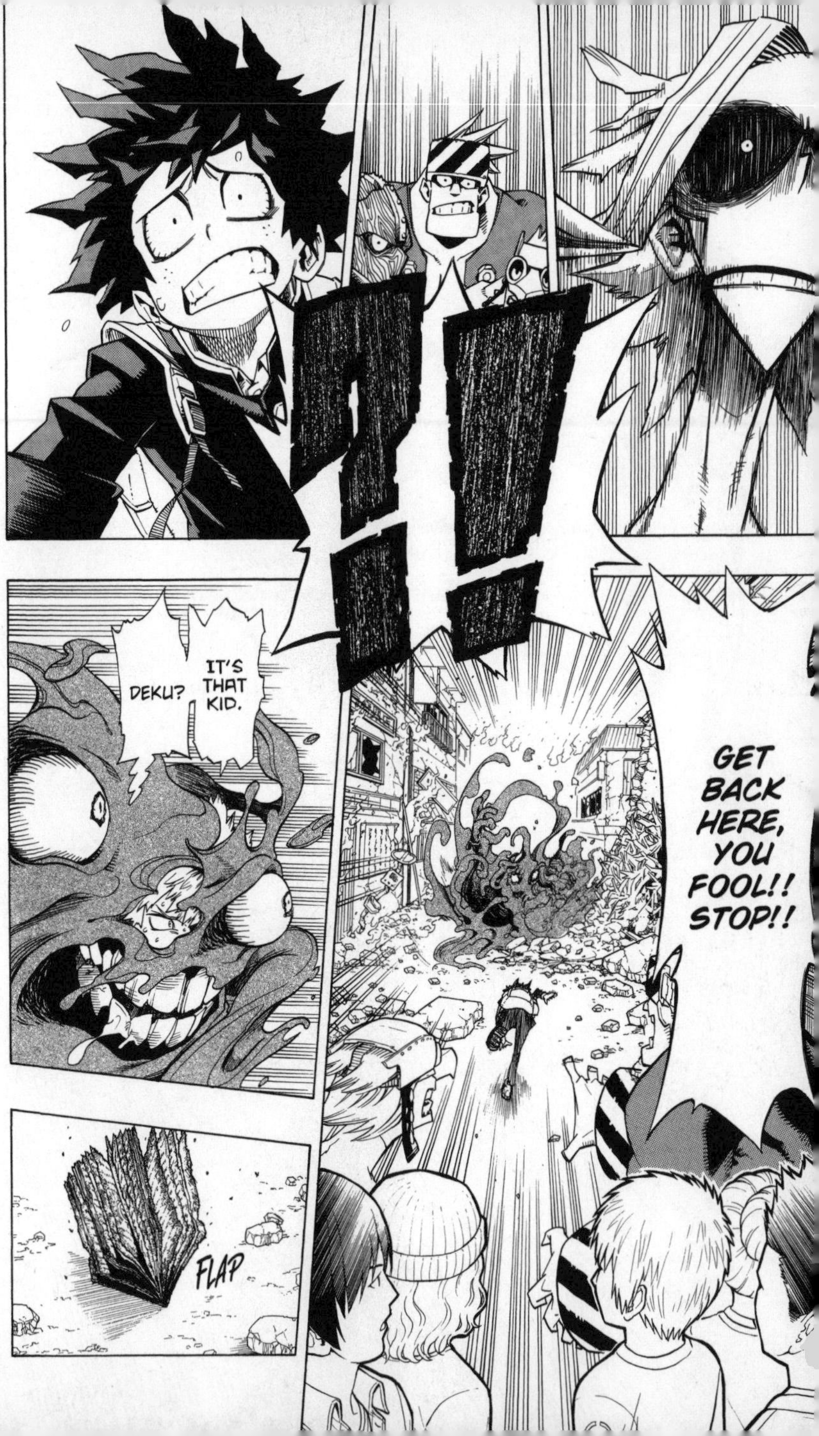
?!
GET BACK HERE, YOU FOOL!! STOP!!
IT'S THAT KID.
DEKU?
FLAP

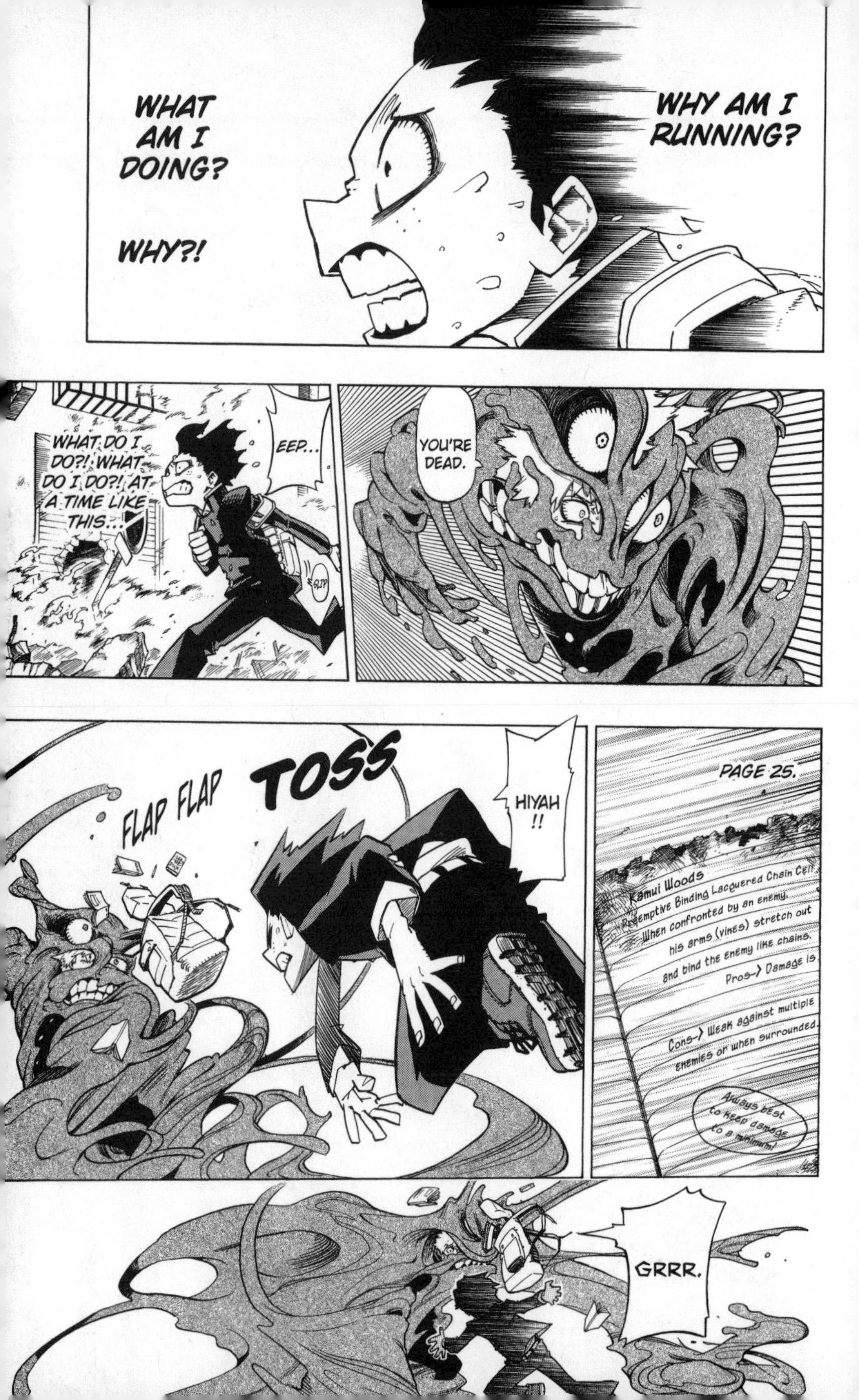
WHY AM I RUNNING?
WHAT AM I DOING?
WHY?!
YOU'RE DEAD.
EEP...
WHAT DO I DO?! WHAT DO I DO?! AT A TIME LIKE THIS...
SLIP
PAGE 25.
Kamui Woods
Preemptive Binding Lacquered Chain Cell
When confronted by an enemy, his arms (vines) stretch out and bind the enemy like chains.
Pros-> Damage is
Cons-> Weak against multiple enemies or when surrounded.
Always best to keep damage to a minimum!
HIYAH !!
TOSS
FLAP FLAP
GRRR.

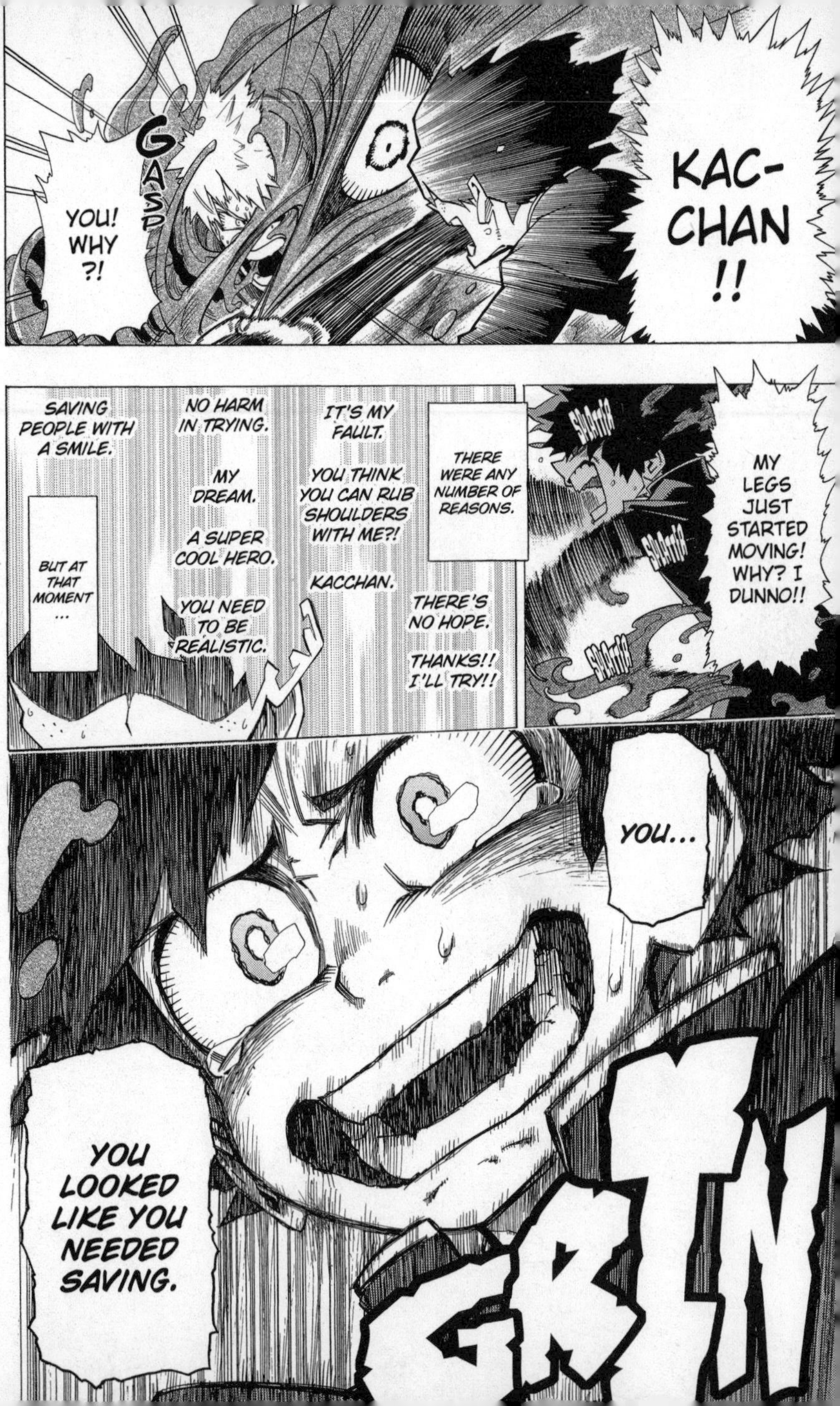
KAC-CHAN!!
GASP
YOU! WHY?!
MY LEGS JUST STARTED MOVING! WHY? I DUNNO!!
SPLOrrSH
SPLOrrSH
SPLOrrSH
THERE WERE ANY NUMBER OF REASONS.
IT'S MY FAULT.
YOU THINK YOU CAN RUB SHOULDERS WITH ME?!
KACCHAN.
THERE'S NO HOPE.
THANKS!! I'LL TRY!!
NO HARM IN TRYING.
MY DREAM.
A SUPER COOL HERO.
YOU NEED TO BE REALISTIC.
SAVING PEOPLE WITH A SMILE.
BUT AT THAT MOMENT ...
YOU...
GRIN
YOU LOOKED LIKE YOU NEEDED SAVING.

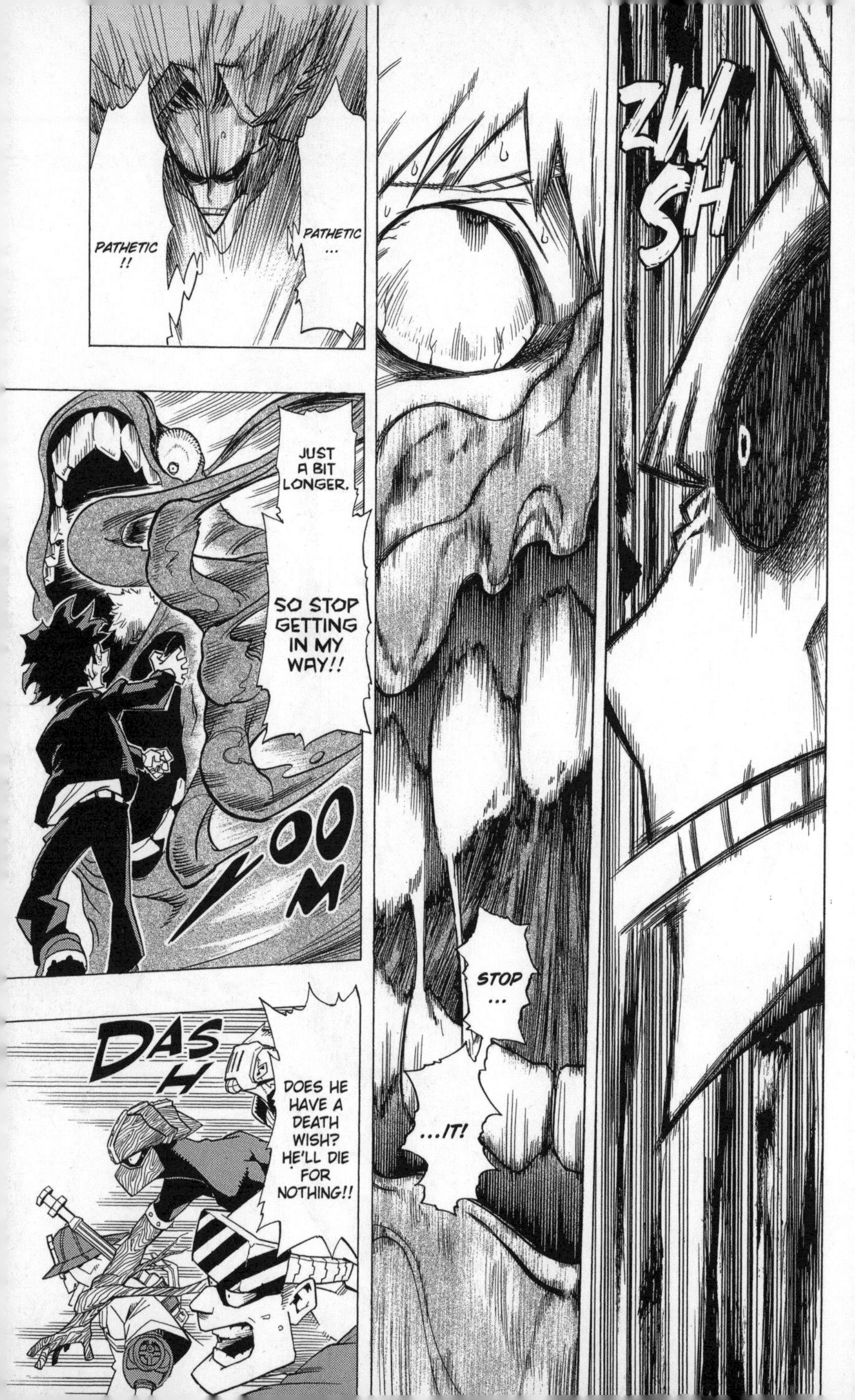
ZWSH
STOP...
...IT!
PATHETIC...
PATHETIC!!
JUST A BIT LONGER.
SO STOP GETTING IN MY WAY!!
ZOOM
DASH
DOES HE HAVE A DEATH WISH? HE'LL DIE FOR NOTHING!!

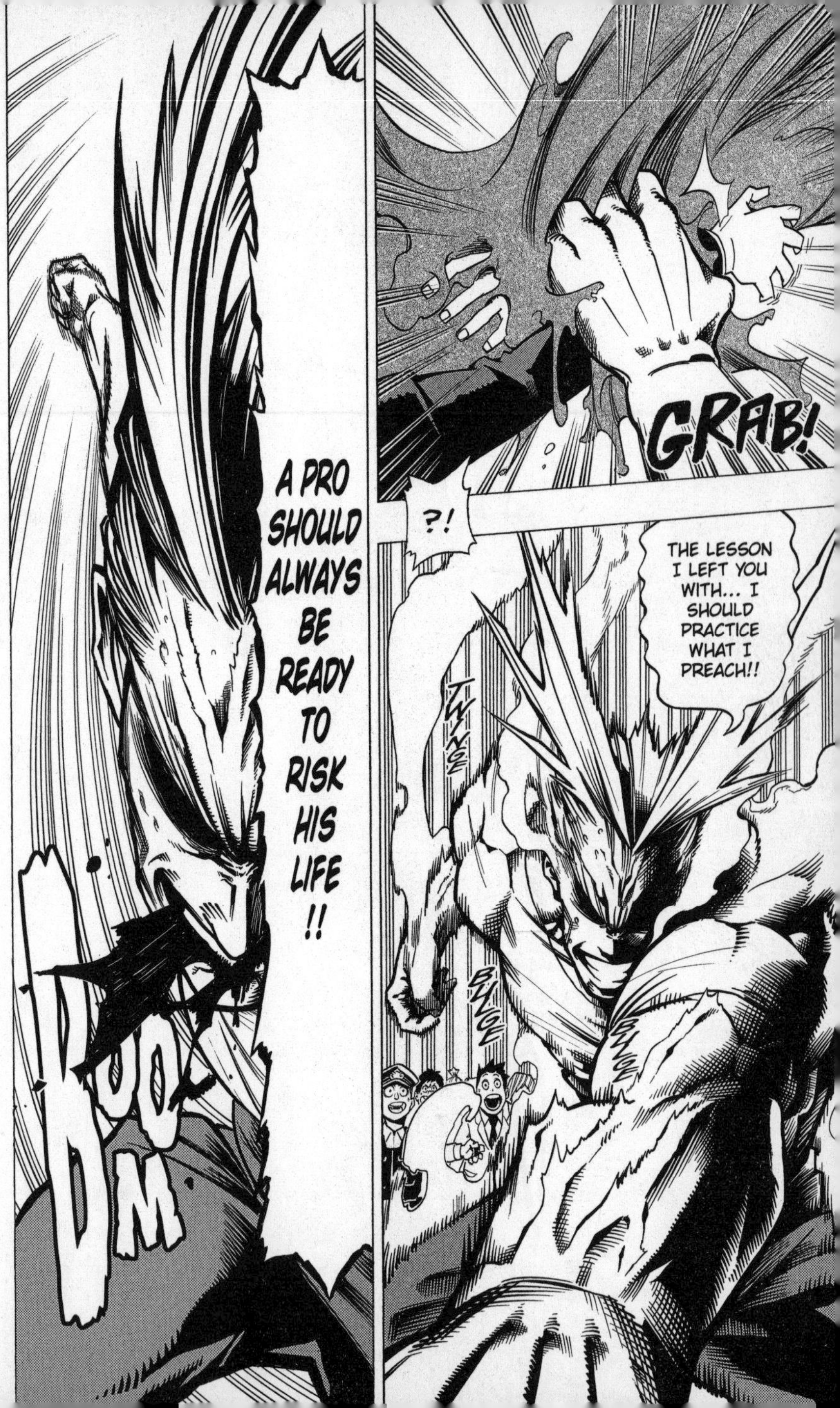
GRAB!
?!
THE LESSON I LEFT YOU WITH... I SHOULD PRACTICE WHAT I PREACH!!
TWINGE
BULGE
A PRO SHOULD ALWAYS BE READY TO RISK HIS LIFE!!
BOOM

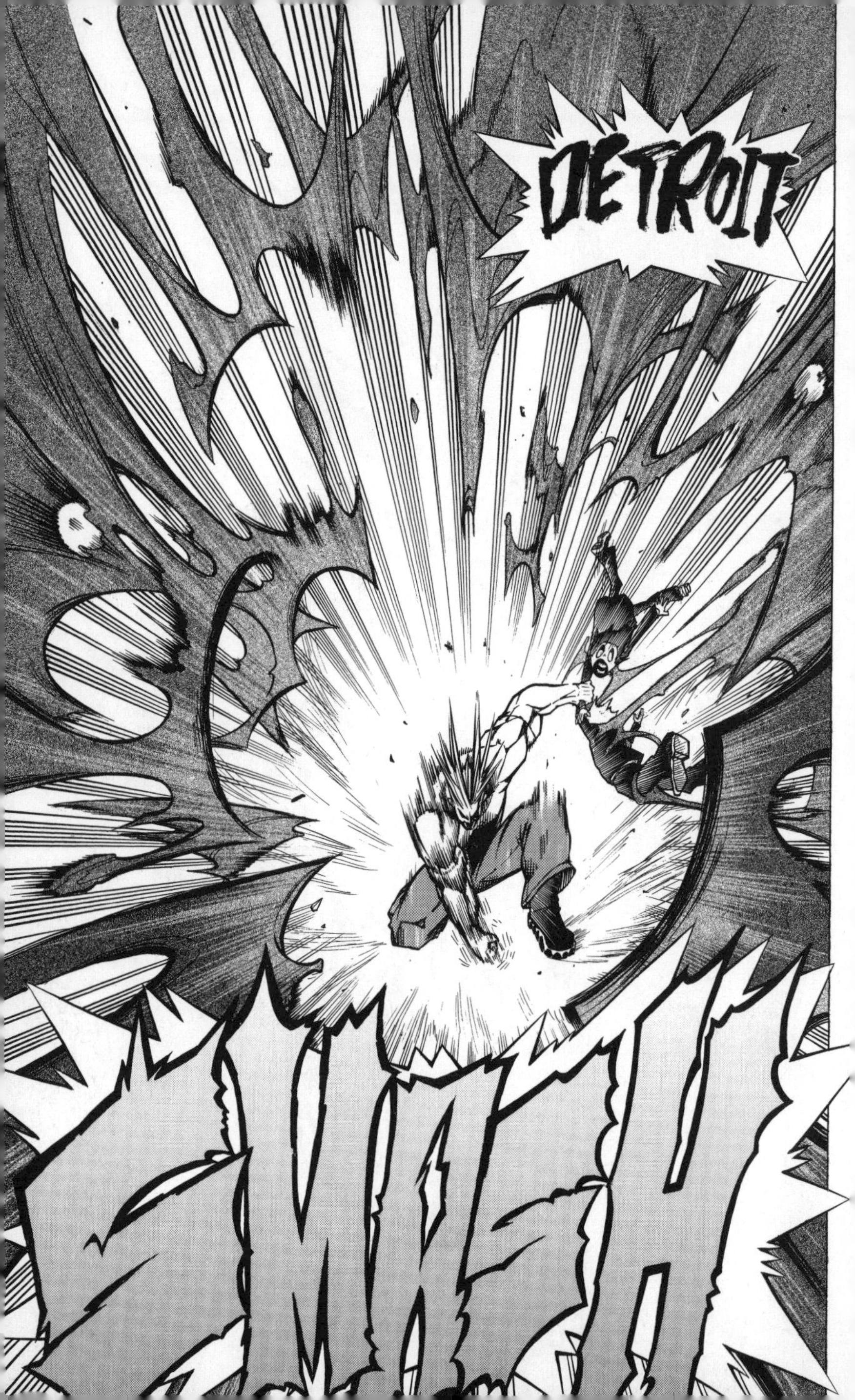
DETROIT
SMASH

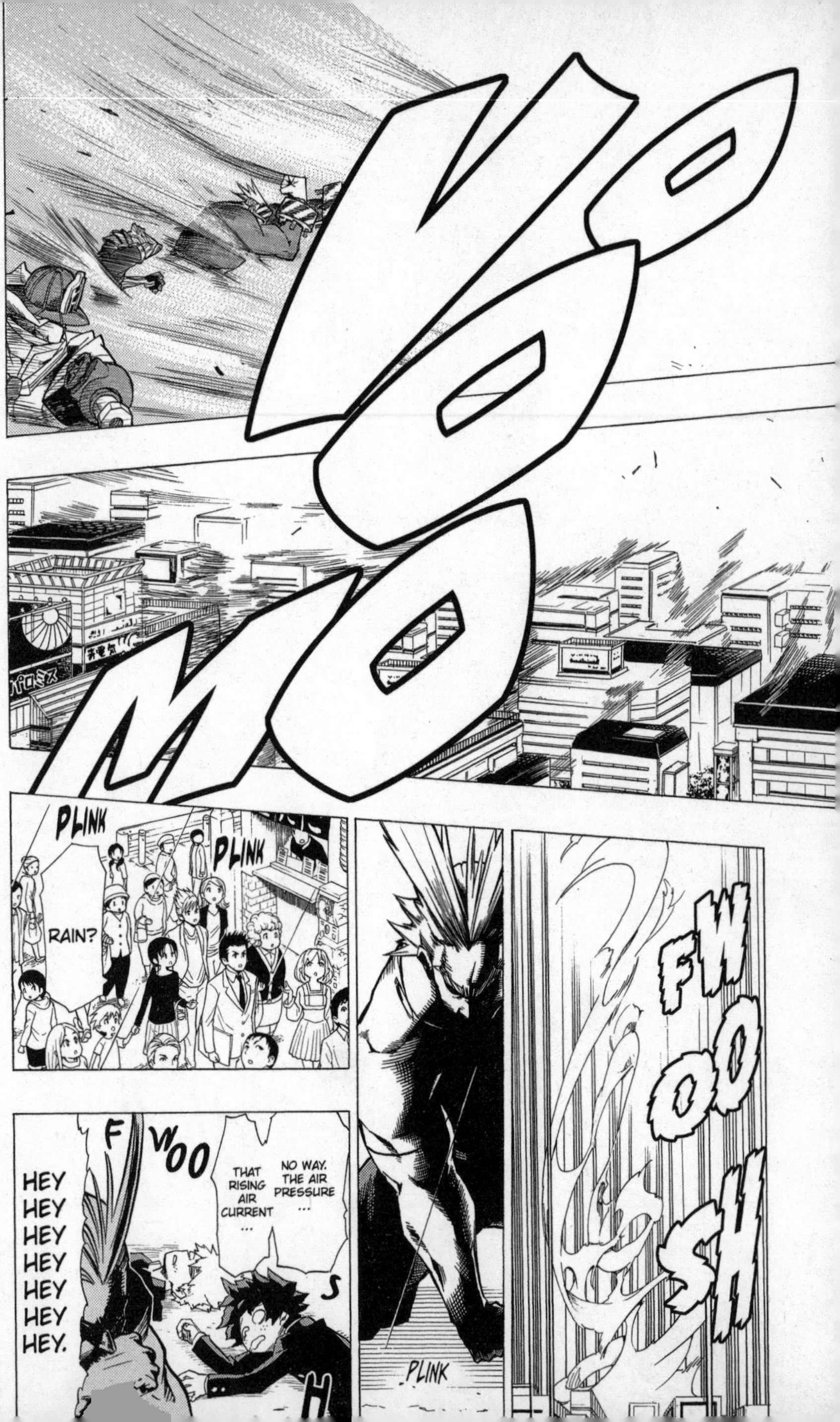
FWOOOSH
PLINK
PLINK
PLINK
RAIN?
FWOO
NO WAY. THE AIR PRESSURE ...
THAT RISING AIR CURRENT ...
HEY HEY HEY HEY HEY HEY HEY.

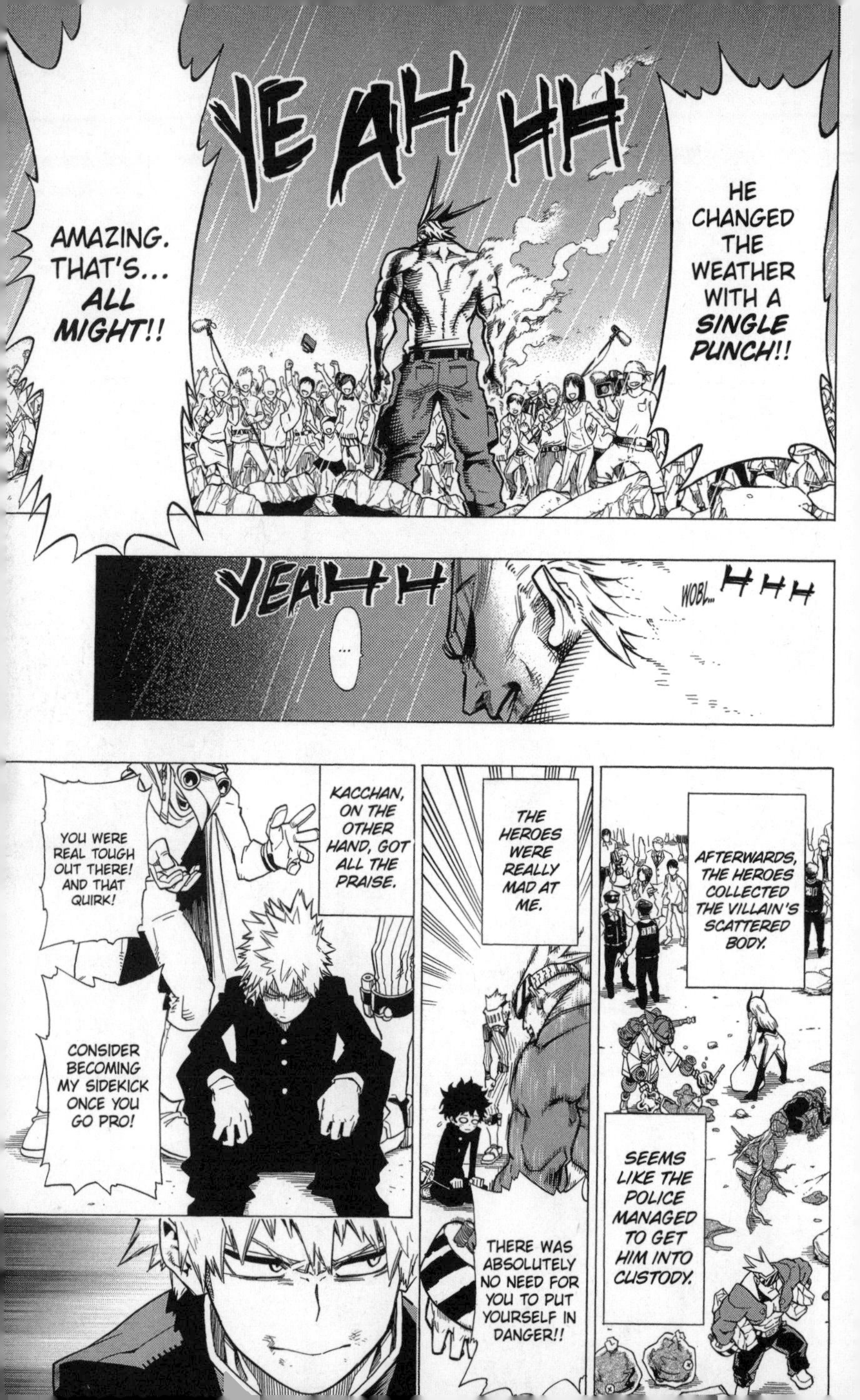
HE CHANGED THE WEATHER WITH A SINGLE PUNCH!!
YEAHHH
AMAZING. THAT'S... ALL MIGHT!!
WOBL... HHH
YEAHHH
...
AFTERWARDS, THE HEROES COLLECTED THE VILLAIN'S SCATTERED BODY.
SEEMS LIKE THE POLICE MANAGED TO GET HIM INTO CUSTODY.
THE HEROES WERE REALLY MAD AT ME.
THERE WAS ABSOLUTELY NO NEED FOR YOU TO PUT YOURSELF IN DANGER!!
KACCHAN, ON THE OTHER HAND, GOT ALL THE PRAISE.
YOU WERE REAL TOUGH OUT THERE! AND THAT QUIRK!
CONSIDER BECOMING MY SIDEKICK ONCE YOU GO PRO!

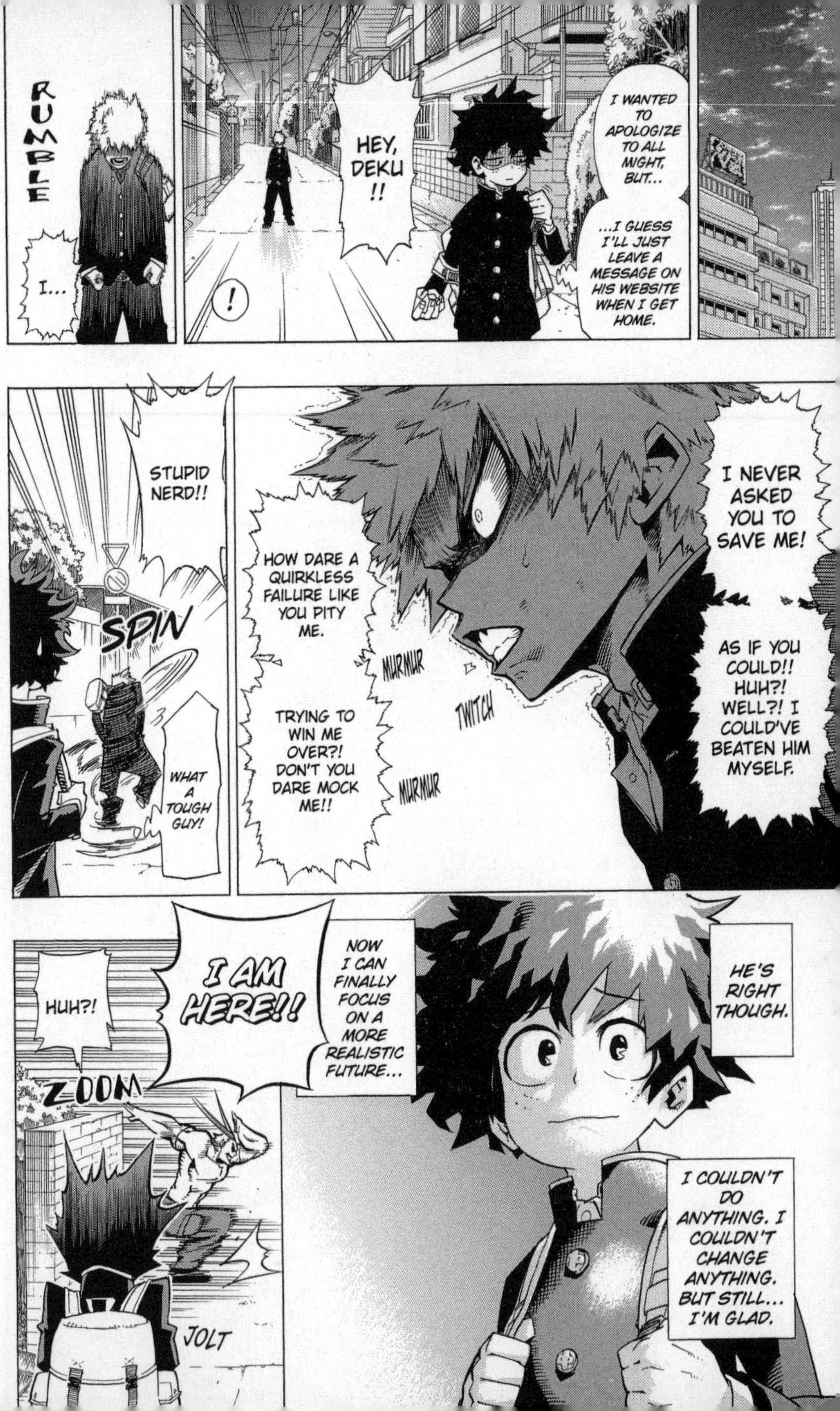
I WANTED TO APOLOGIZE TO ALL MIGHT, BUT...
...I GUESS I'LL JUST LEAVE A MESSAGE ON HIS WEBSITE WHEN I GET HOME.
HEY, DEKU!!
!
RUMBLE
I...
I NEVER ASKED YOU TO SAVE ME!
AS IF YOU COULD!! HUH?! WELL?! I COULD'VE BEATEN HIM MYSELF.
HOW DARE A QUIRKLESS FAILURE LIKE YOU PITY ME.
MURMUR
TWITCH
TRYING TO WIN ME OVER?! DON'T YOU DARE MOCK ME!!
MURMUR
STUPID NERD!!
SPIN
WHAT A TOUGH GUY!
HE'S RIGHT THOUGH.
I COULDN'T DO ANYTHING. I COULDN'T CHANGE ANYTHING. BUT STILL... I'M GLAD.
NOW I CAN FINALLY FOCUS ON A MORE REALISTIC FUTURE...
I AM HERE!!
HUH?!
ZOOM
JOLT

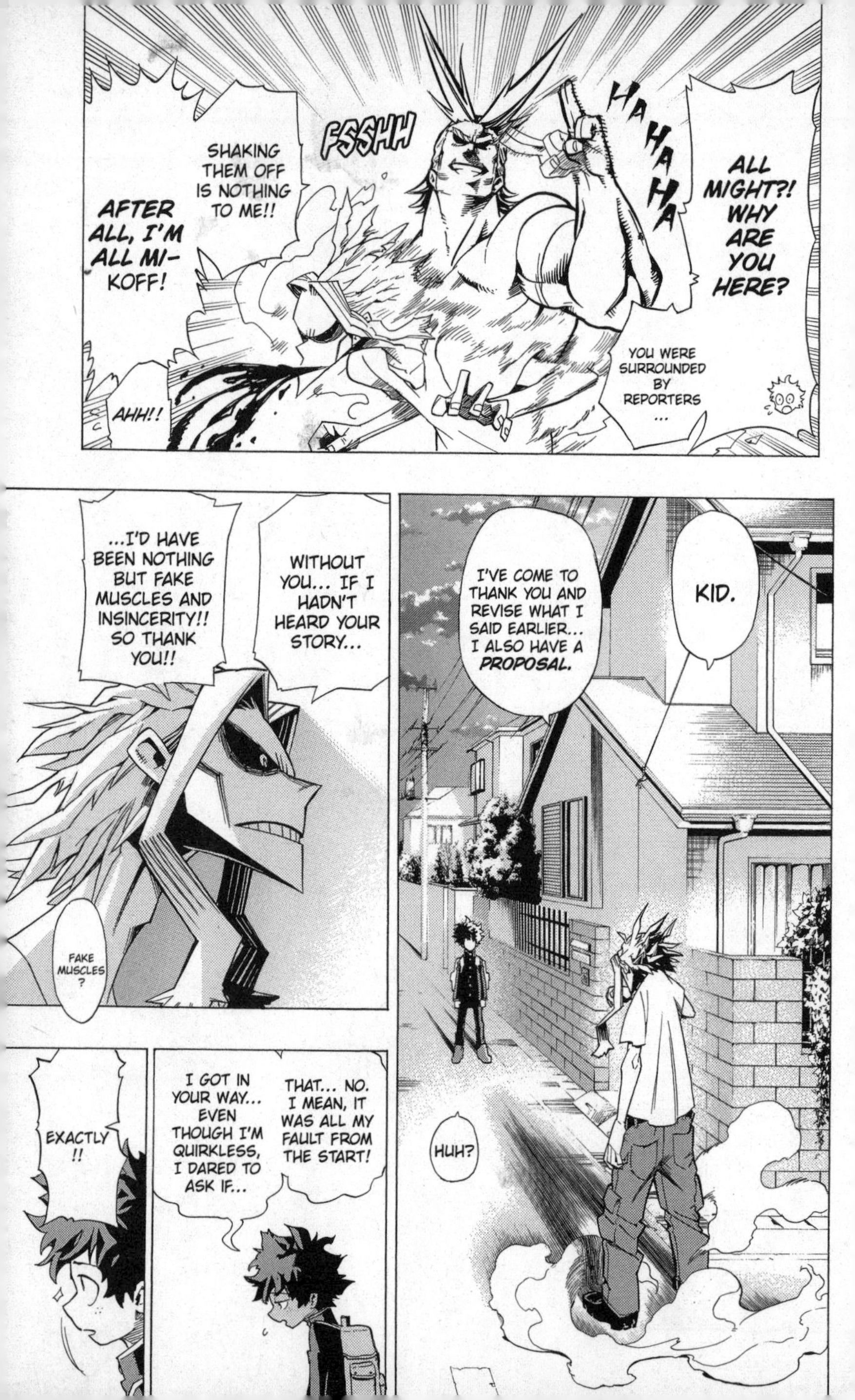
ALL MIGHT?! WHY ARE YOU HERE?
HAHAHAHA
YOU WERE SURROUNDED BY REPORTERS ...
FSSHH
SHAKING THEM OFF IS NOTHING TO ME!!
AFTER ALL, I'M ALL MI- KOFF!
AHH!!
KID.
I'VE COME TO THANK YOU AND REVISE WHAT I SAID EARLIER... I ALSO HAVE A PROPOSAL.
HUH?
WITHOUT YOU... IF I HADN'T HEARD YOUR STORY...
...I'D HAVE BEEN NOTHING BUT FAKE MUSCLES AND INSINCERITY!! SO THANK YOU!!
FAKE MUSCLES ?
THAT... NO. I MEAN, IT WAS ALL MY FAULT FROM THE START!
I GOT IN YOUR WAY... EVEN THOUGH I'M QUIRKLESS, I DARED TO ASK IF...
EXACTLY !!

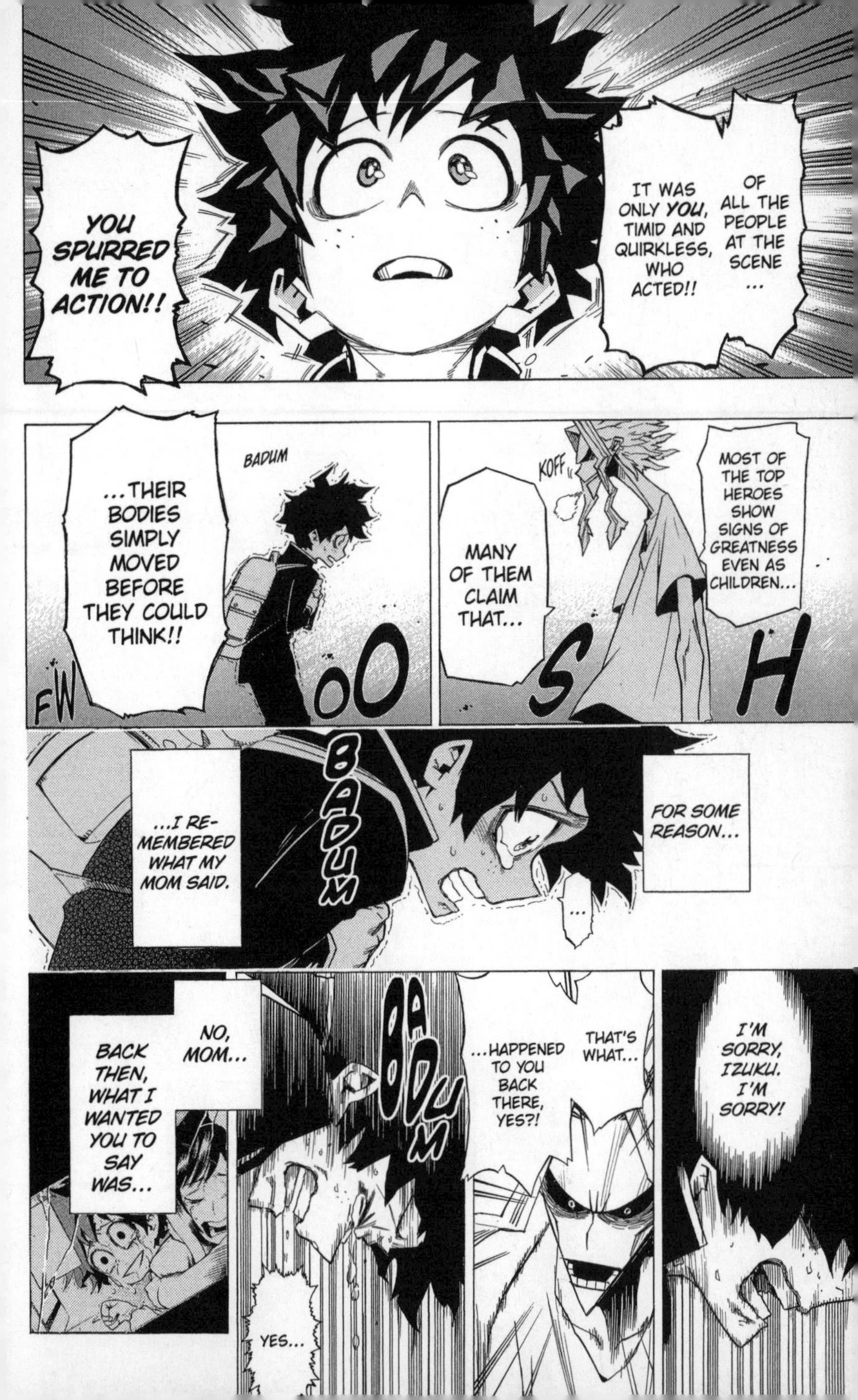
OF ALL THE PEOPLE AT THE SCENE...
IT WAS ONLY YOU, TIMID AND QUIRKLESS, WHO ACTED!!
YOU SPURRED ME TO ACTION!!
MOST OF THE TOP HEROES SHOW SIGNS OF GREATNESS EVEN AS CHILDREN...
KOFF
MANY OF THEM CLAIM THAT...
H S
BADUM
...THEIR BODIES SIMPLY MOVED BEFORE THEY COULD THINK!!
OO FW
FOR SOME REASON...
...
BADUM
...I RE-MEMBERED WHAT MY MOM SAID.
I'M SORRY, IZUKU. I'M SORRY!
THAT'S WHAT...
...HAPPENED TO YOU BACK THERE, YES?!
BADUM
YES...
NO, MOM...
BACK THEN, WHAT I WANTED YOU TO SAY WAS...

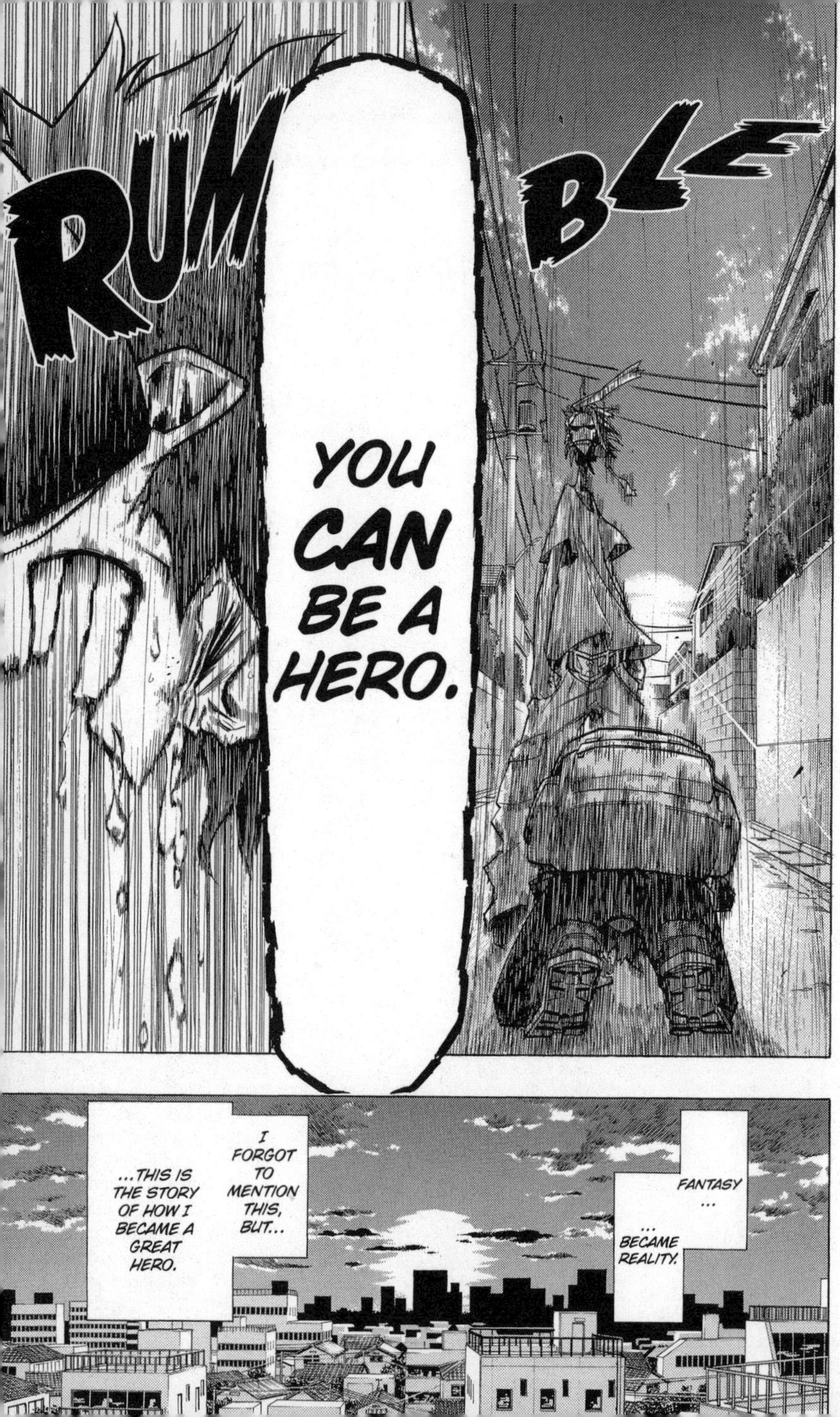
RUMBLE
YOU CAN BE A HERO.
FANTASY ...
... BECAME REALITY.
I FORGOT TO MENTION THIS, BUT...
...THIS IS THE STORY OF HOW I BECAME A GREAT HERO.

ALL MIGHT (AGE: ?)

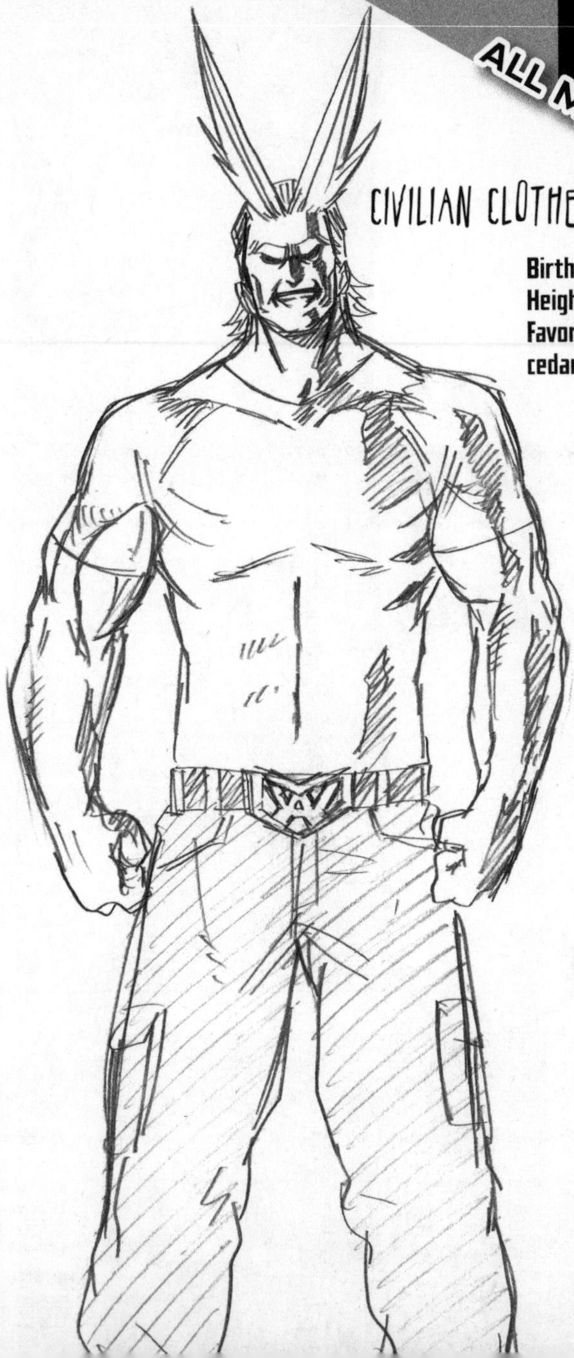
CIVILIAN CLOTHES

Birthday: 6/10
Height: 220 cm
Favorite Things: Yakushima cedars, movies

BEHIND THE SCENES

Drawing a single frontal shot of him uses up one or two pen nibs. He's terrible for my fuel economy.

I thought he was really cool when I first drew him, but at the meeting with the editorial department, they said, "Who'd look up to this old guy? I don't wanna be like him," and "Wouldn't he be better as a pretty boy?" My manga buddies said, "Who's this weird, cheerful old dude?" But their criticism only fanned my flames. Thanks to them, now I give it my all when drawing him. So thanks for that, guys.

THE SUPPLEMENT

The whites of his eyes are all black when in his True Form (skinny). He's so gaunt that they're perpetually in shadow. Only his pupils glisten, reflecting the true strength and dignity of this "symbol of peace." It's like everything that his Muscle Form represents is condensed into those pupils. But I'm really not a good enough artist to properly express that. Sorry.

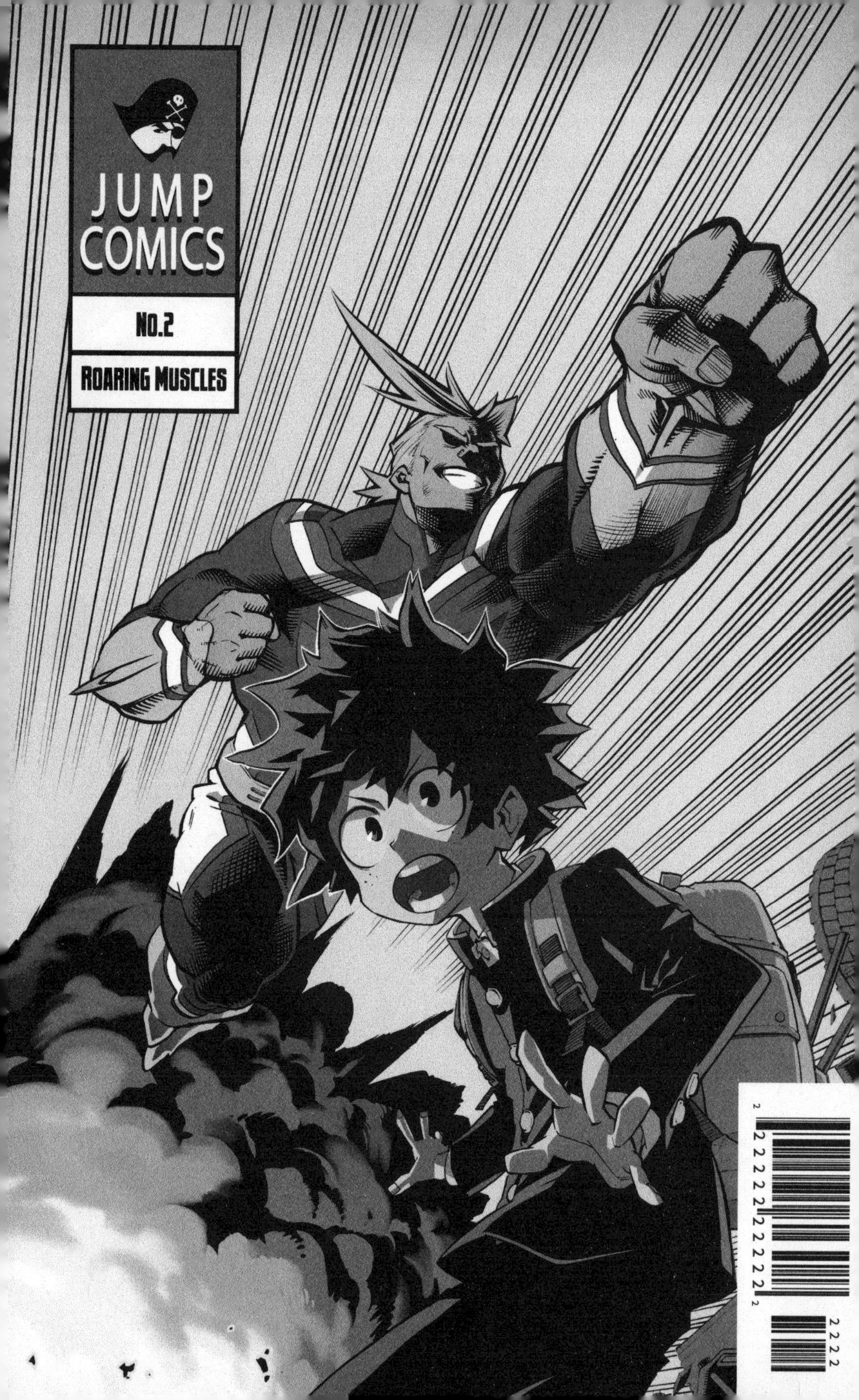
JUMP
COMICS
NO.2
ROARING MUSCLES

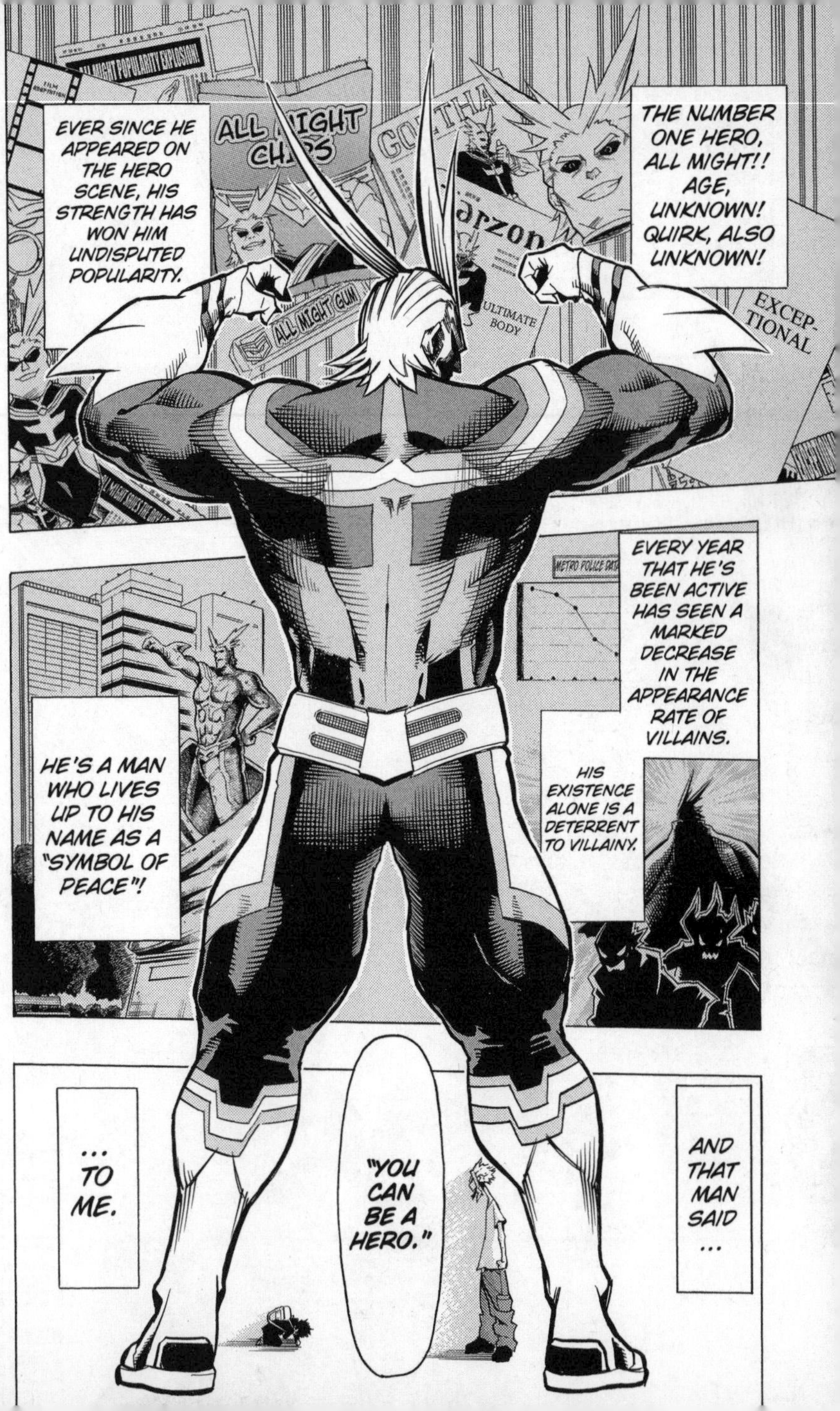
THE NUMBER ONE HERO, ALL MIGHT!! AGE, UNKNOWN! QUIRK, ALSO UNKNOWN!
EXCEP-TIONAL
ULTIMATE BODY
ALL MIGHT GUM
ALL MIGHT CHIPS
EVER SINCE HE APPEARED ON THE HERO SCENE, HIS STRENGTH HAS WON HIM UNDISPUTED POPULARITY.
FILM ADAPTATION
EVERY YEAR THAT HE'S BEEN ACTIVE HAS SEEN A MARKED DECREASE IN THE APPEARANCE RATE OF VILLAINS.
HIS EXISTENCE ALONE IS A DETERRENT TO VILLAINY.
HE'S A MAN WHO LIVES UP TO HIS NAME AS A "SYMBOL OF PEACE"!
AND THAT MAN SAID ...
"YOU CAN BE A HERO."
... TO ME.

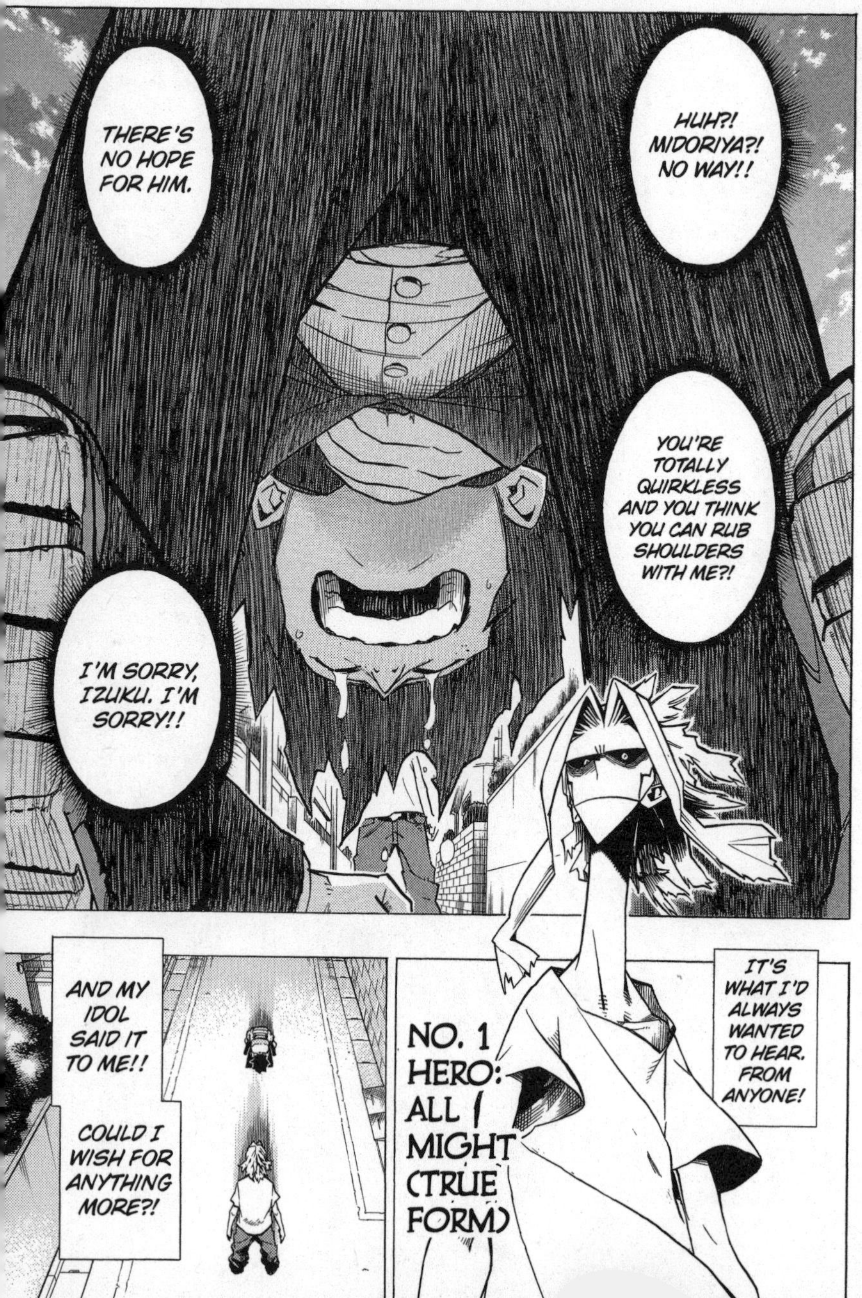
HUH?! MIDORIYA?! NO WAY!!
THERE'S NO HOPE FOR HIM.
YOU'RE TOTALLY QUIRKLESS AND YOU THINK YOU CAN RUB SHOULDERS WITH ME?!
I'M SORRY, IZUKU. I'M SORRY!!
IT'S WHAT I'D ALWAYS WANTED TO HEAR. FROM ANYONE!
NO. 1 HERO: ALL MIGHT (TRUE FORM)
AND MY IDOL SAID IT TO ME!!
COULD I WISH FOR ANYTHING MORE?!

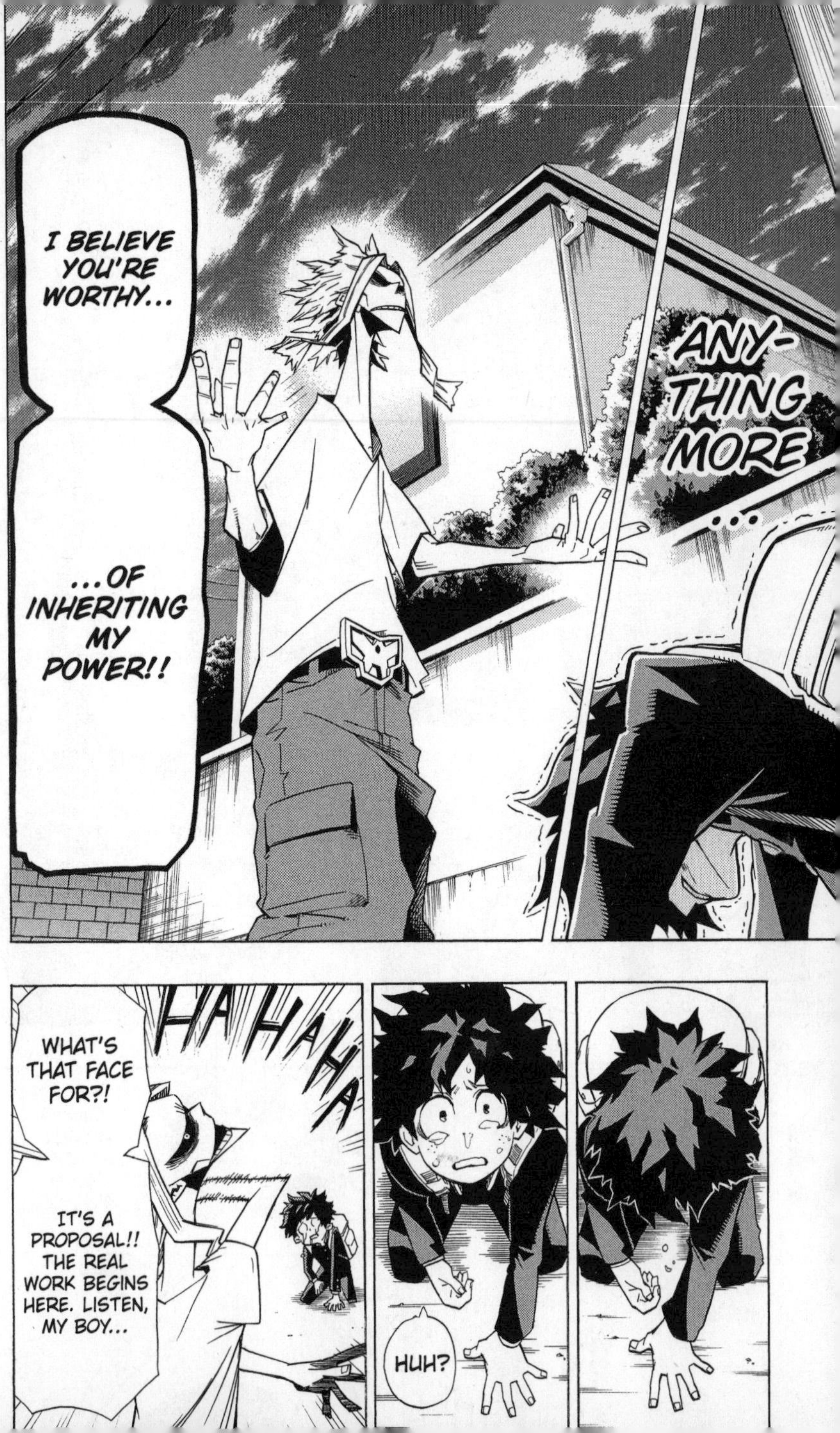
ANY-THING MORE...
I BELIEVE YOU'RE WORTHY...
...OF INHERITING MY POWER!!
HUH?
HAHAHAHA
WHAT'S THAT FACE FOR?!
IT'S A PROPOSAL!! THE REAL WORK BEGINS HERE. LISTEN, MY BOY...

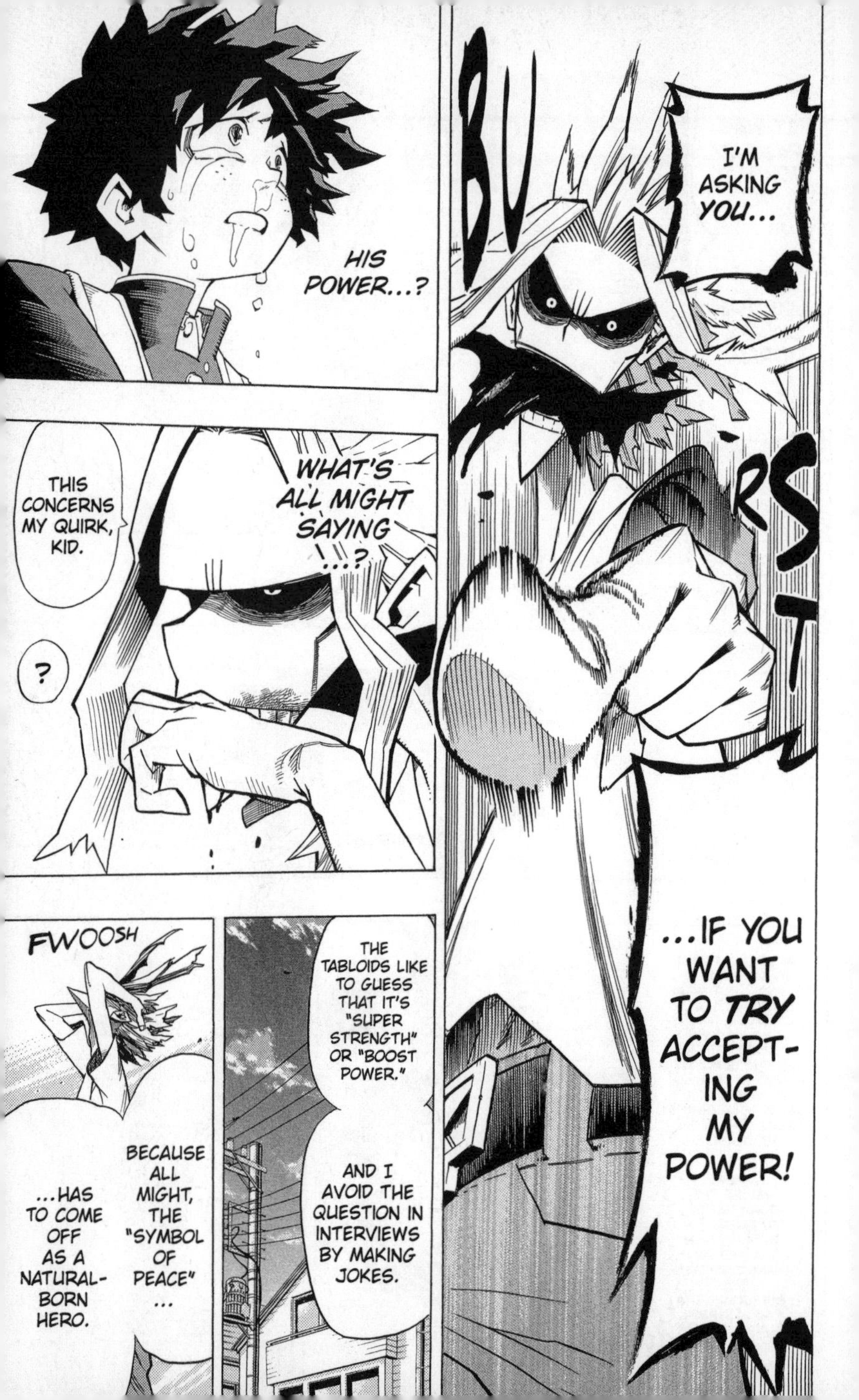
I'M ASKING YOU...
BURST
...IF YOU WANT TO TRY ACCEPTING MY POWER!
HIS POWER...?
THIS CONCERNS MY QUIRK, KID.
WHAT'S ALL MIGHT SAYING ...?
?
THE TABLOIDS LIKE TO GUESS THAT IT'S "SUPER STRENGTH" OR "BOOST POWER."
AND I AVOID THE QUESTION IN INTERVIEWS BY MAKING JOKES.
FWOOSH
BECAUSE ALL MIGHT, THE "SYMBOL OF PEACE" ...
...HAS TO COME OFF AS A NATURAL-BORN HERO.

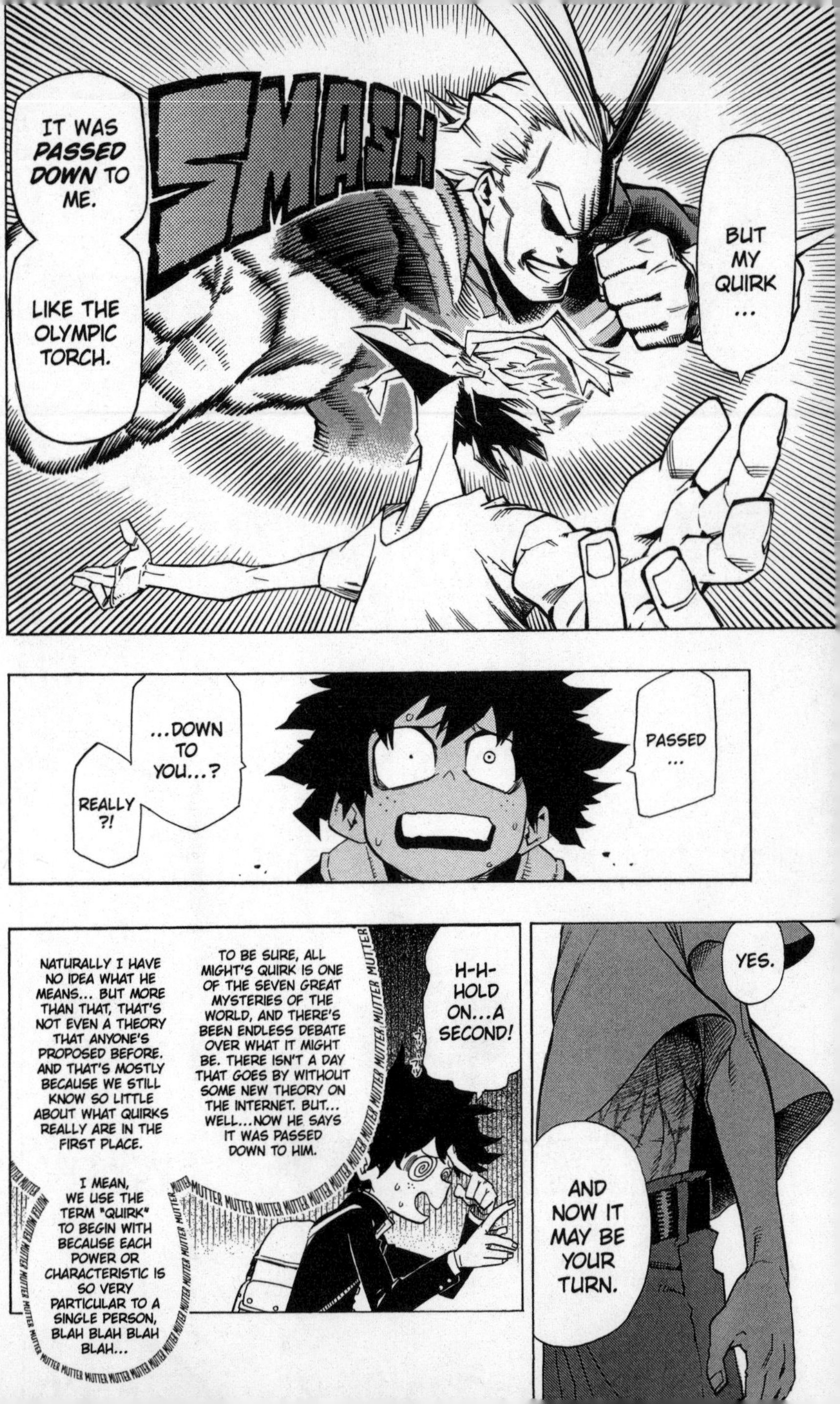
BUT MY QUIRK...
SMASH
IT WAS PASSED DOWN TO ME.
LIKE THE OLYMPIC TORCH.
PASSED...
...DOWN TO YOU...?
REALLY?!
YES.
AND NOW IT MAY BE YOUR TURN.
H-H-HOLD ON...A SECOND!
TO BE SURE, ALL MIGHT'S QUIRK IS ONE OF THE SEVEN GREAT MYSTERIES OF THE WORLD, AND THERE'S BEEN ENDLESS DEBATE OVER WHAT IT MIGHT BE. THERE ISN'T A DAY THAT GOES BY WITHOUT SOME NEW THEORY ON THE INTERNET. BUT... WELL...NOW HE SAYS IT WAS PASSED DOWN TO HIM.
NATURALLY I HAVE NO IDEA WHAT HE MEANS... BUT MORE THAN THAT, THAT'S NOT EVEN A THEORY THAT ANYONE'S PROPOSED BEFORE. AND THAT'S MOSTLY BECAUSE WE STILL KNOW SO LITTLE ABOUT WHAT QUIRKS REALLY ARE IN THE FIRST PLACE.
I MEAN, WE USE THE TERM "QUIRK" TO BEGIN WITH BECAUSE EACH POWER OR CHARACTERISTIC IS SO VERY PARTICULAR TO A SINGLE PERSON, BLAH BLAH BLAH BLAH...
MUTTER MUTTER MUTTER MUTTER

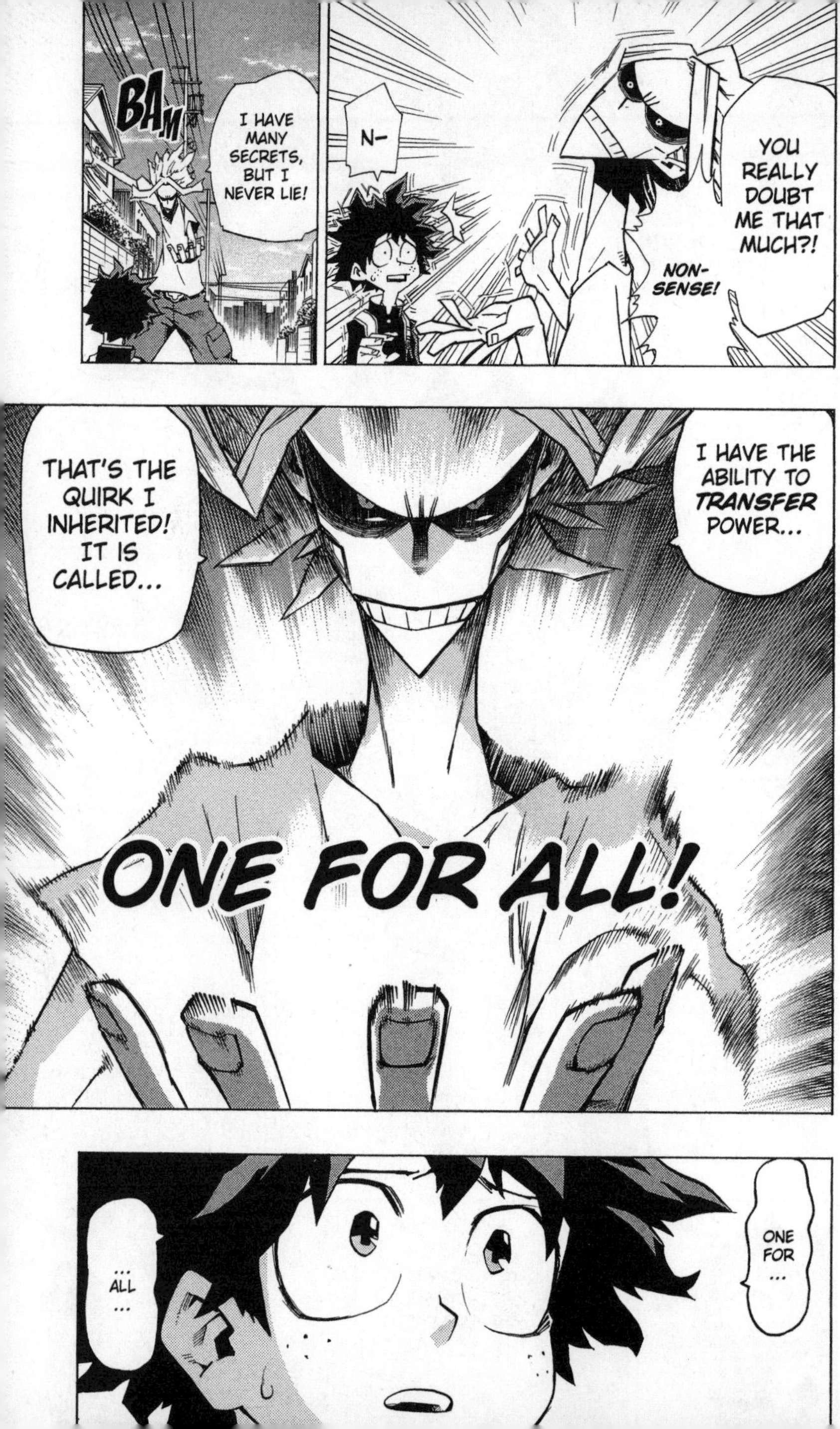
YOU REALLY DOUBT ME THAT MUCH?!
NON-SENSE!
N-
BAM
I HAVE MANY SECRETS, BUT I NEVER LIE!
I HAVE THE ABILITY TO *TRANSFER* POWER...
THAT'S THE QUIRK I INHERITED! IT IS CALLED...
ONE FOR ALL!
ONE FOR ...
... ALL ...

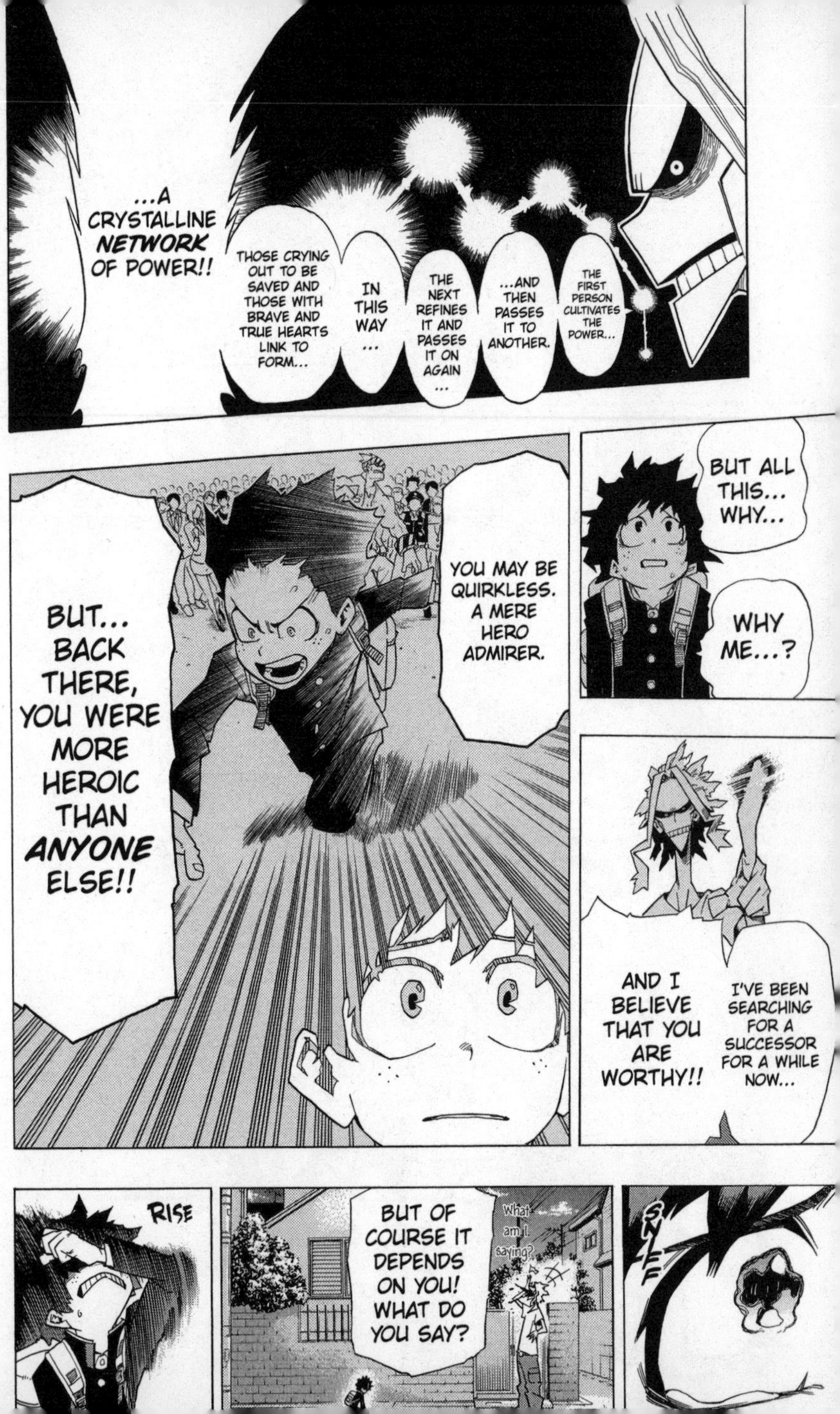
THE FIRST PERSON CULTIVATES THE POWER...
...AND THEN PASSES IT TO ANOTHER.
THE NEXT REFINES IT AND PASSES IT ON AGAIN ...
IN THIS WAY ...
THOSE CRYING OUT TO BE SAVED AND THOSE WITH BRAVE AND TRUE HEARTS LINK TO FORM...
...A CRYSTALLINE NETWORK OF POWER!!
BUT ALL THIS... WHY...
WHY ME...?
I'VE BEEN SEARCHING FOR A SUCCESSOR FOR A WHILE NOW...
AND I BELIEVE THAT YOU ARE WORTHY!!
YOU MAY BE QUIRKLESS. A MERE HERO ADMIRER.
BUT... BACK THERE, YOU WERE MORE HEROIC THAN ANYONE ELSE!!
SNIFF
BUT OF COURSE IT DEPENDS ON YOU! WHAT DO YOU SAY?
What am I saying?
RISE

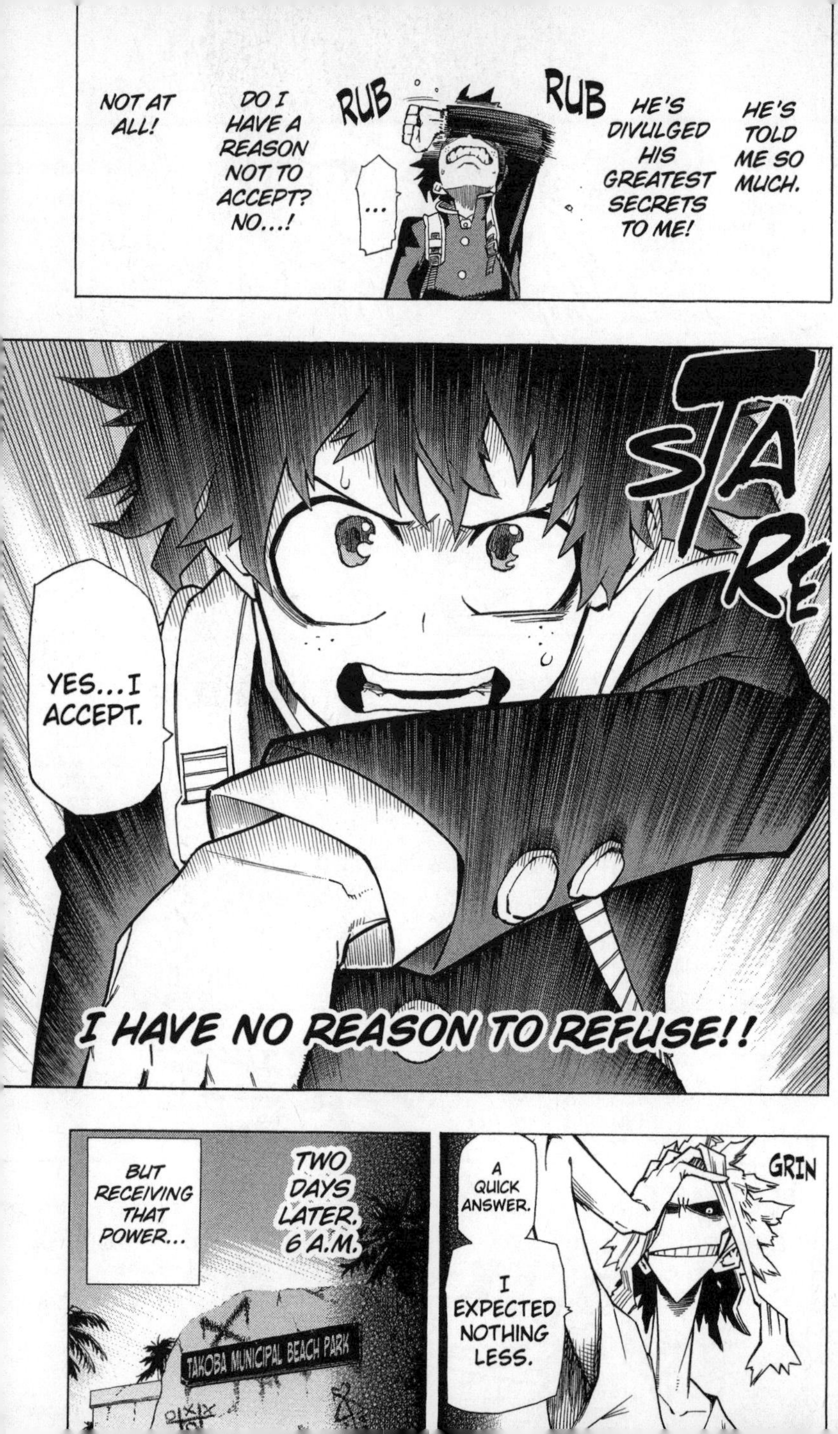
HE'S TOLD ME SO MUCH.
HE'S DIVULGED HIS GREATEST SECRETS TO ME!
RUB
RUB
...
DO I HAVE A REASON NOT TO ACCEPT? NO...!
NOT AT ALL!
STARE
YES...I ACCEPT.
I HAVE NO REASON TO REFUSE!!
GRIN
A QUICK ANSWER.
I EXPECTED NOTHING LESS.
BUT RECEIVING THAT POWER...
TWO DAYS LATER, 6 A.M.
TAKOBA MUNICIPAL BEACH PARK

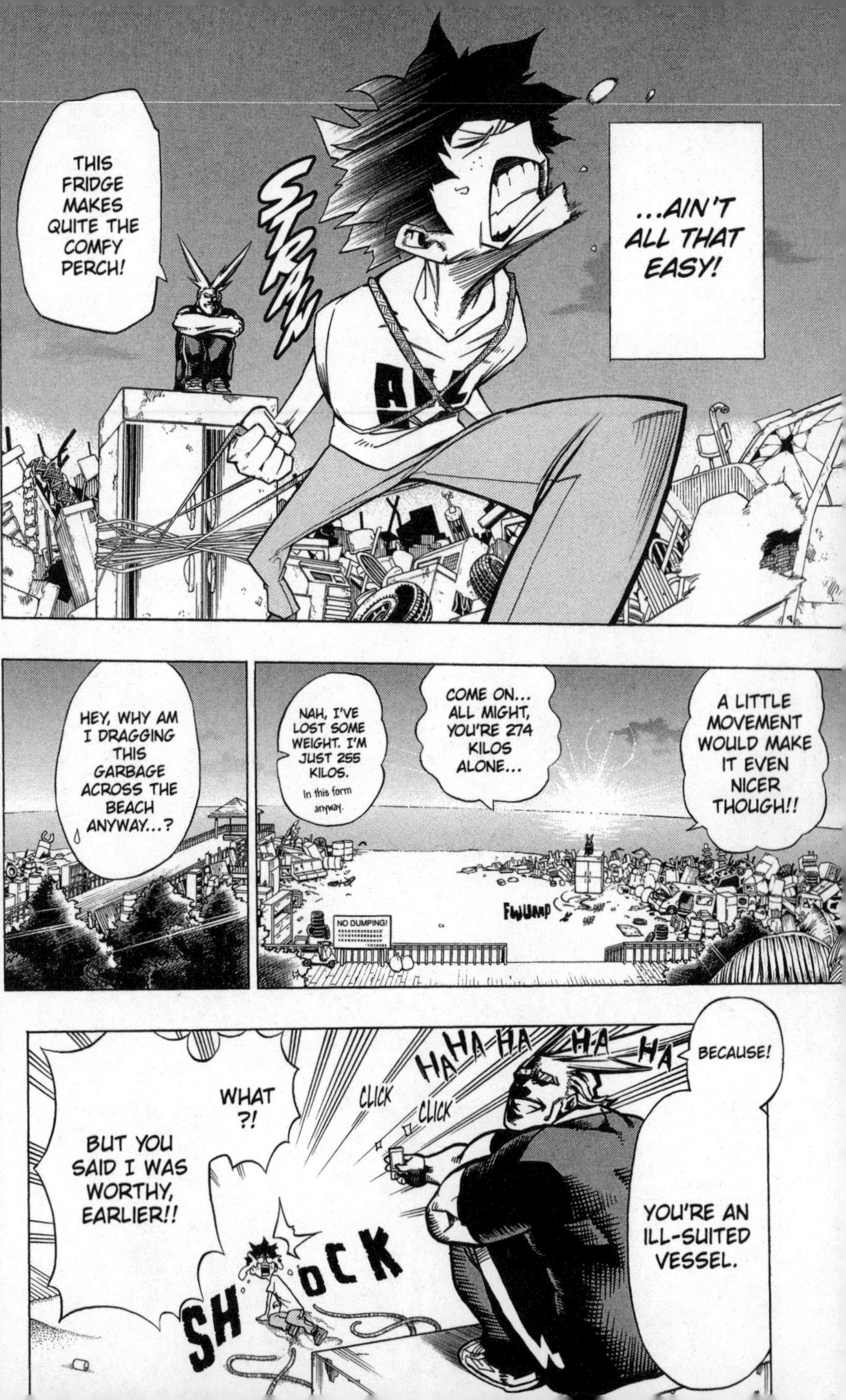
...AIN'T ALL THAT EASY!
THIS FRIDGE MAKES QUITE THE COMFY PERCH!
A LITTLE MOVEMENT WOULD MAKE IT EVEN NICER THOUGH!!
COME ON... ALL MIGHT, YOU'RE 274 KILOS ALONE...
NAH, I'VE LOST SOME WEIGHT. I'M JUST 255 KILOS.
In this form anyway.
NO DUMPING!
FWUMP
HEY, WHY AM I DRAGGING THIS GARBAGE ACROSS THE BEACH ANYWAY...?
BECAUSE!
HA HA HA HA HA HA
CLICK
CLICK
YOU'RE AN ILL-SUITED VESSEL.
WHAT?!
BUT YOU SAID I WAS WORTHY, EARLIER!!
SHOCK

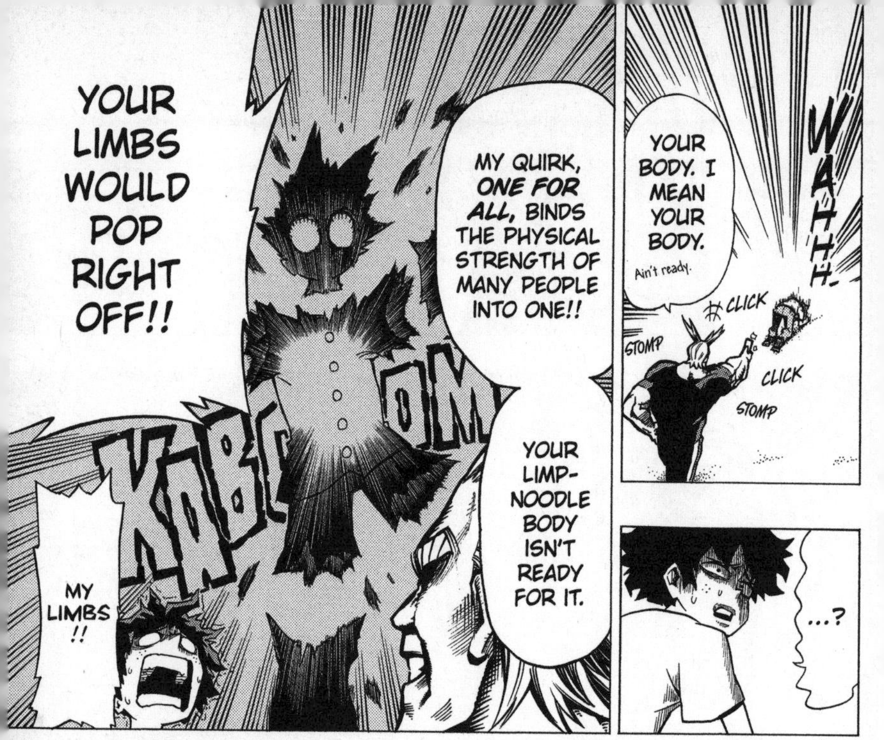
WAHHH
YOUR BODY. I MEAN YOUR BODY.
Ain't ready.
CLICK
STOMP
CLICK
STOMP
...?
MY QUIRK, ONE FOR ALL, BINDS THE PHYSICAL STRENGTH OF MANY PEOPLE INTO ONE!!
YOUR LIMP-NOODLE BODY ISN'T READY FOR IT.
YOUR LIMBS WOULD POP RIGHT OFF!!
KABOOM
MY LIMBS!!

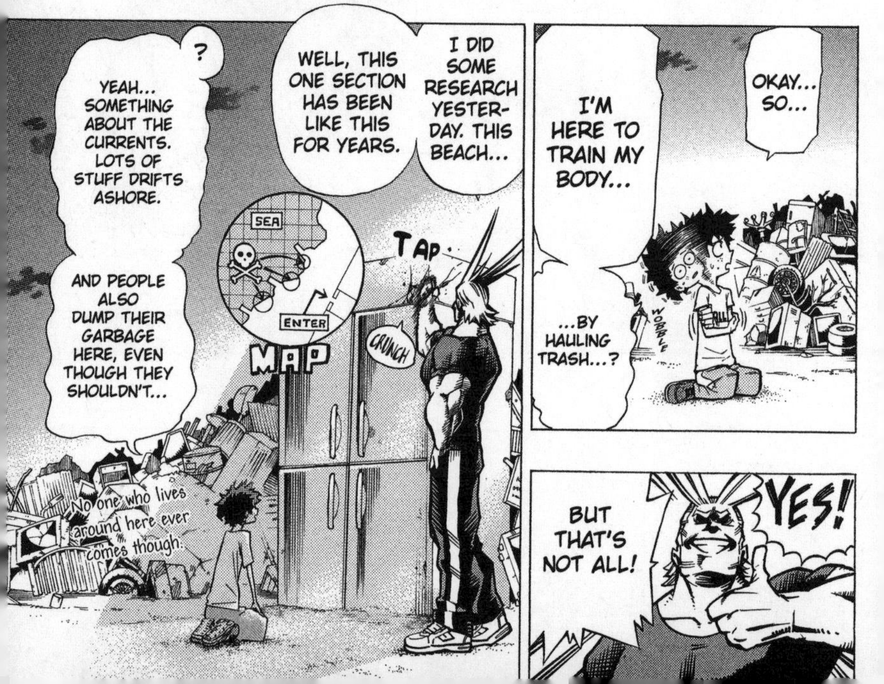
OKAY... SO...
I'M HERE TO TRAIN MY BODY...
...BY HAULING TRASH...?
WOBBLE
YES!
BUT THAT'S NOT ALL!
I DID SOME RESEARCH YESTER-DAY. THIS BEACH...
WELL, THIS ONE SECTION HAS BEEN LIKE THIS FOR YEARS.
?
YEAH... SOMETHING ABOUT THE CURRENTS. LOTS OF STUFF DRIFTS ASHORE.
TAP
SEA
ENTER
MAP
CRUNCH
AND PEOPLE ALSO DUMP THEIR GARBAGE HERE, EVEN THOUGH THEY SHOULDN'T...
No one who lives around here ever comes though.

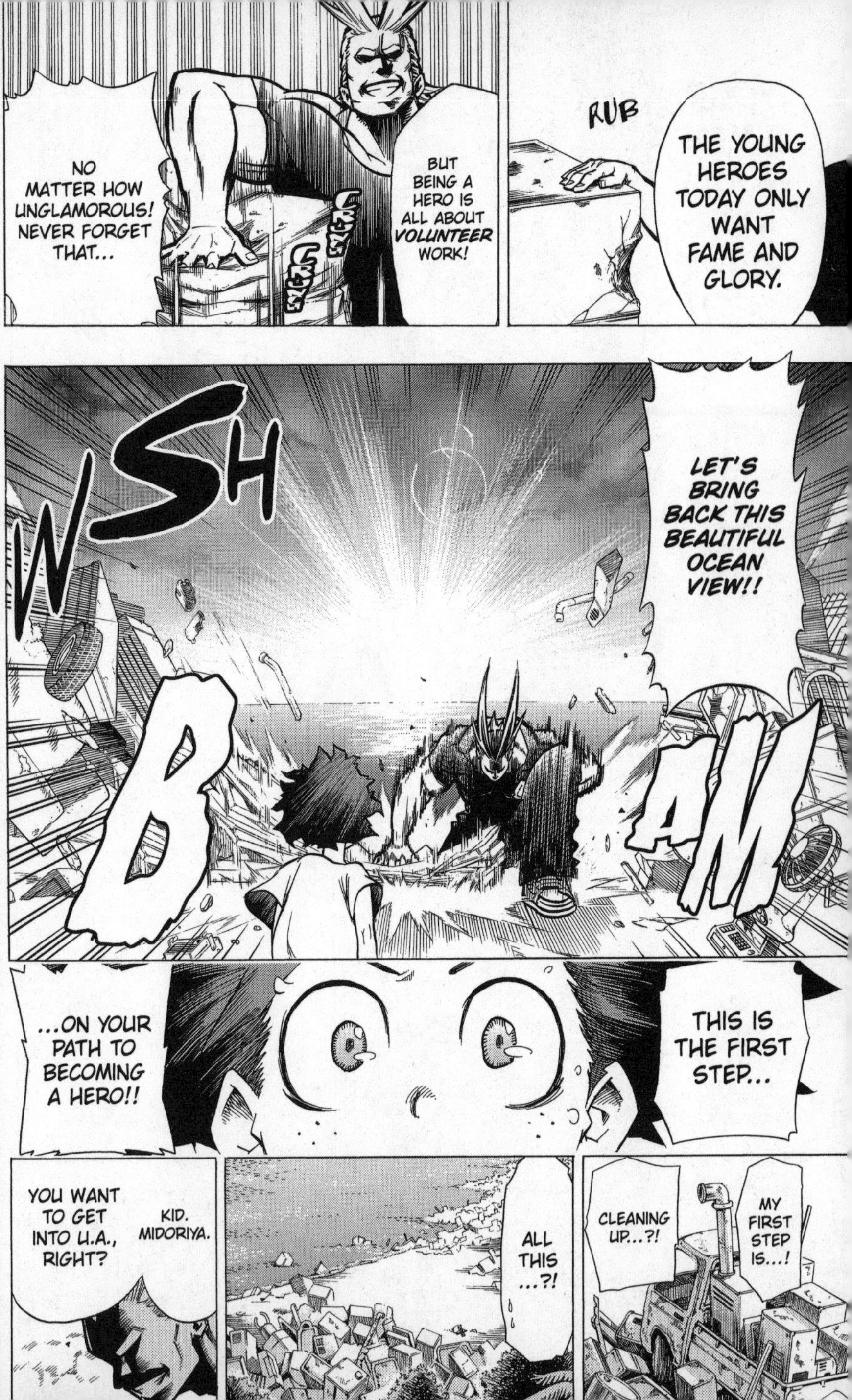
THE YOUNG HEROES TODAY ONLY WANT FAME AND GLORY.
RUB
BUT BEING A HERO IS ALL ABOUT *VOLUNTEER* WORK!
NO MATTER HOW UNGLAMOROUS! NEVER FORGET THAT...
LET'S BRING BACK THIS BEAUTIFUL OCEAN VIEW!!
WSH
BAM
THIS IS THE FIRST STEP...
...ON YOUR PATH TO BECOMING A HERO!!
MY FIRST STEP IS...!
CLEANING UP...?!
ALL THIS ...?!
KID. MIDORIYA.
YOU WANT TO GET INTO U.A., RIGHT?

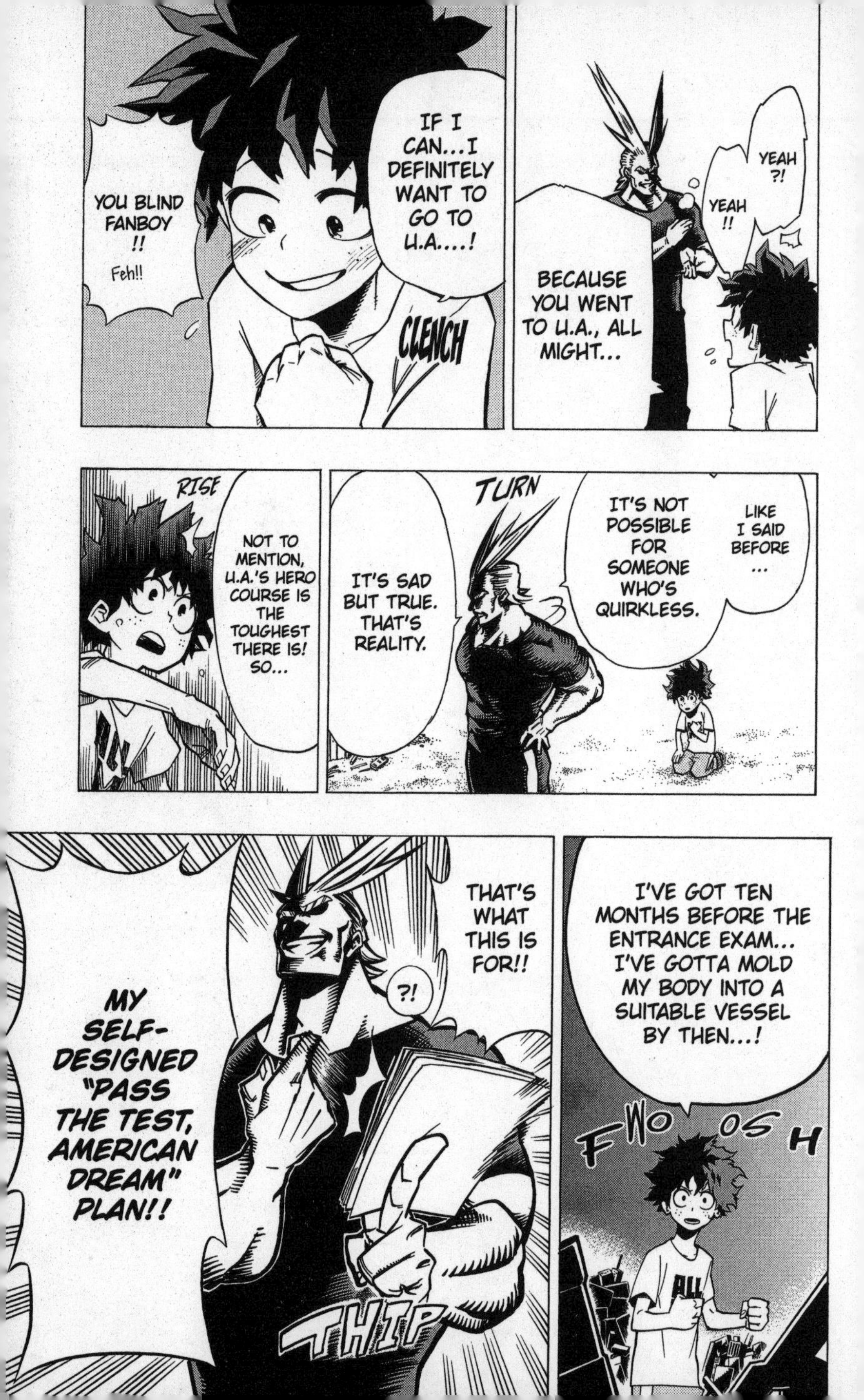
BECAUSE YOU WENT TO U.A., ALL MIGHT...
YEAH ?!
YEAH !!
IF I CAN...I DEFINITELY WANT TO GO TO U.A....!
CLENCH
YOU BLIND FANBOY !!
Feh!!
LIKE I SAID BEFORE ...
IT'S NOT POSSIBLE FOR SOMEONE WHO'S QUIRKLESS.
TURN
IT'S SAD BUT TRUE. THAT'S REALITY.
RISE
NOT TO MENTION, U.A.'S HERO COURSE IS THE TOUGHEST THERE IS! SO...
I'VE GOT TEN MONTHS BEFORE THE ENTRANCE EXAM... I'VE GOTTA MOLD MY BODY INTO A SUITABLE VESSEL BY THEN...!
FWOOSH
THAT'S WHAT THIS IS FOR!!
?!
MY SELF-DESIGNED "PASS THE TEST, AMERICAN DREAM" PLAN!!
THIP

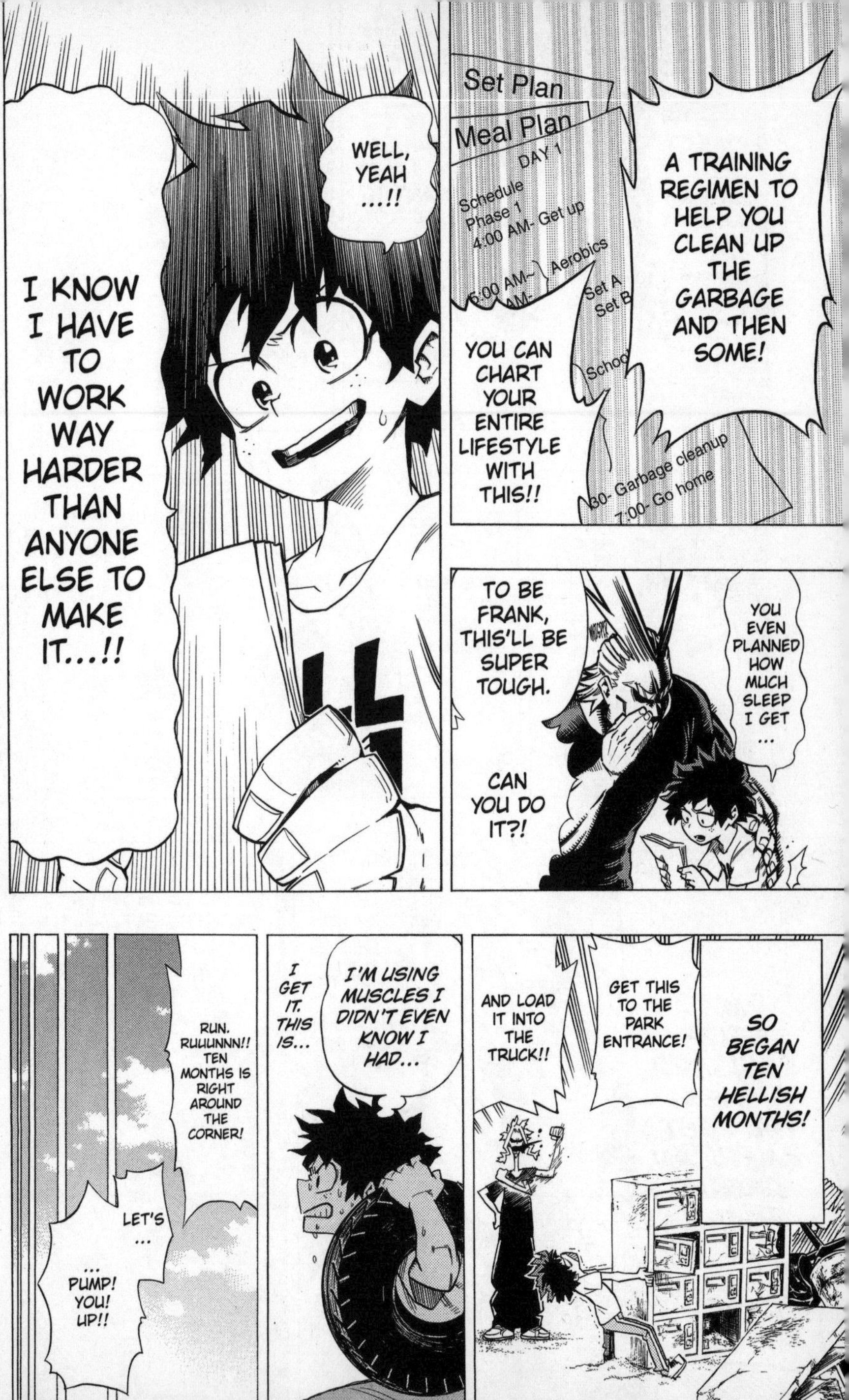
A TRAINING REGIMEN TO HELP YOU CLEAN UP THE GARBAGE AND THEN SOME!
YOU CAN CHART YOUR ENTIRE LIFESTYLE WITH THIS!!
Set Plan
Meal Plan
DAY 1
Schedule
Phase 1
4:00 AM- Get up
6:00 AM- Aerobics
Set A
Set B
-30- Garbage cleanup
7:00- Go home
YOU EVEN PLANNED HOW MUCH SLEEP I GET ...
TO BE FRANK, THIS'LL BE SUPER TOUGH.
CAN YOU DO IT?!
WELL, YEAH ...!!
I KNOW I HAVE TO WORK WAY HARDER THAN ANYONE ELSE TO MAKE IT...!!
SO BEGAN TEN HELLISH MONTHS!
GET THIS TO THE PARK ENTRANCE!
AND LOAD IT INTO THE TRUCK!!
I'M USING MUSCLES I DIDN'T EVEN KNOW I HAD...
I GET IT. THIS IS...
RUN. RUUUNNN!! TEN MONTHS IS RIGHT AROUND THE CORNER!
LET'S ...
... PUMP! YOU! UP!!

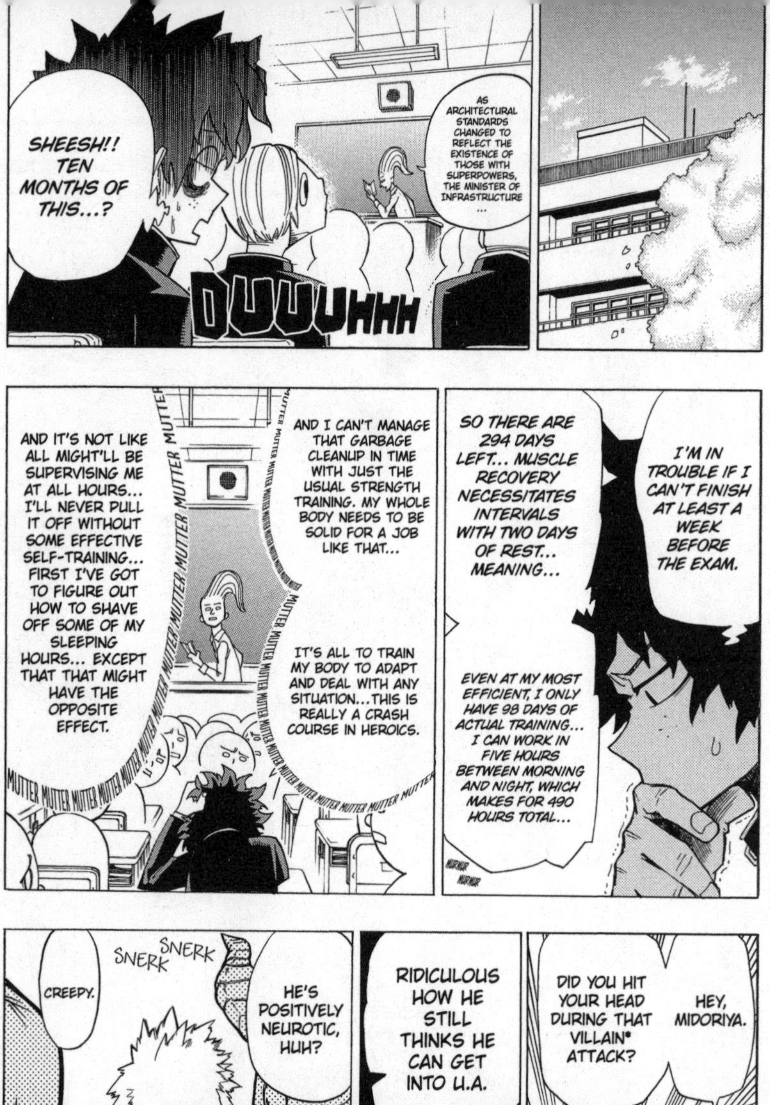
AS ARCHITECTURAL STANDARDS CHANGED TO REFLECT THE EXISTENCE OF THOSE WITH SUPERPOWERS, THE MINISTER OF INFRASTRUCTURE ...
SHEESH!! TEN MONTHS OF THIS...?
DUUUHHH
I'M IN TROUBLE IF I CAN'T FINISH AT LEAST A WEEK BEFORE THE EXAM.
SO THERE ARE 294 DAYS LEFT... MUSCLE RECOVERY NECESSITATES INTERVALS WITH TWO DAYS OF REST... MEANING...
EVEN AT MY MOST EFFICIENT, I ONLY HAVE 98 DAYS OF ACTUAL TRAINING... I CAN WORK IN FIVE HOURS BETWEEN MORNING AND NIGHT, WHICH MAKES FOR 490 HOURS TOTAL...
MURMUR MURMUR
AND I CAN'T MANAGE THAT GARBAGE CLEANUP IN TIME WITH JUST THE USUAL STRENGTH TRAINING. MY WHOLE BODY NEEDS TO BE SOLID FOR A JOB LIKE THAT...
IT'S ALL TO TRAIN MY BODY TO ADAPT AND DEAL WITH ANY SITUATION...THIS IS REALLY A CRASH COURSE IN HEROICS.
AND IT'S NOT LIKE ALL MIGHT'LL BE SUPERVISING ME AT ALL HOURS... I'LL NEVER PULL IT OFF WITHOUT SOME EFFECTIVE SELF-TRAINING... FIRST I'VE GOT TO FIGURE OUT HOW TO SHAVE OFF SOME OF MY SLEEPING HOURS... EXCEPT THAT THAT MIGHT HAVE THE OPPOSITE EFFECT.
MUTTER MUTTER MUTTER MUTTER MUTTER
HEY, MIDORIYA.
DID YOU HIT YOUR HEAD DURING THAT VILLAIN* ATTACK?
BONK
Ah !!
RIDICULOUS HOW HE STILL THINKS HE CAN GET INTO U.A.
THEN THERE'S STUDYING FOR THE ENTRANCE EXAMS.
HE'S POSITIVELY NEUROTIC, HUH?
SNERK SNERK
CREEPY.

*THE MUDMAN FROM CHAPTER 1.

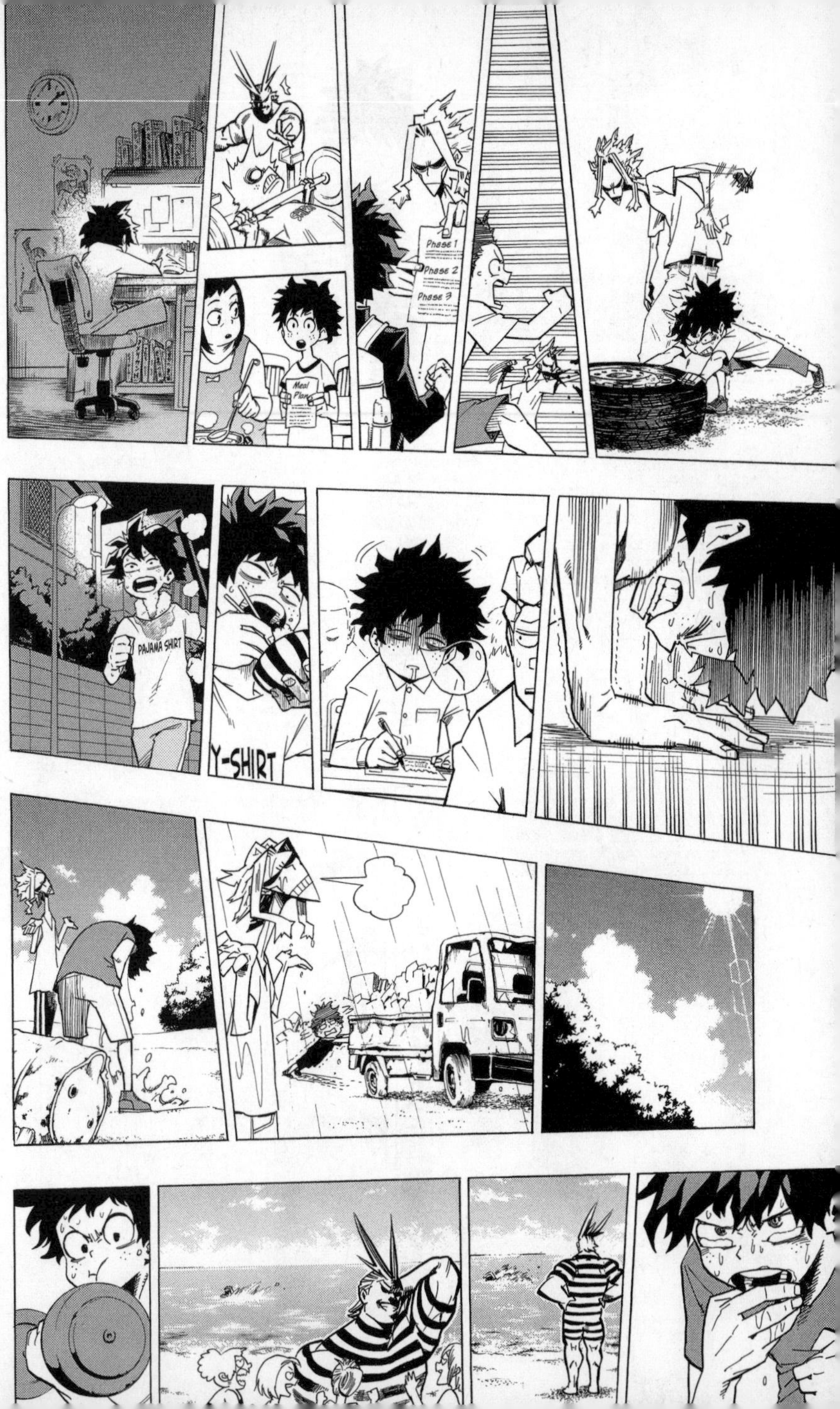
Phase 1
Phase 2
Phase 3
Meal Plan
Y-SHIRT
PAJAMA SHIRT

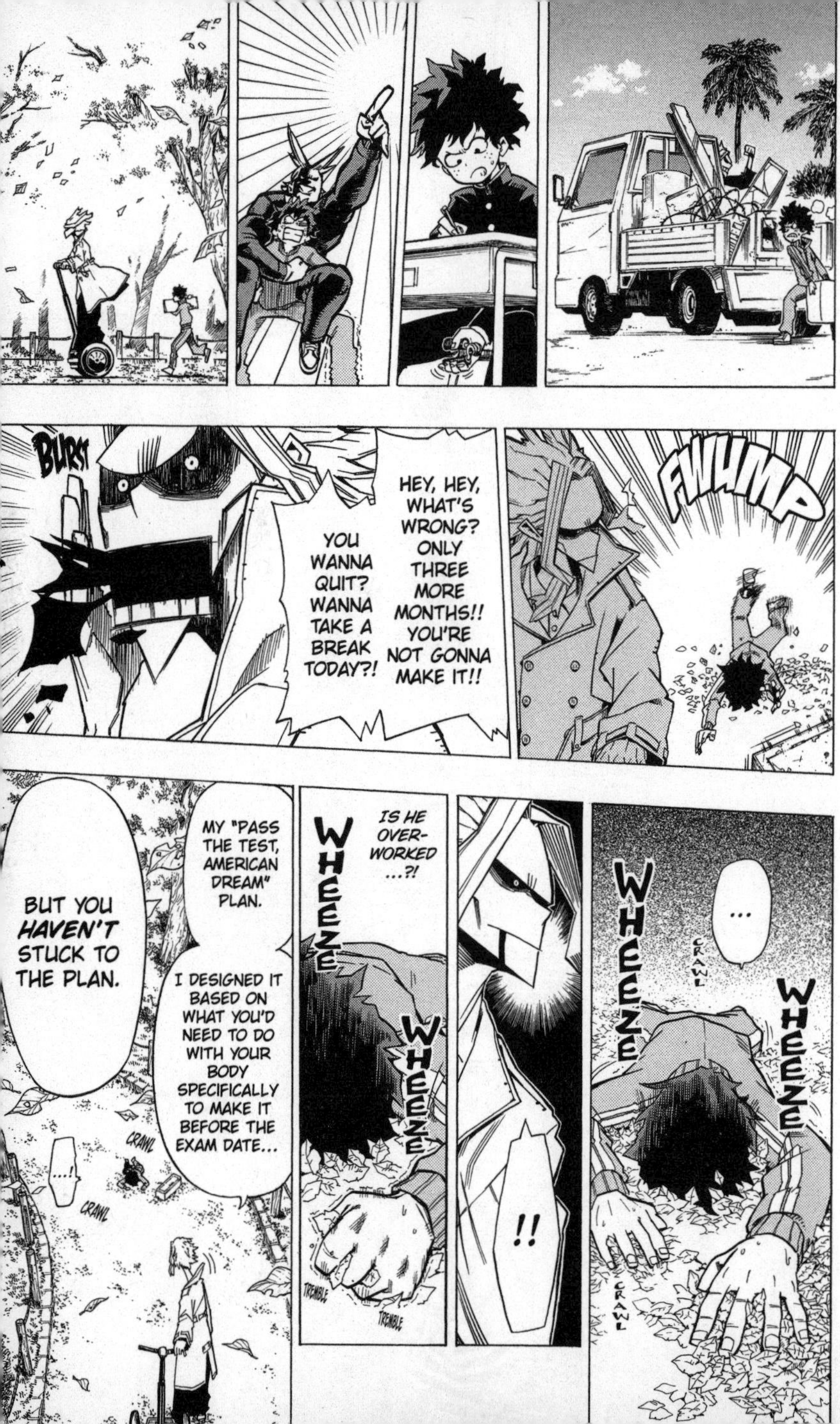
FWUMP
BURST
HEY, HEY, WHAT'S WRONG? ONLY THREE MORE MONTHS!! YOU'RE NOT GONNA MAKE IT!!
YOU WANNA QUIT? WANNA TAKE A BREAK TODAY?!
WHEEZE
WHEEZE
CRAWL
...
!!
WHEEZE
IS HE OVER-WORKED ...?!
WHEEZE
TREMBLE
TREMBLE
MY "PASS THE TEST, AMERICAN DREAM" PLAN.
I DESIGNED IT BASED ON WHAT YOU'D NEED TO DO WITH YOUR BODY SPECIFICALLY TO MAKE IT BEFORE THE EXAM DATE...
BUT YOU *HAVEN'T* STUCK TO THE PLAN.
CRAWL
...!
CRAWL

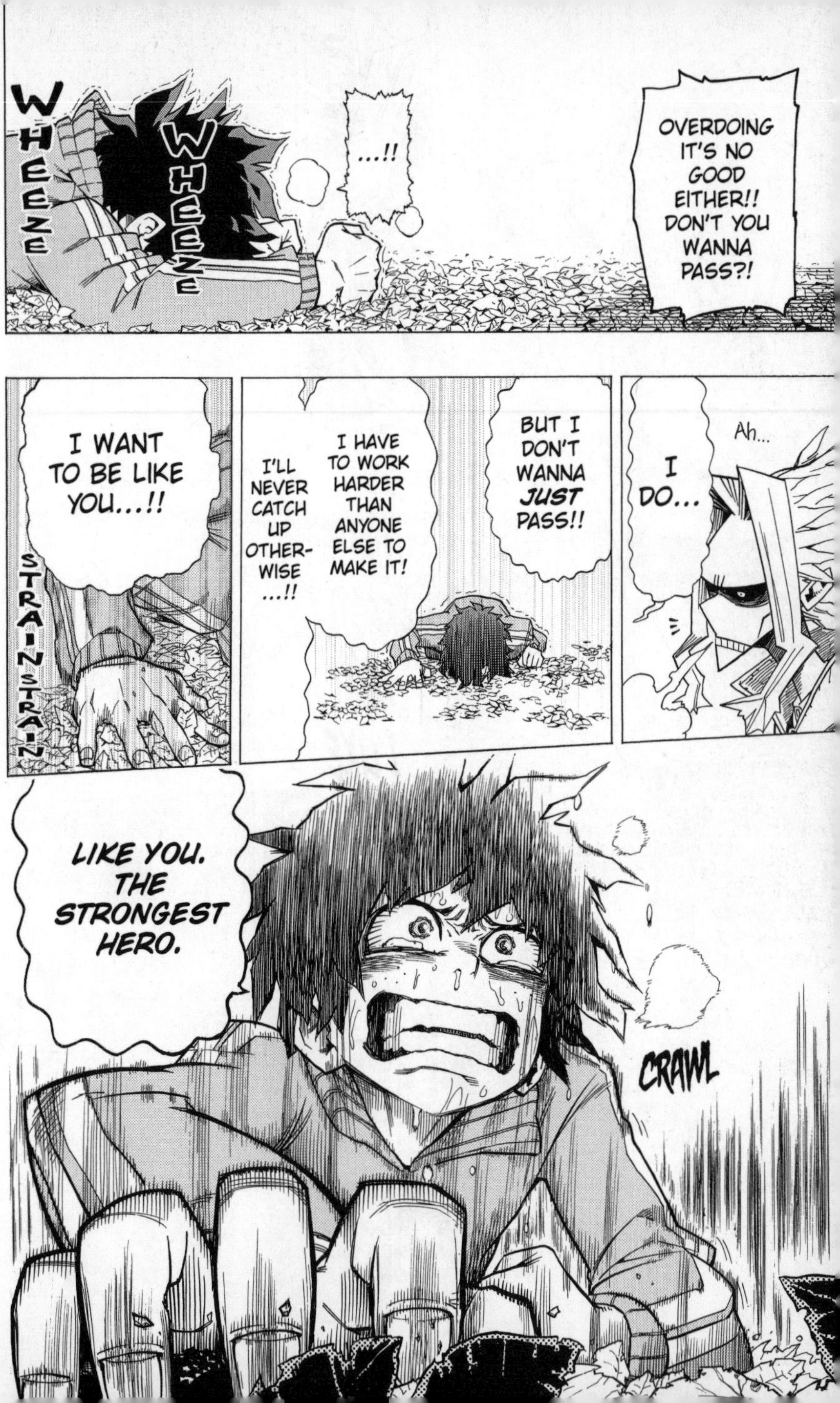
OVERDOING IT'S NO GOOD EITHER!! DON'T YOU WANNA PASS?!
...!!
WHEEZE
WHEEZE
Ah...
I DO...
BUT I DON'T WANNA ***JUST*** PASS!!
I HAVE TO WORK HARDER THAN ANYONE ELSE TO MAKE IT!
I'LL NEVER CATCH UP OTHER-WISE ...!!
I WANT TO BE LIKE YOU...!!
STRAIN STRAIN
LIKE YOU. THE STRONGEST HERO.
CRAWL

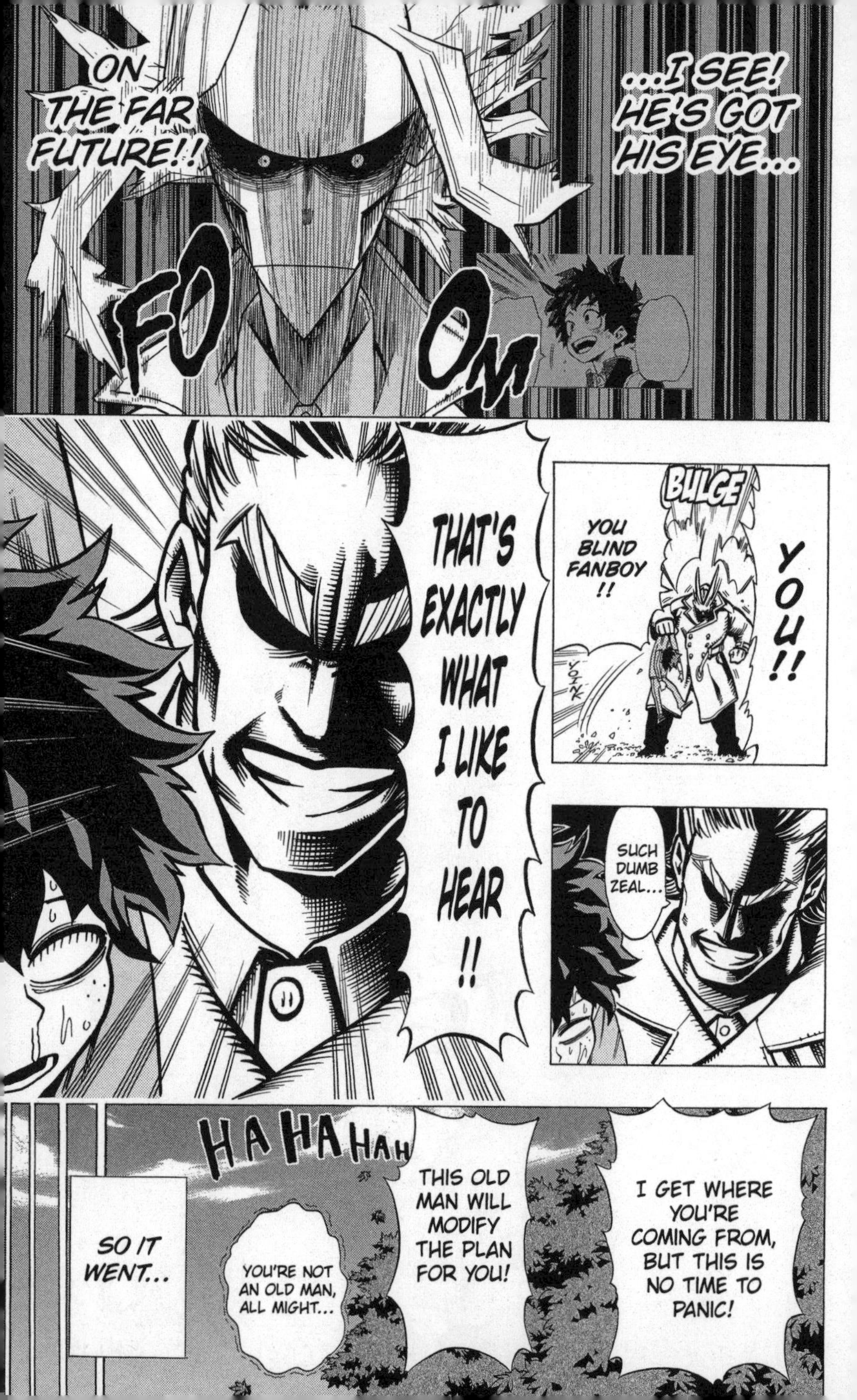
...I SEE! HE'S GOT HIS EYE...
ON THE FAR FUTURE!!
FOOM
YOU!!
BULGE
YOU BLIND FANBOY!!
YOINK
SUCH DUMB ZEAL...
THAT'S EXACTLY WHAT I LIKE TO HEAR!!
I GET WHERE YOU'RE COMING FROM, BUT THIS IS NO TIME TO PANIC!
THIS OLD MAN WILL MODIFY THE PLAN FOR YOU!
HA HA HA HAH
YOU'RE NOT AN OLD MAN, ALL MIGHT...
SO IT WENT...

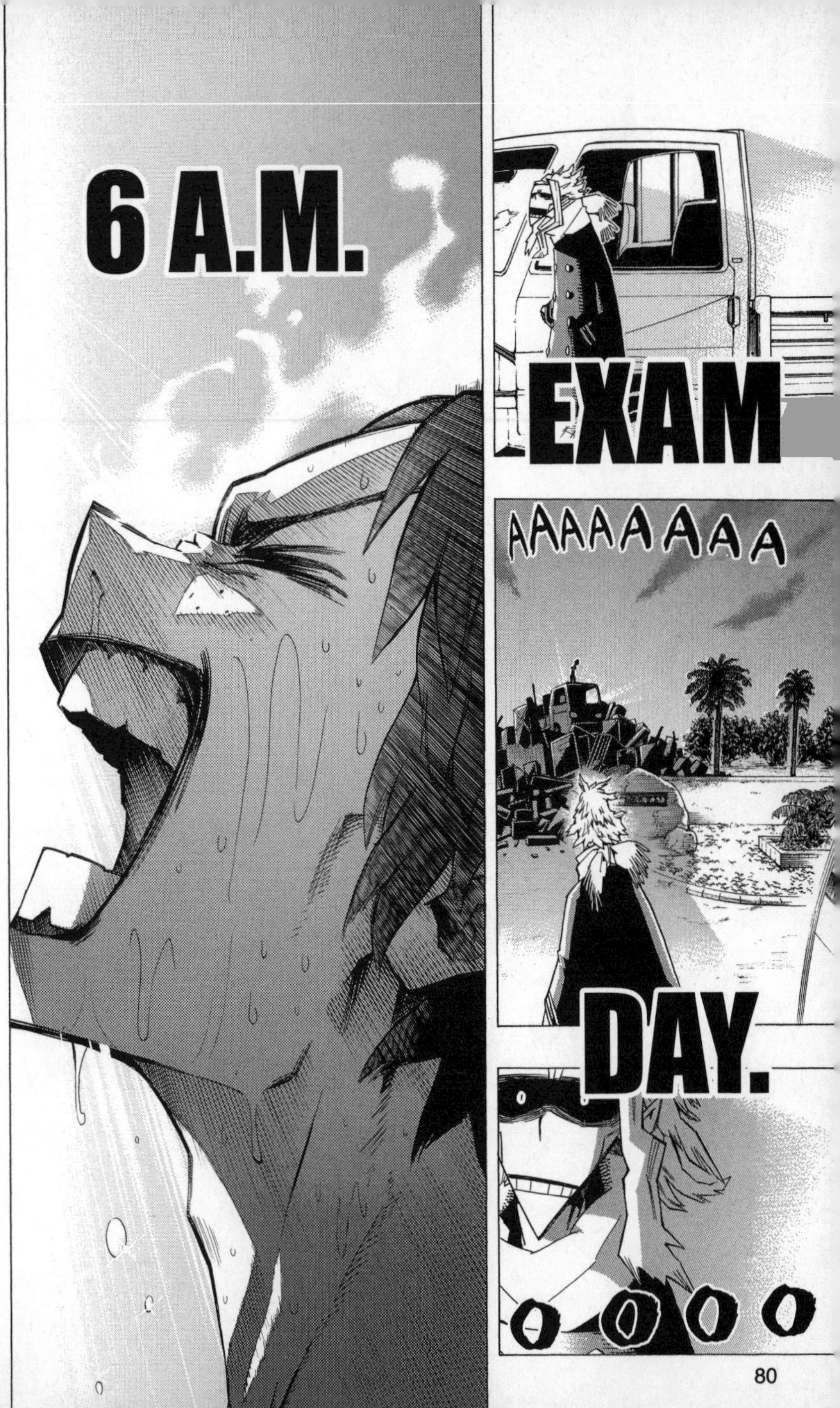
EXAM
AAAAAAAA
DAY.
OOOO
6 A.M.

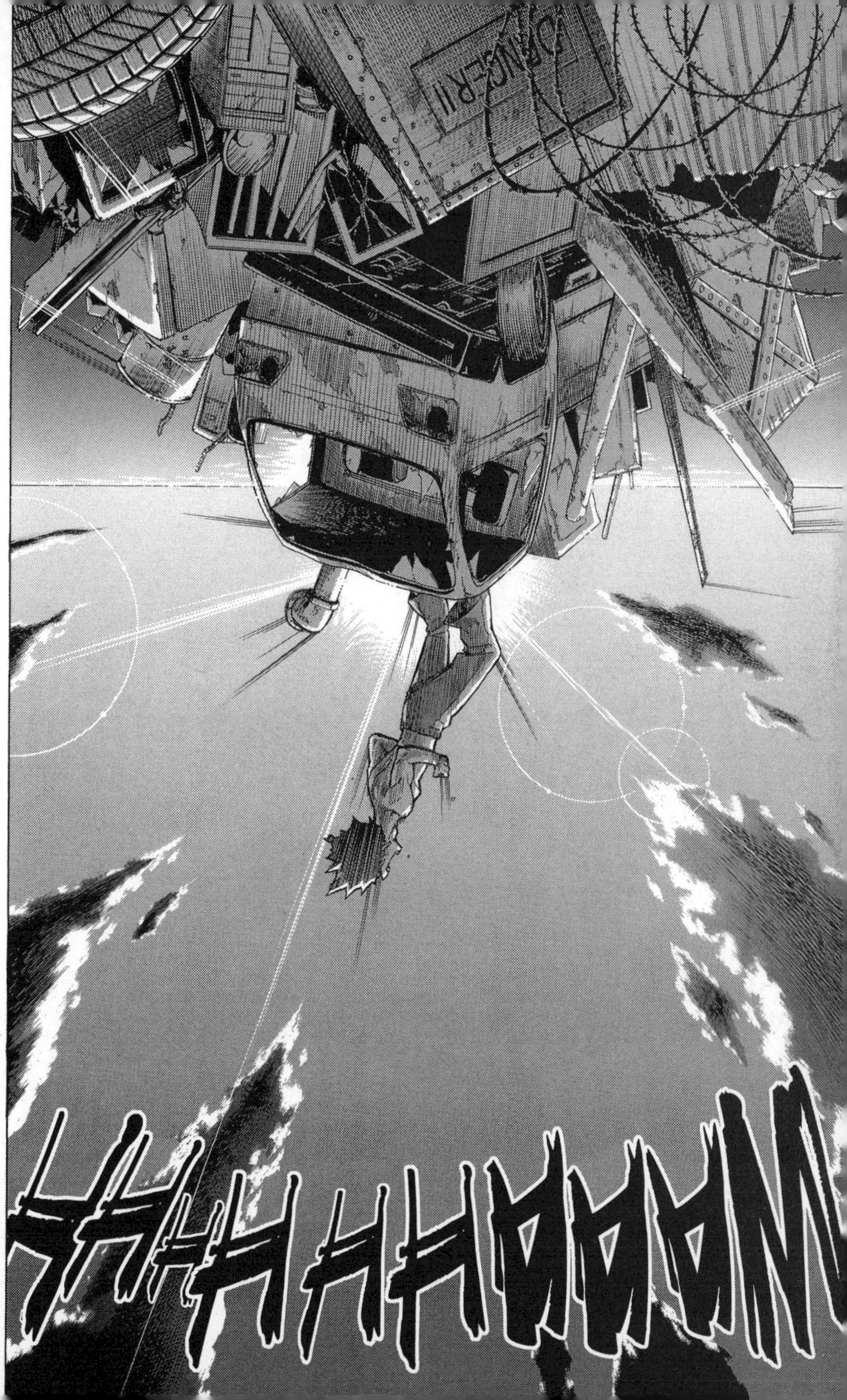
DANGER!!
SHHHHHOOOM

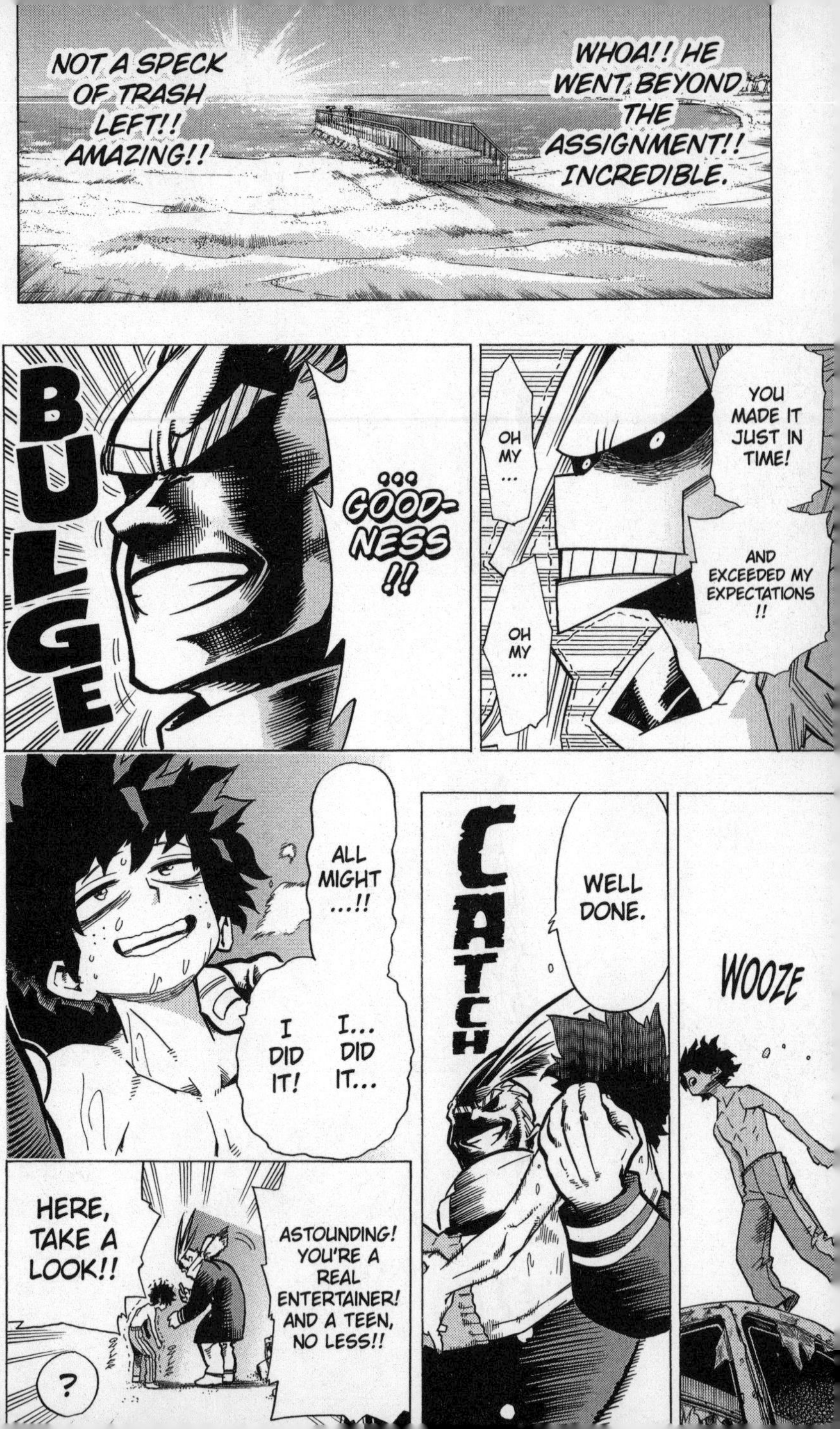
WHOA!! HE WENT BEYOND THE ASSIGNMENT!! INCREDIBLE.
NOT A SPECK OF TRASH LEFT!! AMAZING!!
YOU MADE IT JUST IN TIME!
AND EXCEEDED MY EXPECTATIONS !!
OH MY ...
OH MY ...
...GOOD-NESS !!
BULGE
WOOZE
WELL DONE.
CATCH
ALL MIGHT ...!!
I... DID IT...
I DID IT!
ASTOUNDING! YOU'RE A REAL ENTERTAINER! AND A TEEN, NO LESS!!
HERE, TAKE A LOOK!!
?

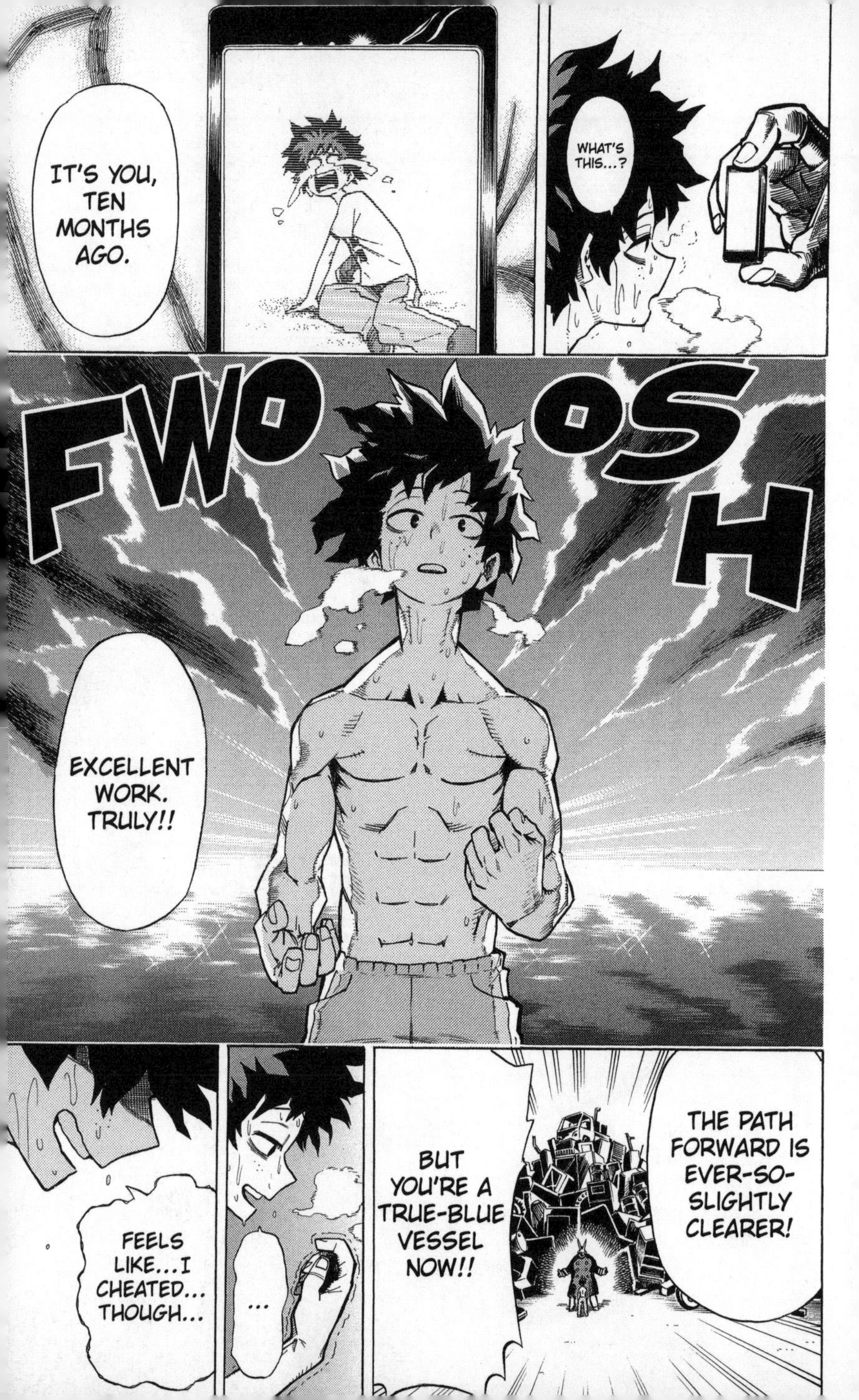
WHAT'S THIS...?
IT'S YOU, TEN MONTHS AGO.
FWOOSH
EXCELLENT WORK. TRULY!!
THE PATH FORWARD IS EVER-SO-SLIGHTLY CLEARER!
BUT YOU'RE A TRUE-BLUE VESSEL NOW!!
...
FEELS LIKE...I CHEATED... THOUGH...

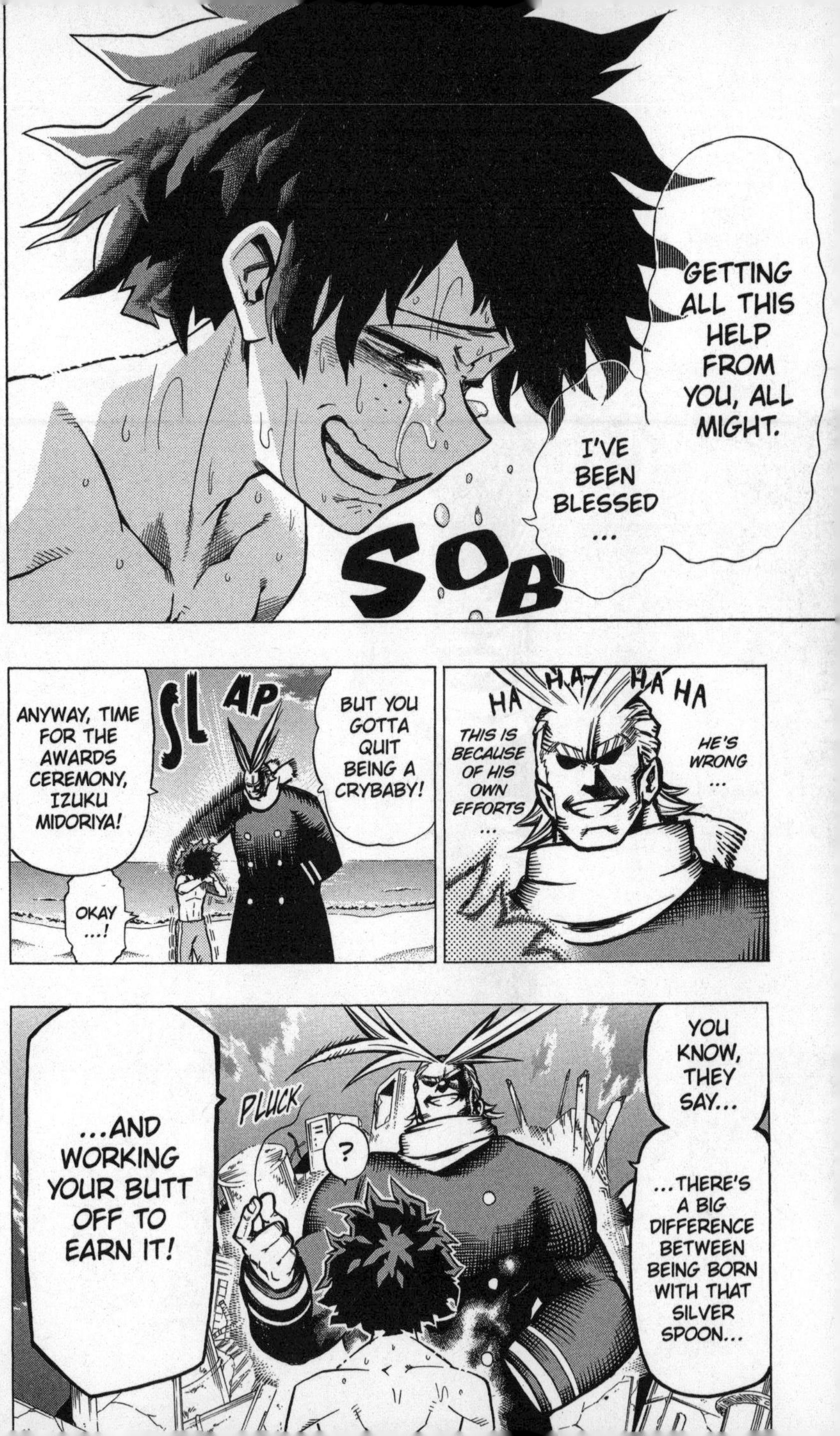
GETTING ALL THIS HELP FROM YOU, ALL MIGHT.
I'VE BEEN BLESSED ...
SOB
HA HA HA HA HA
HE'S WRONG ...
THIS IS BECAUSE OF HIS OWN EFFORTS ...
BUT YOU GOTTA QUIT BEING A CRYBABY!
SLAP
ANYWAY, TIME FOR THE AWARDS CEREMONY, IZUKU MIDORIYA!
OKAY ...!
YOU KNOW, THEY SAY...
...THERE'S A BIG DIFFERENCE BETWEEN BEING BORN WITH THAT SILVER SPOON...
?
PLUCK
...AND WORKING YOUR BUTT OFF TO EARN IT!

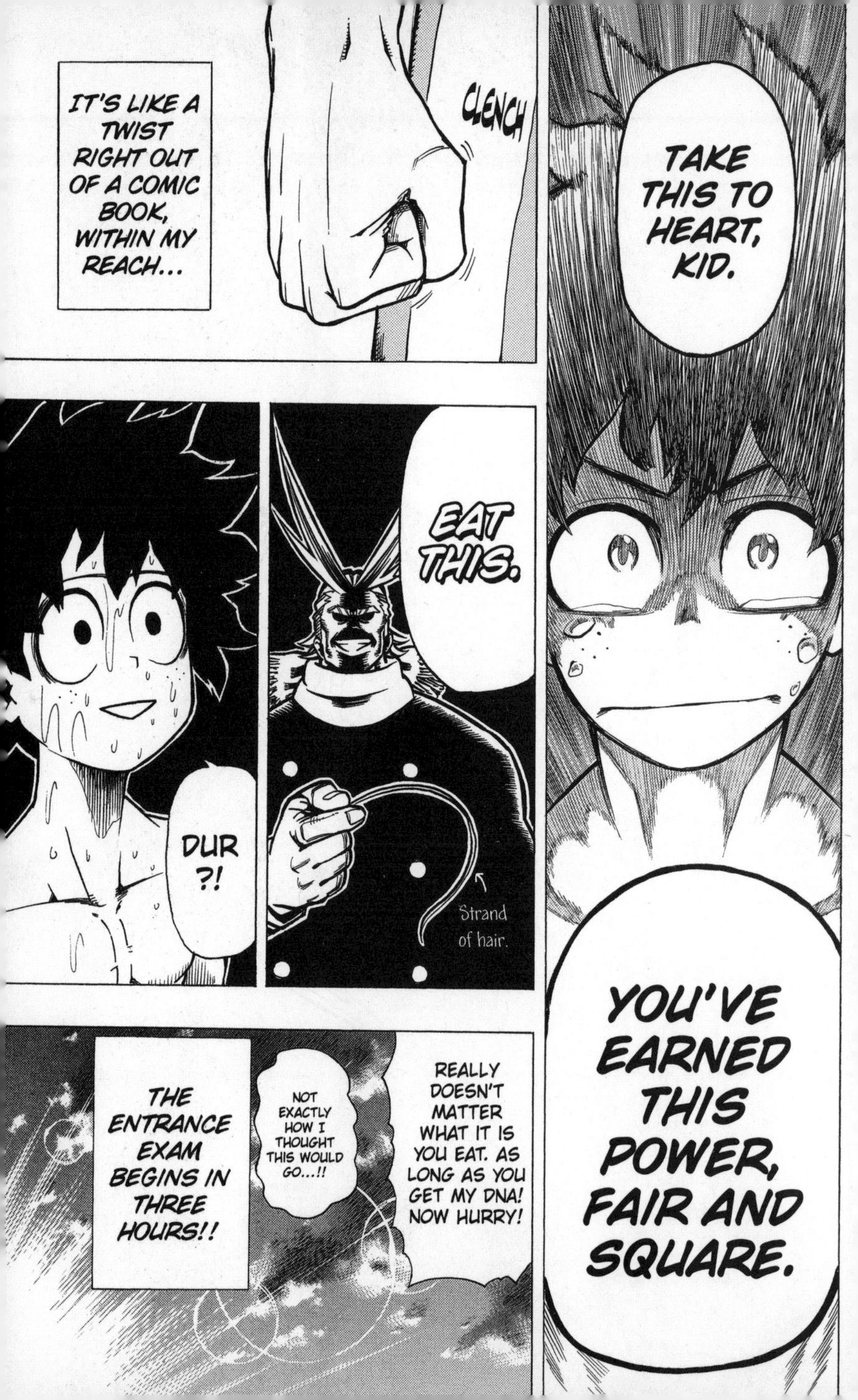
TAKE THIS TO HEART, KID.
YOU'VE EARNED THIS POWER, FAIR AND SQUARE.
CLENCH
IT'S LIKE A TWIST RIGHT OUT OF A COMIC BOOK, WITHIN MY REACH...
EAT THIS.
Strand of hair.
DUR ?!
REALLY DOESN'T MATTER WHAT IT IS YOU EAT. AS LONG AS YOU GET MY DNA! NOW HURRY!
NOT EXACTLY HOW I THOUGHT THIS WOULD GO...!!
THE ENTRANCE EXAM BEGINS IN THREE HOURS!!

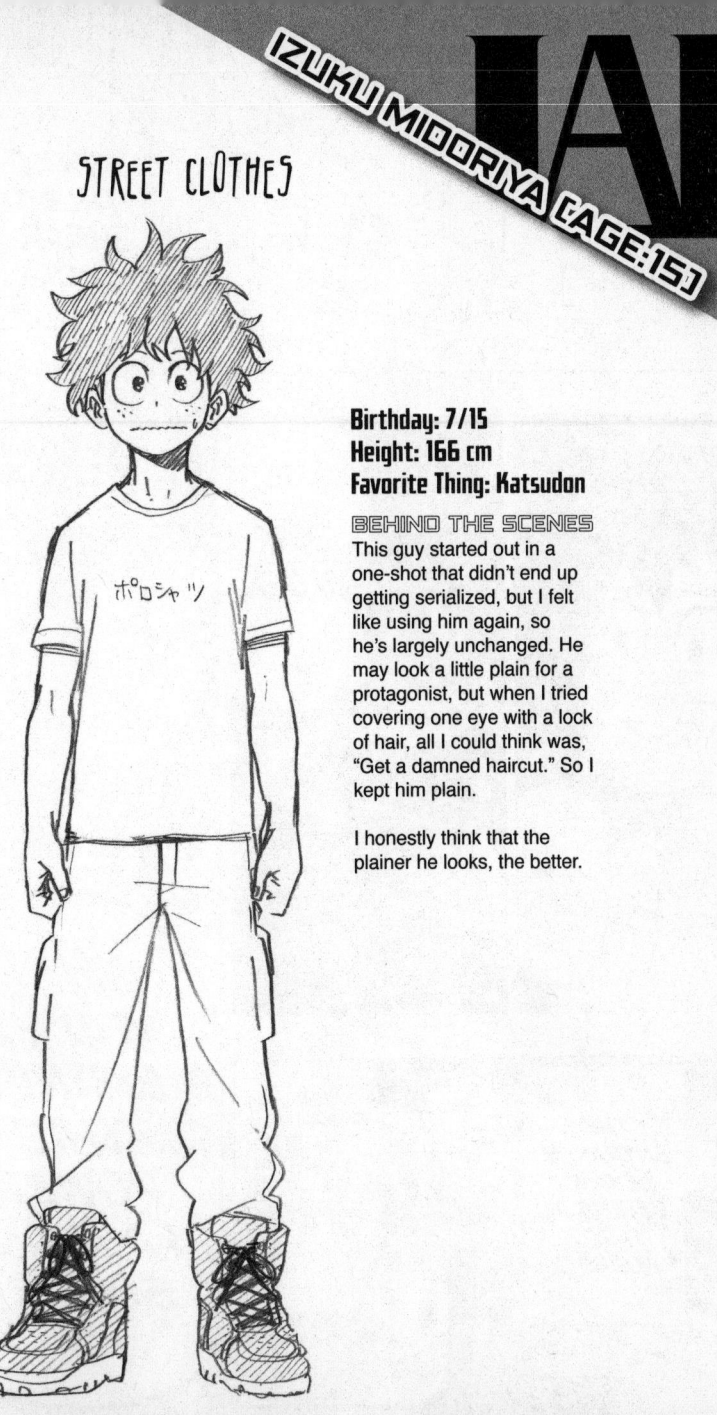

STREET CLOTHES

ポロシャツ

Birthday: 7/15
Height: 166 cm
Favorite Thing: Katsudon

BEHIND THE SCENES

This guy started out in a one-shot that didn't end up getting serialized, but I felt like using him again, so he's largely unchanged. He may look a little plain for a protagonist, but when I tried covering one eye with a lock of hair, all I could think was, "Get a damned haircut." So I kept him plain.

I honestly think that the plainer he looks, the better.

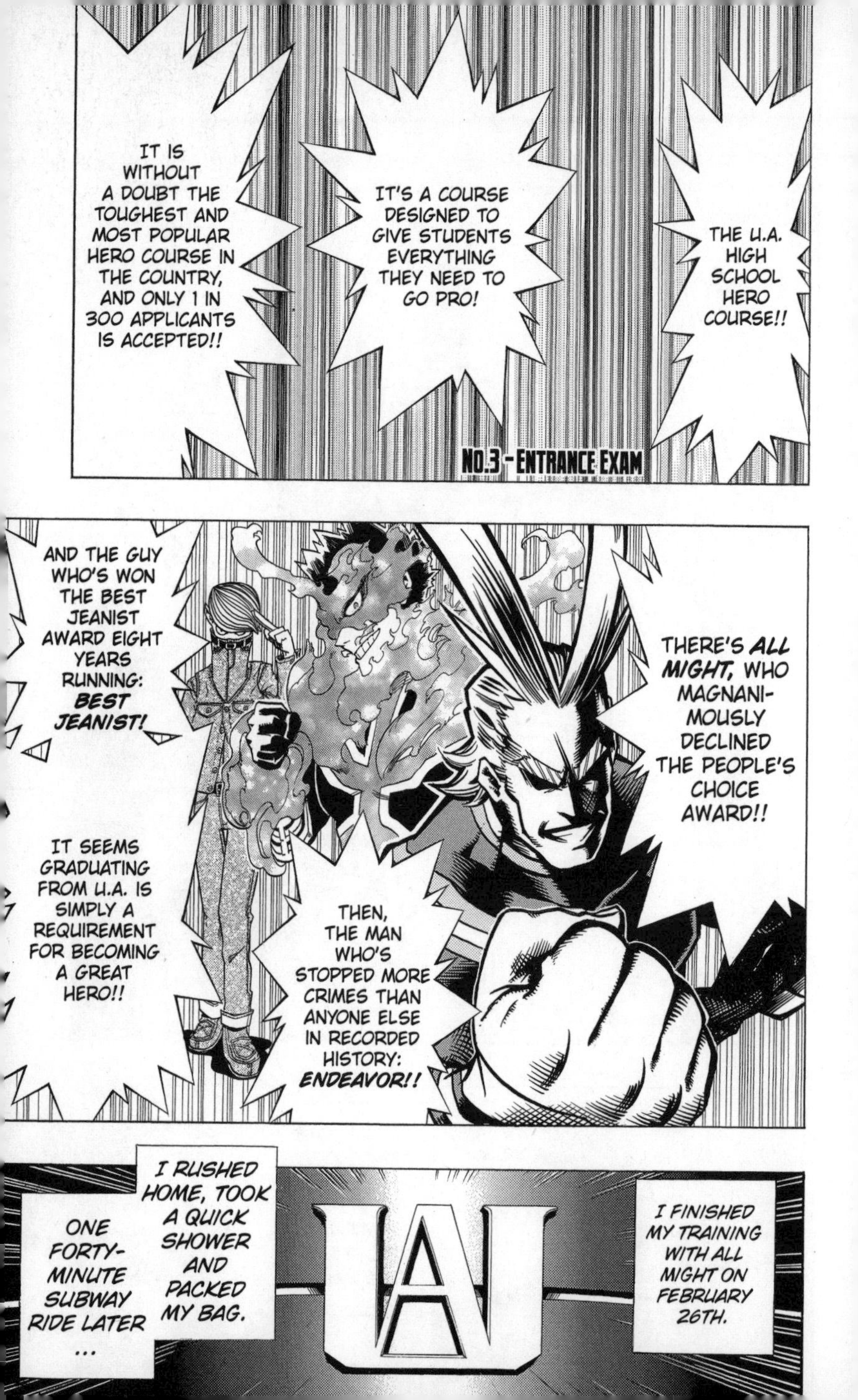
THE U.A. HIGH SCHOOL HERO COURSE!!
IT'S A COURSE DESIGNED TO GIVE STUDENTS EVERYTHING THEY NEED TO GO PRO!
IT IS WITHOUT A DOUBT THE TOUGHEST AND MOST POPULAR HERO COURSE IN THE COUNTRY, AND ONLY 1 IN 300 APPLICANTS IS ACCEPTED!!
NO.3 - ENTRANCE EXAM
THERE'S ALL MIGHT, WHO MAGNANI-MOUSLY DECLINED THE PEOPLE'S CHOICE AWARD!!
AND THE GUY WHO'S WON THE BEST JEANIST AWARD EIGHT YEARS RUNNING: BEST JEANIST!
THEN, THE MAN WHO'S STOPPED MORE CRIMES THAN ANYONE ELSE IN RECORDED HISTORY: ENDEAVOR!!
IT SEEMS GRADUATING FROM U.A. IS SIMPLY A REQUIREMENT FOR BECOMING A GREAT HERO!!
I FINISHED MY TRAINING WITH ALL MIGHT ON FEBRUARY 26TH.
I RUSHED HOME, TOOK A QUICK SHOWER AND PACKED MY BAG.
ONE FORTY-MINUTE SUBWAY RIDE LATER ...

No. 3 - Entrance Exam

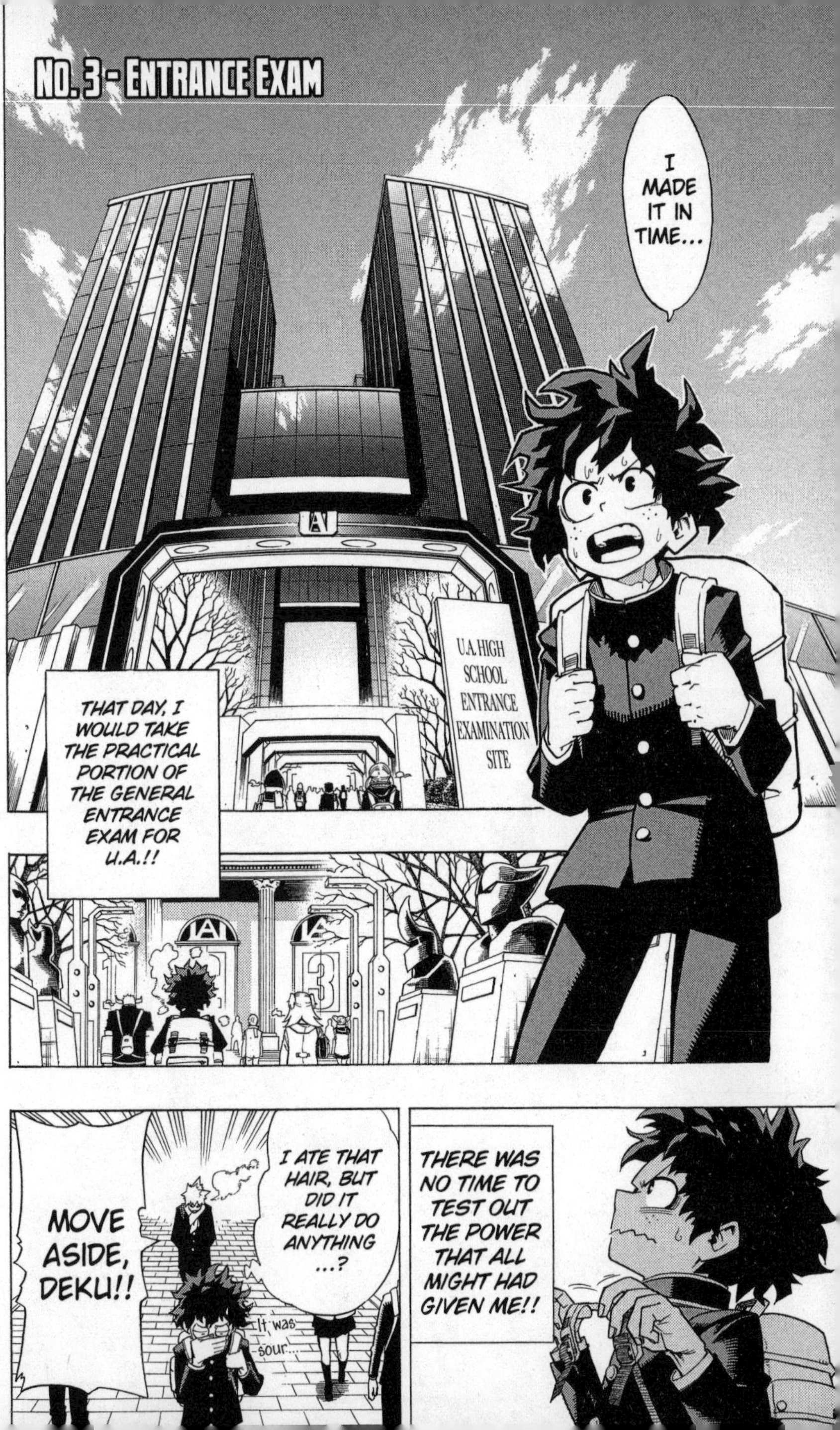

I MADE IT IN TIME...
U.A. HIGH SCHOOL ENTRANCE EXAMINATION SITE
THAT DAY, I WOULD TAKE THE PRACTICAL PORTION OF THE GENERAL ENTRANCE EXAM FOR U.A.!!
THERE WAS NO TIME TO TEST OUT THE POWER THAT ALL MIGHT HAD GIVEN ME!!
I ATE THAT HAIR, BUT DID IT REALLY DO ANYTHING ...?
MOVE ASIDE, DEKU!!
It was sour...

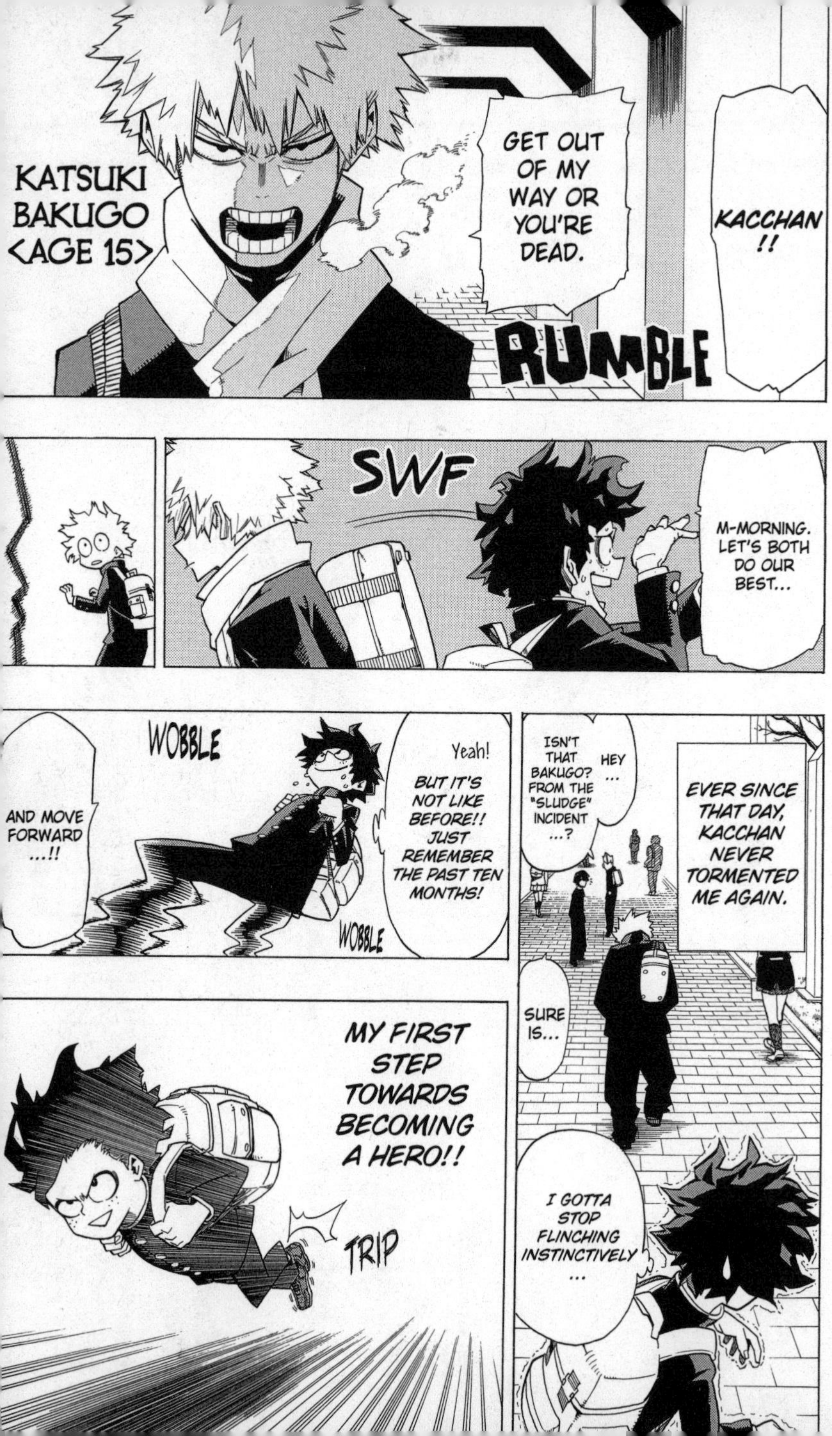
KACCHAN!!
GET OUT OF MY WAY OR YOU'RE DEAD.
RUMBLE
KATSUKI BAKUGO <AGE 15>
M-MORNING. LET'S BOTH DO OUR BEST...
SWF
EVER SINCE THAT DAY, KACCHAN NEVER TORMENTED ME AGAIN.
HEY...
ISN'T THAT BAKUGO? FROM THE "SLUDGE" INCIDENT...?
SURE IS...
I GOTTA STOP FLINCHING INSTINCTIVELY...
Yeah!
BUT IT'S NOT LIKE BEFORE!! JUST REMEMBER THE PAST TEN MONTHS!
WOBBLE
WOBBLE
AND MOVE FORWARD...!!
MY FIRST STEP TOWARDS BECOMING A HERO!!
TRIP

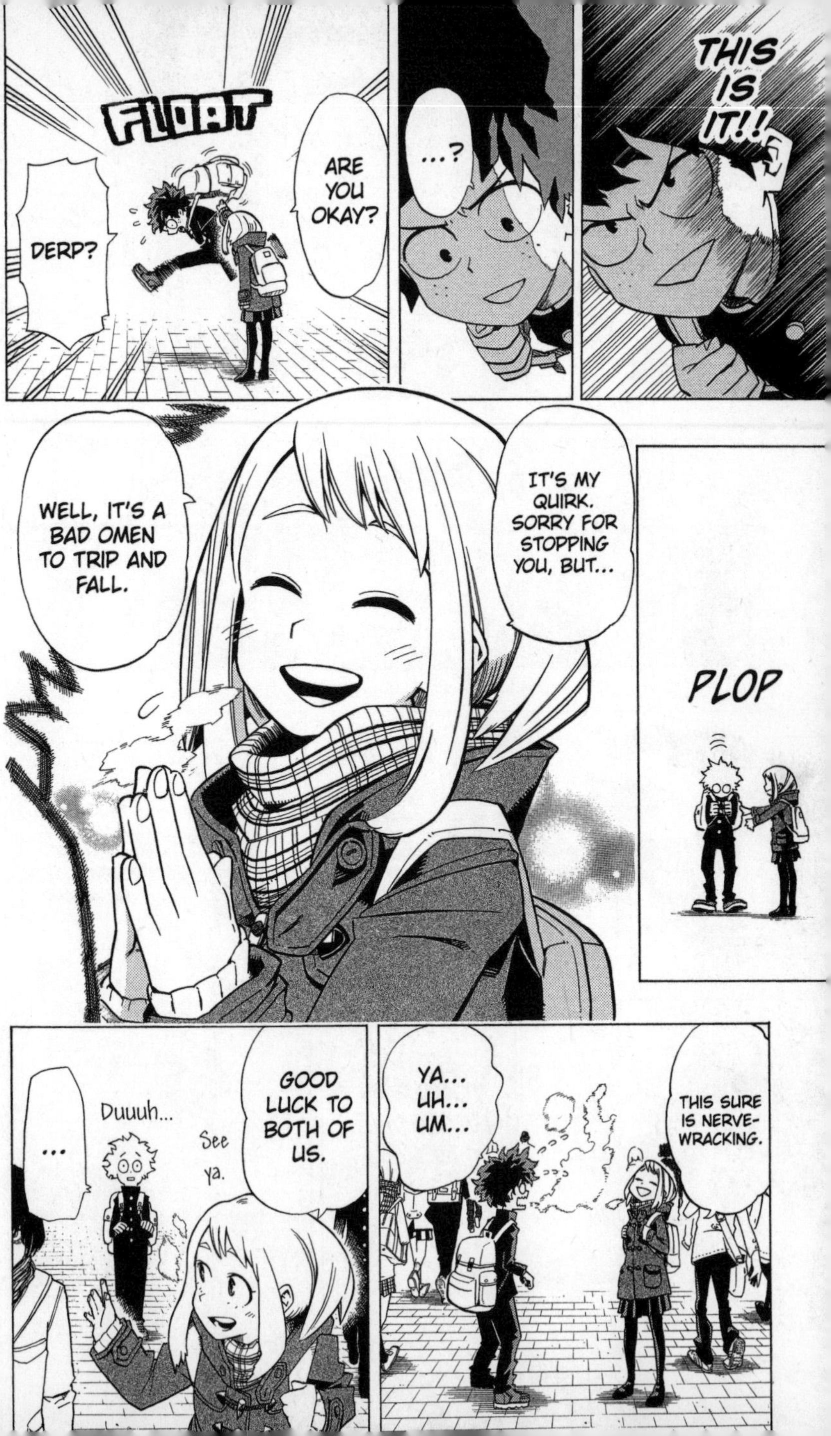
THIS IS IT!!
...?
ARE YOU OKAY?
FLOAT
DERP?
PLOP
IT'S MY QUIRK. SORRY FOR STOPPING YOU, BUT...
WELL, IT'S A BAD OMEN TO TRIP AND FALL.
THIS SURE IS NERVE-WRACKING.
YA... UH... UM...
GOOD LUCK TO BOTH OF US.
See ya.
Duuuh...
...

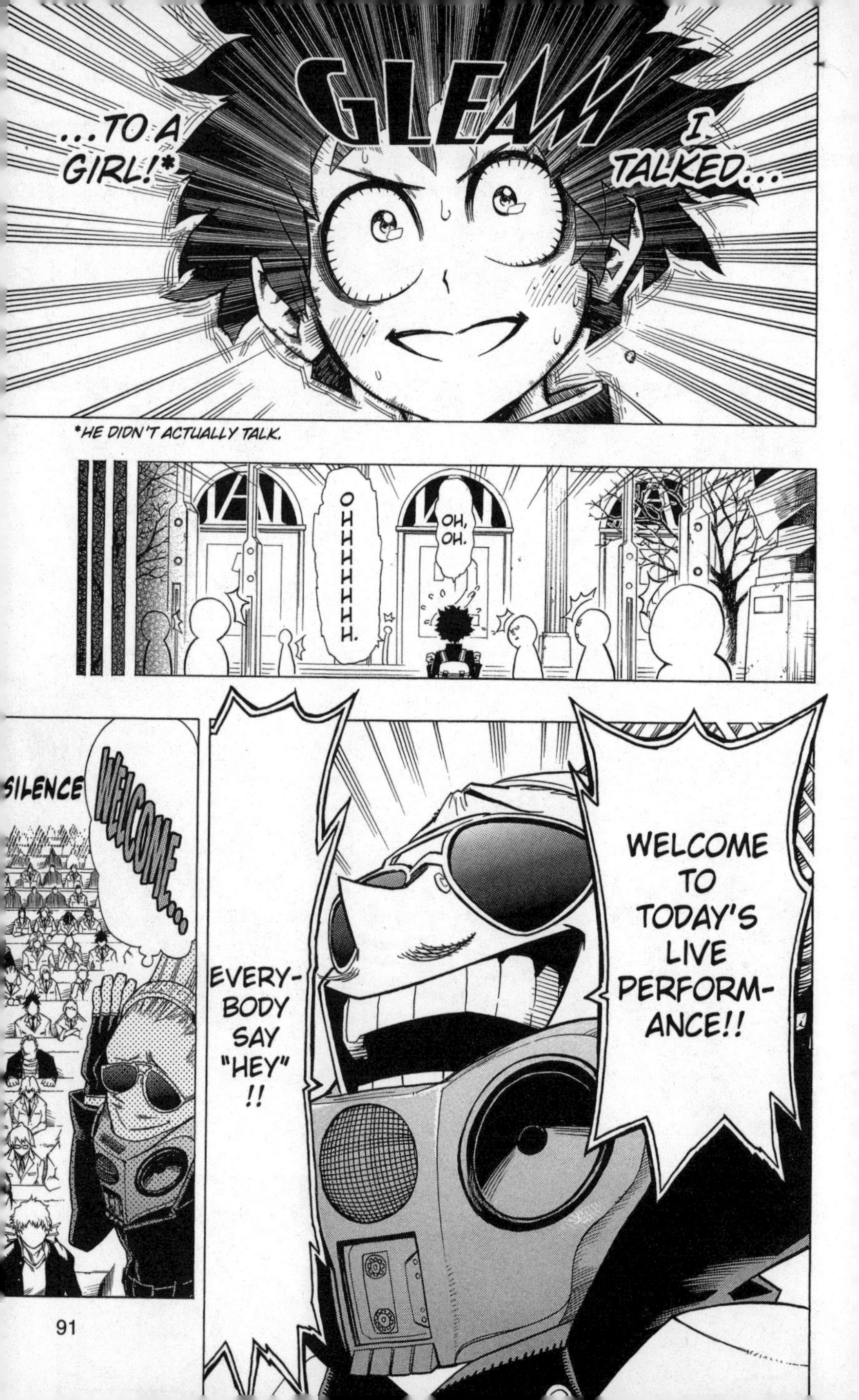
I TALKED...
GLEAM
...TO A GIRL!*
*HE DIDN'T ACTUALLY TALK.
OH, OH.
OHHHHHHHH.
WELCOME TO TODAY'S LIVE PERFORM-ANCE!!
EVERY-BODY SAY "HEY" !!
WELCOME...
SILENCE

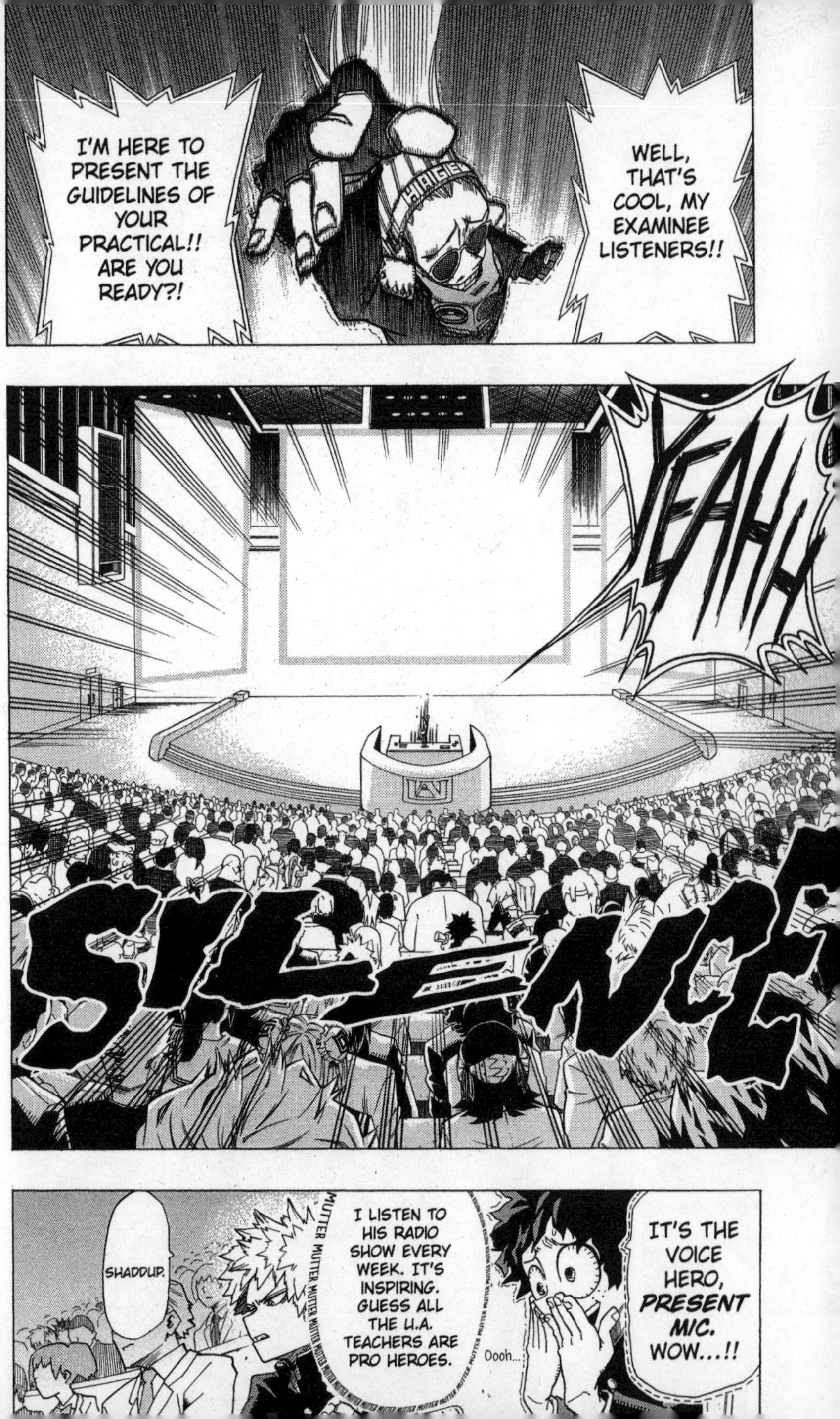
WELL, THAT'S COOL, MY EXAMINEE LISTENERS!!
I'M HERE TO PRESENT THE GUIDELINES OF YOUR PRACTICAL!! ARE YOU READY?!
YEAHH
SILENCE
IT'S THE VOICE HERO, ***PRESENT MIC.*** WOW...!!
Oooh...
I LISTEN TO HIS RADIO SHOW EVERY WEEK. IT'S INSPIRING. GUESS ALL THE U.A. TEACHERS ARE PRO HEROES.
MUTTER MUTTER
SHADDUP.

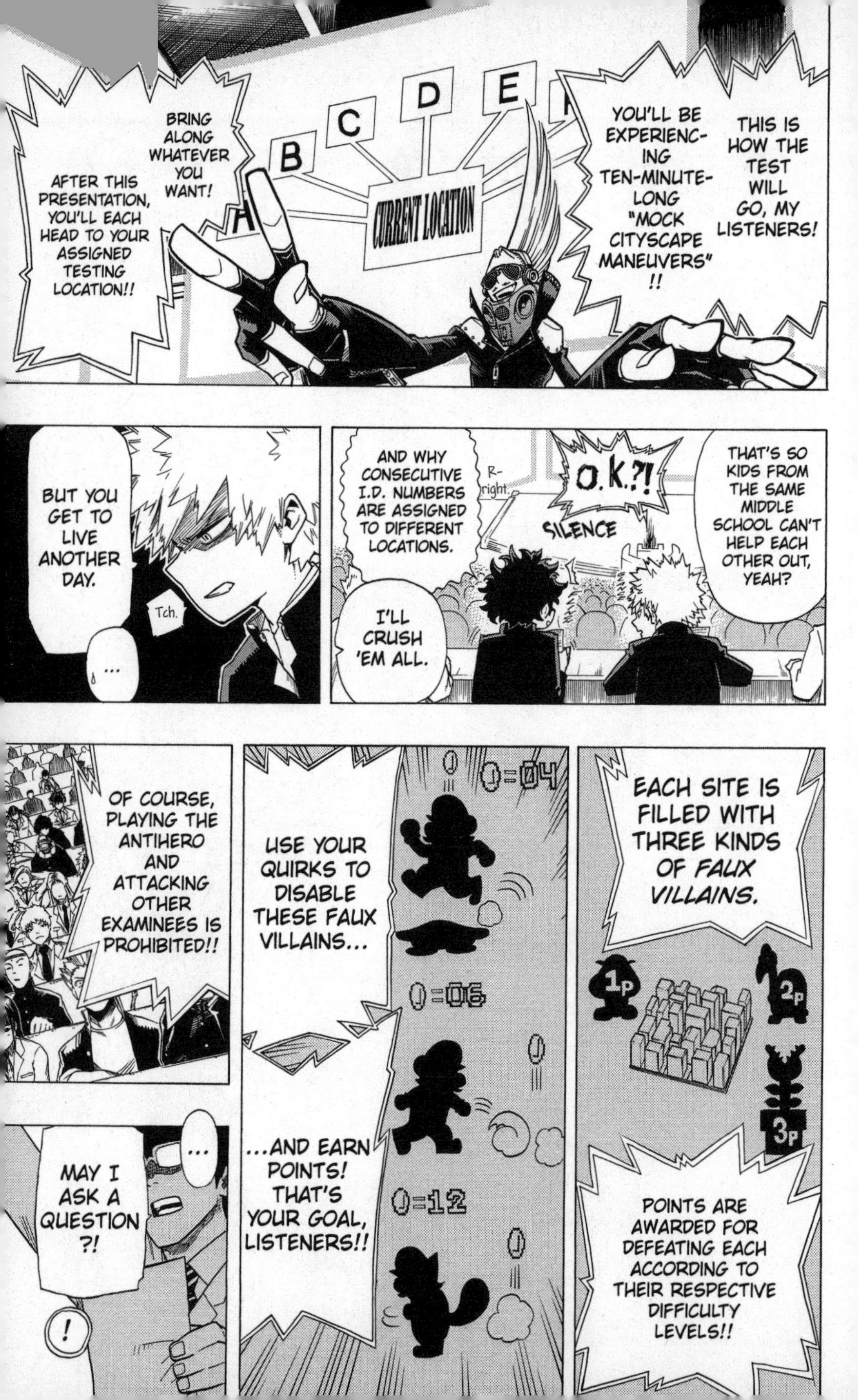
THIS IS HOW THE TEST WILL GO, MY LISTENERS!
YOU'LL BE EXPERIENCING TEN-MINUTE-LONG "MOCK CITYSCAPE MANEUVERS"!!
CURRENT LOCATION
A
B
C
D
E
AFTER THIS PRESENTATION, YOU'LL EACH HEAD TO YOUR ASSIGNED TESTING LOCATION!!
BRING ALONG WHATEVER YOU WANT!
THAT'S SO KIDS FROM THE SAME MIDDLE SCHOOL CAN'T HELP EACH OTHER OUT, YEAH?
O.K.?!
SILENCE
R-right.
AND WHY CONSECUTIVE I.D. NUMBERS ARE ASSIGNED TO DIFFERENT LOCATIONS.
I'LL CRUSH 'EM ALL.
BUT YOU GET TO LIVE ANOTHER DAY.
Tch.
...
EACH SITE IS FILLED WITH THREE KINDS OF FAUX VILLAINS.
1p
2p
3p
POINTS ARE AWARDED FOR DEFEATING EACH ACCORDING TO THEIR RESPECTIVE DIFFICULTY LEVELS!!
0=04
USE YOUR QUIRKS TO DISABLE THESE FAUX VILLAINS...
0=06
...AND EARN POINTS! THAT'S YOUR GOAL, LISTENERS!!
0=12
OF COURSE, PLAYING THE ANTIHERO AND ATTACKING OTHER EXAMINEES IS PROHIBITED!!
...
MAY I ASK A QUESTION?!
!

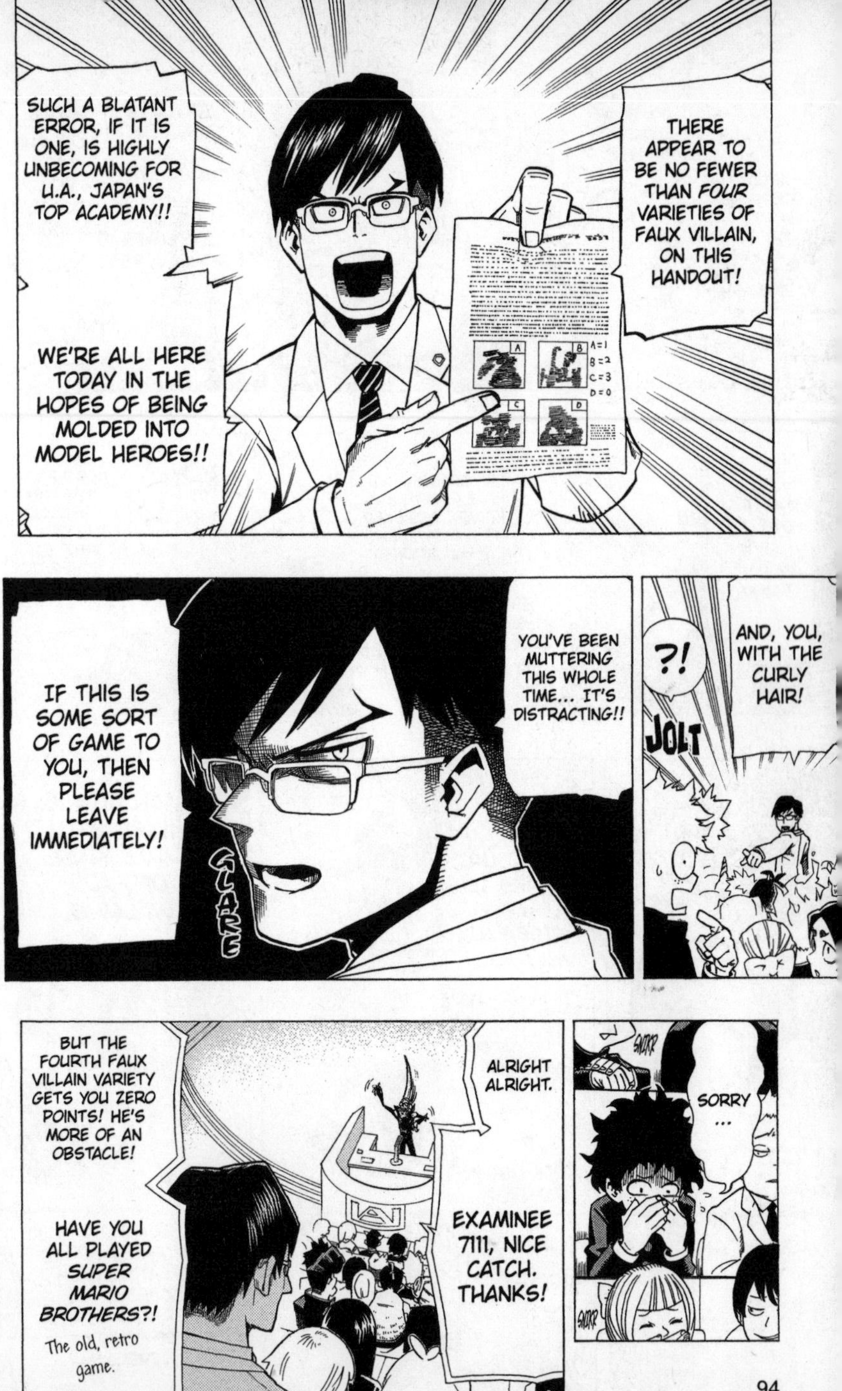
THERE APPEAR TO BE NO FEWER THAN *FOUR* VARIETIES OF FAUX VILLAIN, ON THIS HANDOUT!
SUCH A BLATANT ERROR, IF IT IS ONE, IS HIGHLY UNBECOMING FOR U.A., JAPAN'S TOP ACADEMY!!
WE'RE ALL HERE TODAY IN THE HOPES OF BEING MOLDED INTO MODEL HEROES!!
A=1
B=2
C=3
D=0
AND, YOU, WITH THE CURLY HAIR!
?!
JOLT
YOU'VE BEEN MUTTERING THIS WHOLE TIME... IT'S DISTRACTING!!
IF THIS IS SOME SORT OF GAME TO YOU, THEN PLEASE LEAVE IMMEDIATELY!
GLARE
SNRKR
SORRY...
SNRKR
ALRIGHT ALRIGHT.
BUT THE FOURTH FAUX VILLAIN VARIETY GETS YOU ZERO POINTS! HE'S MORE OF AN OBSTACLE!
EXAMINEE 7111, NICE CATCH. THANKS!
HAVE YOU ALL PLAYED *SUPER MARIO BROTHERS*?!
The old, retro game.

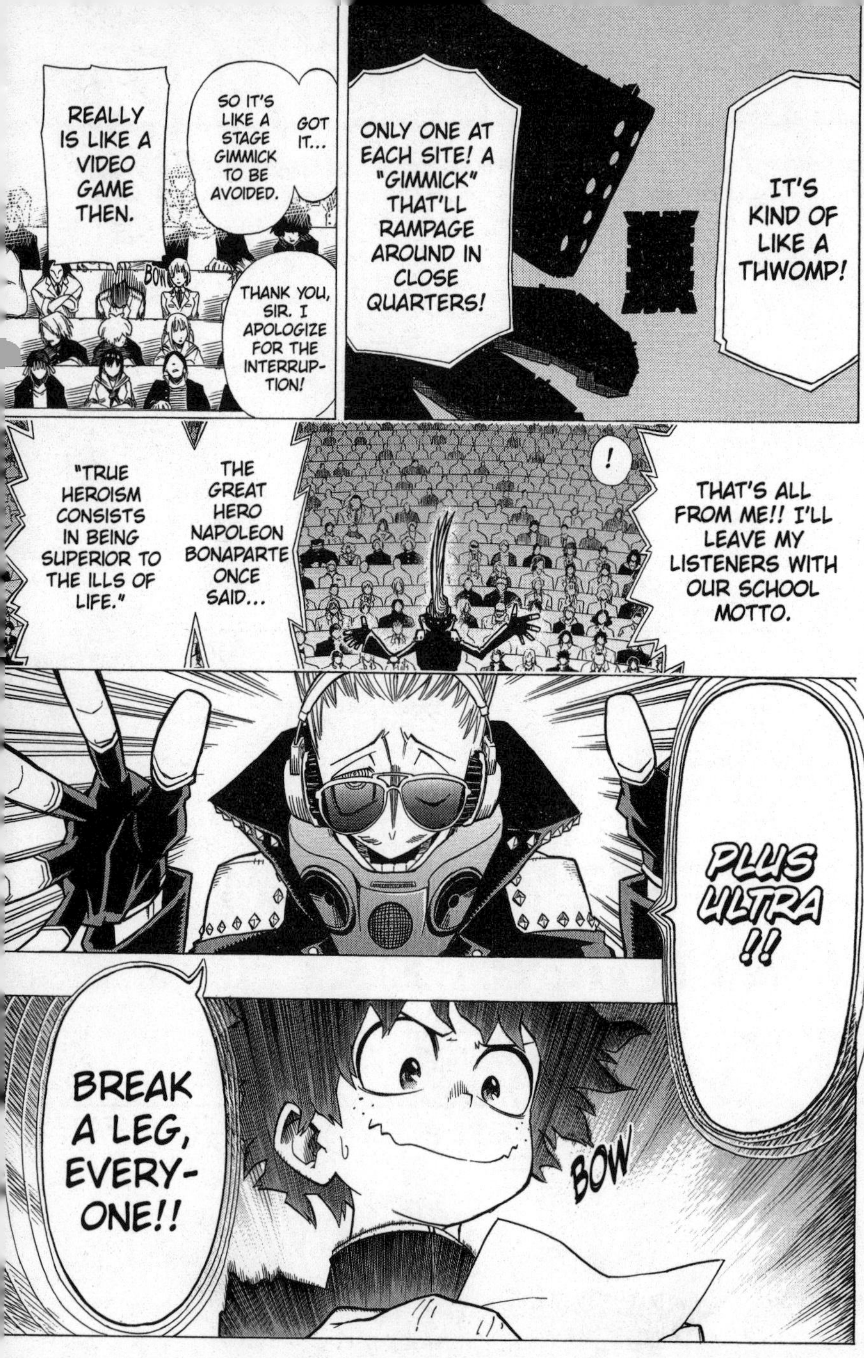
IT'S KIND OF LIKE A THWOMP!
ONLY ONE AT EACH SITE! A "GIMMICK" THAT'LL RAMPAGE AROUND IN CLOSE QUARTERS!
GOT IT...
SO IT'S LIKE A STAGE GIMMICK TO BE AVOIDED.
REALLY IS LIKE A VIDEO GAME THEN.
THANK YOU, SIR. I APOLOGIZE FOR THE INTERRUPTION!
BOW
!
THAT'S ALL FROM ME!! I'LL LEAVE MY LISTENERS WITH OUR SCHOOL MOTTO.
THE GREAT HERO NAPOLEON BONAPARTE ONCE SAID...
"TRUE HEROISM CONSISTS IN BEING SUPERIOR TO THE ILLS OF LIFE."
PLUS ULTRA!!
BOW
BREAK A LEG, EVERYONE!!

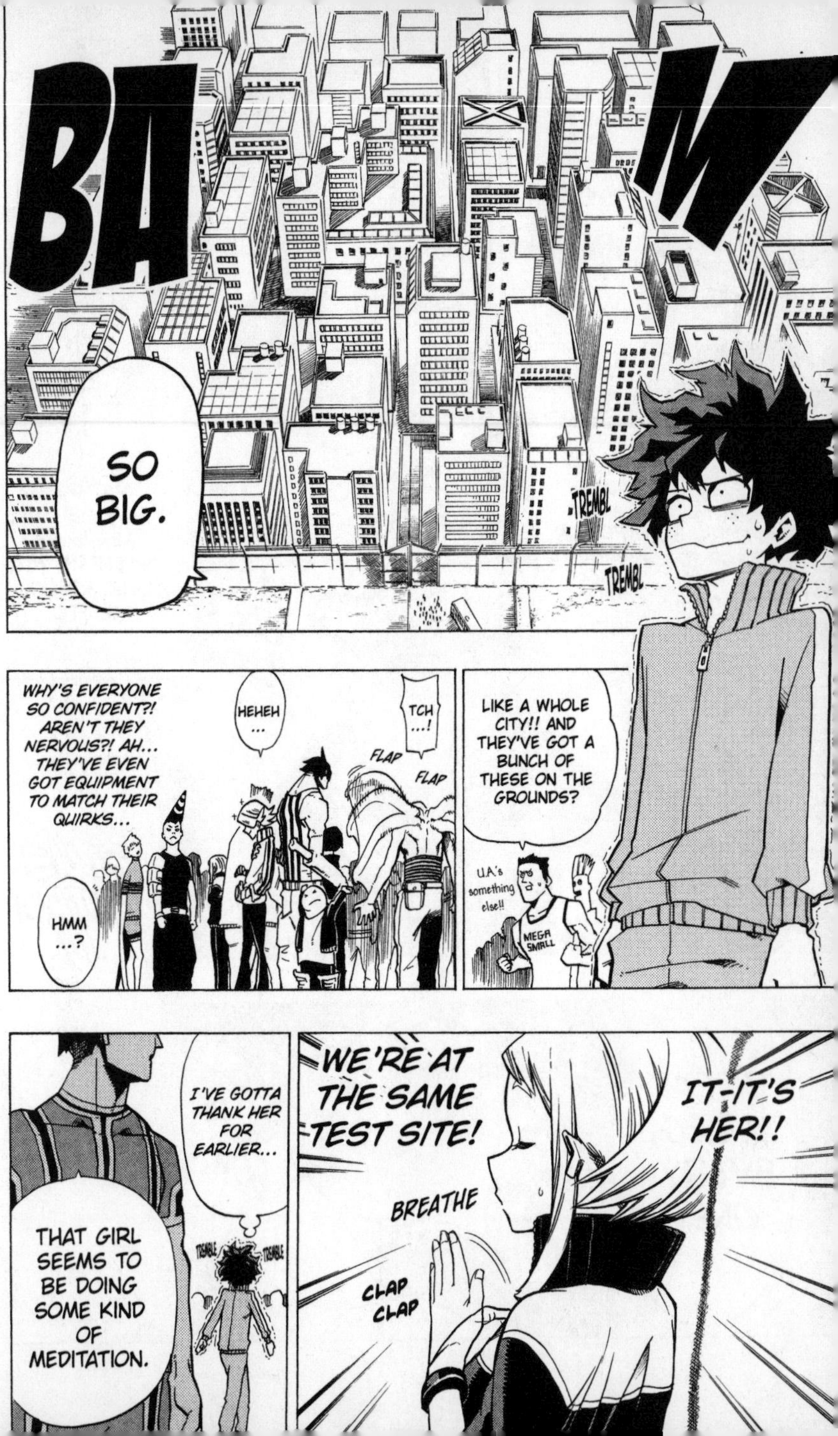
BAM
TREMBL
TREMBL
SO BIG.
LIKE A WHOLE CITY!! AND THEY'VE GOT A BUNCH OF THESE ON THE GROUNDS?
U.A.'s something else!!
MEGA SMALL
TCH ...!
FLAP
FLAP
HEHEH ...
WHY'S EVERYONE SO CONFIDENT?! AREN'T THEY NERVOUS?! AH... THEY'VE EVEN GOT EQUIPMENT TO MATCH THEIR QUIRKS...
HMM ...?
IT-IT'S HER!!
WE'RE AT THE SAME TEST SITE!
BREATHE
CLAP CLAP
I'VE GOTTA THANK HER FOR EARLIER...
TREMBLE
TREMBLE
THAT GIRL SEEMS TO BE DOING SOME KIND OF MEDITATION.

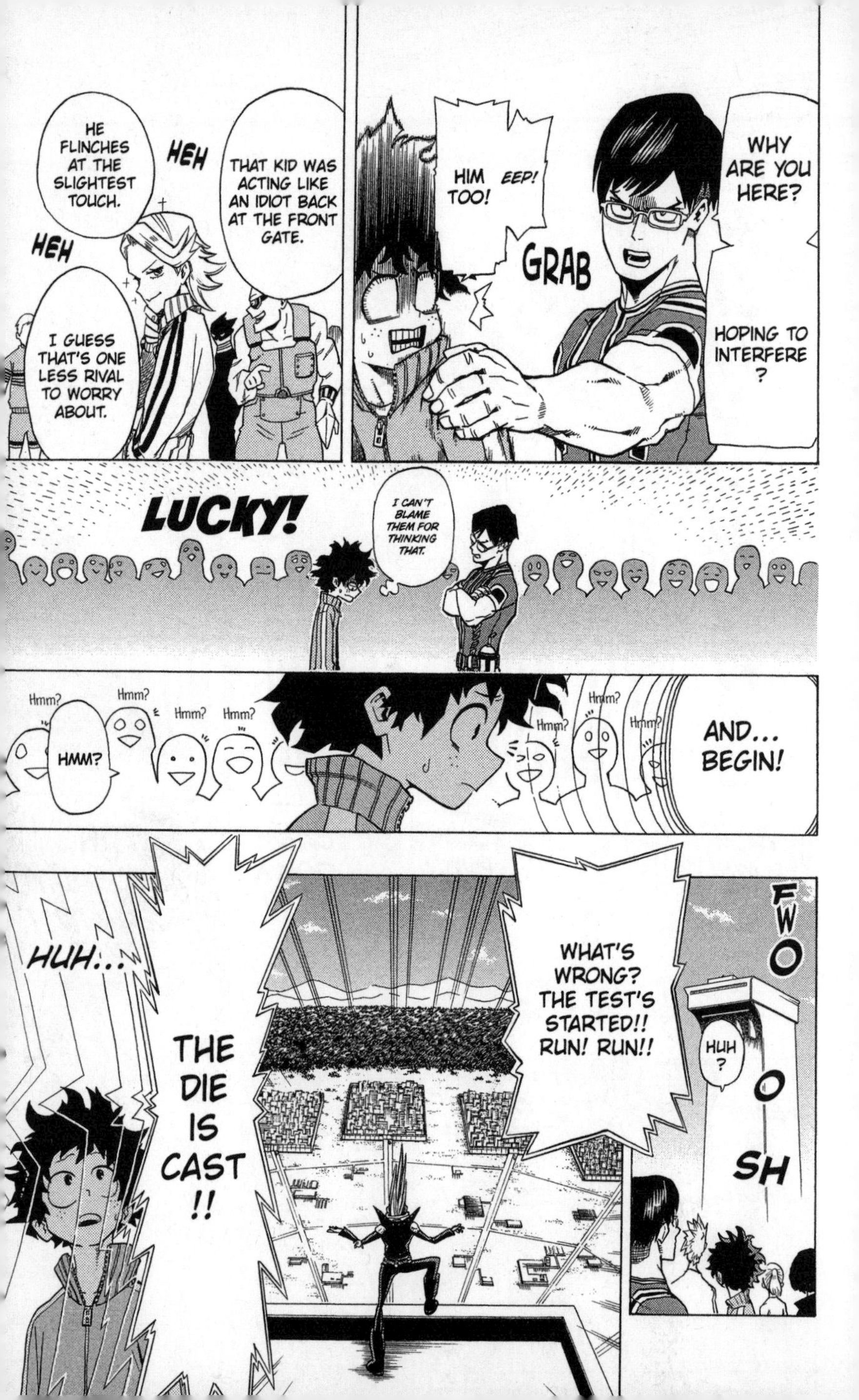
WHY ARE YOU HERE?
HOPING TO INTERFERE?
GRAB
HIM TOO!
EEP!
THAT KID WAS ACTING LIKE AN IDIOT BACK AT THE FRONT GATE.
HEH
HE FLINCHES AT THE SLIGHTEST TOUCH.
HEH
I GUESS THAT'S ONE LESS RIVAL TO WORRY ABOUT.
I CAN'T BLAME THEM FOR THINKING THAT.
LUCKY!
AND... BEGIN!
Hmm?
Hmm?
Hmm?
Hmm?
Hmm?
Hmm?
Hmm?
HMM?
Hmm?
FWOOSH
HUH?
WHAT'S WRONG? THE TEST'S STARTED!! RUN! RUN!!
THE DIE IS CAST!!
HUH...

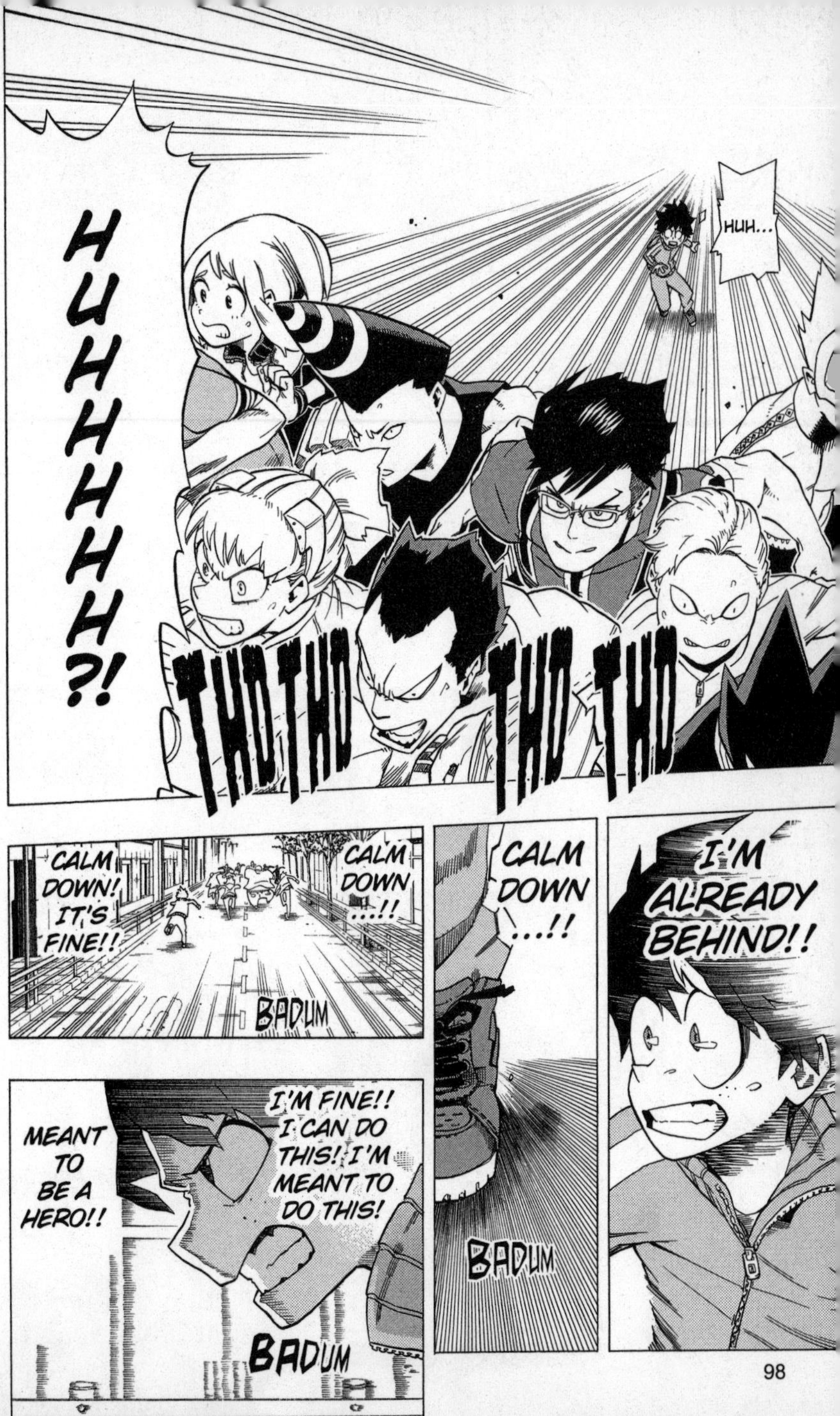
HUH...
HUHHHHHH?!
THD THD
THD THD
I'M ALREADY BEHIND!!
CALM DOWN ...!!
BADUM
CALM DOWN ...!!
CALM DOWN! IT'S FINE!!
BADUM
I'M FINE!! I CAN DO THIS! I'M MEANT TO DO THIS!
MEANT TO BE A HERO!!
BADUM

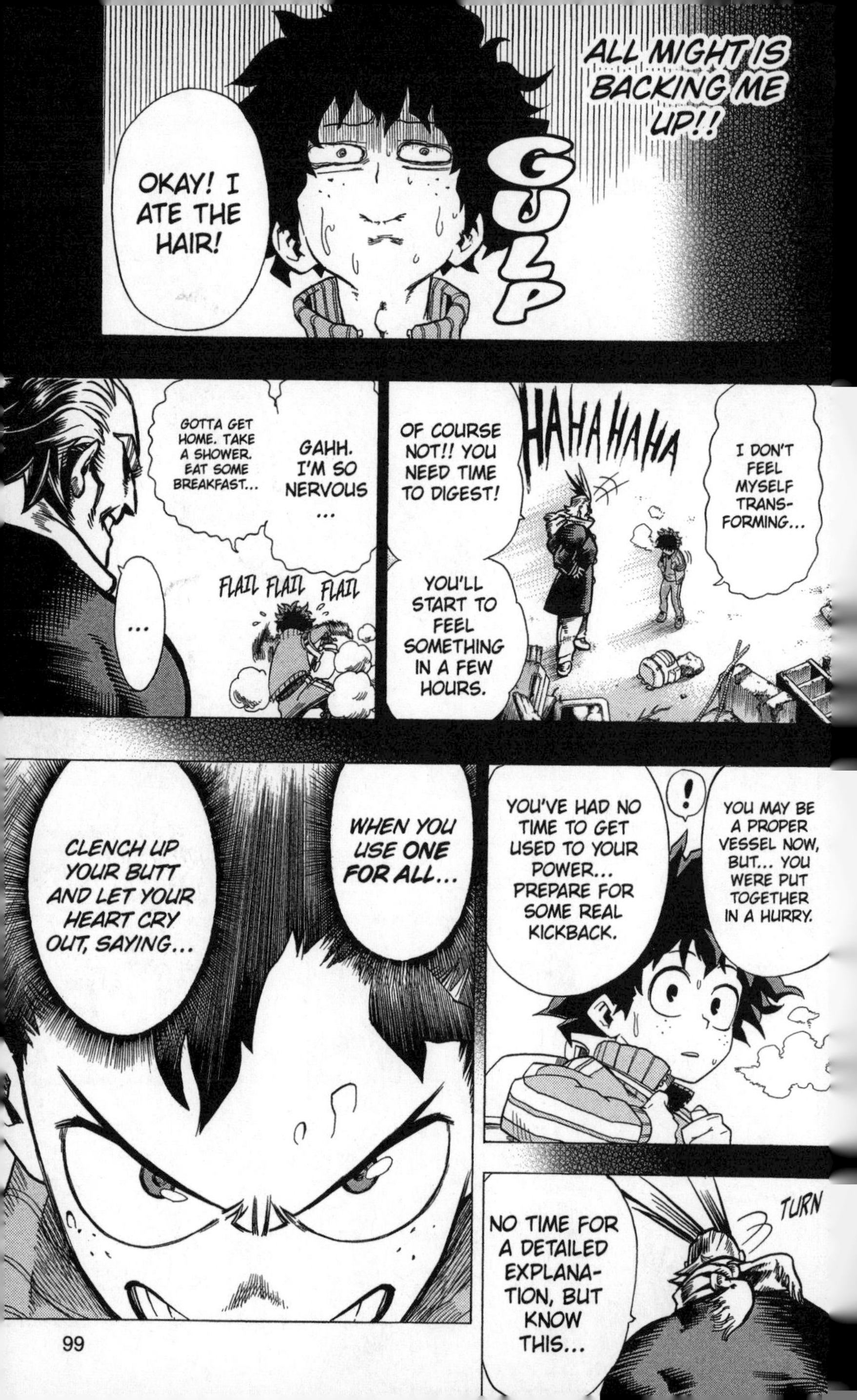
ALL MIGHT IS BACKING ME UP!!
GULP
OKAY! I ATE THE HAIR!
I DON'T FEEL MYSELF TRANS-FORMING...
HAHAHAHA
OF COURSE NOT!! YOU NEED TIME TO DIGEST!
YOU'LL START TO FEEL SOMETHING IN A FEW HOURS.
GAHH. I'M SO NERVOUS...
GOTTA GET HOME. TAKE A SHOWER. EAT SOME BREAKFAST...
FLAIL FLAIL FLAIL
...
YOU MAY BE A PROPER VESSEL NOW, BUT... YOU WERE PUT TOGETHER IN A HURRY.
!
YOU'VE HAD NO TIME TO GET USED TO YOUR POWER... PREPARE FOR SOME REAL KICKBACK.
TURN
NO TIME FOR A DETAILED EXPLANA-TION, BUT KNOW THIS...
WHEN YOU USE ONE FOR ALL...
CLENCH UP YOUR BUTT AND LET YOUR HEART CRY OUT, SAYING...

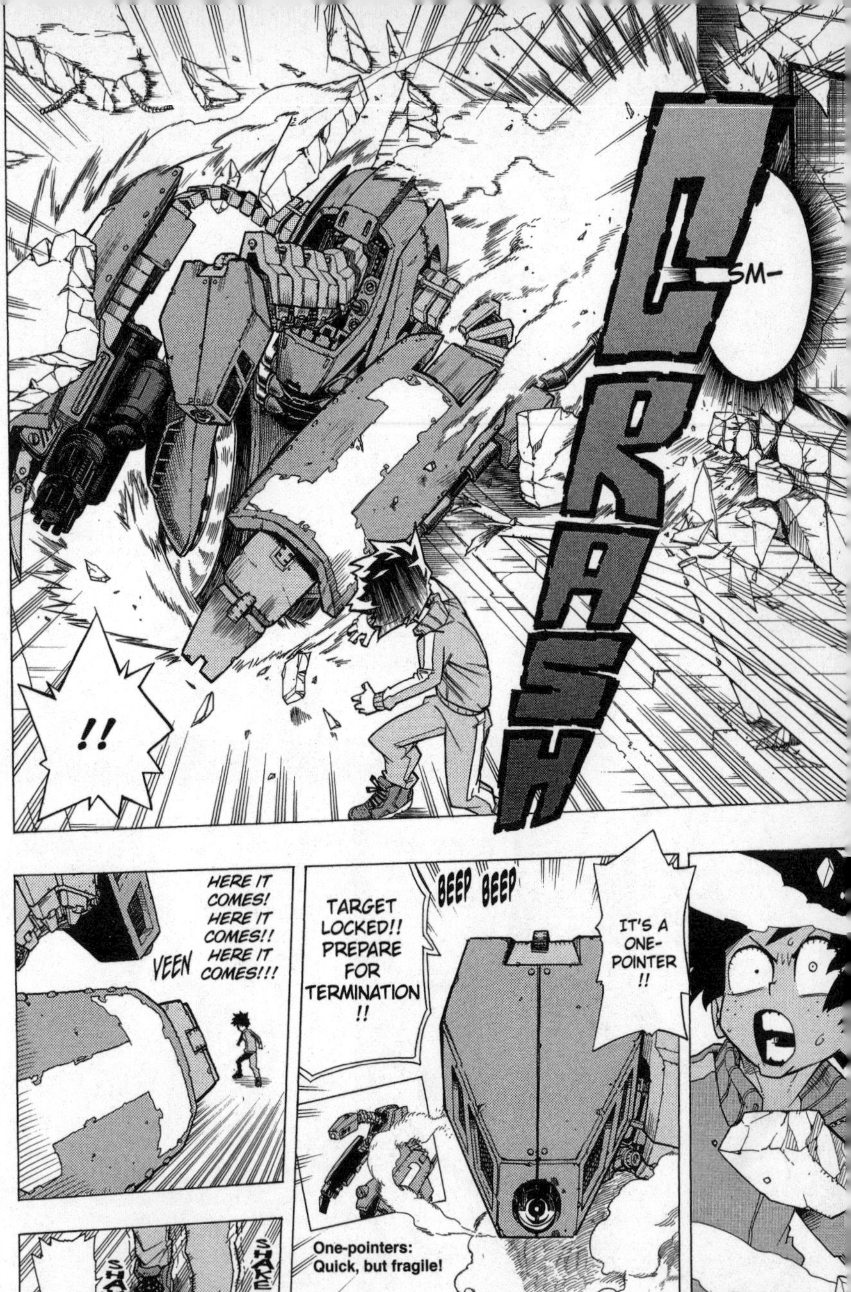
SM-
CRASH
!!
IT'S A ONE-POINTER!!
BEEP BEEP
TARGET LOCKED!! PREPARE FOR TERMINATION!!
One-pointers: Quick, but fragile!
HERE IT COMES! HERE IT COMES!! HERE IT COMES!!!
VEEN
SHAKE SHAKE
SHAKE SHAKE
...!!

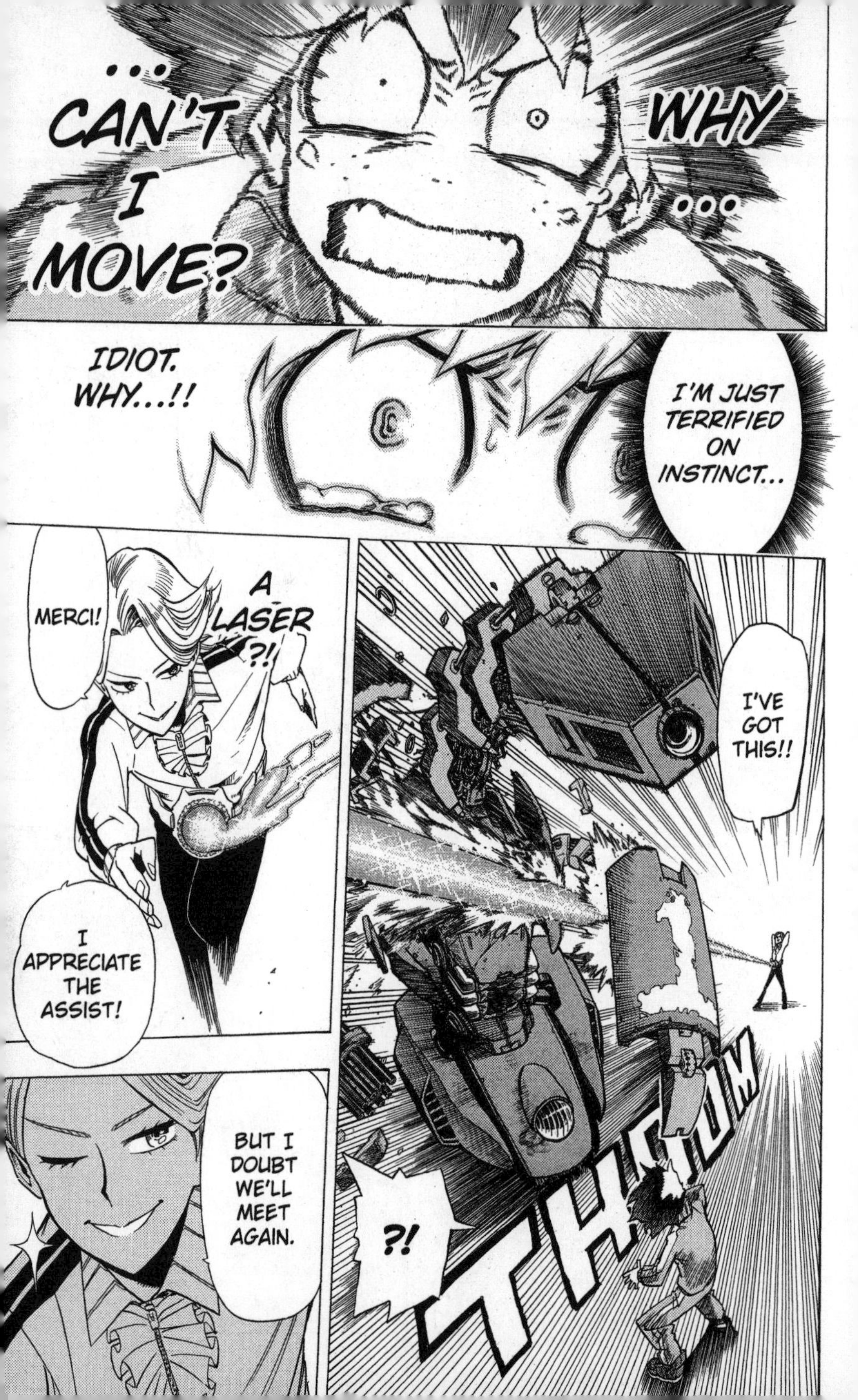
WHY...
...CAN'T I MOVE?
I'M JUST TERRIFIED ON INSTINCT...
IDIOT. WHY...!!
I'VE GOT THIS!!
THOOOM
?!
MERCI!
A LASER?!
I APPRECIATE THE ASSIST!
BUT I DOUBT WE'LL MEET AGAIN.

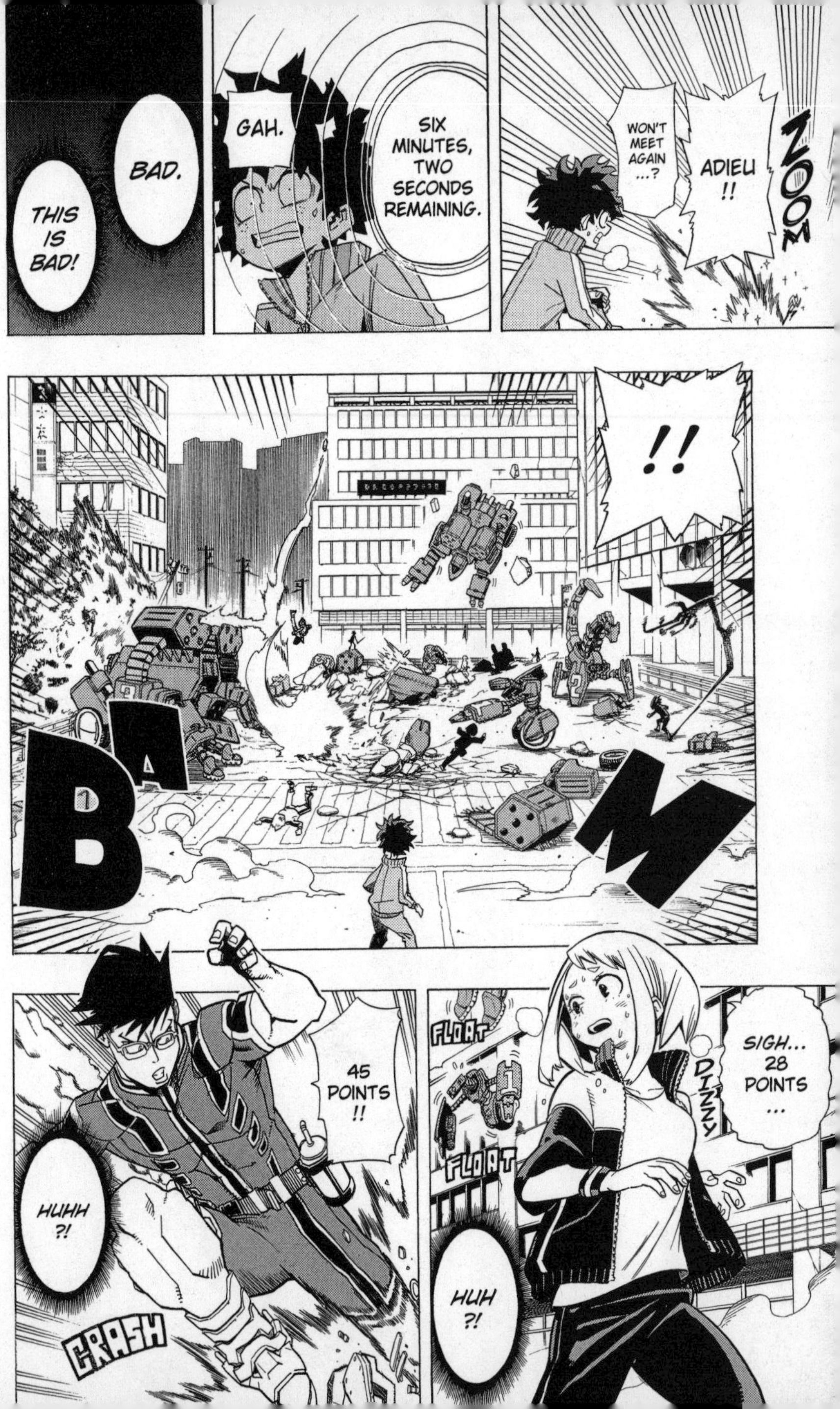
ADIEU !!
WON'T MEET AGAIN ...?
ZOOM
SIX MINUTES, TWO SECONDS REMAINING.
GAH.
BAD.
THIS IS BAD!
!!
BAM
SIGH... 28 POINTS ...
DIZZY
FLOAT
FLOAT
HUH ?!
45 POINTS !!
HUHH ?!
CRASH

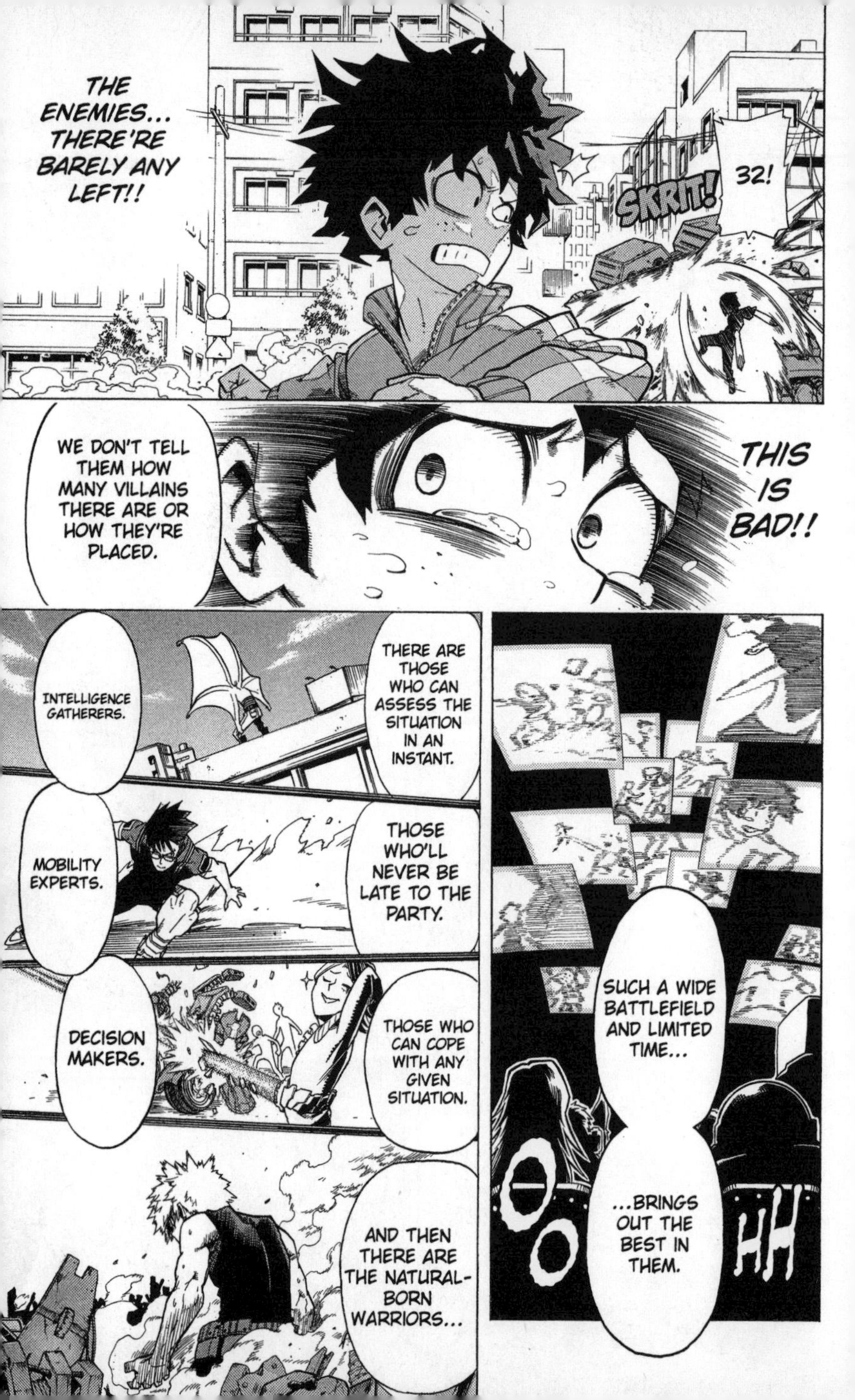
32!
SKRIT!
THE ENEMIES... THERE'RE BARELY ANY LEFT!!
THIS IS BAD!!
WE DON'T TELL THEM HOW MANY VILLAINS THERE ARE OR HOW THEY'RE PLACED.
SUCH A WIDE BATTLEFIELD AND LIMITED TIME...
...BRINGS OUT THE BEST IN THEM.
HH
THERE ARE THOSE WHO CAN ASSESS THE SITUATION IN AN INSTANT.
INTELLIGENCE GATHERERS.
THOSE WHO'LL NEVER BE LATE TO THE PARTY.
MOBILITY EXPERTS.
THOSE WHO CAN COPE WITH ANY GIVEN SITUATION.
DECISION MAKERS.
AND THEN THERE ARE THE NATURAL-BORN WARRIORS...

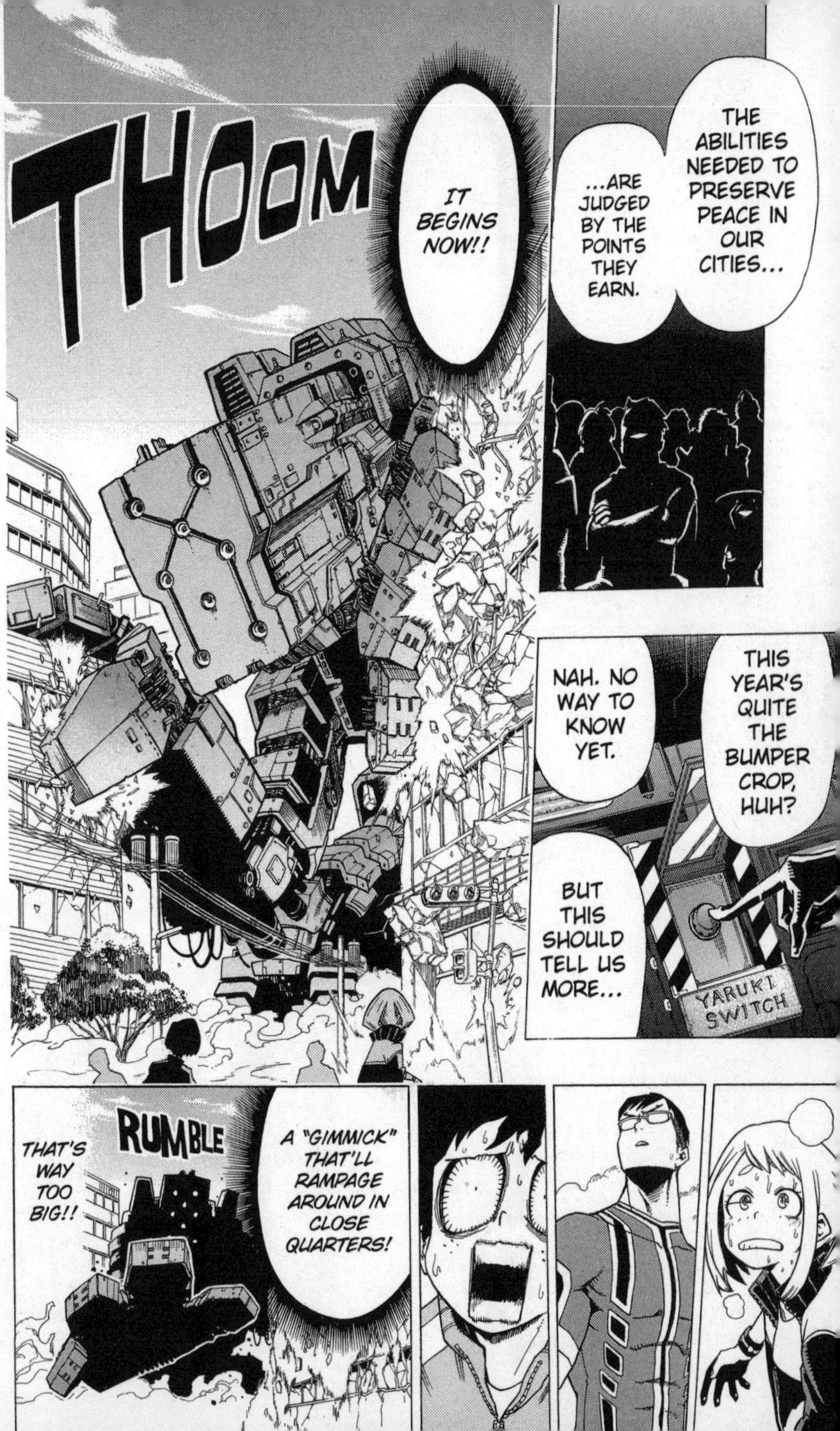
THE ABILITIES NEEDED TO PRESERVE PEACE IN OUR CITIES...
...ARE JUDGED BY THE POINTS THEY EARN.
THIS YEAR'S QUITE THE BUMPER CROP, HUH?
NAH. NO WAY TO KNOW YET.
BUT THIS SHOULD TELL US MORE...
YARUKI SWITCH
IT BEGINS NOW!!
THOOM
A "GIMMICK" THAT'LL RAMPAGE AROUND IN CLOSE QUARTERS!
RUMBLE
THAT'S WAY TOO BIG!!

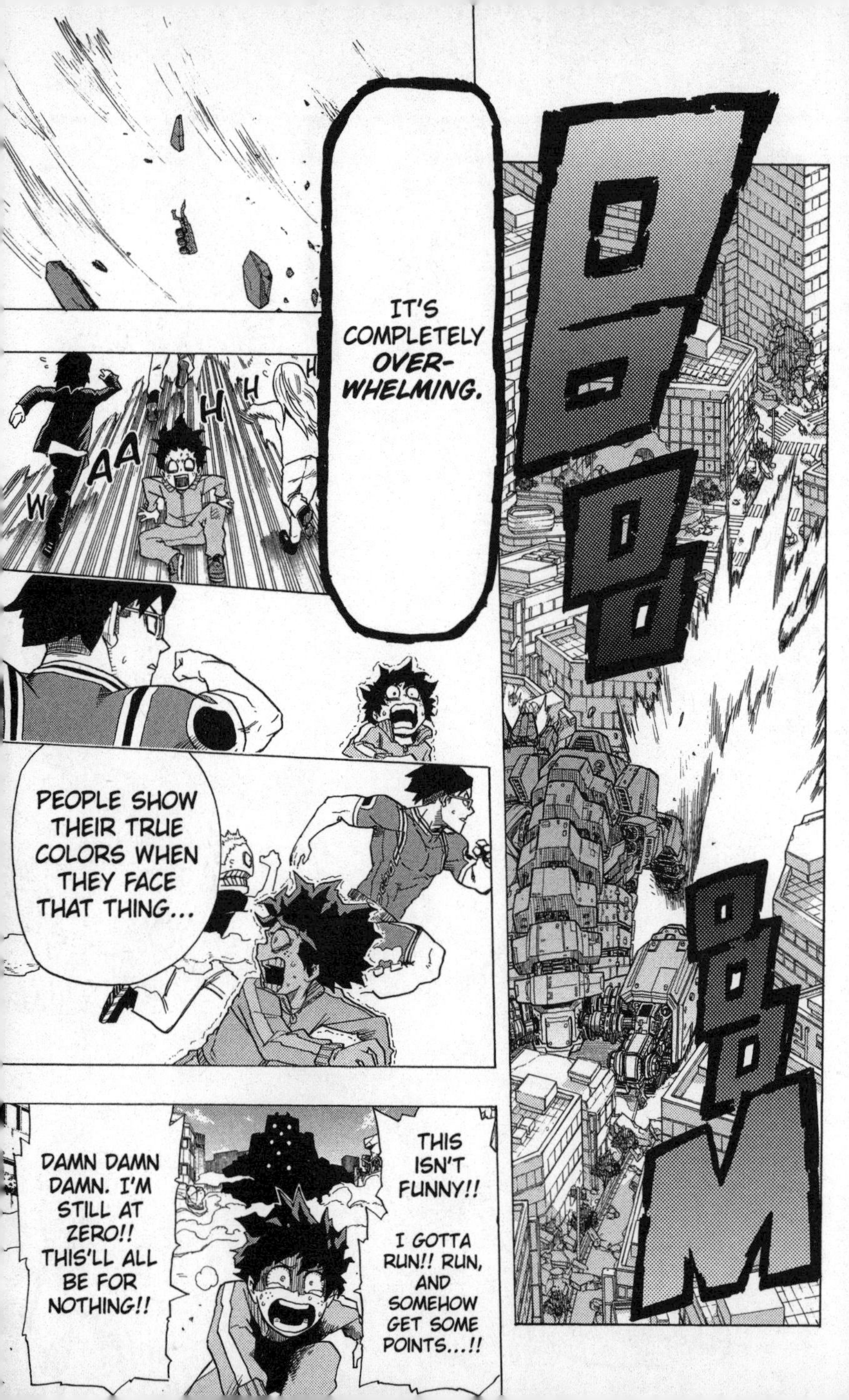
DOOOOOM
IT'S COMPLETELY *OVER-WHELMING.*
WAAHHH
PEOPLE SHOW THEIR TRUE COLORS WHEN THEY FACE THAT THING...
THIS ISN'T FUNNY!!
I GOTTA RUN!! RUN, AND SOMEHOW GET SOME POINTS...!!
DAMN DAMN DAMN. I'M STILL AT ZERO!! THIS'LL ALL BE FOR NOTHING!!

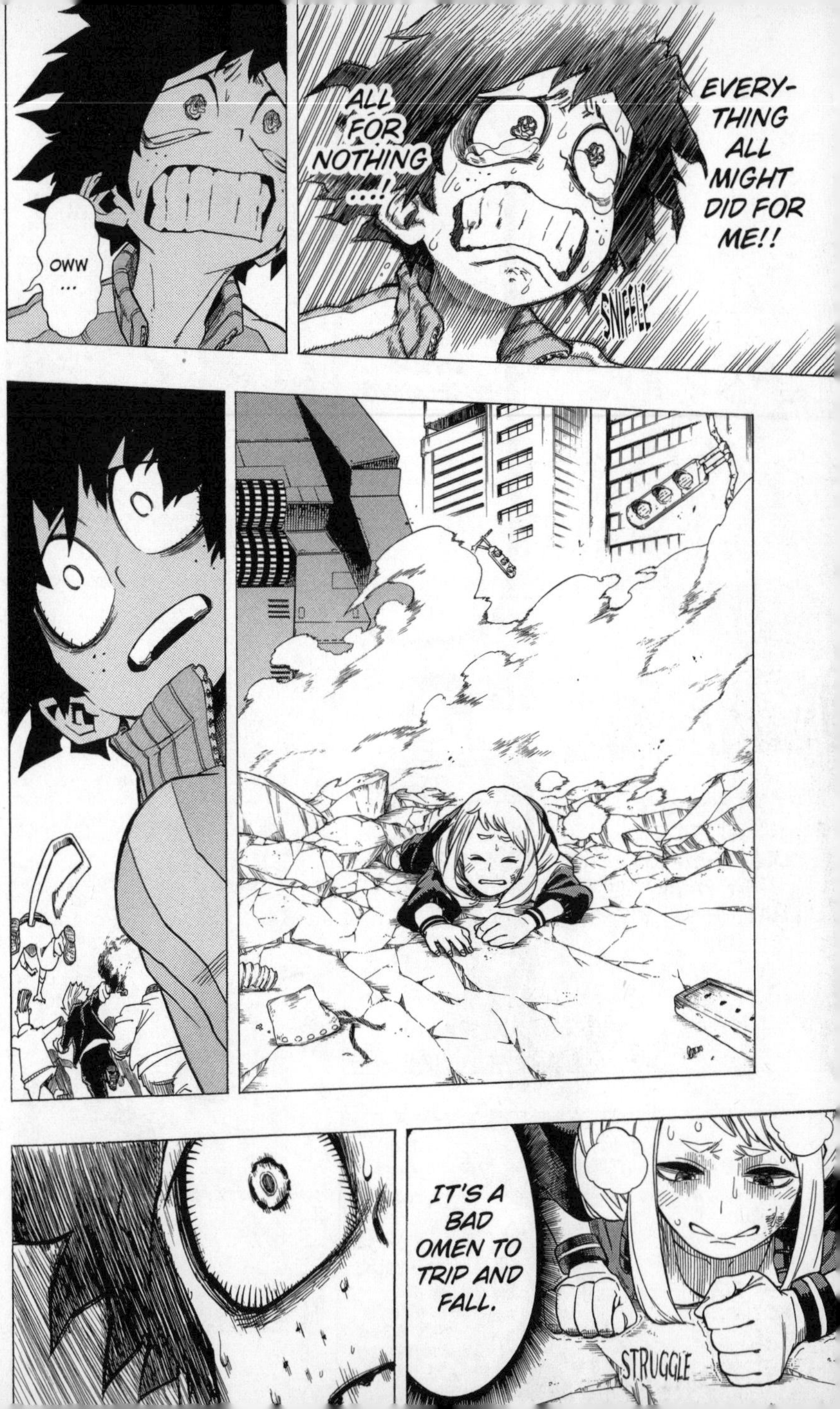
EVERYTHING ALL MIGHT DID FOR ME!!
ALL FOR NOTHING ...!
SNIFFLE
OWW ...
IT'S A BAD OMEN TO TRIP AND FALL.
STRUGGLE

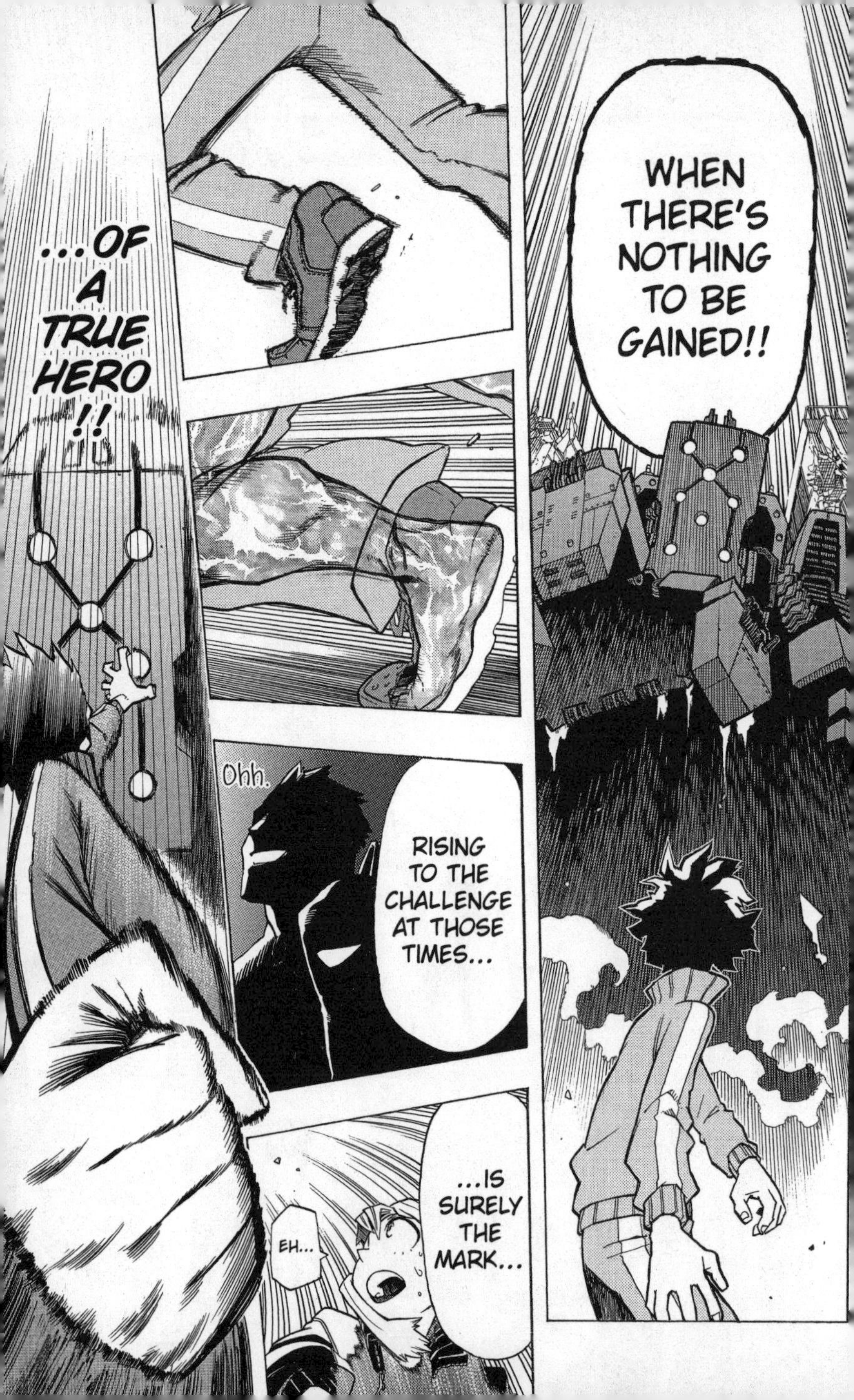
WHEN THERE'S NOTHING TO BE GAINED!!
Ohh.
RISING TO THE CHALLENGE AT THOSE TIMES...
...IS SURELY THE MARK...
EH...
...OF A TRUE HERO!!

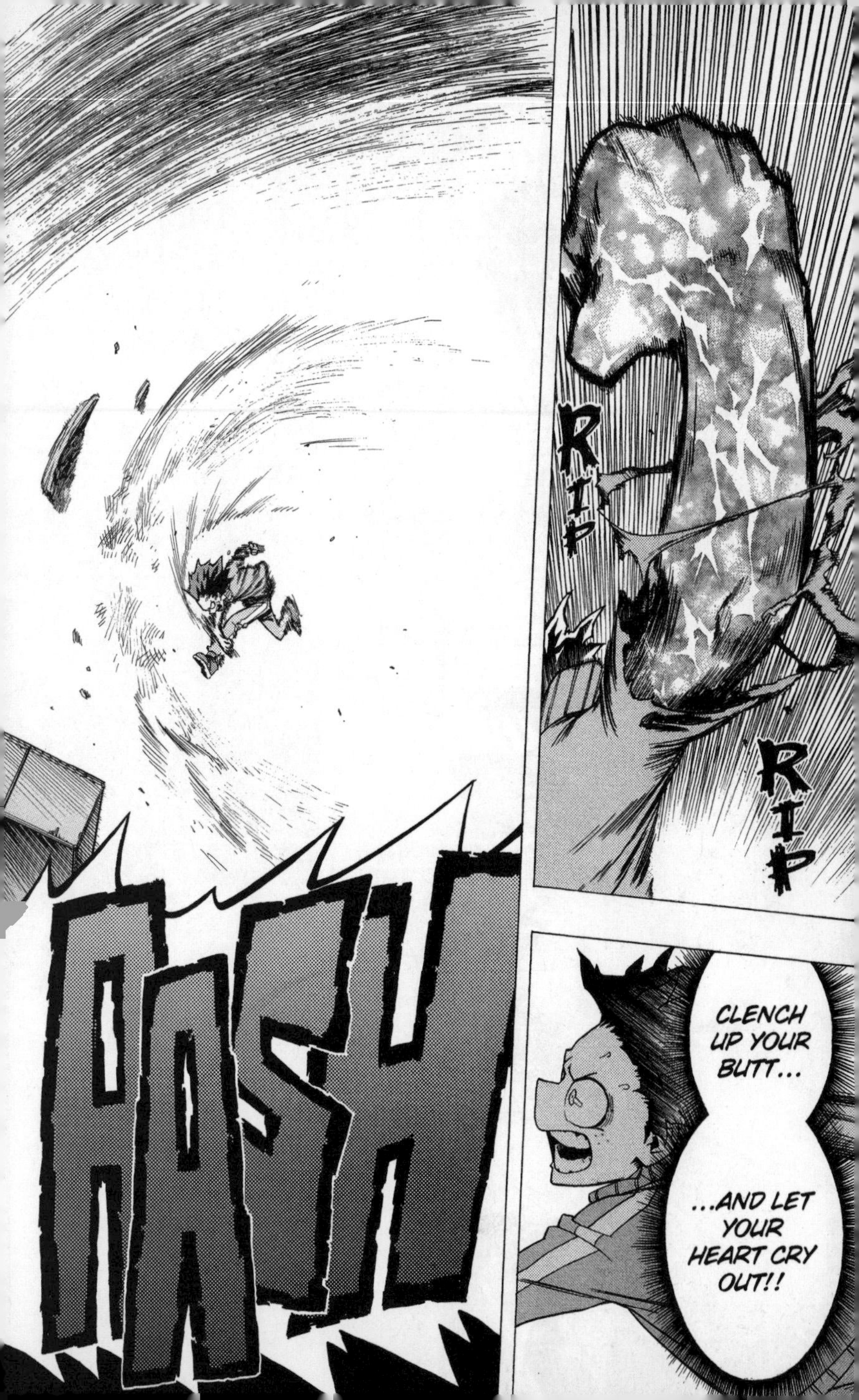
RIP
RIP
CLENCH UP YOUR BUTT...
...AND LET YOUR HEART CRY OUT!!
RASH

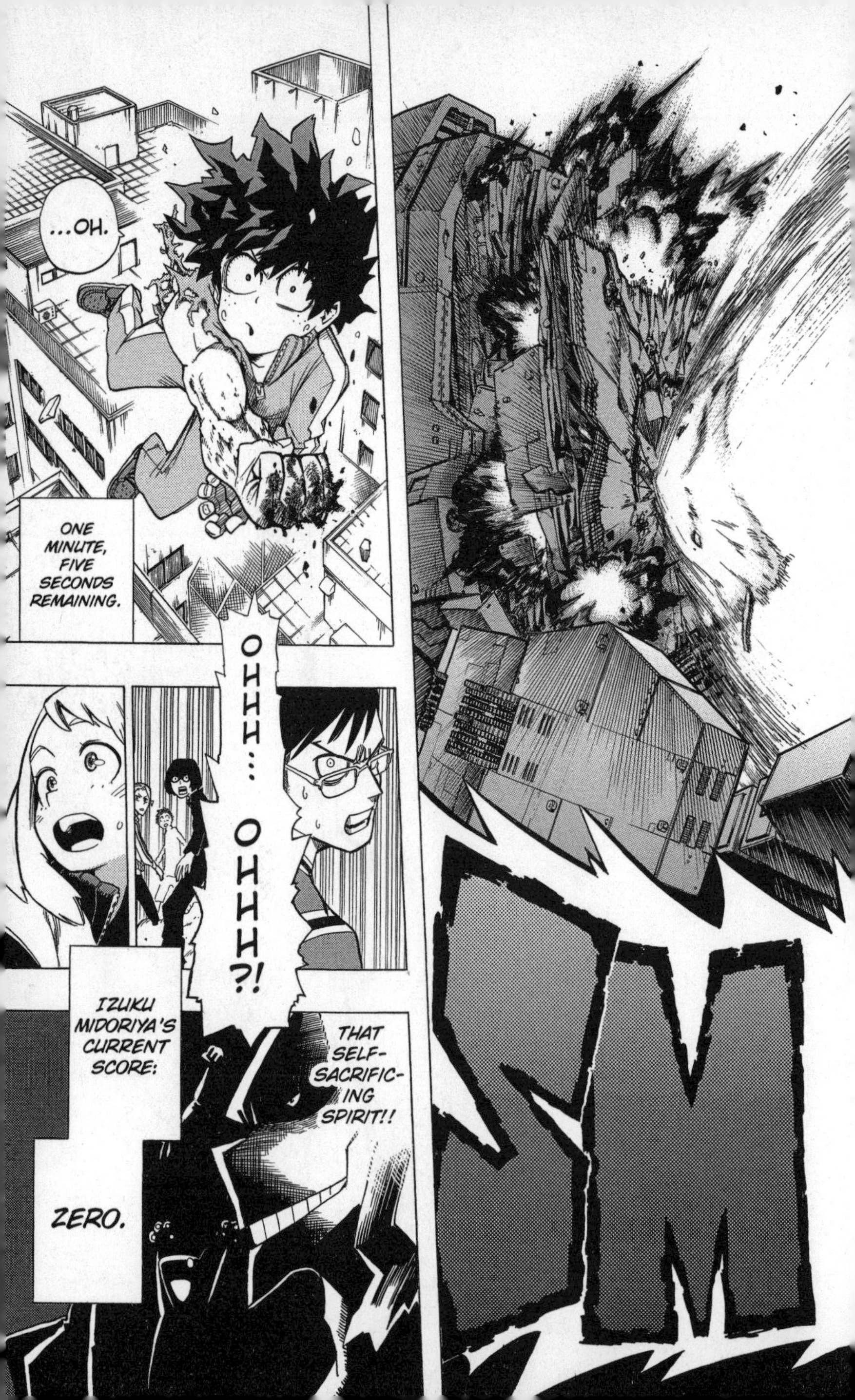
SM
...OH.
ONE MINUTE, FIVE SECONDS REMAINING.
OHHH... OHHHH?!
THAT SELF-SACRIFICING SPIRIT!!
IZUKU MIDORIYA'S CURRENT SCORE:
ZERO.

KATSUKI BAKUGO (AGE: 15)

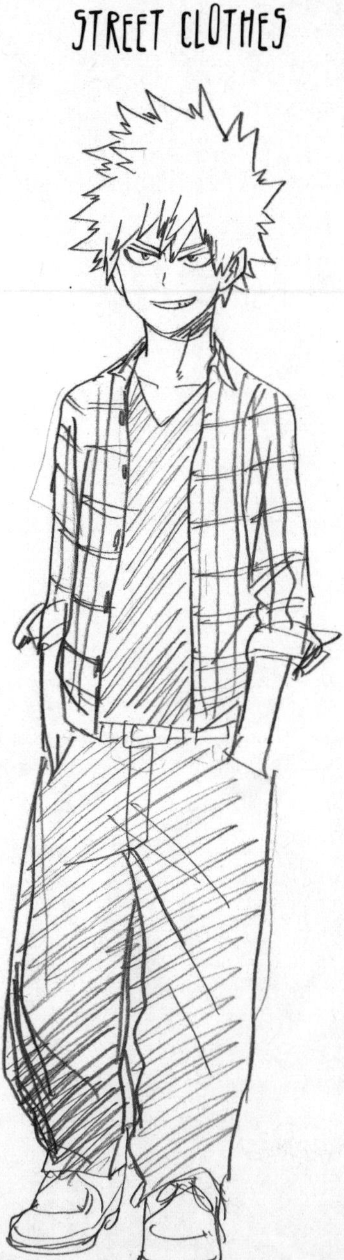
STREET CLOTHES

Birthday: 4/20
Height: 172 cm
Favorite Things: All spicy food, mountain climbing

BEHIND THE SCENES

At first, I made him a natural-born genius who would inadvertently insult people, but that got pretty boring. So I went the other route and turned him into a nasty guy with an explosive personality. I'm glad he came out so unlikable.

His face just screams "I'm a rotten thief."

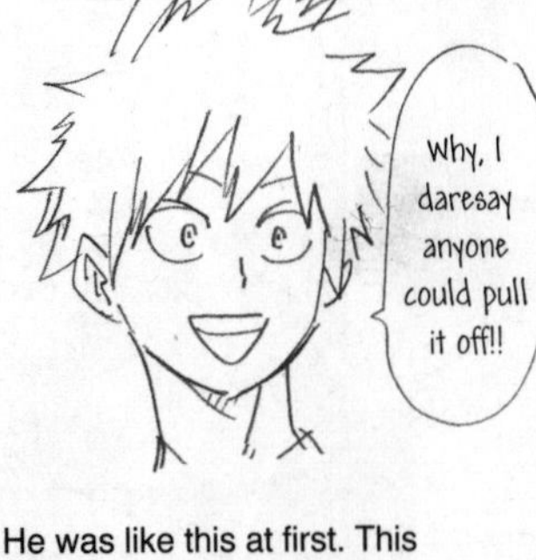
Why, I daresay anyone could pull it off!!

He was like this at first. This version just made me angry though.

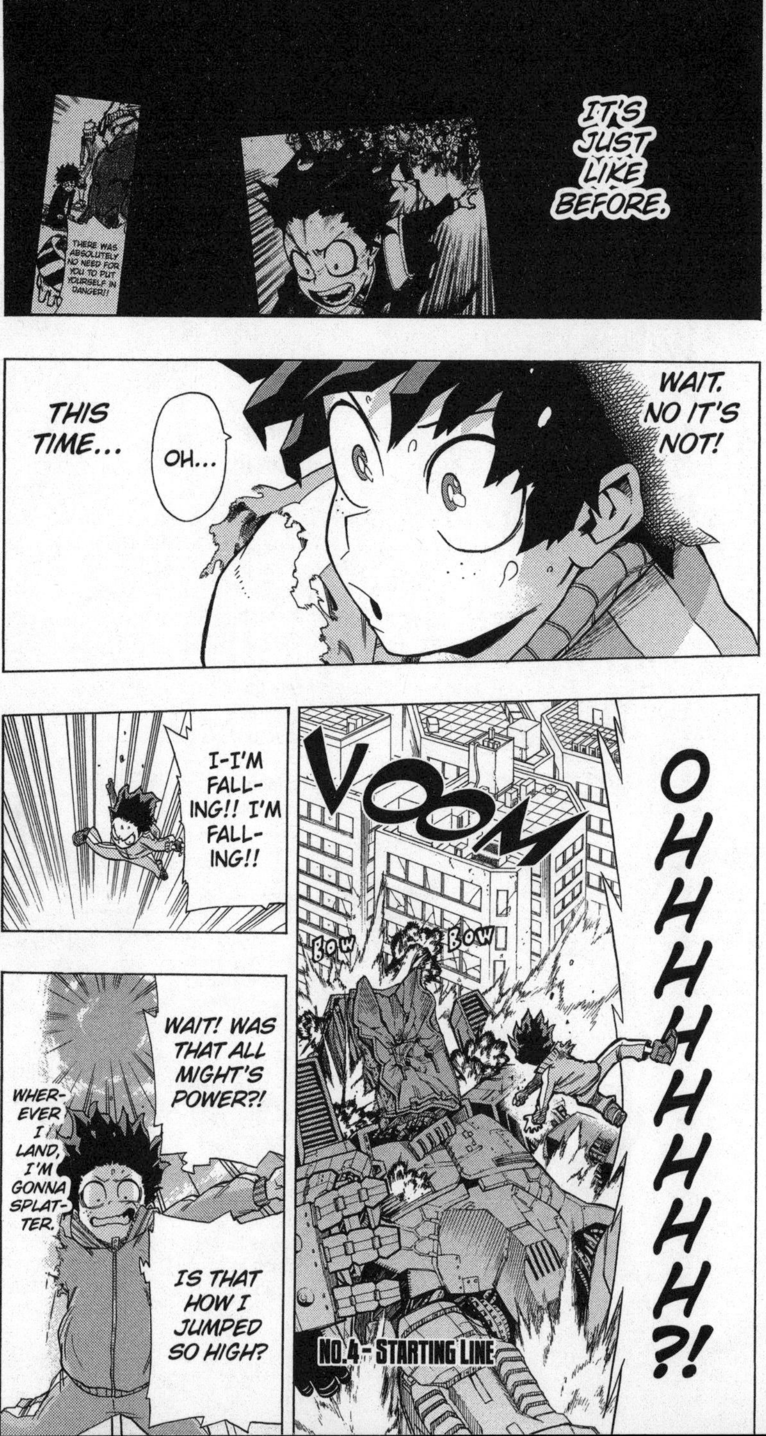
IT'S JUST LIKE BEFORE.
THERE WAS ABSOLUTELY NO NEED FOR YOU TO PUT YOURSELF IN DANGER!!
WAIT. NO IT'S NOT!
OH...
THIS TIME...
OHHHHHHHHH?!
VOOM
BOW
BOW
NO.4 - STARTING LINE
I-I'M FALLING!! I'M FALLING!!
WAIT! WAS THAT ALL MIGHT'S POWER?!
WHEREVER I LAND, I'M GONNA SPLATTER.
IS THAT HOW I JUMPED SO HIGH?

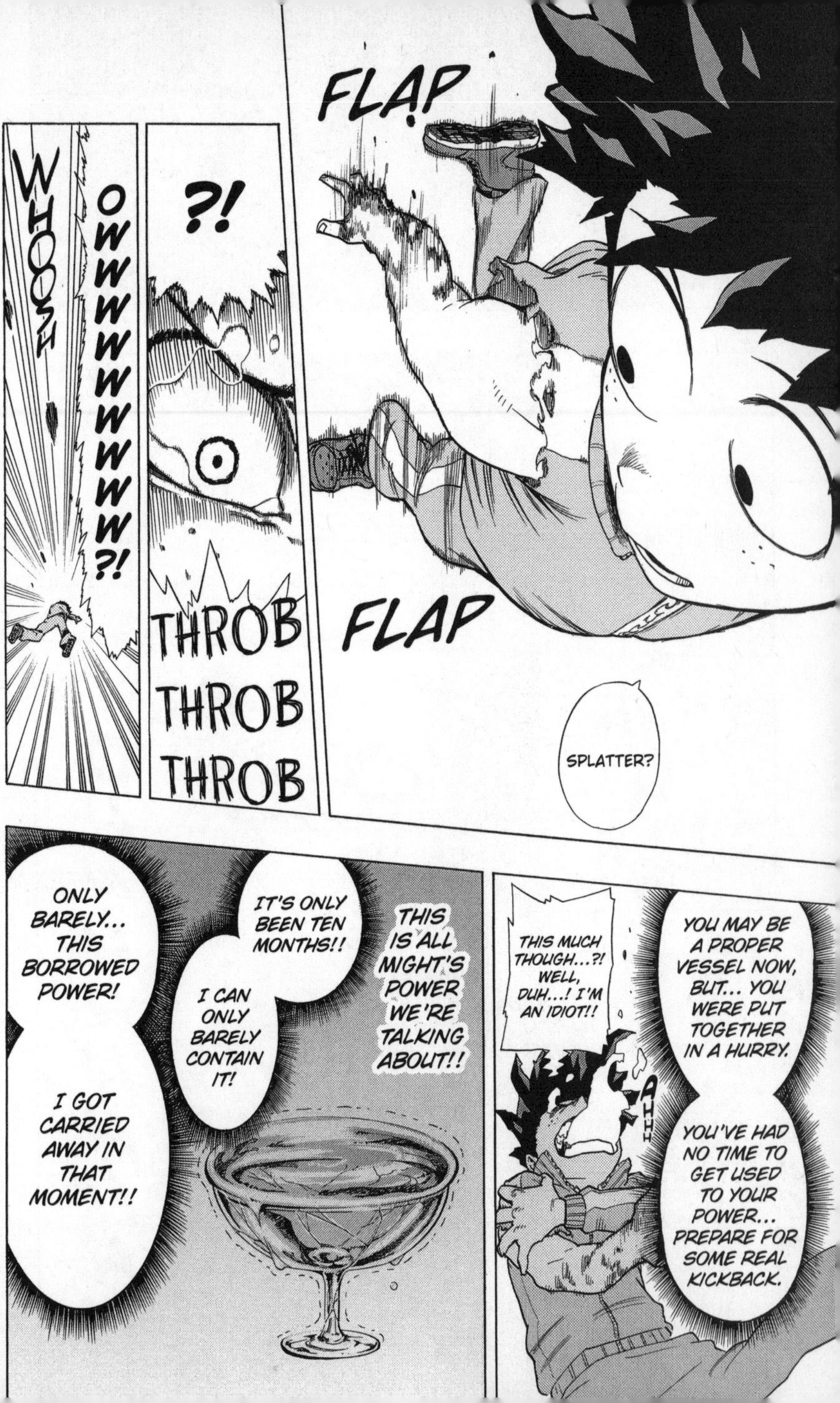
FLAP
FLAP
SPLATTER?
THROB
THROB
THROB
?!
WHOOSH
OWWWWWWWWWWWWW?!
YOU MAY BE A PROPER VESSEL NOW, BUT... YOU WERE PUT TOGETHER IN A HURRY.
YOU'VE HAD NO TIME TO GET USED TO YOUR POWER... PREPARE FOR SOME REAL KICKBACK.
THIS MUCH THOUGH...?! WELL, DUH...! I'M AN IDIOT!!
AHH
THIS IS ALL MIGHT'S POWER WE'RE TALKING ABOUT!!
IT'S ONLY BEEN TEN MONTHS!!
I CAN ONLY BARELY CONTAIN IT!
ONLY BARELY... THIS BORROWED POWER!
I GOT CARRIED AWAY IN THAT MOMENT!!

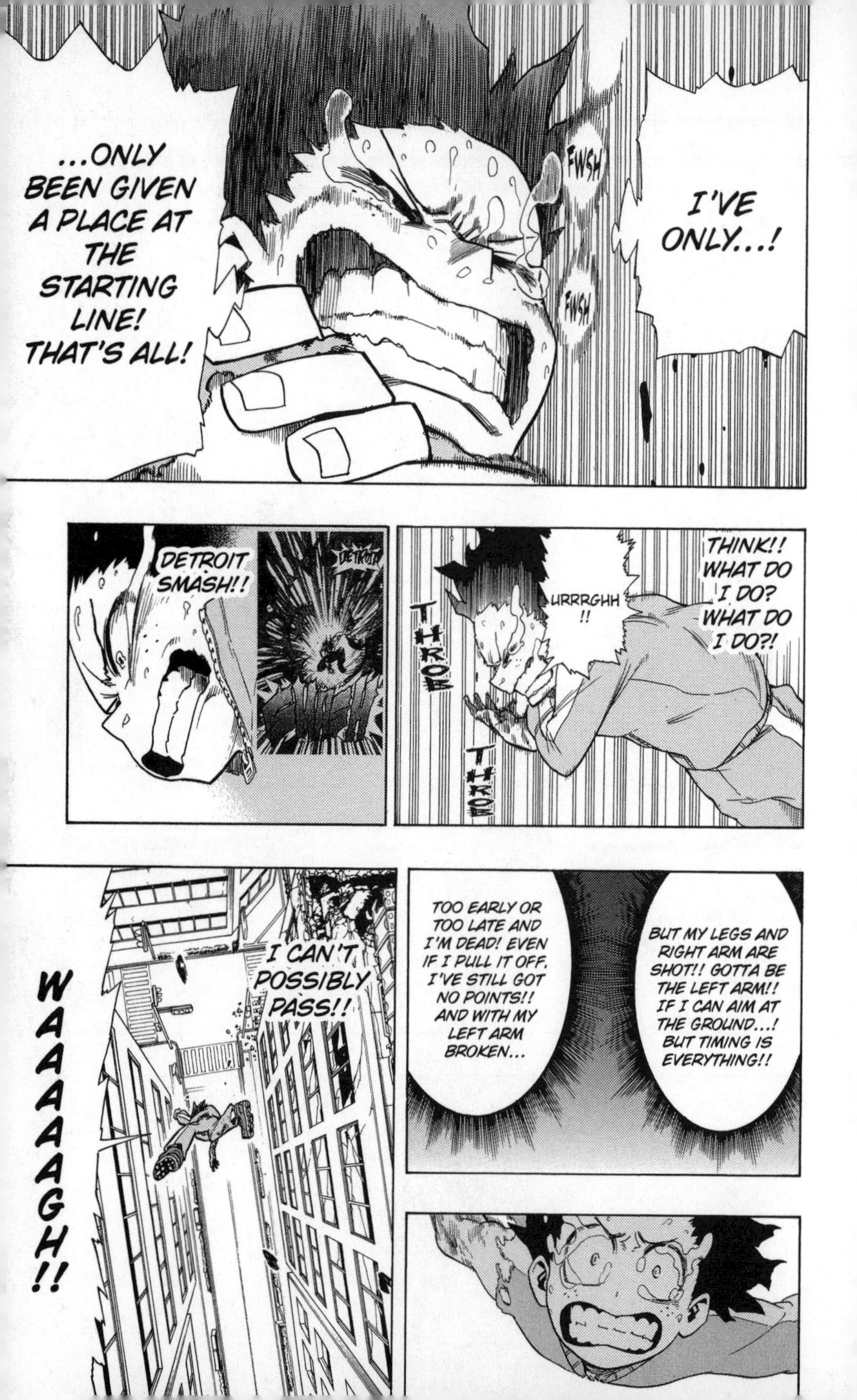
I'VE ONLY...!
...ONLY BEEN GIVEN A PLACE AT THE STARTING LINE! THAT'S ALL!
FWSH
FWSH
THINK!! WHAT DO I DO? WHAT DO I DO?!
URRRGHH !!
THROB
THROB
DETROIT SMASH!!
DETROIT
BUT MY LEGS AND RIGHT ARM ARE SHOT!! GOTTA BE THE LEFT ARM!! IF I CAN AIM AT THE GROUND...! BUT TIMING IS EVERYTHING!!
TOO EARLY OR TOO LATE AND I'M DEAD! EVEN IF I PULL IT OFF, I'VE STILL GOT NO POINTS!! AND WITH MY LEFT ARM BROKEN...
I CAN'T POSSIBLY PASS!!
WAAAAAAAGH!!

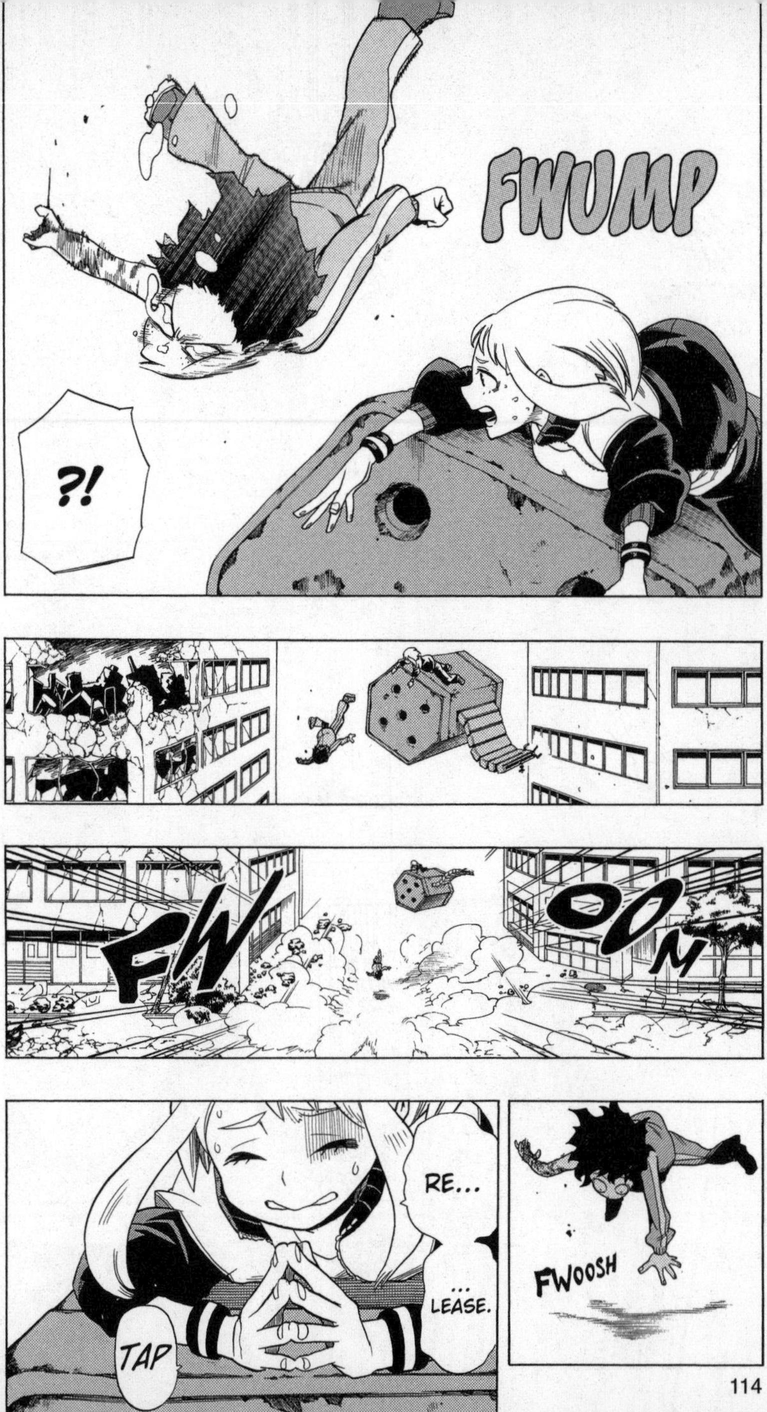
FWUMP
?!
FWOOM
FWOOSH
RE...
...LEASE.
TAP

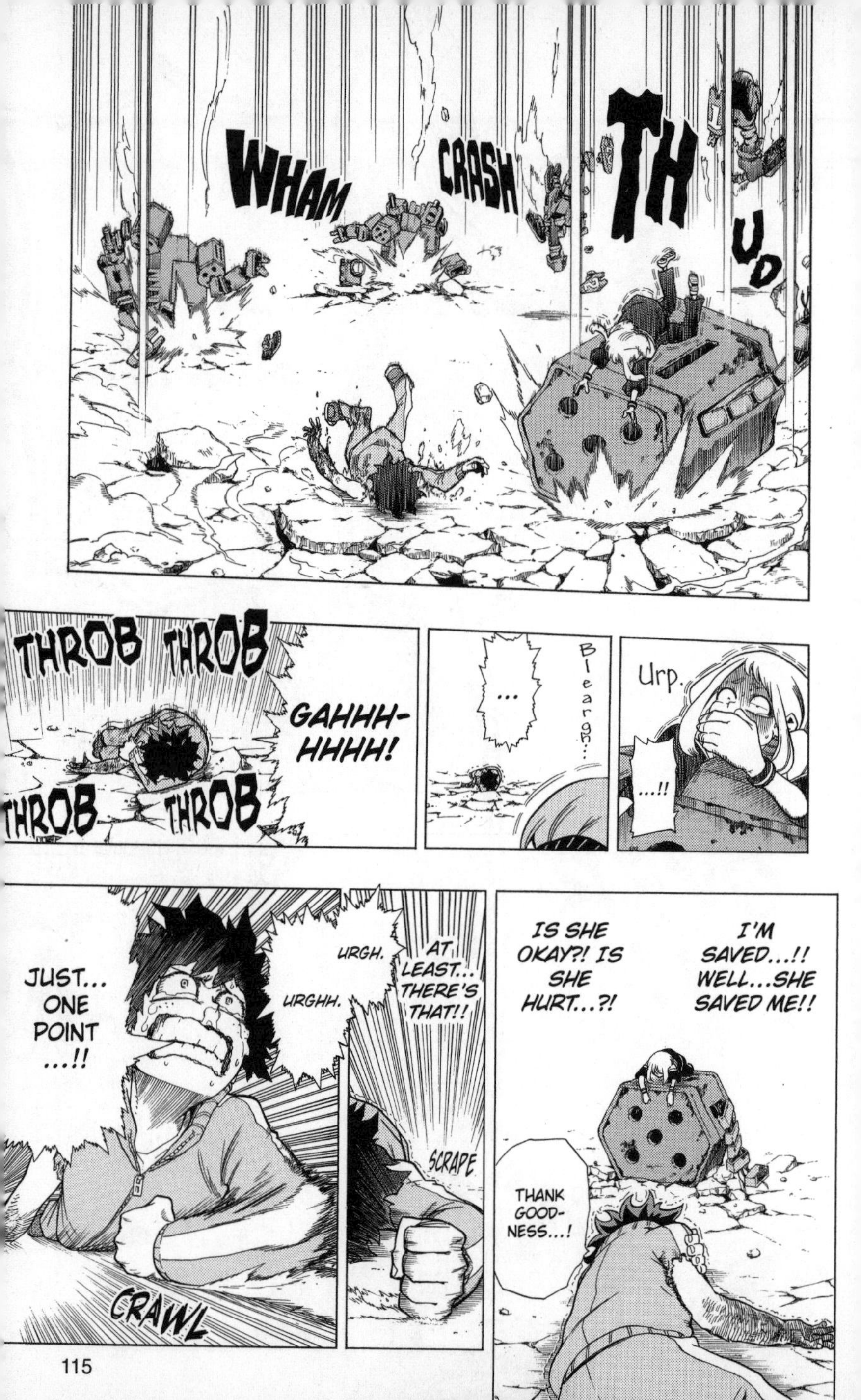
THUD
CRASH
WHAM
Urp.
...!!
Bleargh...
...
GAHHH-HHHH!
THROB THROB
THROB THROB
I'M SAVED...!! WELL...SHE SAVED ME!!
IS SHE OKAY?! IS SHE HURT...?!
THANK GOODNESS...!
AT LEAST... THERE'S THAT!!
URGH.
URGHH.
SCRAPE
JUST... ONE POINT ...!!
CRAWL

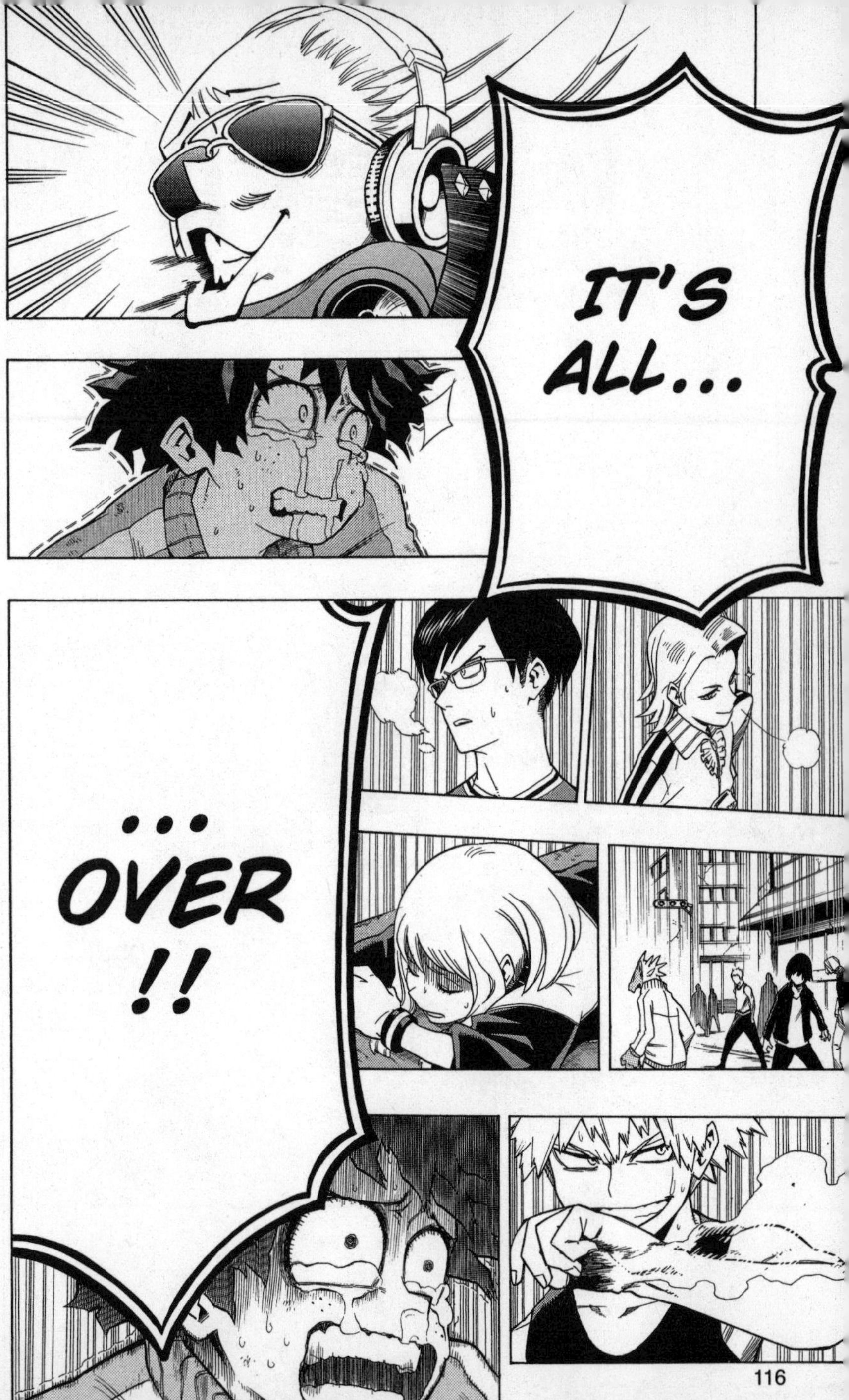
IT'S ALL...
...OVER!!

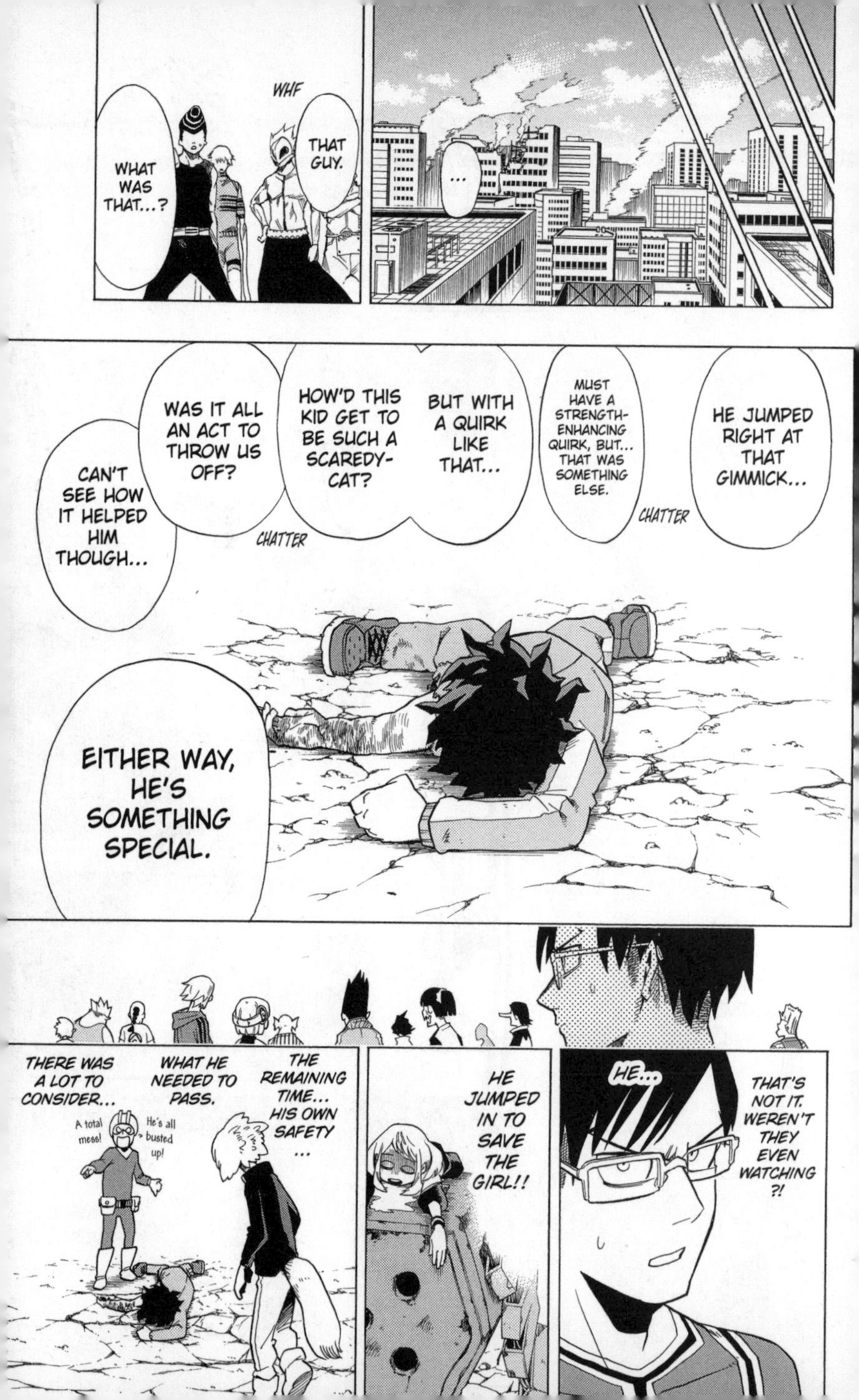
...
WHF
THAT GUY.
WHAT WAS THAT...?
HE JUMPED RIGHT AT THAT GIMMICK...
MUST HAVE A STRENGTH-ENHANCING QUIRK, BUT... THAT WAS SOMETHING ELSE.
CHATTER
BUT WITH A QUIRK LIKE THAT...
HOW'D THIS KID GET TO BE SUCH A SCAREDY-CAT?
WAS IT ALL AN ACT TO THROW US OFF?
CHATTER
CAN'T SEE HOW IT HELPED HIM THOUGH...
EITHER WAY, HE'S SOMETHING SPECIAL.
HE...
THAT'S NOT IT. WEREN'T THEY EVEN WATCHING ?!
HE JUMPED IN TO SAVE THE GIRL!!
THE REMAINING TIME... HIS OWN SAFETY ...
WHAT HE NEEDED TO PASS.
THERE WAS A LOT TO CONSIDER...
He's all busted up!
A total mess!

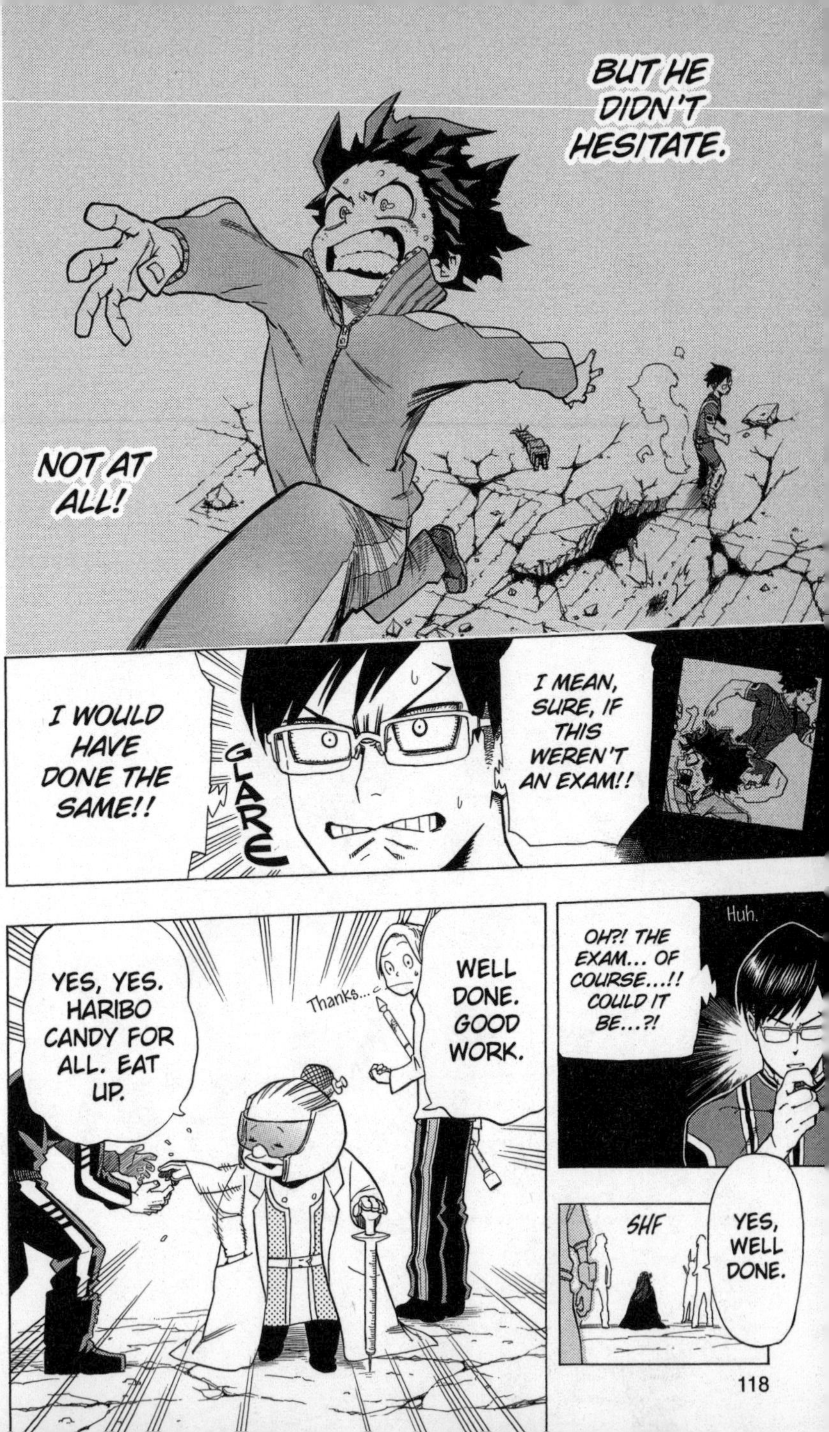
BUT HE DIDN'T HESITATE.
NOT AT ALL!
I MEAN, SURE, IF THIS WEREN'T AN EXAM!!
GLARE
I WOULD HAVE DONE THE SAME!!
Huh.
OH?! THE EXAM... OF COURSE...!! COULD IT BE...?!
SHF
YES, WELL DONE.
WELL DONE. GOOD WORK.
Thanks...
YES, YES. HARIBO CANDY FOR ALL. EAT UP.

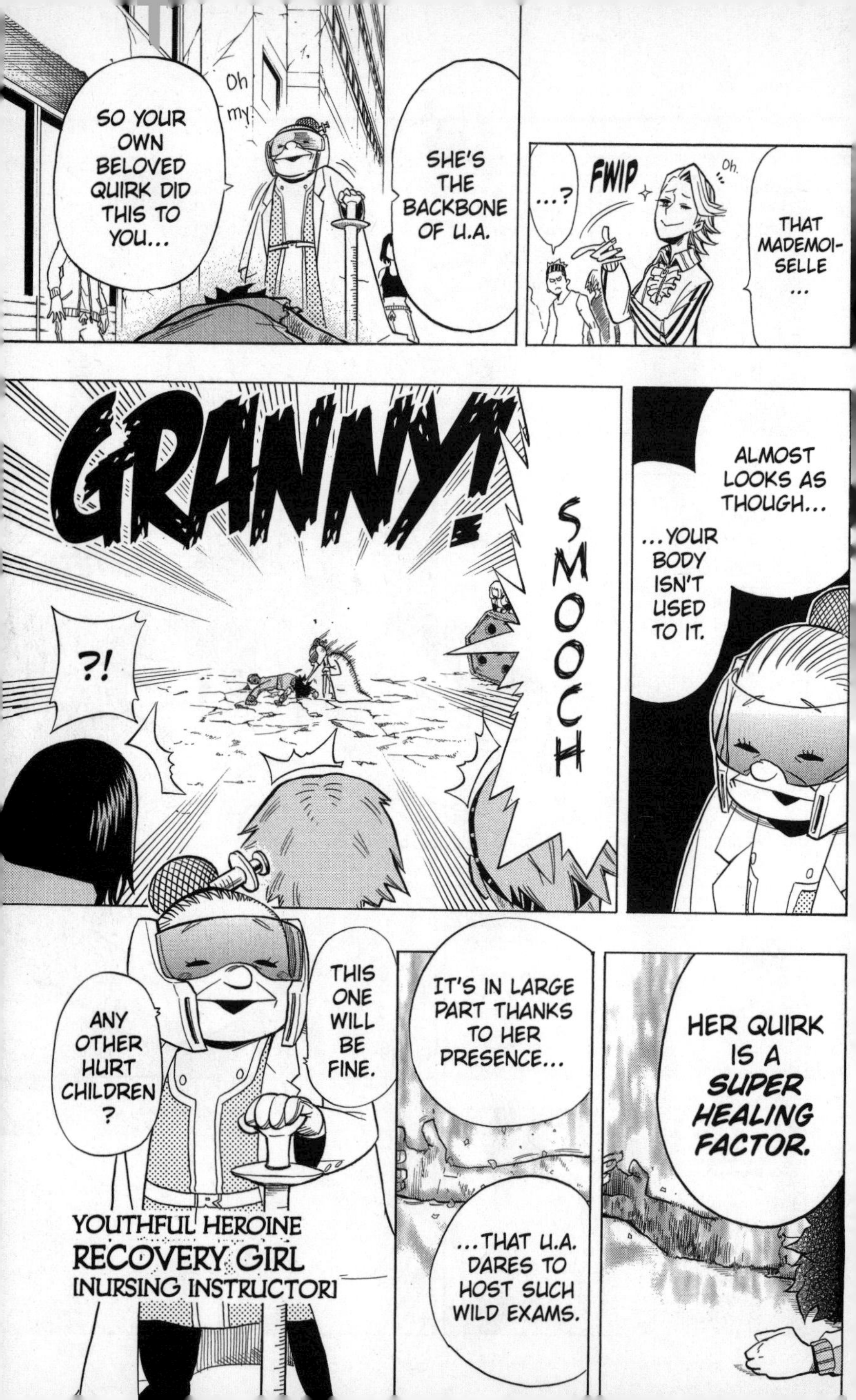
THAT MADEMOI-SELLE ...
Oh.
FWIP
...?
SHE'S THE BACKBONE OF U.A.
Oh my.
SO YOUR OWN BELOVED QUIRK DID THIS TO YOU...
ALMOST LOOKS AS THOUGH...
...YOUR BODY ISN'T USED TO IT.
SMOOCH
GRANNY!
?!
HER QUIRK IS A *SUPER HEALING FACTOR.*
IT'S IN LARGE PART THANKS TO HER PRESENCE...
...THAT U.A. DARES TO HOST SUCH WILD EXAMS.
THIS ONE WILL BE FINE.
ANY OTHER HURT CHILDREN ?
YOUTHFUL HEROINE
RECOVERY GIRL
[NURSING INSTRUCTOR]

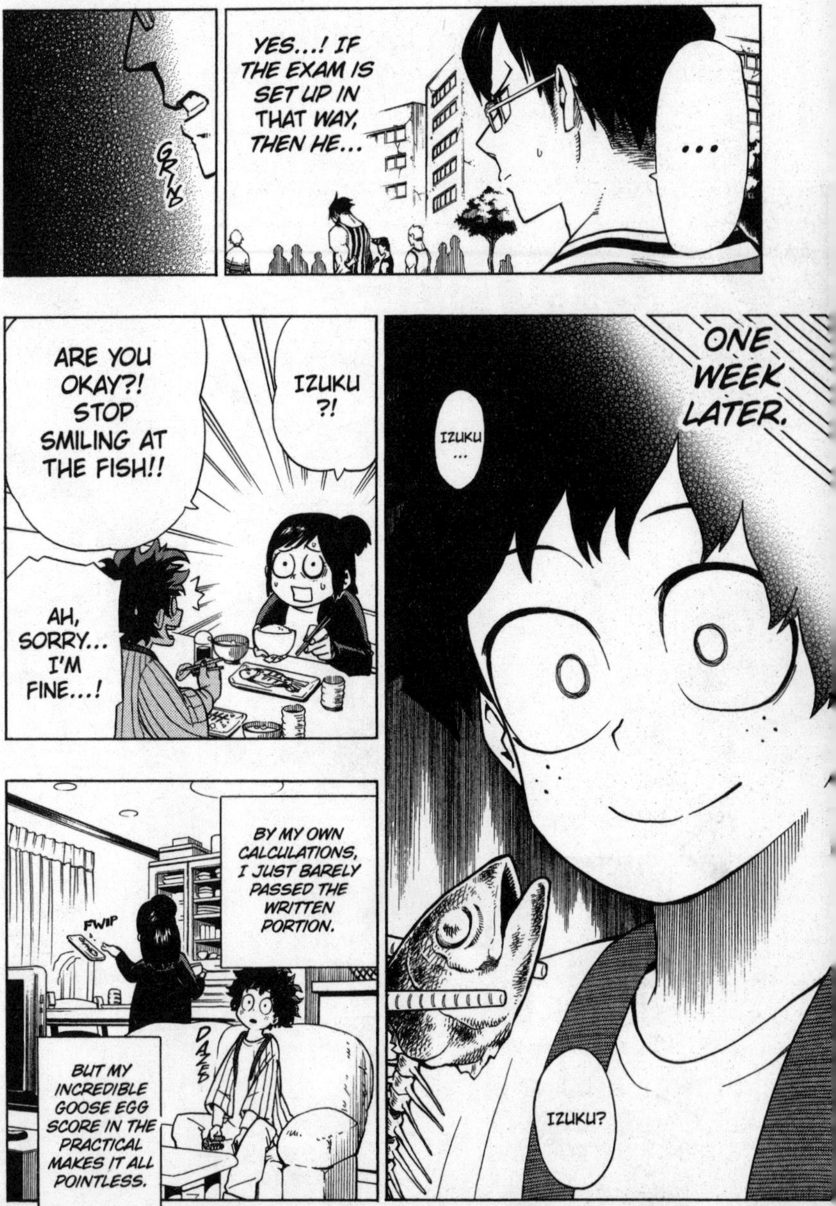
...
YES...! IF THE EXAM IS SET UP IN THAT WAY, THEN HE...
GRIND
ONE WEEK LATER.
IZUKU ...
IZUKU?
ARE YOU OKAY?! STOP SMILING AT THE FISH!!
IZUKU ?!
AH, SORRY... I'M FINE...!
BY MY OWN CALCULATIONS, I JUST BARELY PASSED THE WRITTEN PORTION.
FWIP
DAZED
BUT MY INCREDIBLE GOOSE EGG SCORE IN THE PRACTICAL MAKES IT ALL POINTLESS.

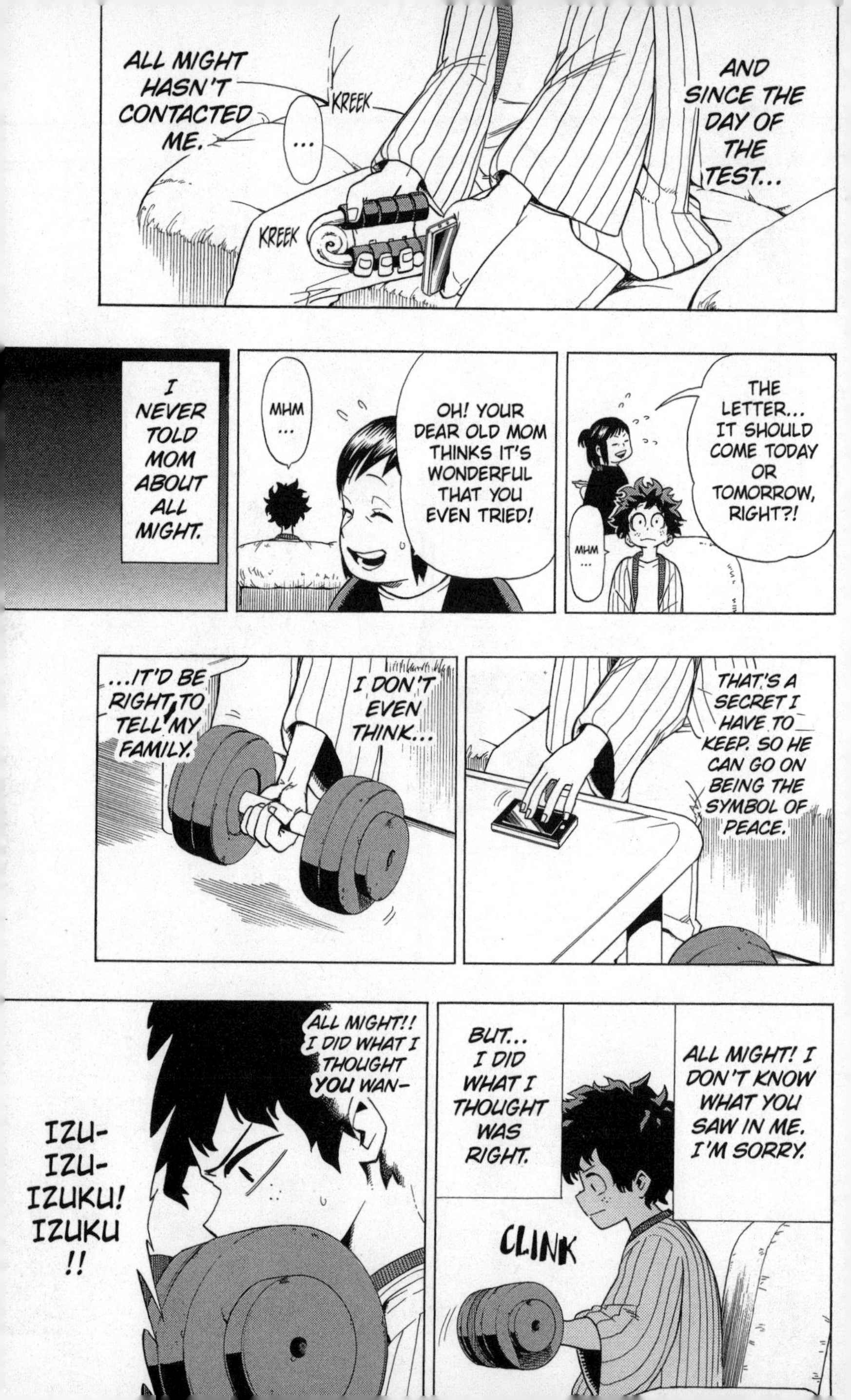
AND SINCE THE DAY OF THE TEST...
KREEK
...
ALL MIGHT HASN'T CONTACTED ME.
KREEK
THE LETTER... IT SHOULD COME TODAY OR TOMORROW, RIGHT?!
MHM ...
OH! YOUR DEAR OLD MOM THINKS IT'S WONDERFUL THAT YOU EVEN TRIED!
MHM ...
I NEVER TOLD MOM ABOUT ALL MIGHT.
THAT'S A SECRET I HAVE TO KEEP. SO HE CAN GO ON BEING THE SYMBOL OF PEACE.
I DON'T EVEN THINK...
...IT'D BE RIGHT TO TELL MY FAMILY.
ALL MIGHT! I DON'T KNOW WHAT YOU SAW IN ME. I'M SORRY.
BUT... I DID WHAT I THOUGHT WAS RIGHT.
CLINK
ALL MIGHT!! I DID WHAT I THOUGHT YOU WAN-
IZU- IZU- IZUKU! IZUKU !!

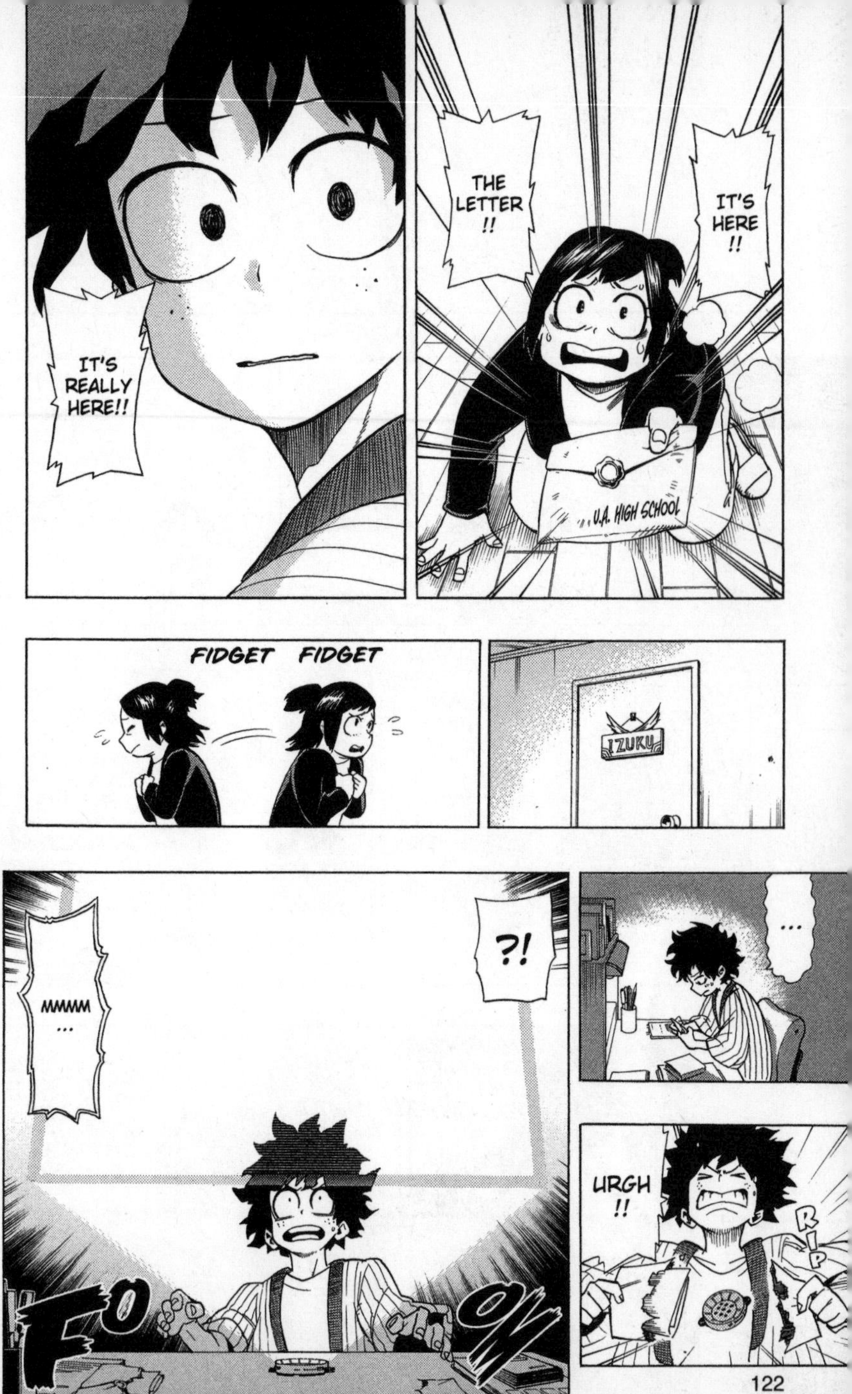
IT'S HERE !!
THE LETTER !!
U.A. HIGH SCHOOL
IT'S REALLY HERE!!
IZUKU
FIDGET FIDGET
...
URGH !!
RIP
?!
MMMM ...
FO
%

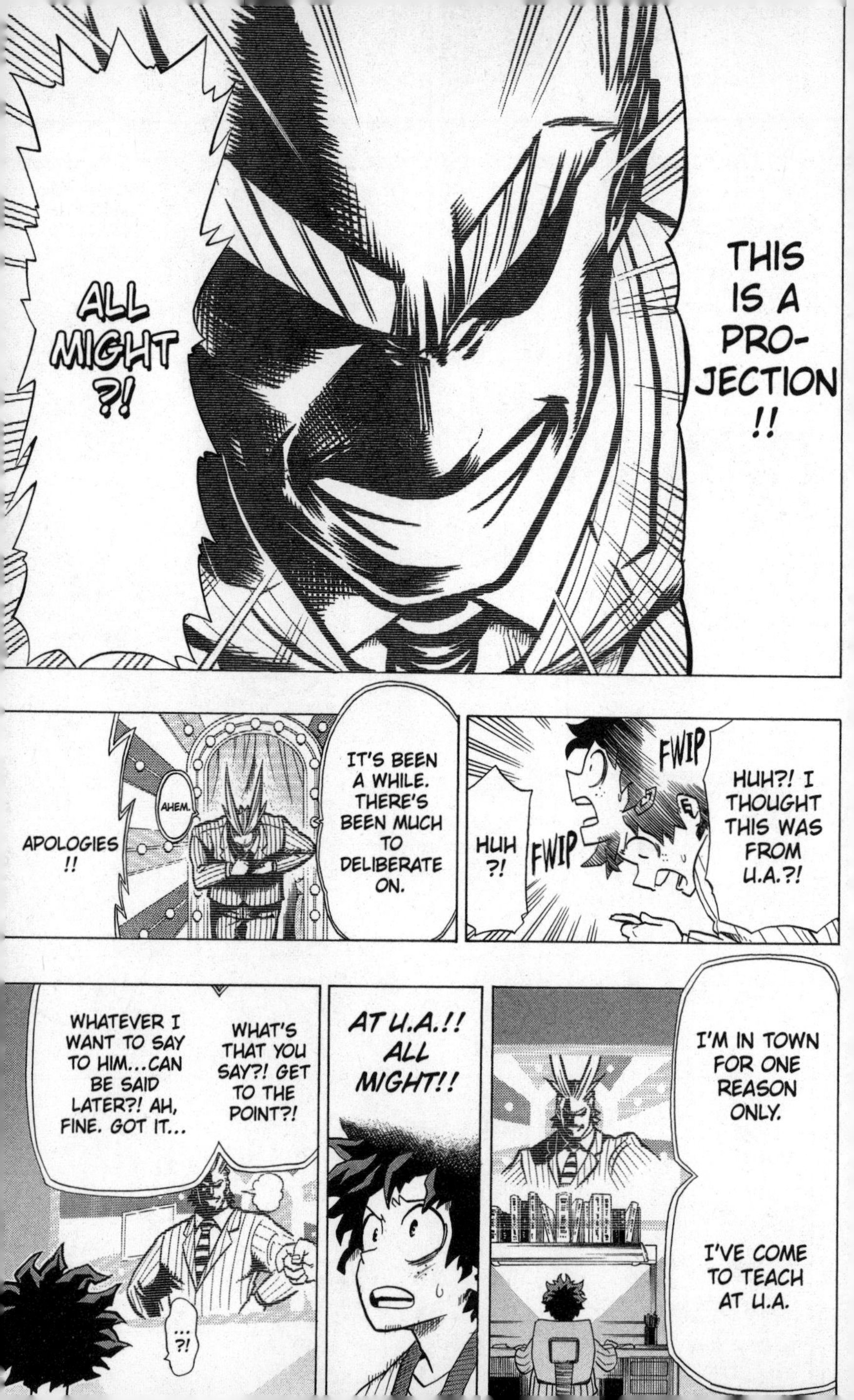
THIS IS A PRO-JECTION !!
ALL MIGHT ?!
HUH?! I THOUGHT THIS WAS FROM U.A.?!
FWIP
FWIP
HUH ?!
IT'S BEEN A WHILE. THERE'S BEEN MUCH TO DELIBERATE ON.
AHEM.
APOLOGIES !!
I'M IN TOWN FOR ONE REASON ONLY.
I'VE COME TO TEACH AT U.A.
AT U.A.!! ALL MIGHT!!
WHAT'S THAT YOU SAY?! GET TO THE POINT?!
WHATEVER I WANT TO SAY TO HIM...CAN BE SAID LATER?! AH, FINE. GOT IT...
...?!

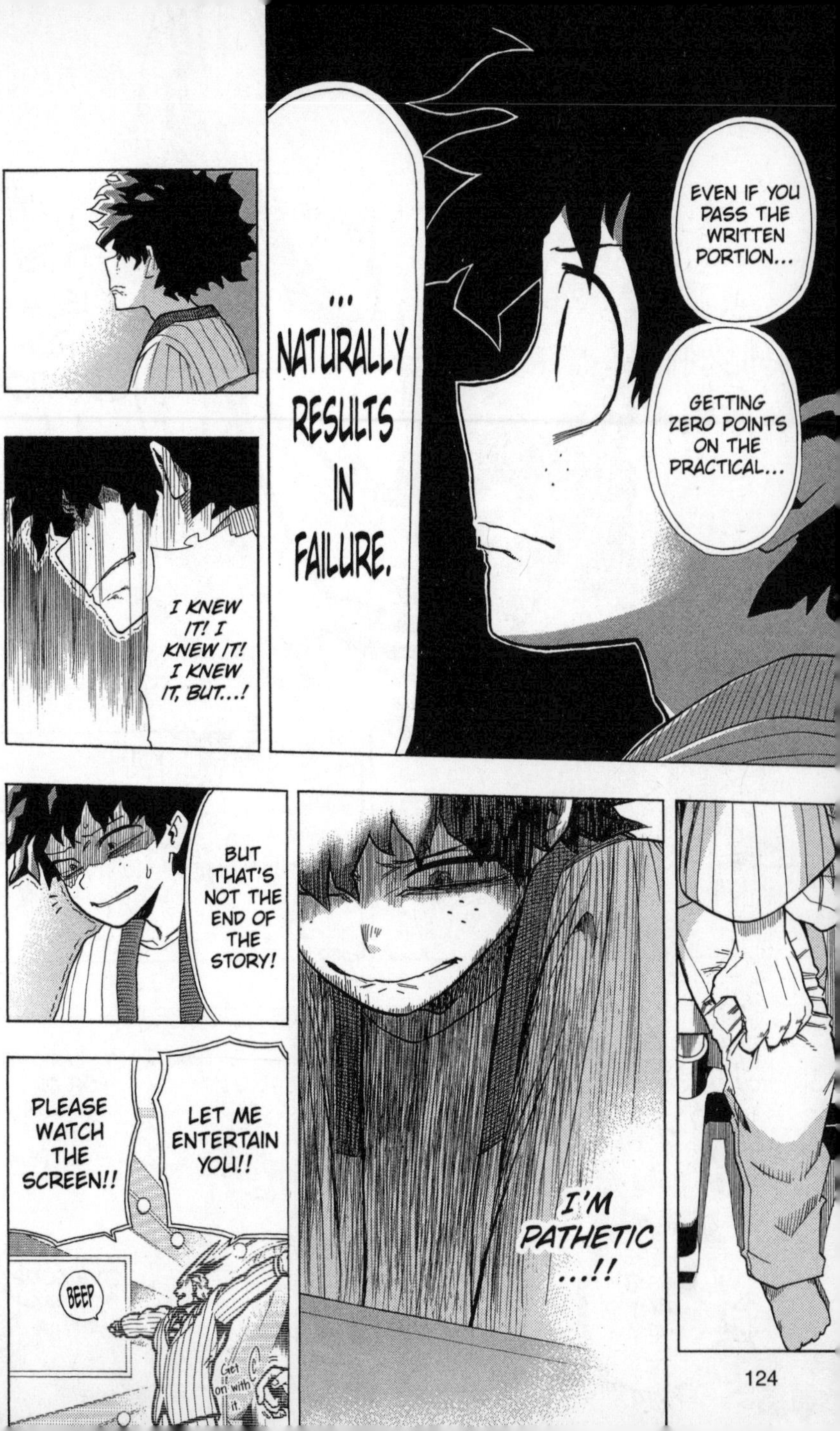
EVEN IF YOU PASS THE WRITTEN PORTION...
GETTING ZERO POINTS ON THE PRACTICAL...
... NATURALLY RESULTS IN FAILURE.
I KNEW IT! I KNEW IT! I KNEW IT, BUT...!
I'M PATHETIC ...!!
BUT THAT'S NOT THE END OF THE STORY!
LET ME ENTERTAIN YOU!!
PLEASE WATCH THE SCREEN!!
BEEP
Get on with it

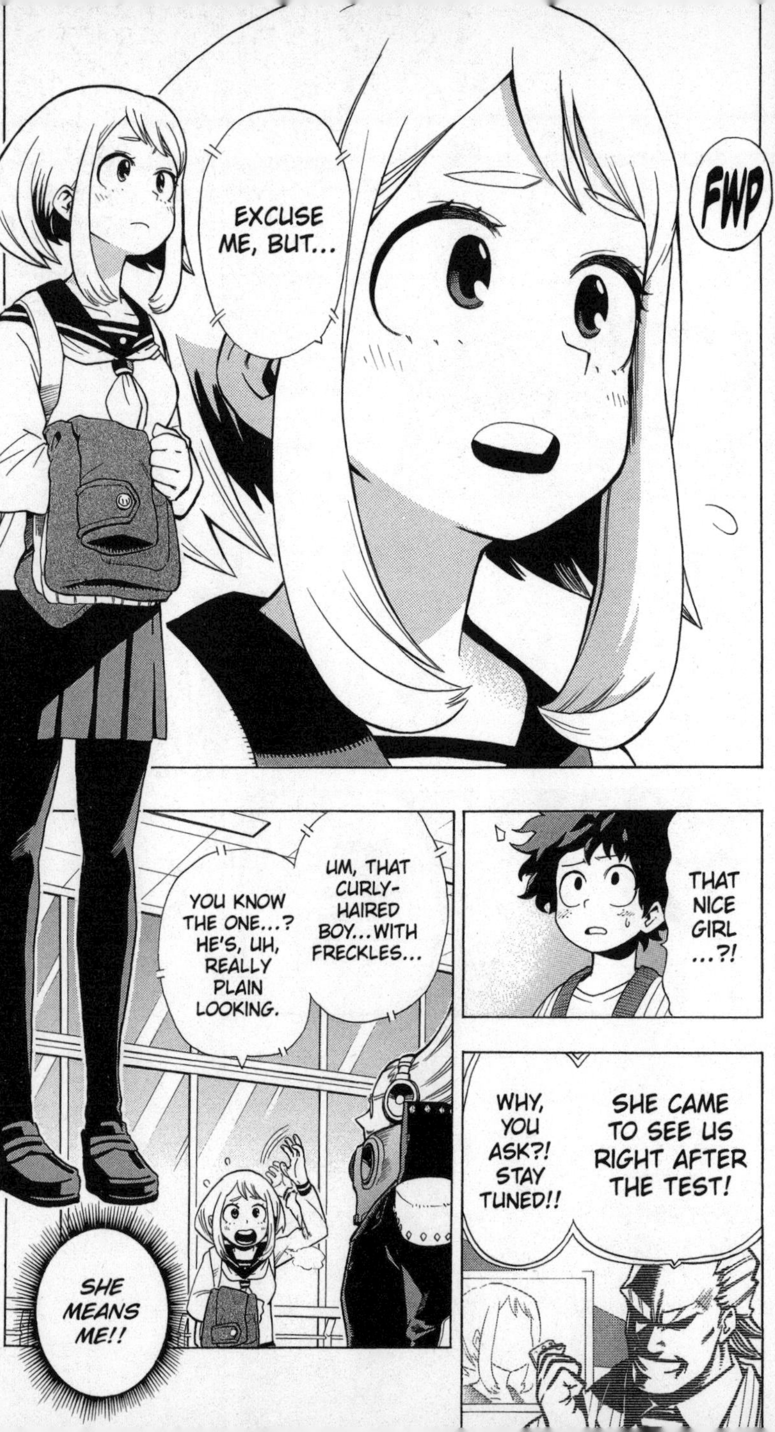
FWP
EXCUSE ME, BUT...
THAT NICE GIRL ...?!
UM, THAT CURLY-HAIRED BOY...WITH FRECKLES...
YOU KNOW THE ONE...? HE'S, UH, REALLY PLAIN LOOKING.
SHE MEANS ME!!
SHE CAME TO SEE US RIGHT AFTER THE TEST!
WHY, YOU ASK?! STAY TUNED!!

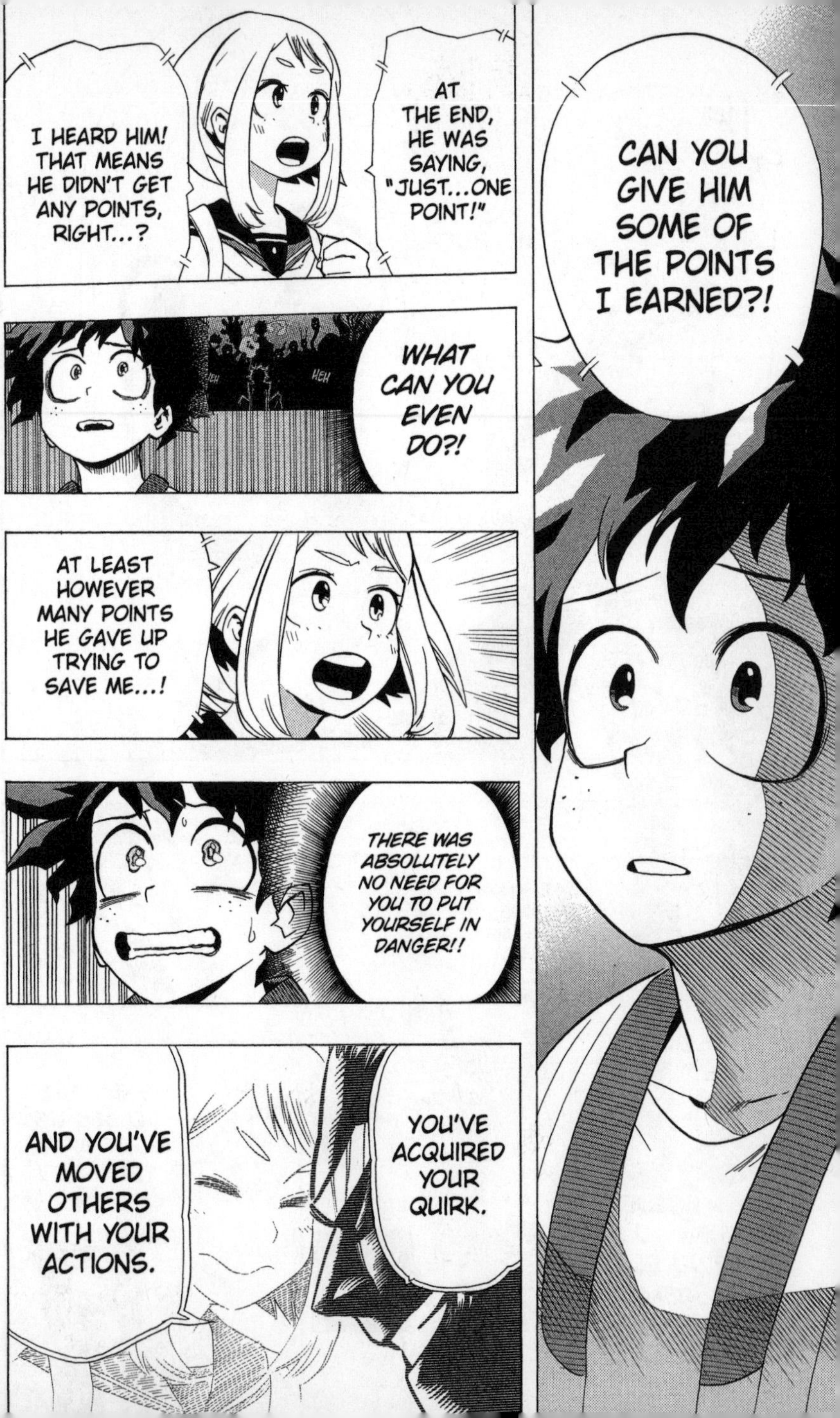
CAN YOU GIVE HIM SOME OF THE POINTS I EARNED?!
AT THE END, HE WAS SAYING, "JUST...ONE POINT!"
I HEARD HIM! THAT MEANS HE DIDN'T GET ANY POINTS, RIGHT...?
WHAT CAN YOU EVEN DO?!
HEH
HEH
AT LEAST HOWEVER MANY POINTS HE GAVE UP TRYING TO SAVE ME...!
THERE WAS ABSOLUTELY NO NEED FOR YOU TO PUT YOURSELF IN DANGER!!
YOU'VE ACQUIRED YOUR QUIRK.
AND YOU'VE MOVED OTHERS WITH YOUR ACTIONS.

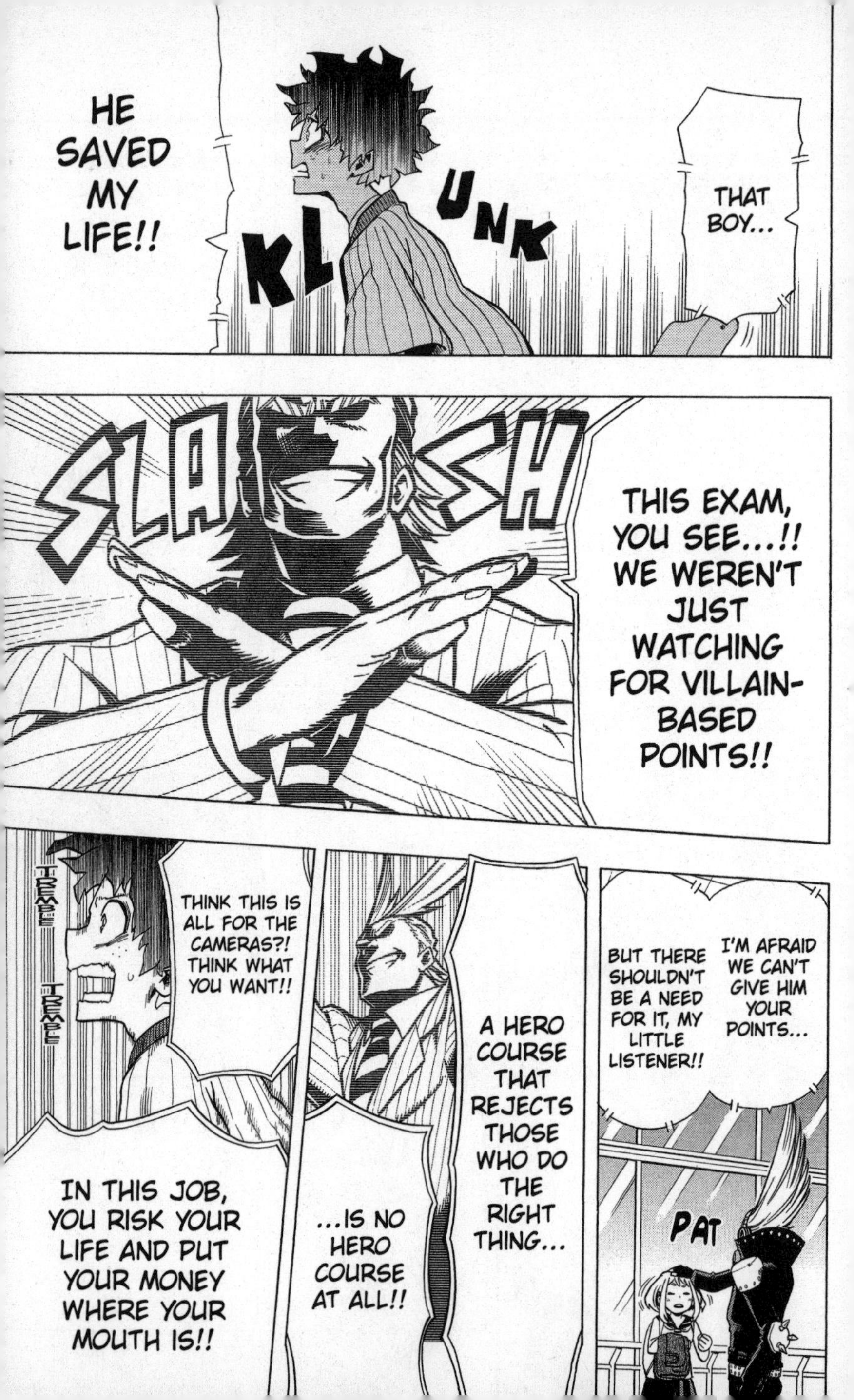
THAT BOY...
HE SAVED MY LIFE!!
KLUNK
THIS EXAM, YOU SEE...!! WE WEREN'T JUST WATCHING FOR VILLAIN-BASED POINTS!!
SLASH
I'M AFRAID WE CAN'T GIVE HIM YOUR POINTS...
BUT THERE SHOULDN'T BE A NEED FOR IT, MY LITTLE LISTENER!!
PAT
A HERO COURSE THAT REJECTS THOSE WHO DO THE RIGHT THING...
...IS NO HERO COURSE AT ALL!!
TREMBLE
TREMBLE
THINK THIS IS ALL FOR THE CAMERAS?! THINK WHAT YOU WANT!!
IN THIS JOB, YOU RISK YOUR LIFE AND PUT YOUR MONEY WHERE YOUR MOUTH IS!!

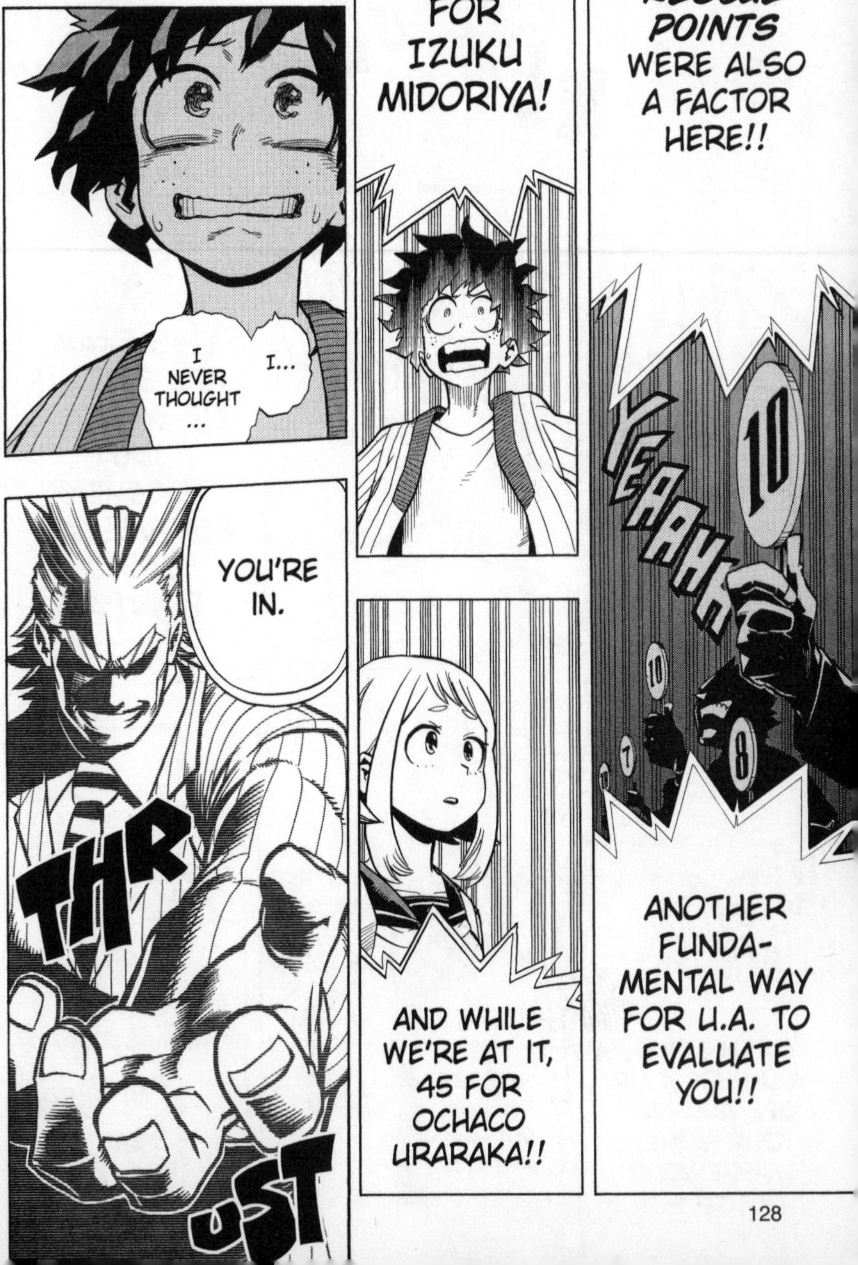
RESCUE POINTS WERE ALSO A FACTOR HERE!!
YEAAHH
10
10
8
7
ANOTHER FUNDAMENTAL WAY FOR U.A. TO EVALUATE YOU!!
SIXTY POINTS FOR IZUKU MIDORIYA!
AND WHILE WE'RE AT IT, 45 FOR OCHACO URARAKA!!
I... I NEVER THOUGHT...
YOU'RE IN.
THRUST

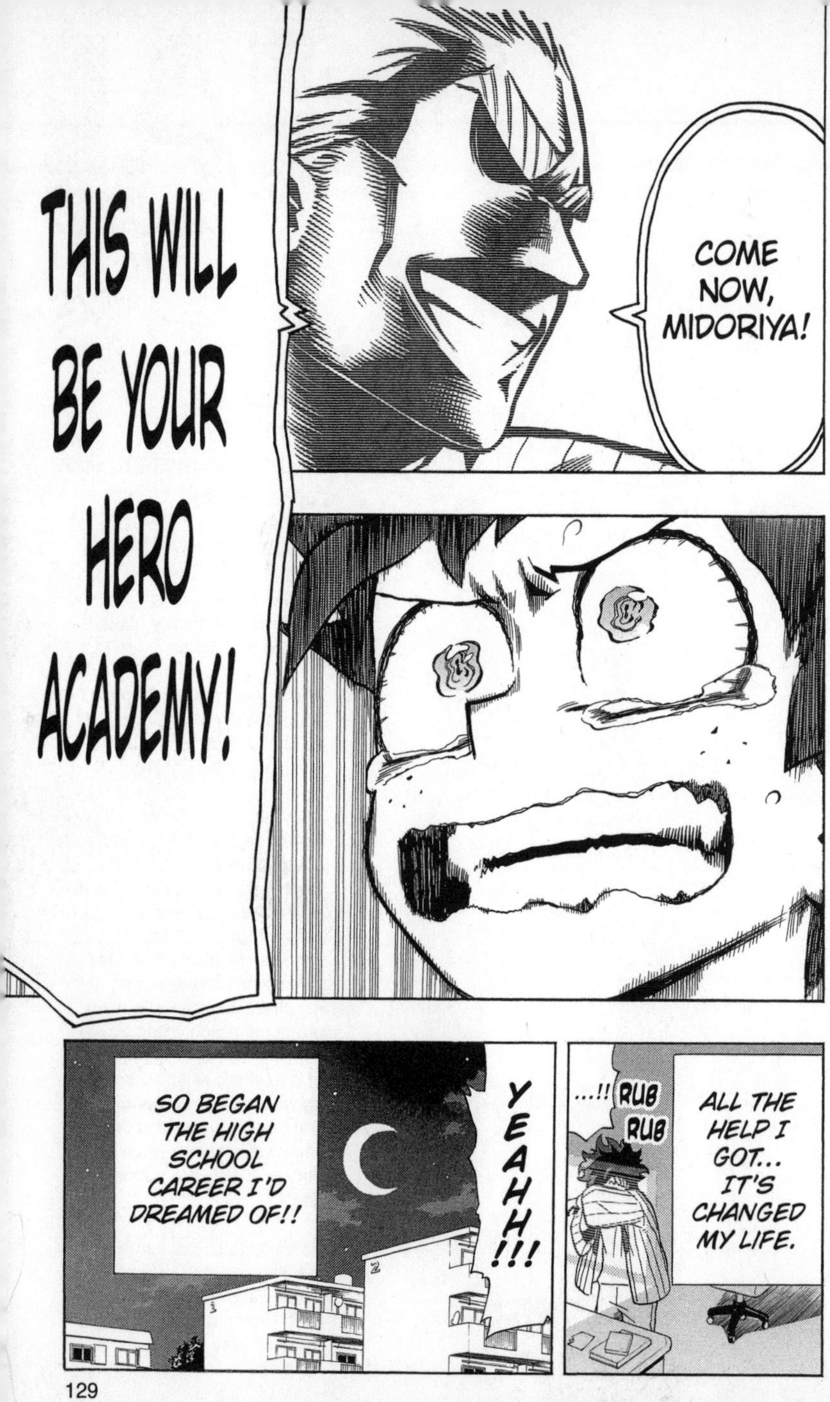
COME NOW, MIDORIYA!
THIS WILL BE YOUR HERO ACADEMY!
ALL THE HELP I GOT... IT'S CHANGED MY LIFE.
...!! RUB RUB
YEAHH!!!
SO BEGAN THE HIGH SCHOOL CAREER I'D DREAMED OF!!

OCHACO URARAKA [AGE:15]

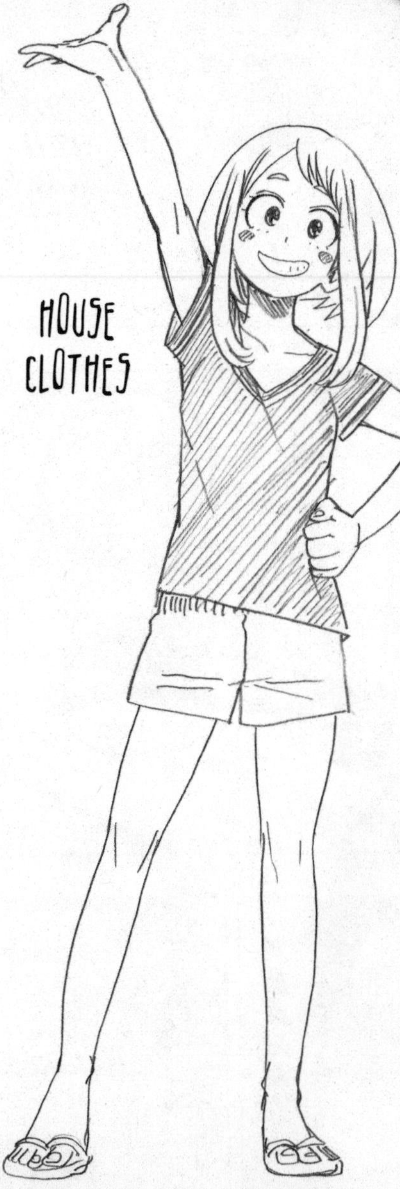
HOUSE CLOTHES

Birthday: 12/27
Height: 156 cm
Favorite Things: Starry skies, Japanese food

BEHIND THE SCENES

I'd planned to have her appear with Izuku a lot, so she needed to be cheery enough to drive their conversations.

She's unexpectedly brazen and frank. Proof that there's no hidden side to her, if you catch my drift.

Early on, Mt. Lady (who appeared in chapter 1) was going to be the heroine, but when it comes to a girl whose only power is growing… Taking that to its logical conclusions just brought about all sorts of problems, and the character started getting pretty dark. So I changed her.

The moment when I came up with her name was the first time in my manga career when I thought myself a true genius. It's such a nuanced name.

Editor's Note: Her name literally means "Tea-Girl Pretty-Day," with her last name being a homophone with one way to say "beautiful."

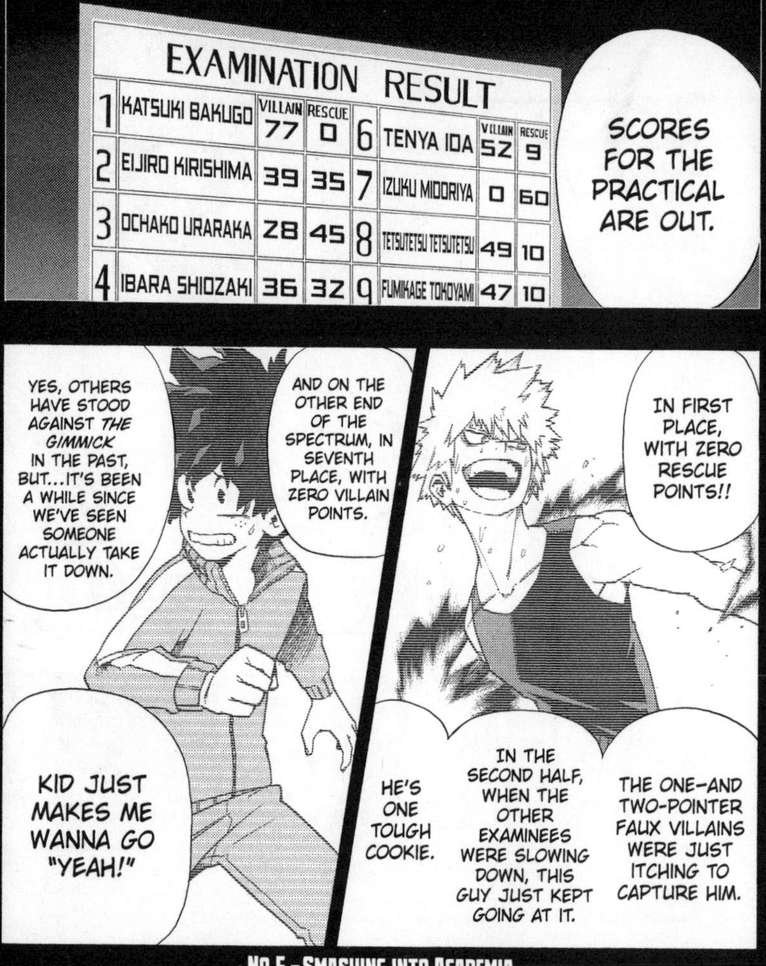
EXAMINATION RESULT
1 KATSUKI BAKUGO VILLAIN 77 RESCUE 0
2 EIJIRO KIRISHIMA 39 35
3 OCHAKO URARAKA 28 45
4 IBARA SHIOZAKI 36 32
6 TENYA IDA VILLAIN 52 RESCUE 9
7 IZUKU MIDORIYA 0 60
8 TETSUTETSU TETSUTETSU 49 10
9 FUMIKAGE TOKOYAMI 47 10
SCORES FOR THE PRACTICAL ARE OUT.
IN FIRST PLACE, WITH ZERO RESCUE POINTS!!
THE ONE-AND TWO-POINTER FAUX VILLAINS WERE JUST ITCHING TO CAPTURE HIM.
IN THE SECOND HALF, WHEN THE OTHER EXAMINEES WERE SLOWING DOWN, THIS GUY JUST KEPT GOING AT IT.
HE'S ONE TOUGH COOKIE.
AND ON THE OTHER END OF THE SPECTRUM, IN SEVENTH PLACE, WITH ZERO VILLAIN POINTS.
YES, OTHERS HAVE STOOD AGAINST *THE GIMMICK* IN THE PAST, BUT...IT'S BEEN A WHILE SINCE WE'VE SEEN SOMEONE ACTUALLY TAKE IT DOWN.
KID JUST MAKES ME WANNA GO "YEAH!"

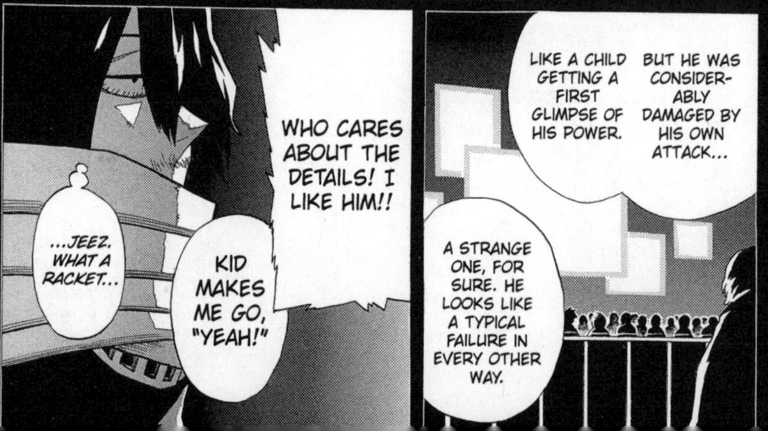
LIKE A CHILD GETTING A FIRST GLIMPSE OF HIS POWER. BUT HE WAS CONSIDER-ABLY DAMAGED BY HIS OWN ATTACK...
A STRANGE ONE, FOR SURE. HE LOOKS LIKE A TYPICAL FAILURE IN EVERY OTHER WAY.
WHO CARES ABOUT THE DETAILS! I LIKE HIM!!
KID MAKES ME GO, "YEAH!"
...JEEZ. WHAT A RACKET...

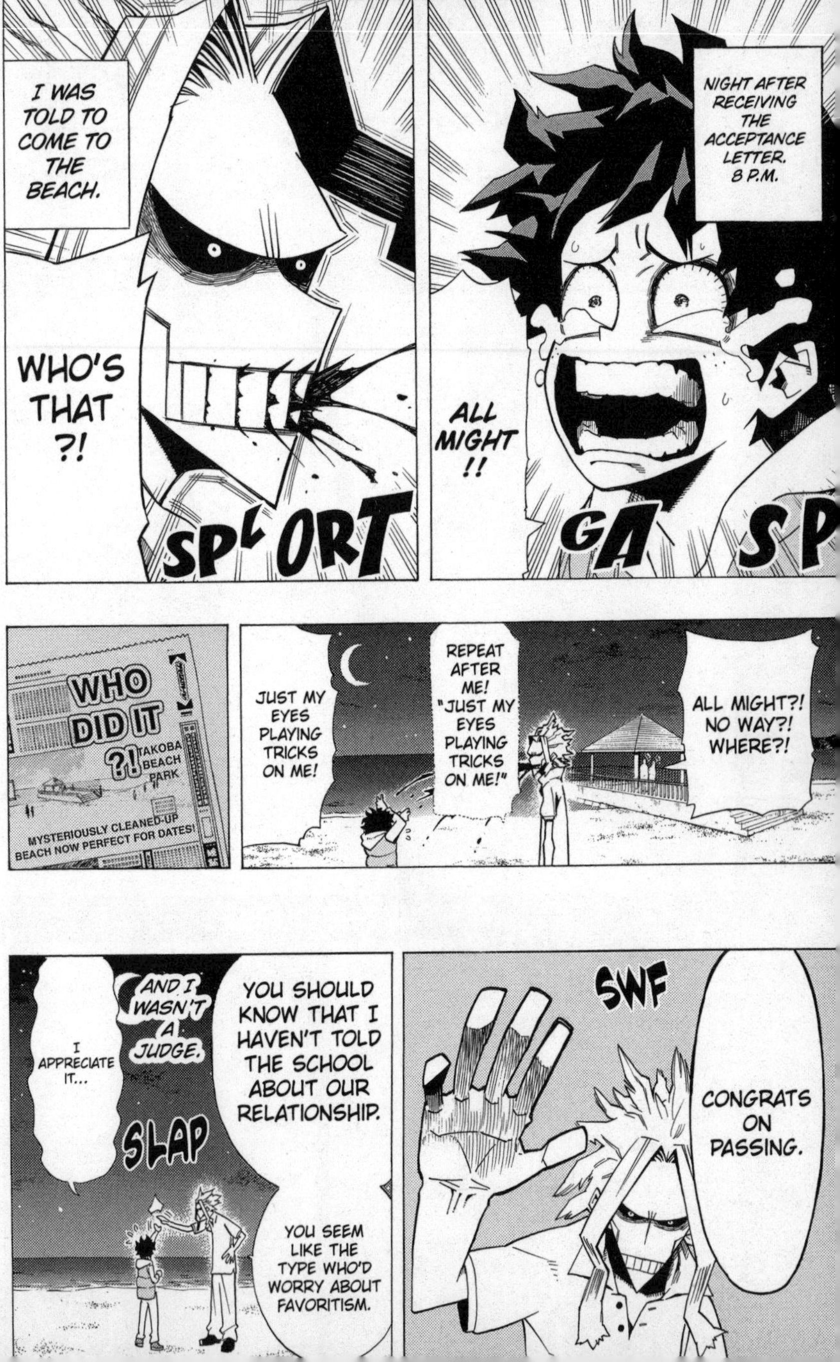
NIGHT AFTER RECEIVING THE ACCEPTANCE LETTER. 8 P.M.
ALL MIGHT!!
GA SP
I WAS TOLD TO COME TO THE BEACH.
WHO'S THAT ?!
SPLORT
ALL MIGHT?! NO WAY?! WHERE?!
REPEAT AFTER ME! "JUST MY EYES PLAYING TRICKS ON ME!"
JUST MY EYES PLAYING TRICKS ON ME!
WHO DID IT ?!
TAKOBA BEACH PARK
MYSTERIOUSLY CLEANED-UP BEACH NOW PERFECT FOR DATES!
SWF
CONGRATS ON PASSING.
YOU SHOULD KNOW THAT I HAVEN'T TOLD THE SCHOOL ABOUT OUR RELATIONSHIP.
YOU SEEM LIKE THE TYPE WHO'D WORRY ABOUT FAVORITISM.
AND I WASN'T A JUDGE.
I APPRECIATE IT...
SLAP

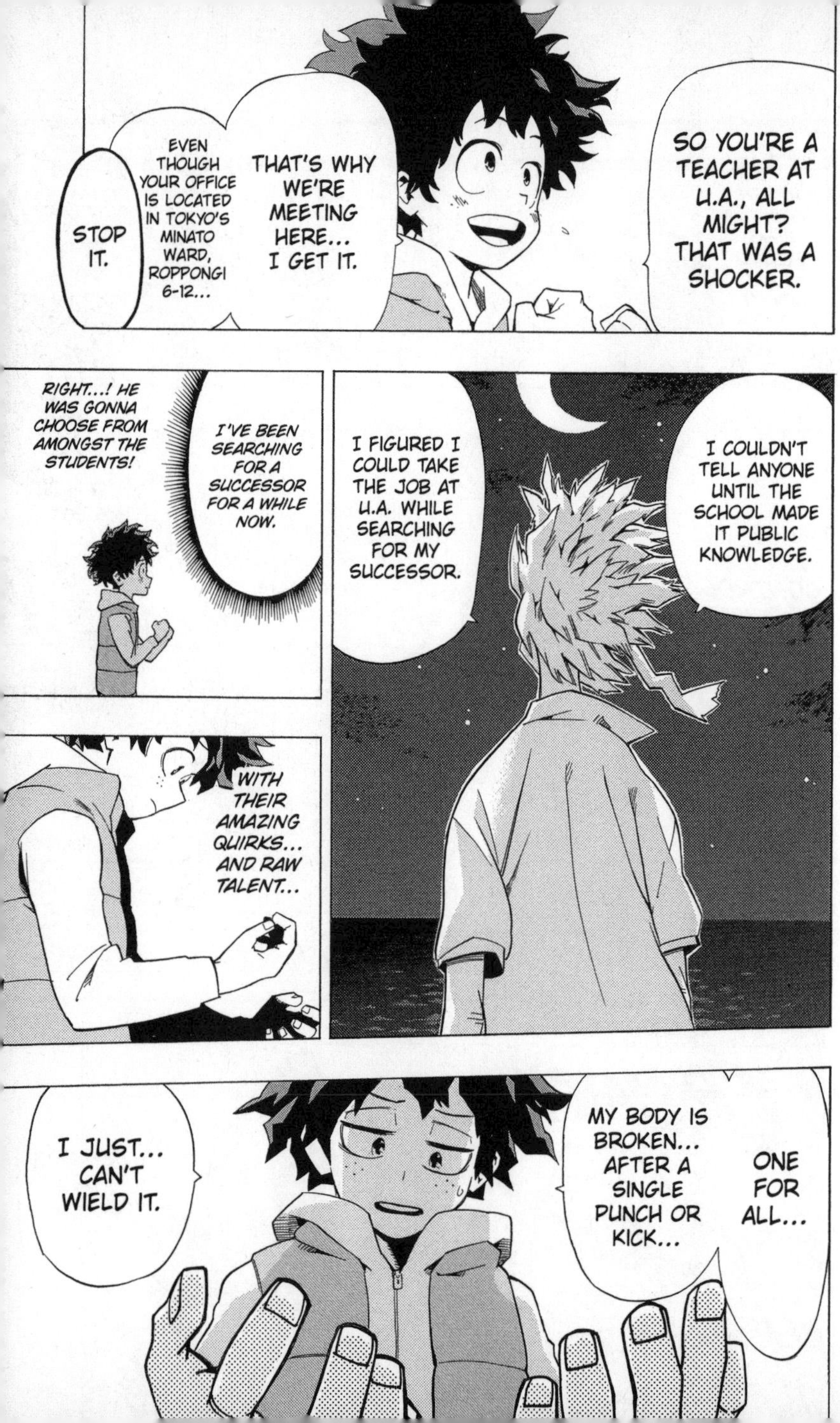
SO YOU'RE A TEACHER AT U.A., ALL MIGHT? THAT WAS A SHOCKER.
THAT'S WHY WE'RE MEETING HERE... I GET IT.
EVEN THOUGH YOUR OFFICE IS LOCATED IN TOKYO'S MINATO WARD, ROPPONGI 6-12...
STOP IT.
I COULDN'T TELL ANYONE UNTIL THE SCHOOL MADE IT PUBLIC KNOWLEDGE.
I FIGURED I COULD TAKE THE JOB AT U.A. WHILE SEARCHING FOR MY SUCCESSOR.
I'VE BEEN SEARCHING FOR A SUCCESSOR FOR A WHILE NOW.
RIGHT...! HE WAS GONNA CHOOSE FROM AMONGST THE STUDENTS!
WITH THEIR AMAZING QUIRKS... AND RAW TALENT...
ONE FOR ALL...
MY BODY IS BROKEN... AFTER A SINGLE PUNCH OR KICK...
I JUST... CAN'T WIELD IT.

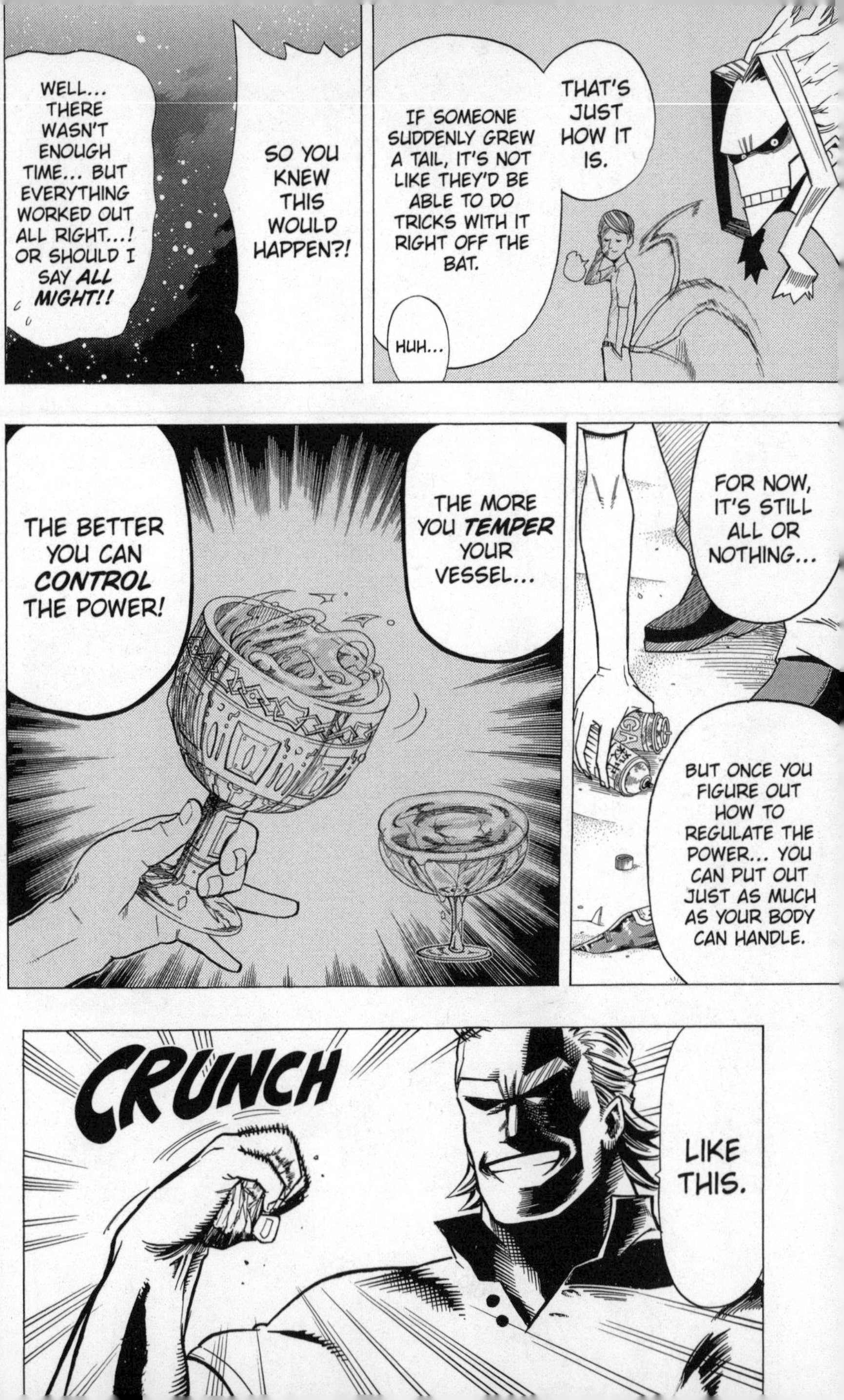
THAT'S JUST HOW IT IS.
IF SOMEONE SUDDENLY GREW A TAIL, IT'S NOT LIKE THEY'D BE ABLE TO DO TRICKS WITH IT RIGHT OFF THE BAT.
HUH...
SO YOU KNEW THIS WOULD HAPPEN?!
WELL... THERE WASN'T ENOUGH TIME... BUT EVERYTHING WORKED OUT ALL RIGHT...! OR SHOULD I SAY ALL MIGHT!!
FOR NOW, IT'S STILL ALL OR NOTHING...
BUT ONCE YOU FIGURE OUT HOW TO REGULATE THE POWER... YOU CAN PUT OUT JUST AS MUCH AS YOUR BODY CAN HANDLE.
THE MORE YOU TEMPER YOUR VESSEL...
THE BETTER YOU CAN CONTROL THE POWER!
LIKE THIS.
CRUNCH

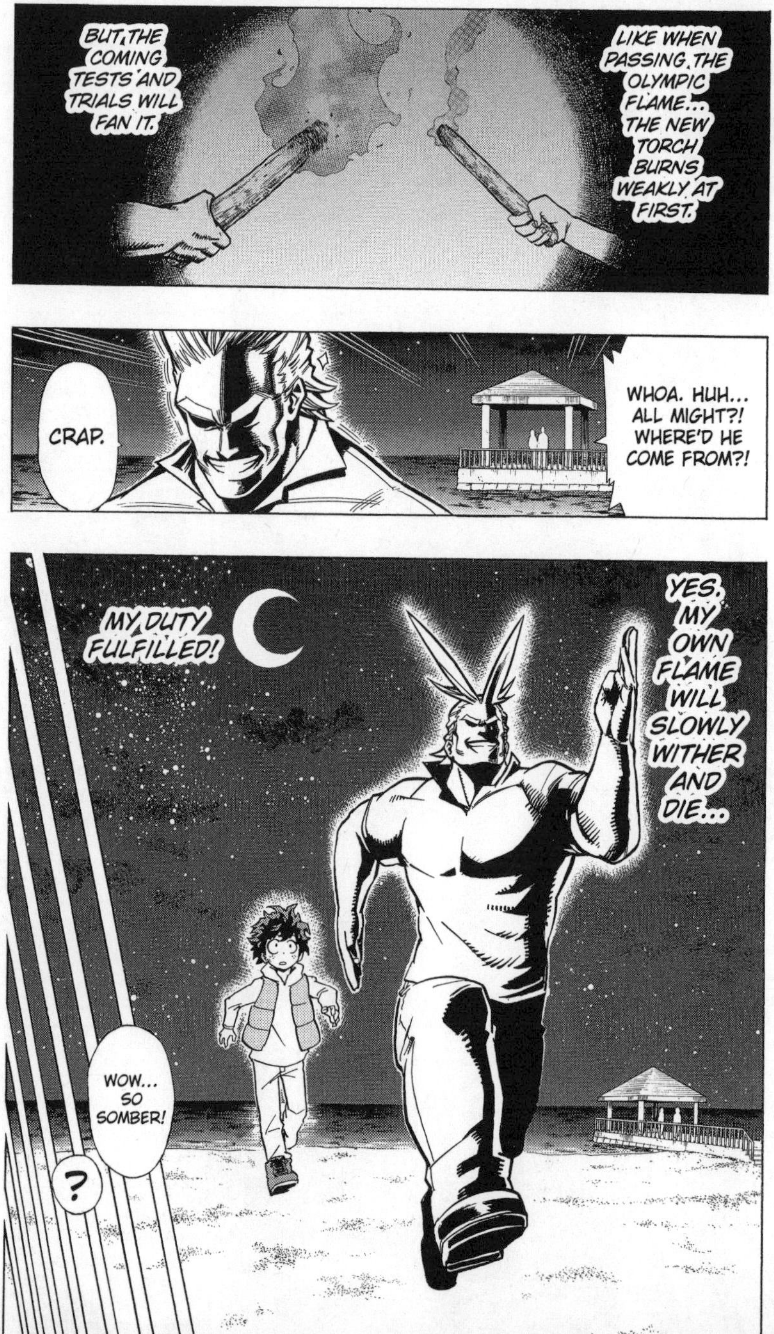
LIKE WHEN PASSING THE OLYMPIC FLAME... THE NEW TORCH BURNS WEAKLY AT FIRST.
BUT THE COMING TESTS AND TRIALS WILL FAN IT.
WHOA. HUH... ALL MIGHT?! WHERE'D HE COME FROM?!
CRAP.
YES. MY OWN FLAME WILL SLOWLY WITHER AND DIE...
MY DUTY FULFILLED!
WOW... SO SOMBER!
?

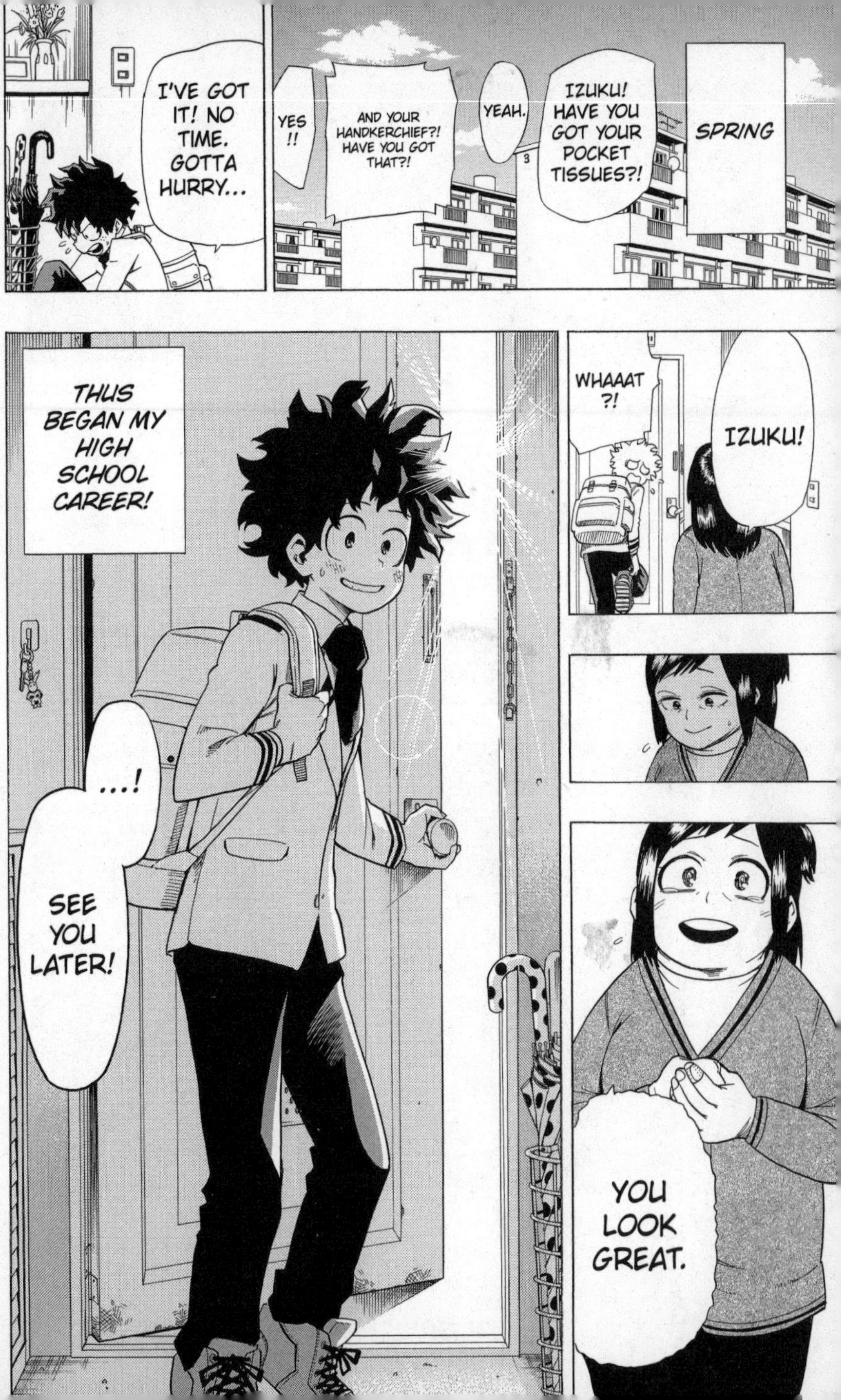
SPRING
IZUKU! HAVE YOU GOT YOUR POCKET TISSUES?!
YEAH.
AND YOUR HANDKERCHIEF?! HAVE YOU GOT THAT?!
YES !!
I'VE GOT IT! NO TIME. GOTTA HURRY...
IZUKU!
WHAAAT ?!
YOU LOOK GREAT.
THUS BEGAN MY HIGH SCHOOL CAREER!
...!
SEE YOU LATER!

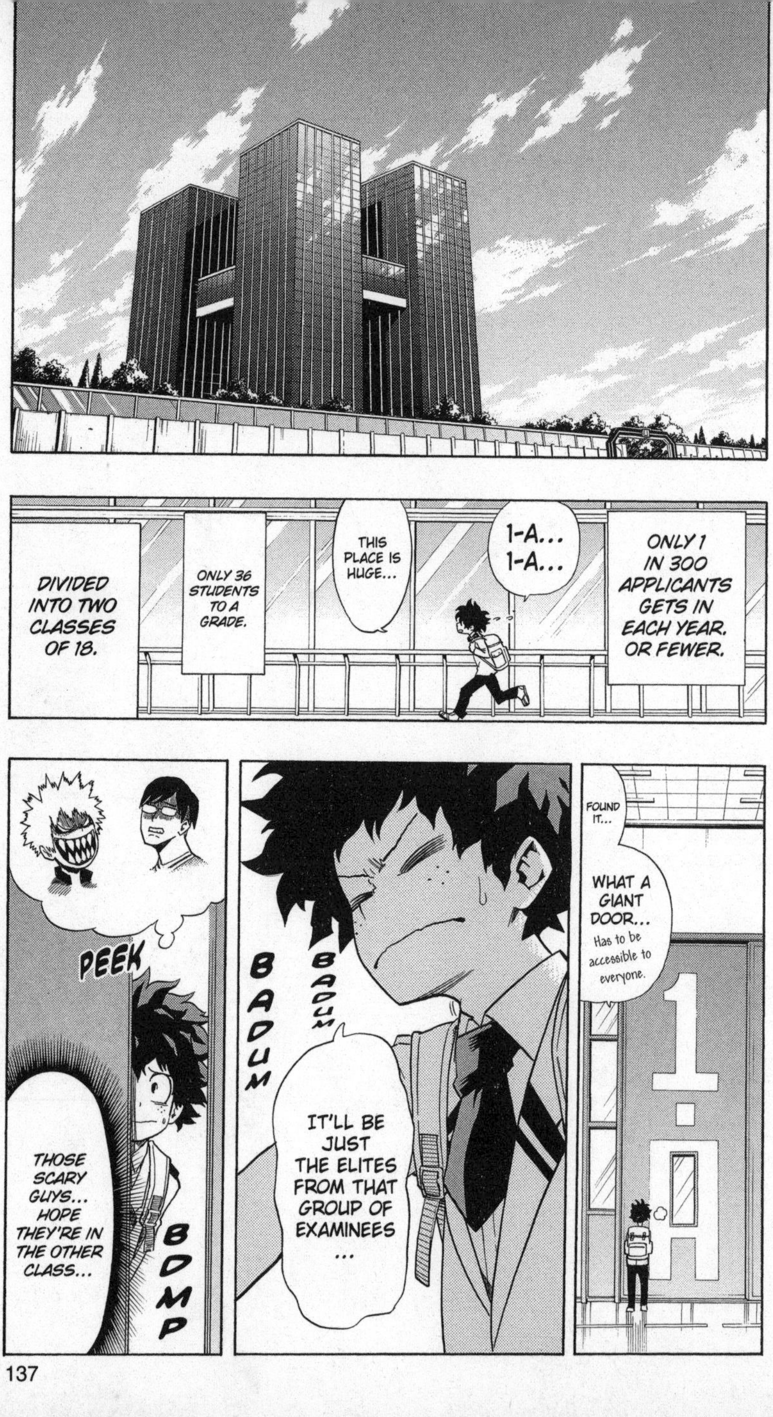
ONLY 1 IN 300 APPLICANTS GETS IN EACH YEAR. OR FEWER.
1-A... 1-A...
THIS PLACE IS HUGE...
ONLY 36 STUDENTS TO A GRADE.
DIVIDED INTO TWO CLASSES OF 18.
FOUND IT...
WHAT A GIANT DOOR...
Has to be accessible to everyone.
BADUM
BADUM
IT'LL BE JUST THE ELITES FROM THAT GROUP OF EXAMINEES ...
PEEK
BDMP
THOSE SCARY GUYS... HOPE THEY'RE IN THE OTHER CLASS...

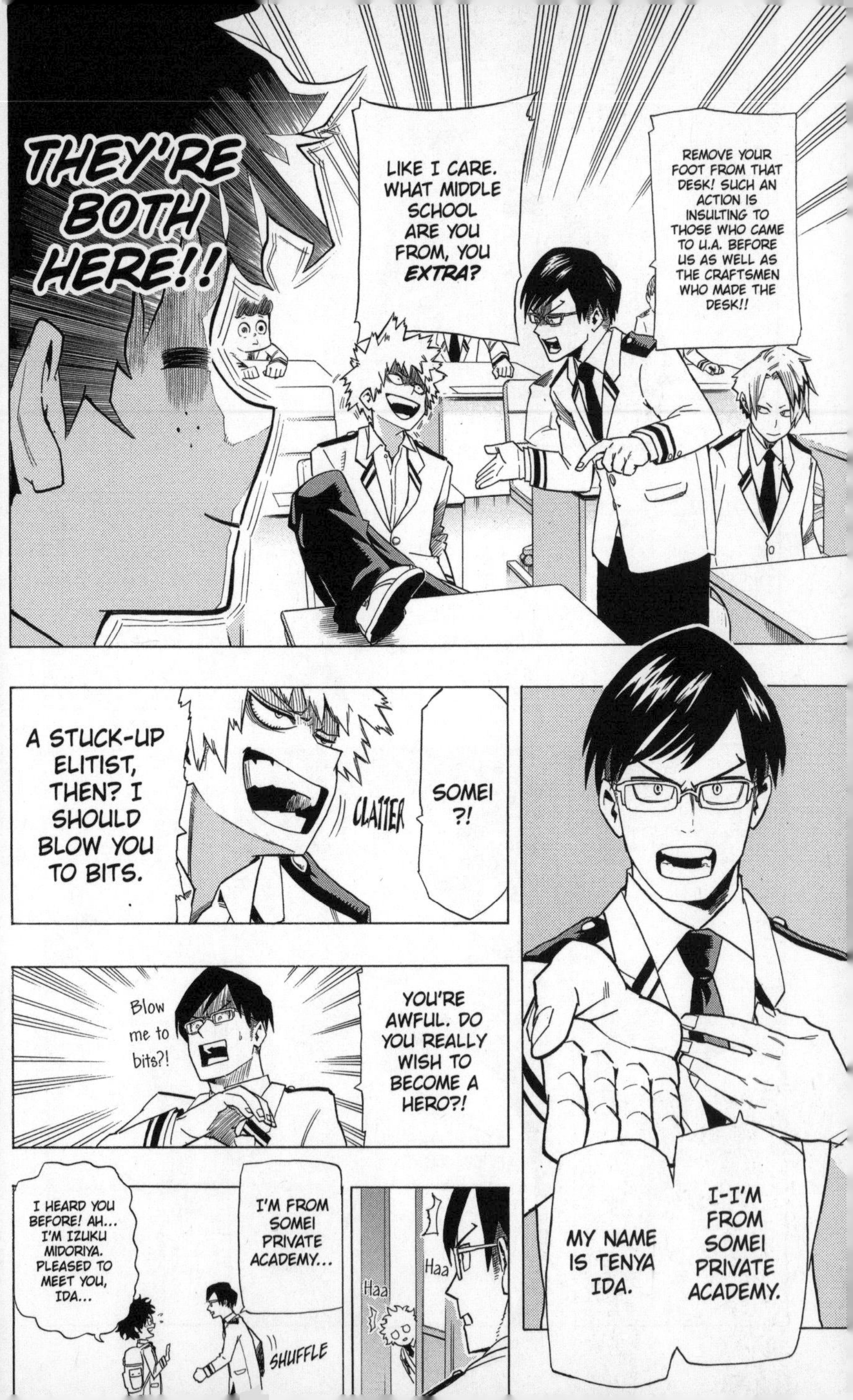
REMOVE YOUR FOOT FROM THAT DESK! SUCH AN ACTION IS INSULTING TO THOSE WHO CAME TO U.A. BEFORE US AS WELL AS THE CRAFTSMEN WHO MADE THE DESK!!
LIKE I CARE. WHAT MIDDLE SCHOOL ARE YOU FROM, YOU *EXTRA?*
THEY'RE BOTH HERE!!
I-I'M FROM SOMEI PRIVATE ACADEMY.
MY NAME IS TENYA IDA.
SOMEI ?!
CLATTER
A STUCK-UP ELITIST, THEN? I SHOULD BLOW YOU TO BITS.
YOU'RE AWFUL. DO YOU REALLY WISH TO BECOME A HERO?!
Blow me to bits?!
Haa
Haa
I'M FROM SOMEI PRIVATE ACADEMY...
SHUFFLE
I HEARD YOU BEFORE! AH... I'M IZUKU MIDORIYA. PLEASED TO MEET YOU, IDA...

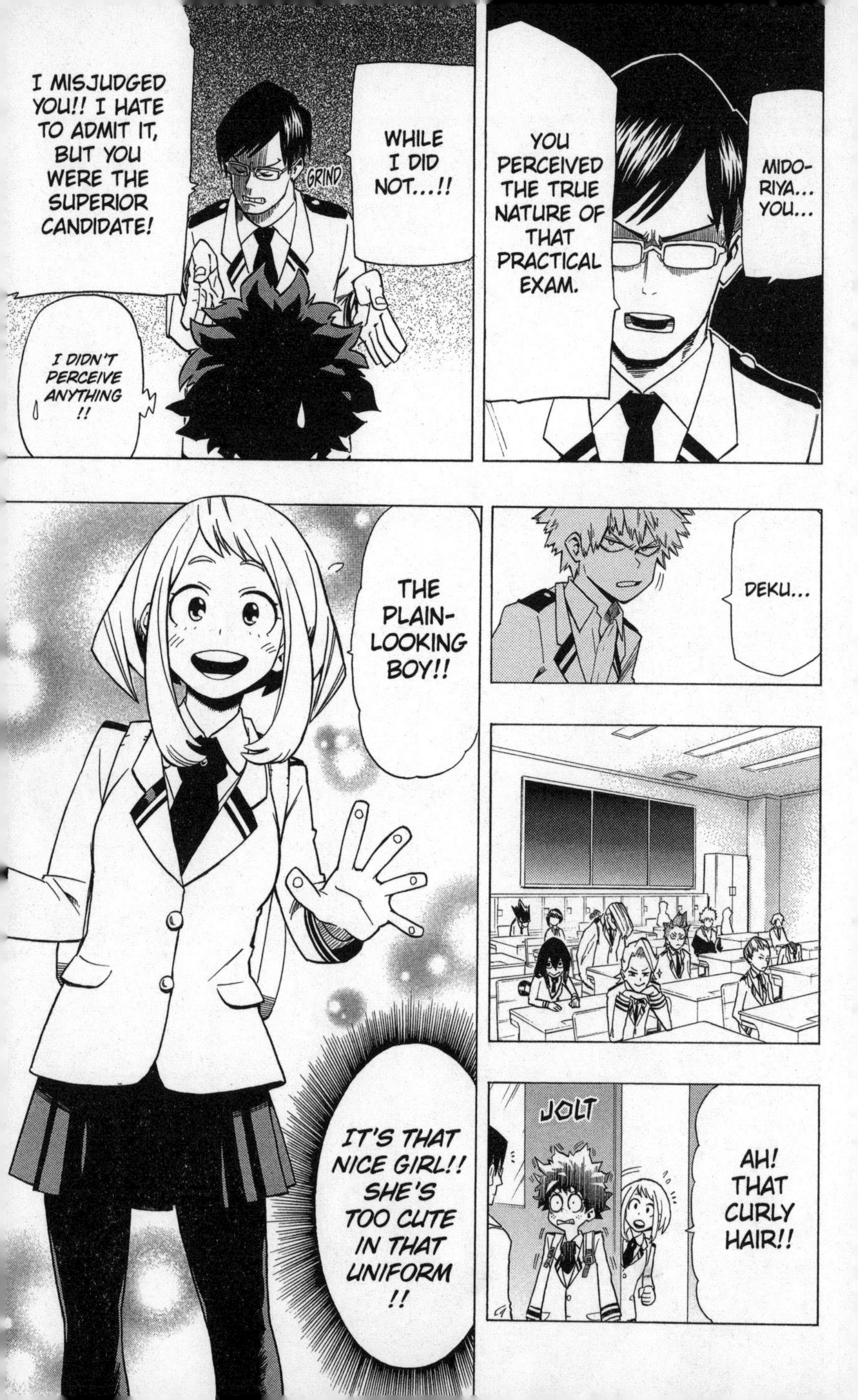
MIDO-RIYA... YOU...
YOU PERCEIVED THE TRUE NATURE OF THAT PRACTICAL EXAM.
WHILE I DID NOT...!!
I MISJUDGED YOU!! I HATE TO ADMIT IT, BUT YOU WERE THE SUPERIOR CANDIDATE!
GRIND
I DIDN'T PERCEIVE ANYTHING !!
DEKU...
AH! THAT CURLY HAIR!!
JOLT
THE PLAIN-LOOKING BOY!!
IT'S THAT NICE GIRL!! SHE'S TOO CUTE IN THAT UNIFORM !!

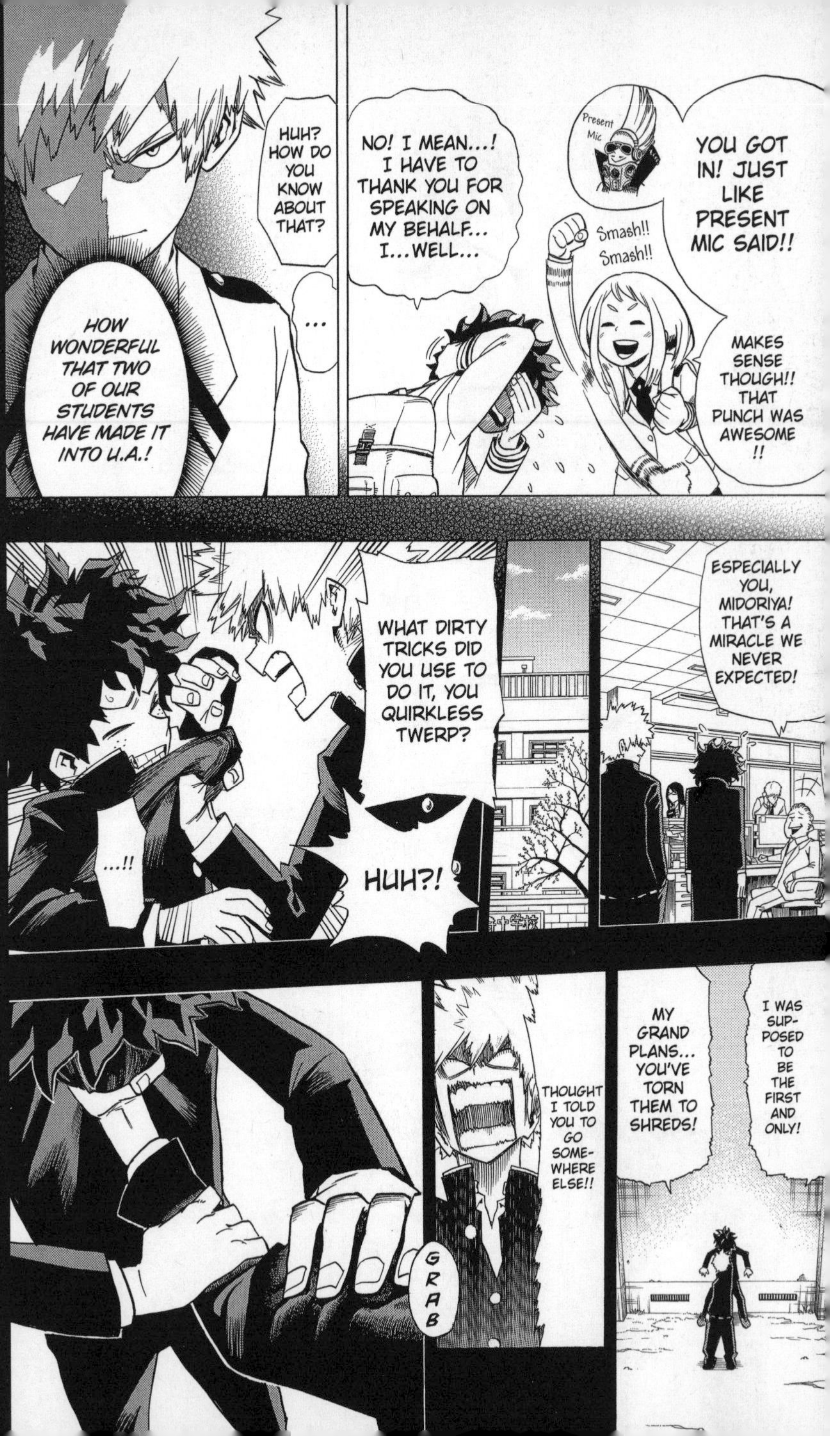
YOU GOT IN! JUST LIKE PRESENT MIC SAID!!
Present Mic
Smash!! Smash!!
MAKES SENSE THOUGH!! THAT PUNCH WAS AWESOME!!
NO! I MEAN...! I HAVE TO THANK YOU FOR SPEAKING ON MY BEHALF... I...WELL...
HUH? HOW DO YOU KNOW ABOUT THAT?
HOW WONDERFUL THAT TWO OF OUR STUDENTS HAVE MADE IT INTO U.A.!
...
ESPECIALLY YOU, MIDORIYA! THAT'S A MIRACLE WE NEVER EXPECTED!
WHAT DIRTY TRICKS DID YOU USE TO DO IT, YOU QUIRKLESS TWERP?
HUH?!
...!!
I WAS SUPPOSED TO BE THE FIRST AND ONLY!
MY GRAND PLANS... YOU'VE TORN THEM TO SHREDS!
THOUGHT I TOLD YOU TO GO SOMEWHERE ELSE!!
GRAB

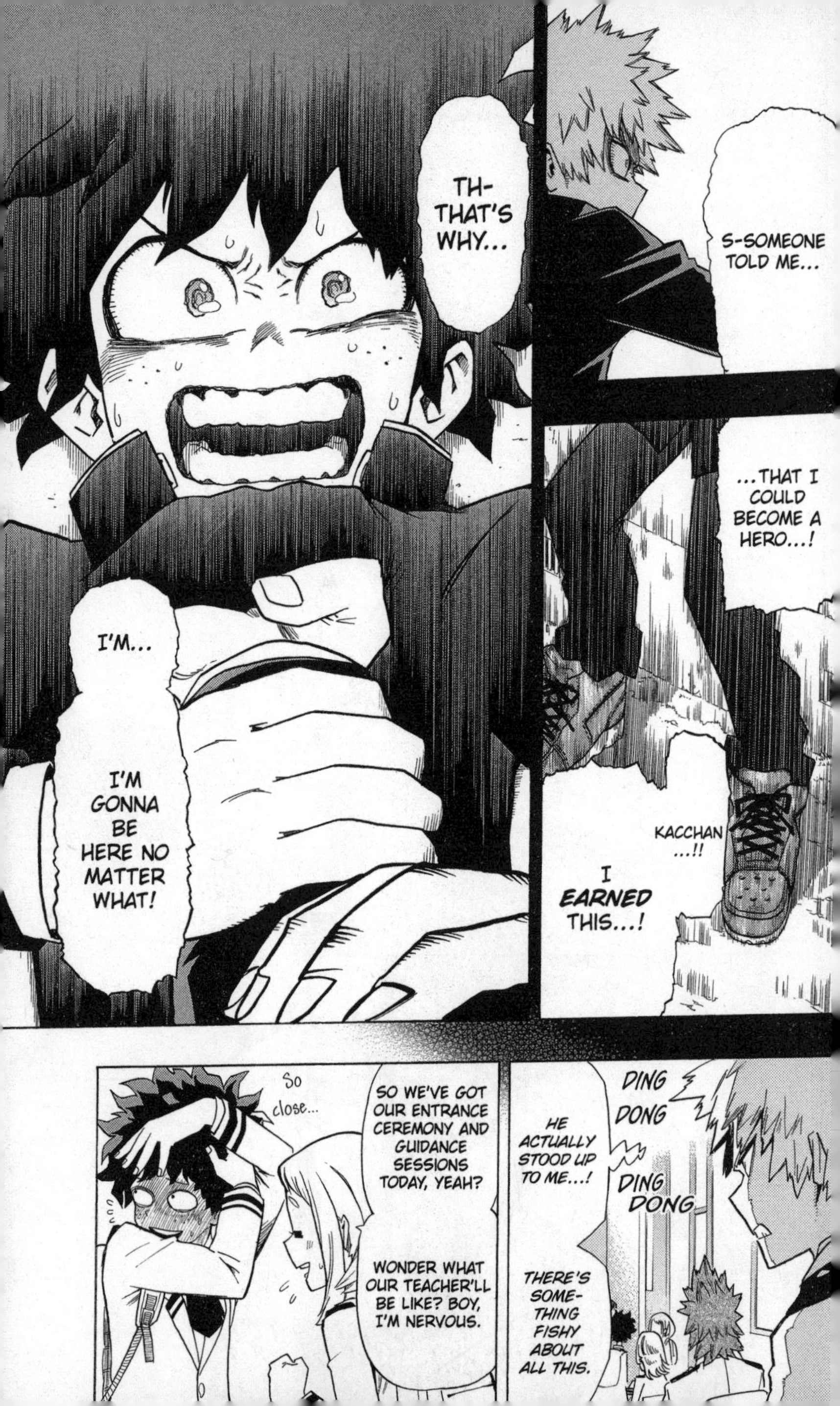
S-SOMEONE TOLD ME...
...THAT I COULD BECOME A HERO...!
KACCHAN ...!!
I **EARNED** THIS...!
TH- THAT'S WHY...
I'M...
I'M GONNA BE HERE NO MATTER WHAT!
DING DONG
HE ACTUALLY STOOD UP TO ME...!
DING DONG
THERE'S SOME-THING FISHY ABOUT ALL THIS.
So close...
SO WE'VE GOT OUR ENTRANCE CEREMONY AND GUIDANCE SESSIONS TODAY, YEAH?
WONDER WHAT OUR TEACHER'LL BE LIKE? BOY, I'M NERVOUS.

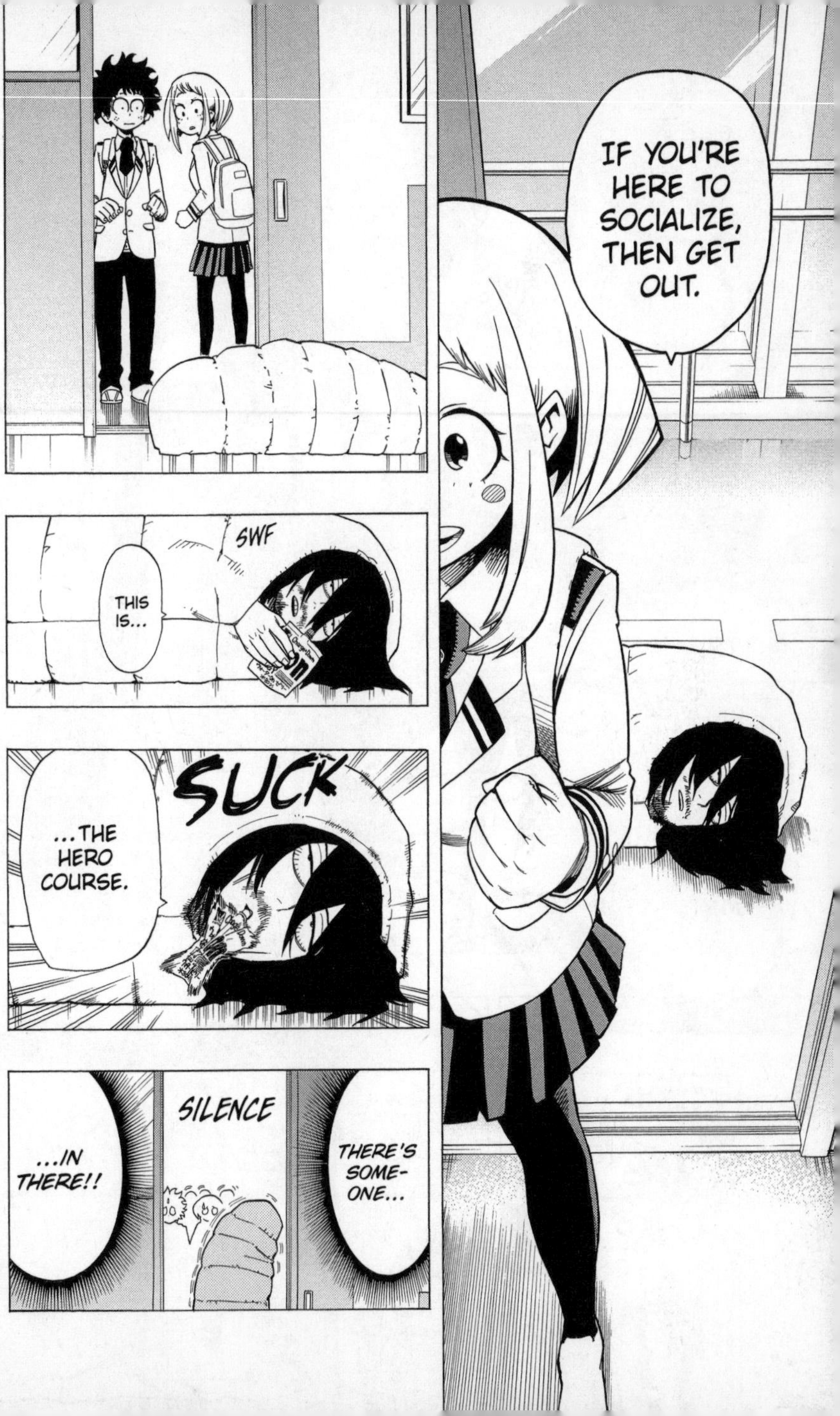
IF YOU'RE HERE TO SOCIALIZE, THEN GET OUT.
SWF
THIS IS...
SUCK
...THE HERO COURSE.
THERE'S SOME-ONE...
SILENCE
...IN THERE!!

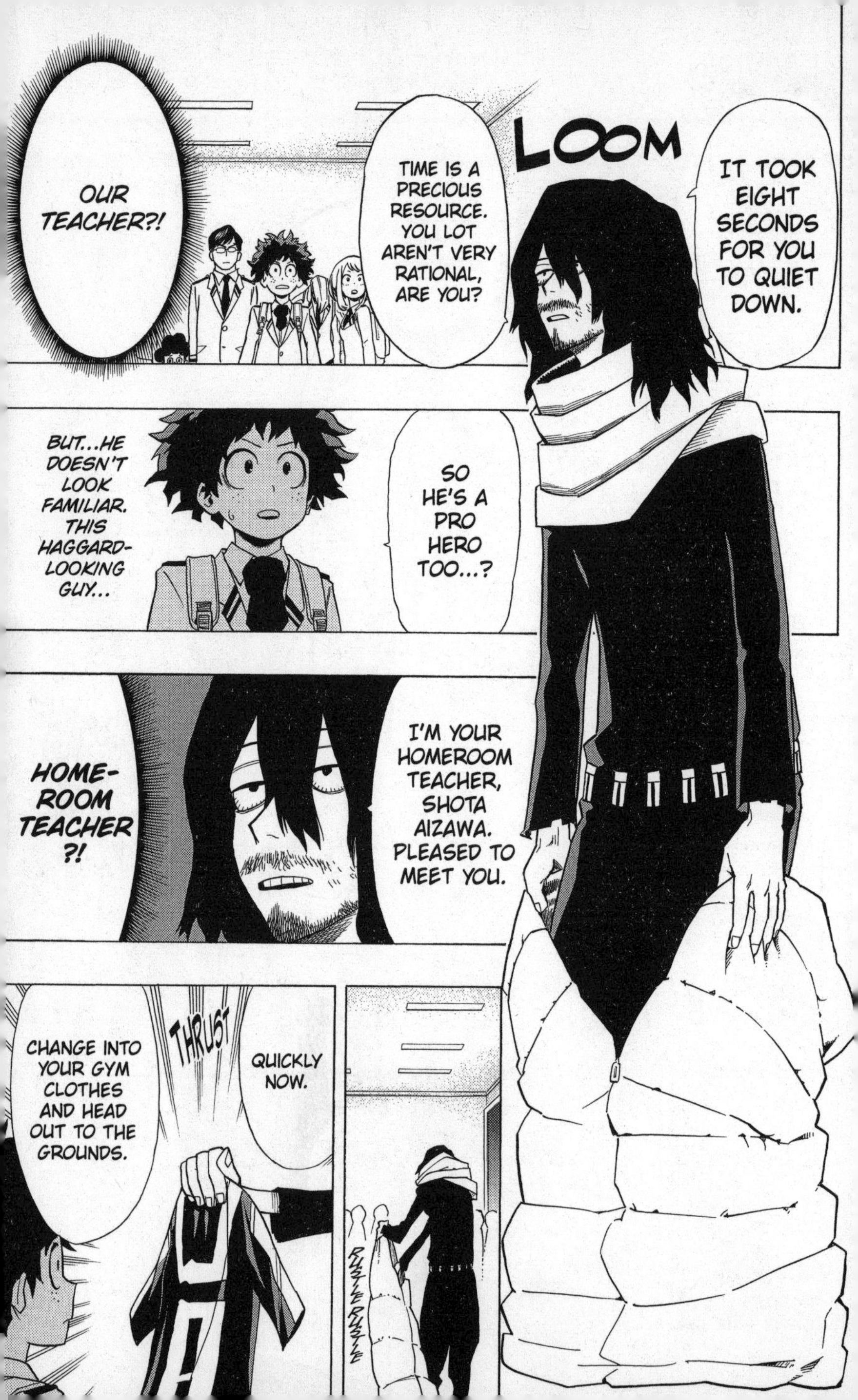
LOOM
IT TOOK EIGHT SECONDS FOR YOU TO QUIET DOWN.
TIME IS A PRECIOUS RESOURCE. YOU LOT AREN'T VERY RATIONAL, ARE YOU?
OUR TEACHER?!
SO HE'S A PRO HERO TOO...?
BUT...HE DOESN'T LOOK FAMILIAR. THIS HAGGARD-LOOKING GUY...
I'M YOUR HOMEROOM TEACHER, SHOTA AIZAWA. PLEASED TO MEET YOU.
HOME-ROOM TEACHER?!
RUSTLE RUSTLE
QUICKLY NOW.
THRUST
CHANGE INTO YOUR GYM CLOTHES AND HEAD OUT TO THE GROUNDS.

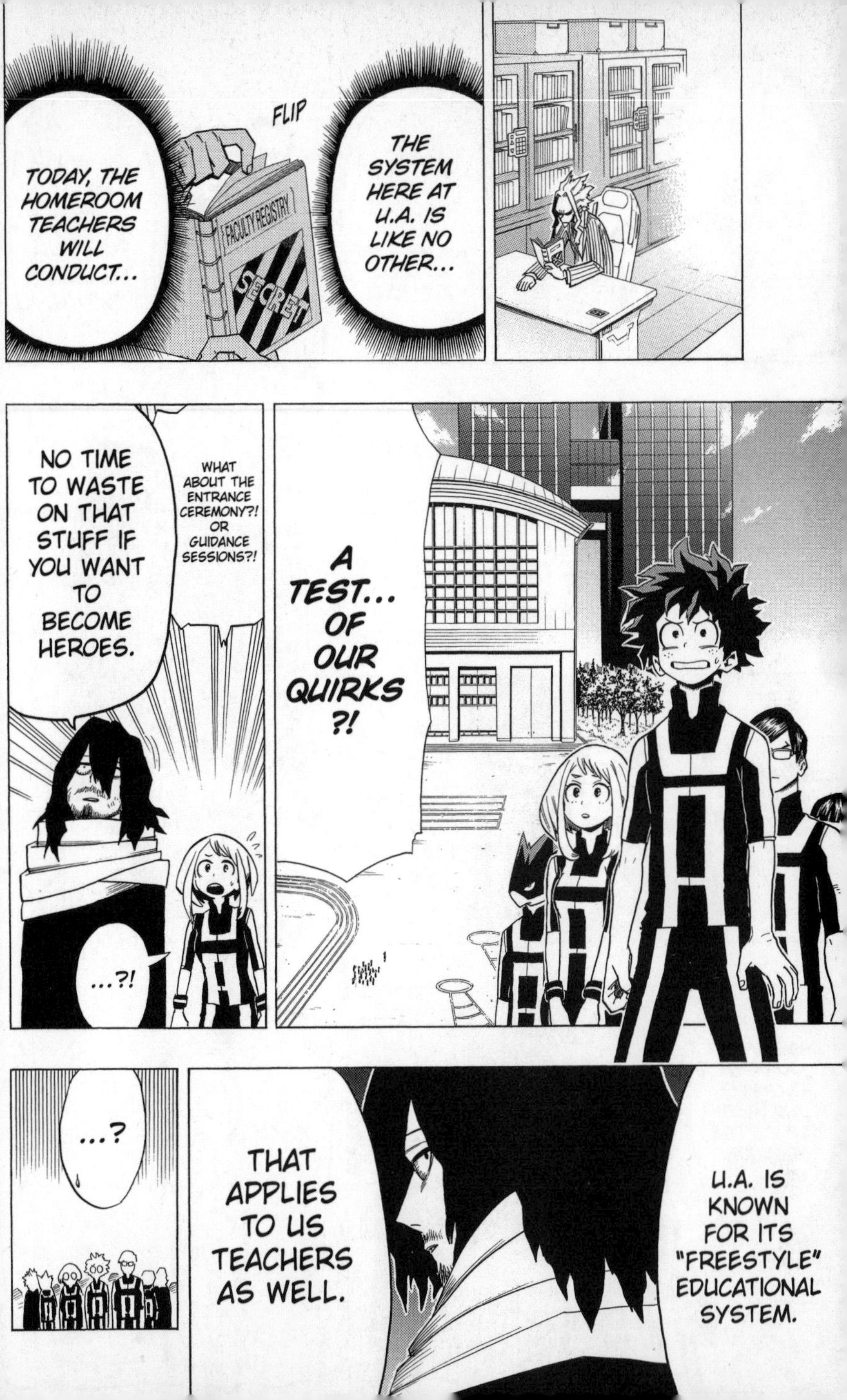
THE SYSTEM HERE AT U.A. IS LIKE NO OTHER...
FLIP
TODAY, THE HOMEROOM TEACHERS WILL CONDUCT...
FACULTY REGISTRY
SECRET
A TEST... OF OUR QUIRKS ?!
WHAT ABOUT THE ENTRANCE CEREMONY?! OR GUIDANCE SESSIONS?!
NO TIME TO WASTE ON THAT STUFF IF YOU WANT TO BECOME HEROES.
...?!
U.A. IS KNOWN FOR ITS "FREESTYLE" EDUCATIONAL SYSTEM.
THAT APPLIES TO US TEACHERS AS WELL.
...?

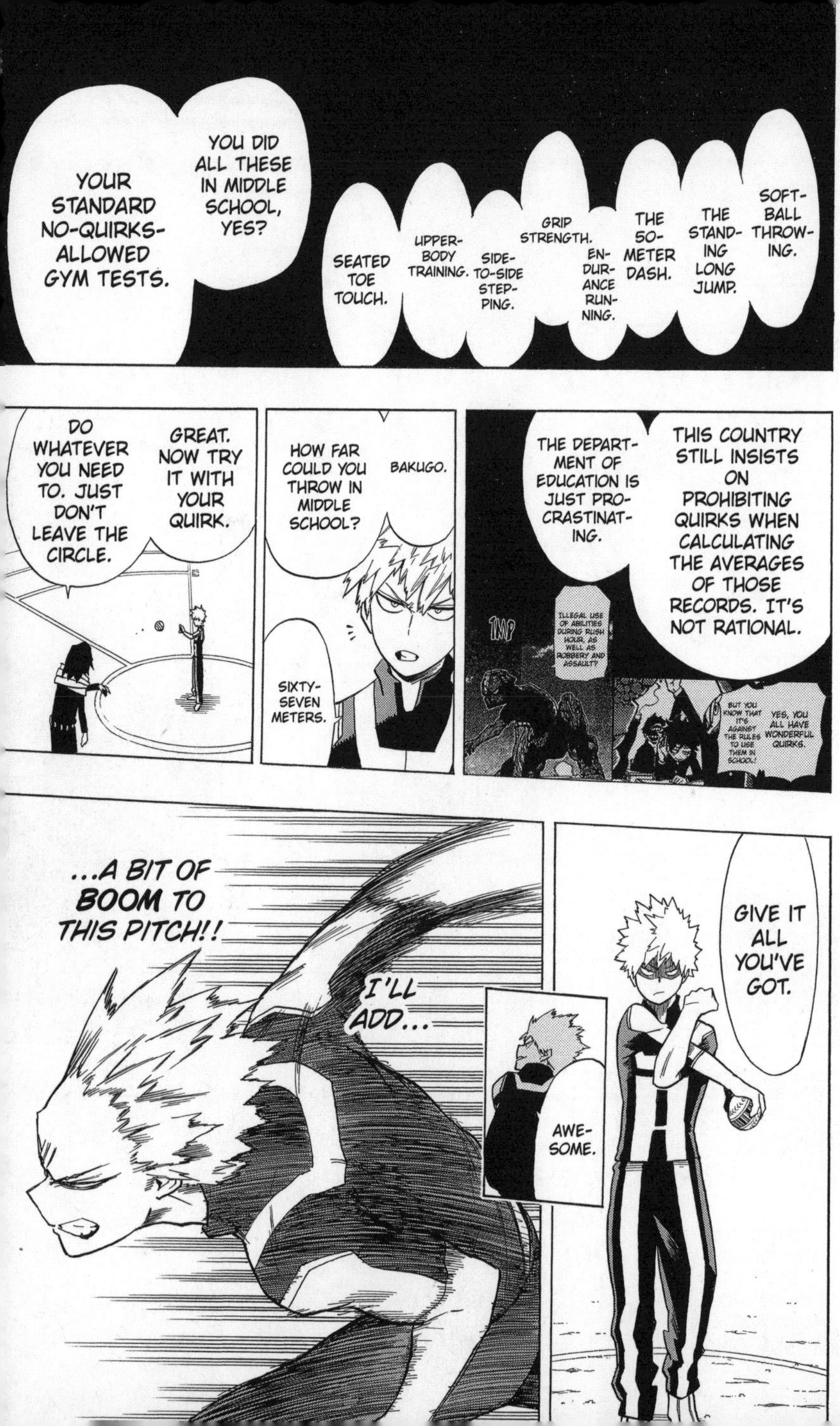
SOFT-BALL THROWING.
THE STANDING LONG JUMP.
THE 50-METER DASH.
ENDURANCE RUNNING.
GRIP STRENGTH.
SIDE-TO-SIDE STEPPING.
UPPER-BODY TRAINING.
SEATED TOE TOUCH.
YOU DID ALL THESE IN MIDDLE SCHOOL, YES?
YOUR STANDARD NO-QUIRKS-ALLOWED GYM TESTS.
THIS COUNTRY STILL INSISTS ON PROHIBITING QUIRKS WHEN CALCULATING THE AVERAGES OF THOSE RECORDS. IT'S NOT RATIONAL.
THE DEPARTMENT OF EDUCATION IS JUST PROCRASTINATING.
ILLEGAL USE OF ABILITIES DURING RUSH HOUR, AS WELL AS ROBBERY AND ASSAULT?
TMP
YES, YOU ALL HAVE WONDERFUL QUIRKS.
BUT YOU KNOW THAT IT'S AGAINST THE RULES TO USE THEM IN SCHOOL!
BAKUGO.
HOW FAR COULD YOU THROW IN MIDDLE SCHOOL?
SIXTY-SEVEN METERS.
GREAT. NOW TRY IT WITH YOUR QUIRK.
DO WHATEVER YOU NEED TO. JUST DON'T LEAVE THE CIRCLE.
GIVE IT ALL YOU'VE GOT.
AWESOME.
I'LL ADD...
...A BIT OF BOOM TO THIS PITCH!!

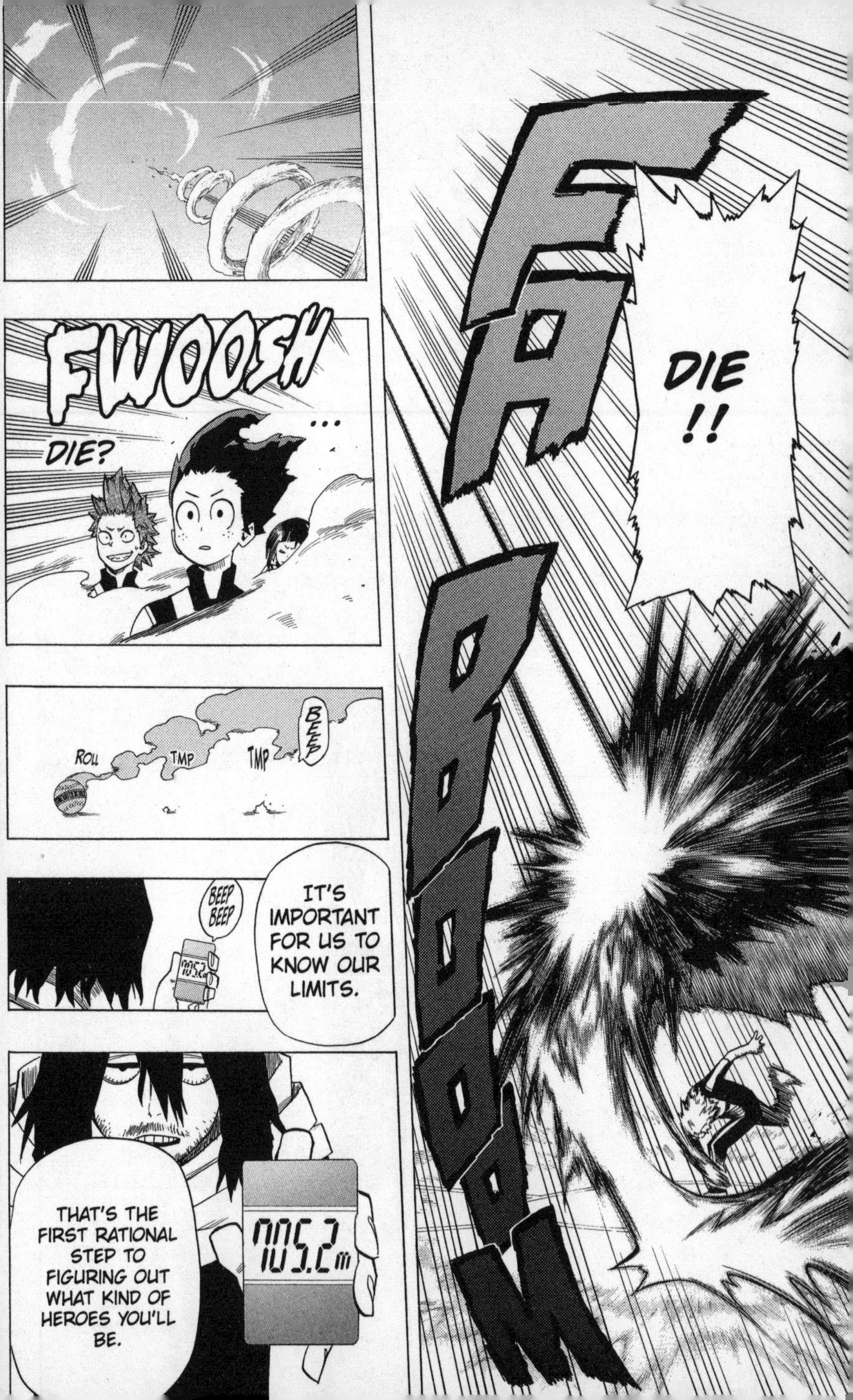
DIE !!
FWOOSH
...
DIE?
ROLL
TMP
TMP
BEEP
BEEP BEEP
IT'S IMPORTANT FOR US TO KNOW OUR LIMITS.
705.2m
THAT'S THE FIRST RATIONAL STEP TO FIGURING OUT WHAT KIND OF HEROES YOU'LL BE.

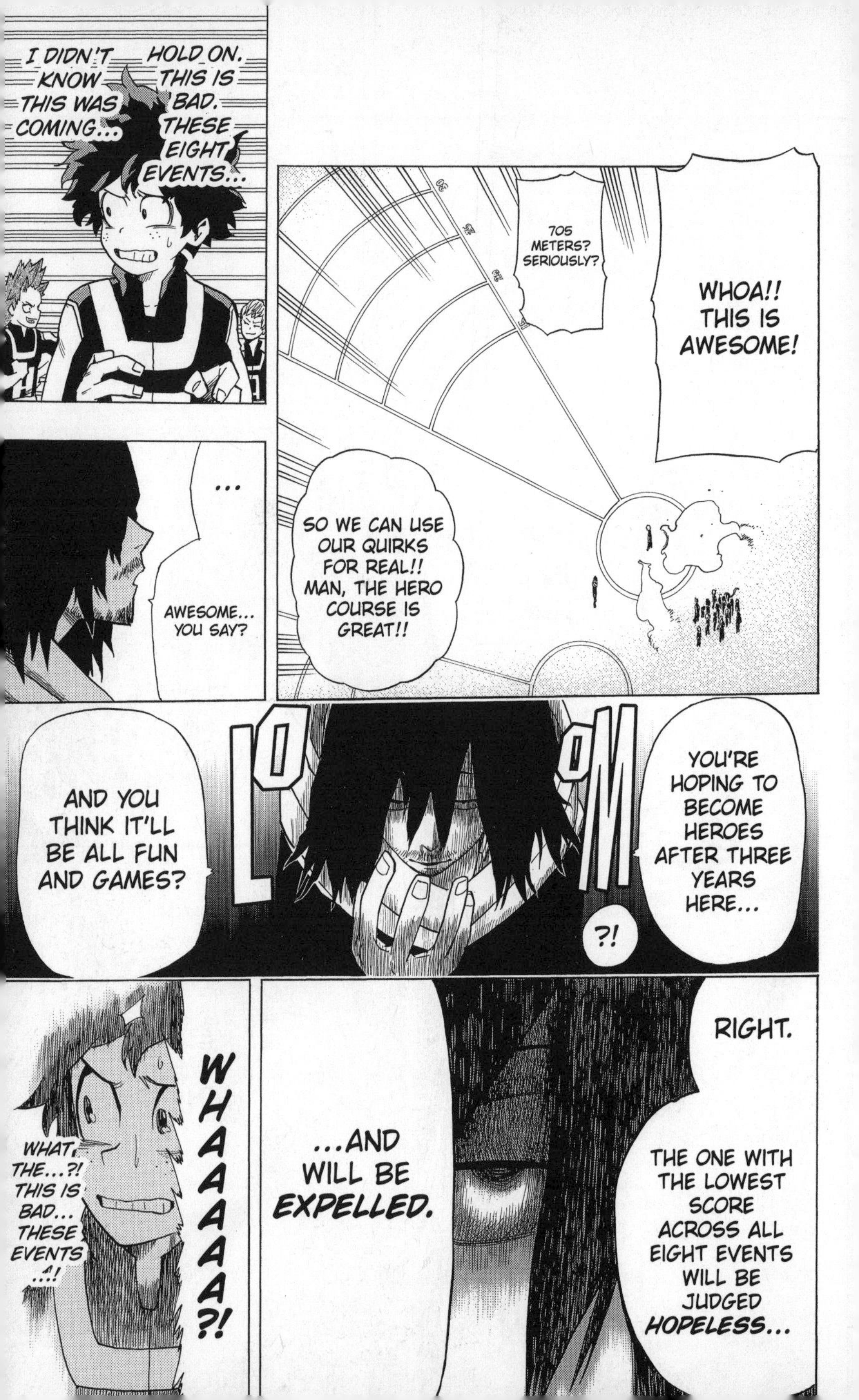
WHOA!! THIS IS AWESOME!
705 METERS? SERIOUSLY?
SO WE CAN USE OUR QUIRKS FOR REAL!! MAN, THE HERO COURSE IS GREAT!!
HOLD ON. THIS IS BAD. THESE EIGHT EVENTS...
I DIDN'T KNOW THIS WAS COMING...
...
AWESOME... YOU SAY?
YOU'RE HOPING TO BECOME HEROES AFTER THREE YEARS HERE...
LOOM
?!
AND YOU THINK IT'LL BE ALL FUN AND GAMES?
RIGHT.
THE ONE WITH THE LOWEST SCORE ACROSS ALL EIGHT EVENTS WILL BE JUDGED HOPELESS...
...AND WILL BE EXPELLED.
WHAAAAAAA?!
WHAT THE...?! THIS IS BAD... THESE EVENTS...!

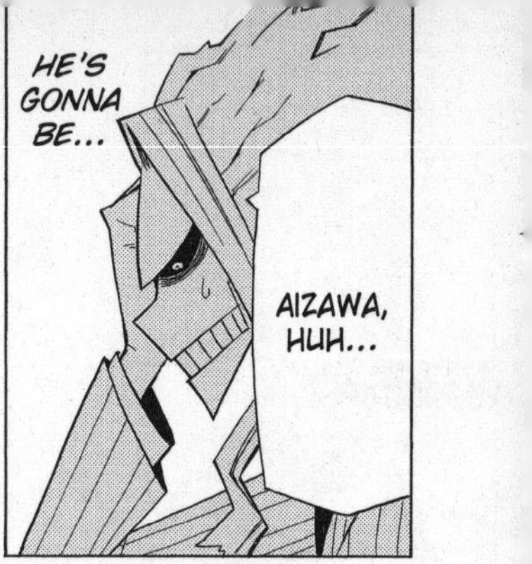
AIZAWA, HUH...
HE'S GONNA BE...

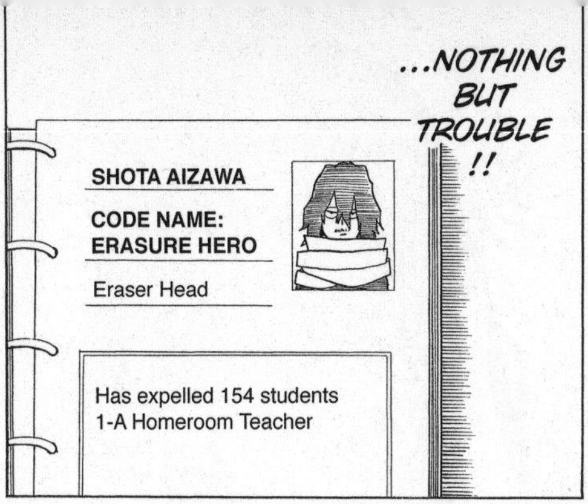
...NOTHING BUT TROUBLE !!
SHOTA AIZAWA
CODE NAME: ERASURE HERO
Eraser Head
Has expelled 154 students
1-A Homeroom Teacher

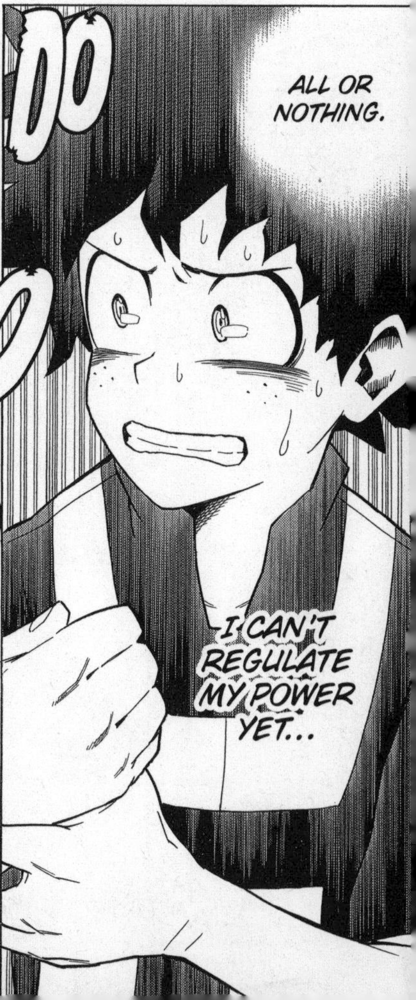
DO
ALL OR NOTHING.
I CAN'T REGULATE MY POWER YET...

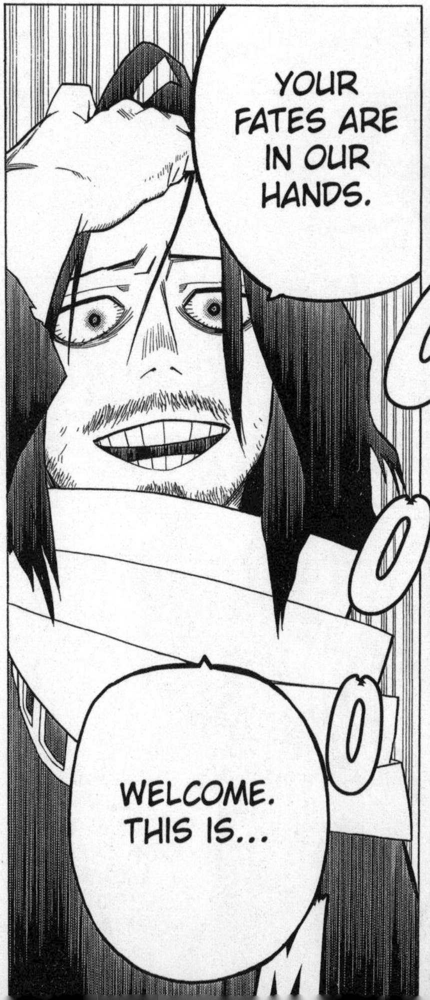
YOUR FATES ARE IN OUR HANDS.
WELCOME. THIS IS...

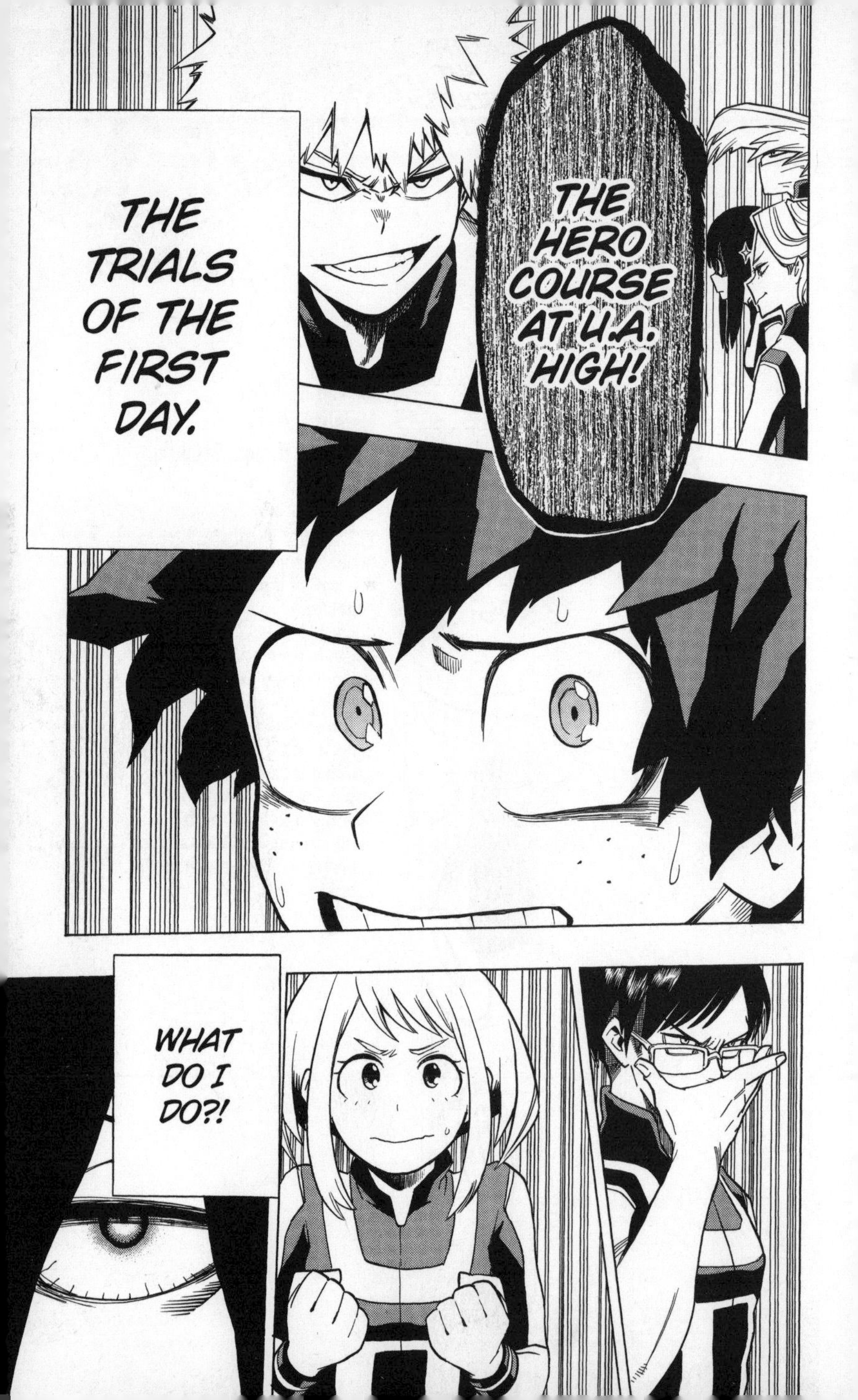
THE HERO COURSE AT U.A. HIGH!
THE TRIALS OF THE FIRST DAY.
WHAT DO I DO?!

CIVILIAN CLOTHES

IAI

TENYA IDA (AGE: 15)

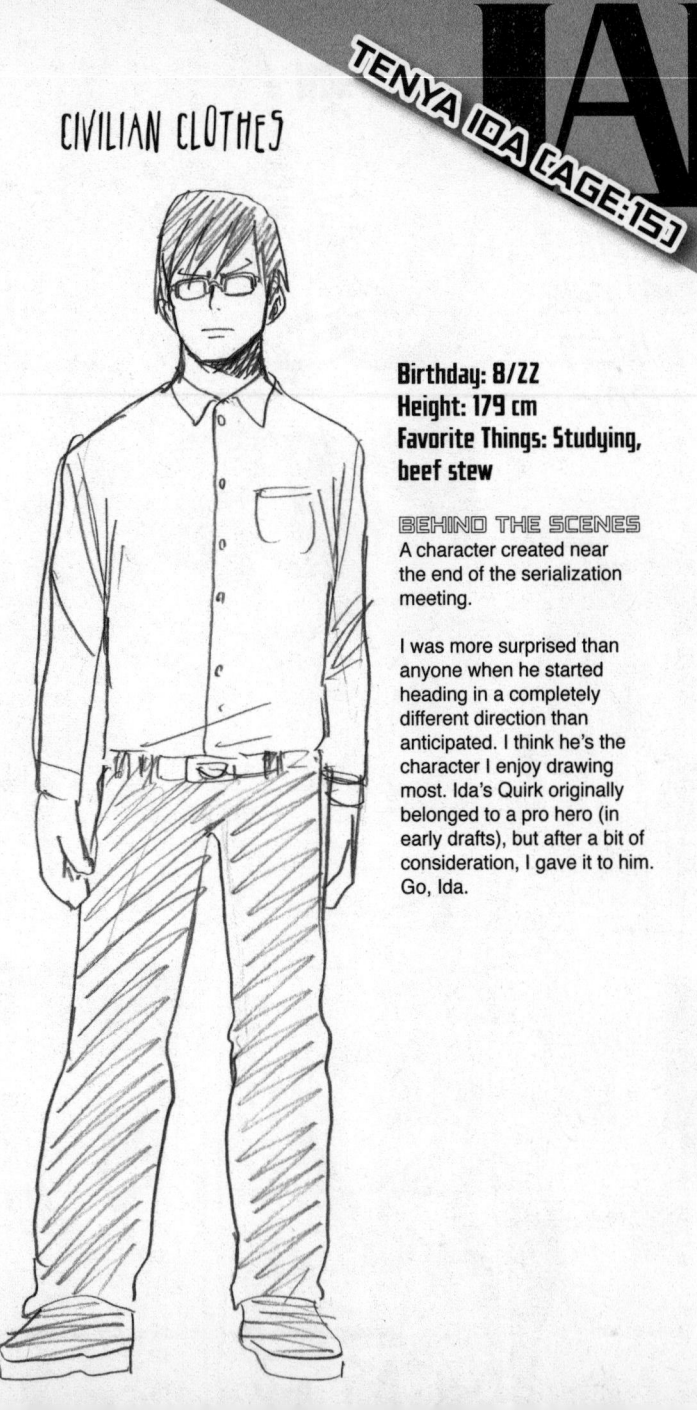

Birthday: 8/22
Height: 179 cm
Favorite Things: Studying,
beef stew

BEHIND THE SCENES
A character created near
the end of the serialization
meeting.

I was more surprised than
anyone when he started
heading in a completely
different direction than
anticipated. I think he's the
character I enjoy drawing
most. Ida's Quirk originally
belonged to a pro hero (in
early drafts), but after a bit of
consideration, I gave it to him.
Go, Ida.

No.6 – What I Can Do for Now

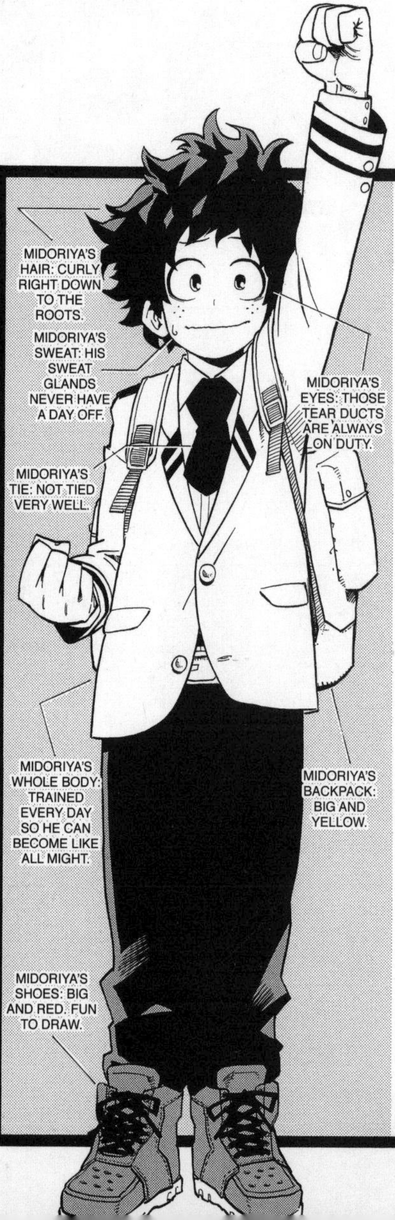

MIDORIYA'S HAIR: CURLY RIGHT DOWN TO THE ROOTS.
MIDORIYA'S SWEAT: HIS SWEAT GLANDS NEVER HAVE A DAY OFF.
MIDORIYA'S EYES: THOSE TEAR DUCTS ARE ALWAYS ON DUTY.
MIDORIYA'S TIE: NOT TIED VERY WELL.
MIDORIYA'S WHOLE BODY: TRAINED EVERY DAY SO HE CAN BECOME LIKE ALL MIGHT.
MIDORIYA'S BACKPACK: BIG AND YELLOW.
MIDORIYA'S SHOES: BIG AND RED. FUN TO DRAW.

U.A. FILE.01

CLASS No.18
IZUKU MIDORIYA

Quirk [TBD]

ONE FOR ALL

A crystalline power network containing the strength of many others! Allows for unbelievable bursts of strength, but only for an instant!

But Midoriya… Well, it's still too much for the kid to bear, so using 100 percent of the power would break him in two!

He's got to work on regulating it!

Good luck, kid!

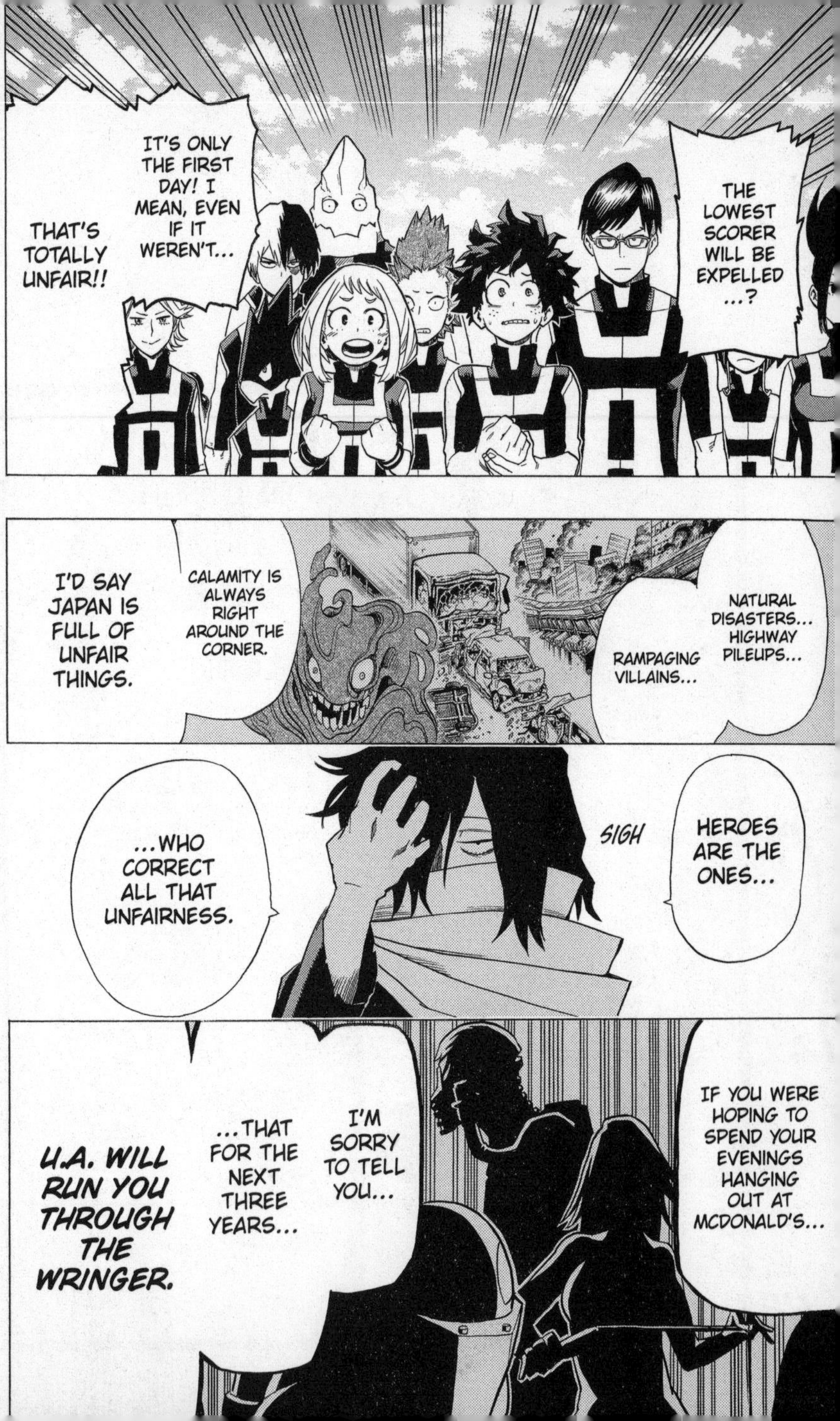
THE LOWEST SCORER WILL BE EXPELLED ...?
IT'S ONLY THE FIRST DAY! I MEAN, EVEN IF IT WEREN'T...
THAT'S TOTALLY UNFAIR!!
NATURAL DISASTERS... HIGHWAY PILEUPS...
RAMPAGING VILLAINS...
CALAMITY IS ALWAYS RIGHT AROUND THE CORNER.
I'D SAY JAPAN IS FULL OF UNFAIR THINGS.
HEROES ARE THE ONES...
SIGH
...WHO CORRECT ALL THAT UNFAIRNESS.
IF YOU WERE HOPING TO SPEND YOUR EVENINGS HANGING OUT AT MCDONALD'S...
I'M SORRY TO TELL YOU...
...THAT FOR THE NEXT THREE YEARS...
U.A. WILL RUN YOU THROUGH THE WRINGER.

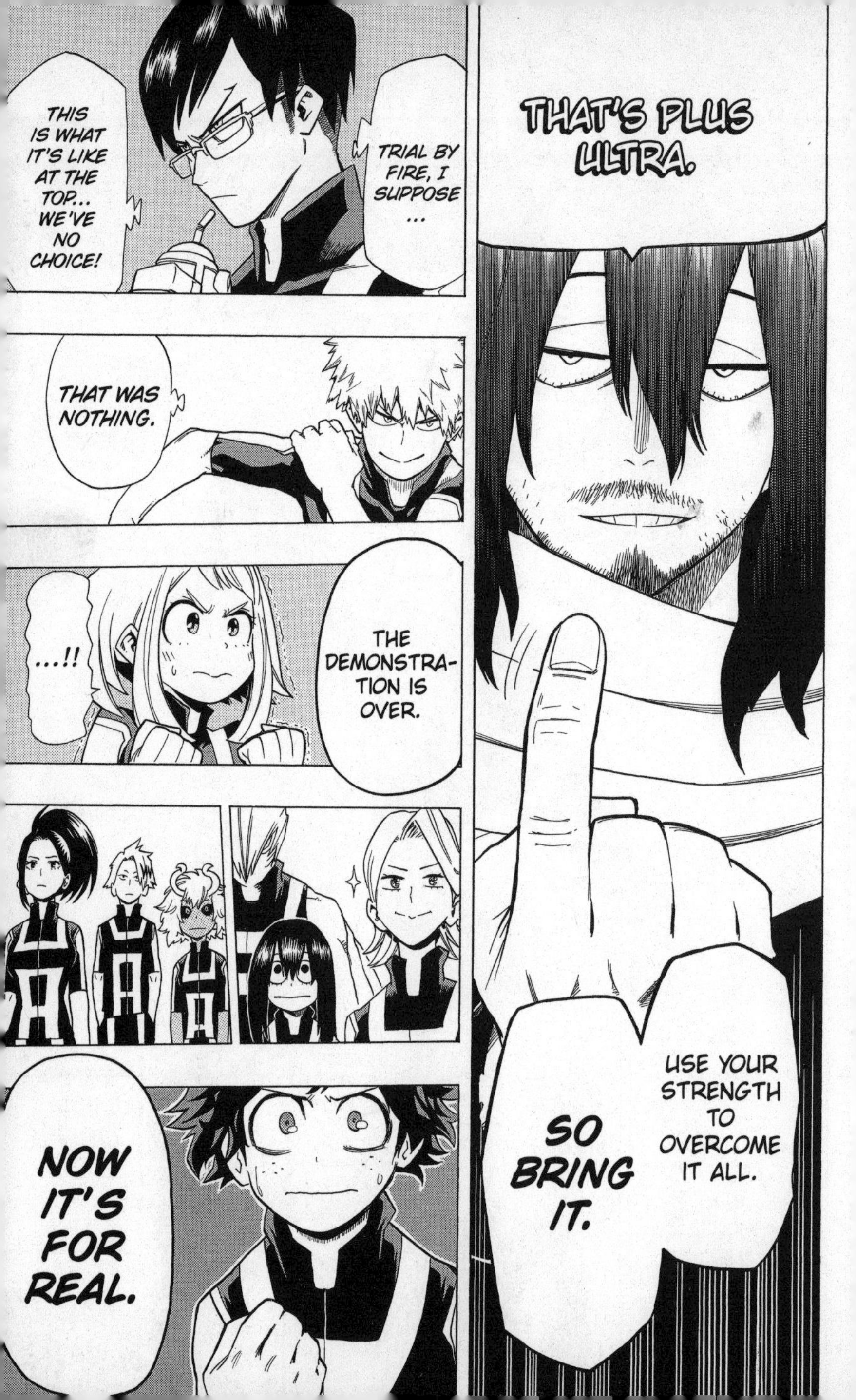
THAT'S PLUS ULTRA.
USE YOUR STRENGTH TO OVERCOME IT ALL.
SO BRING IT.
TRIAL BY FIRE, I SUPPOSE...
THIS IS WHAT IT'S LIKE AT THE TOP... WE'VE NO CHOICE!
THAT WAS NOTHING.
THE DEMONSTRATION IS OVER.
...!!
NOW IT'S FOR REAL.

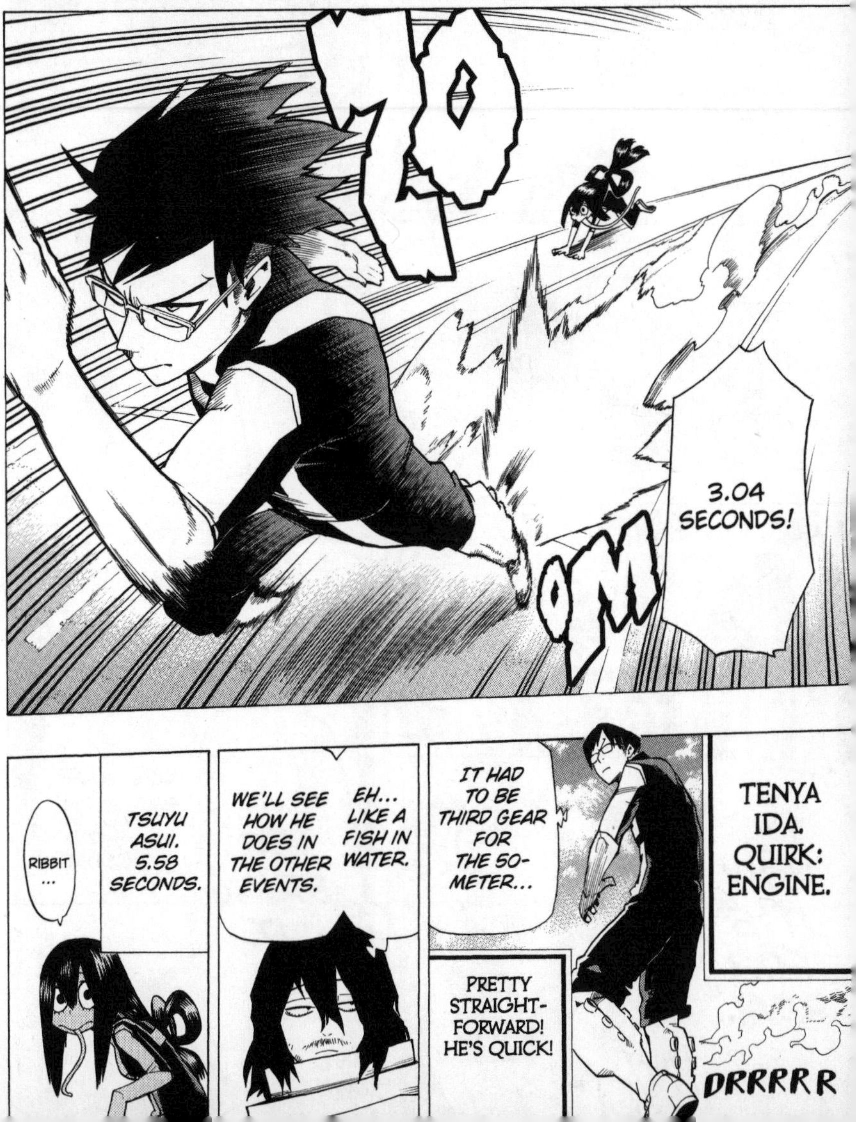
3.04 SECONDS!
TENYA IDA. QUIRK: ENGINE.
DRRRRR
IT HAD TO BE THIRD GEAR FOR THE 50-METER...
PRETTY STRAIGHT-FORWARD! HE'S QUICK!
EH... LIKE A FISH IN WATER.
WE'LL SEE HOW HE DOES IN THE OTHER EVENTS.
TSUYU ASUI. 5.58 SECONDS.
RIBBIT...

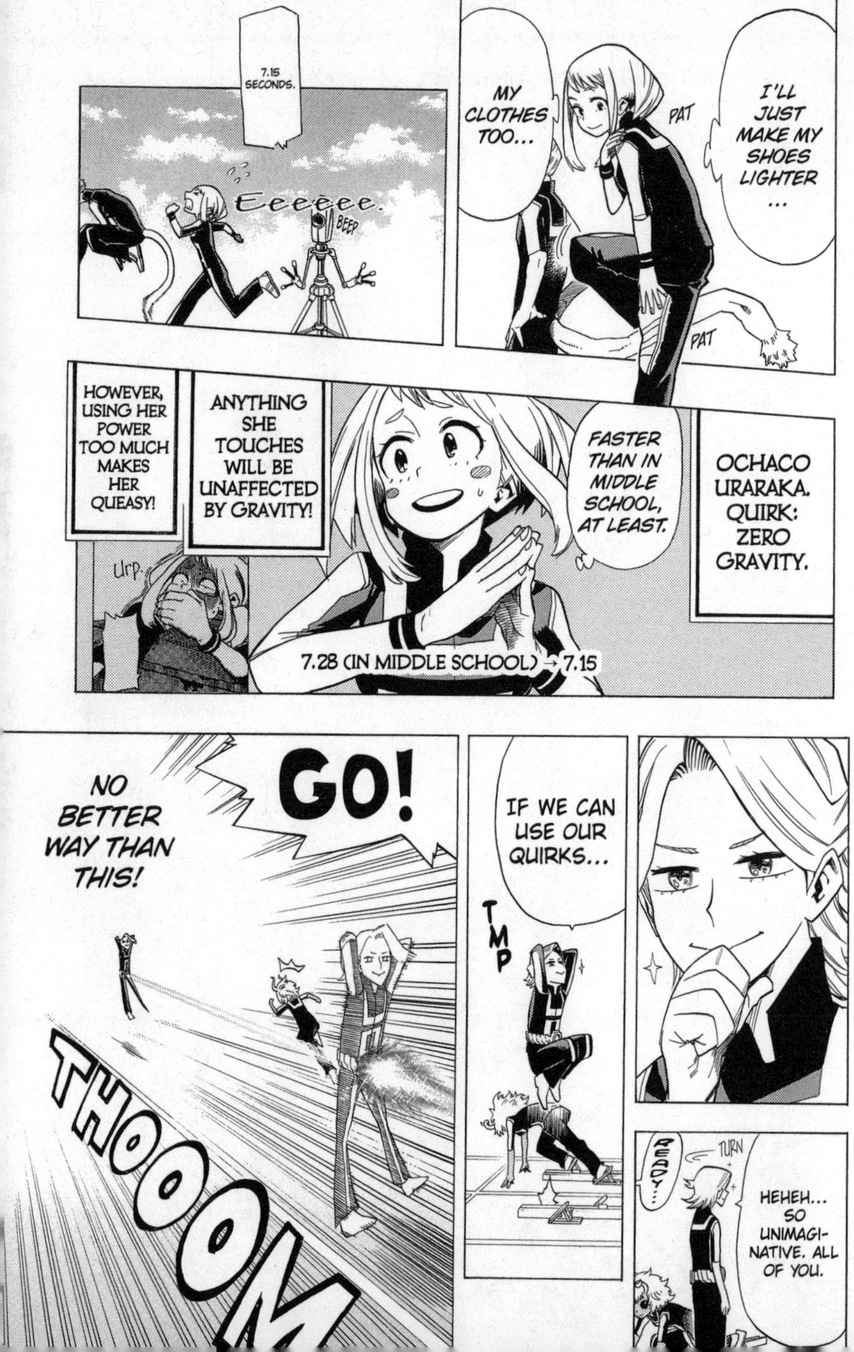
I'LL JUST MAKE MY SHOES LIGHTER ...
PAT
MY CLOTHES TOO...
PAT
7.15 SECONDS.
Eeeeee.
BEEP
OCHACO URARAKA. QUIRK: ZERO GRAVITY.
FASTER THAN IN MIDDLE SCHOOL, AT LEAST.
ANYTHING SHE TOUCHES WILL BE UNAFFECTED BY GRAVITY!
HOWEVER, USING HER POWER TOO MUCH MAKES HER QUEASY!
Urp.
7.28 (IN MIDDLE SCHOOL) → 7.15
HEHEH... SO UNIMAGI-NATIVE. ALL OF YOU.
TURN
READY...
IF WE CAN USE OUR QUIRKS...
TMP
GO!
NO BETTER WAY THAN THIS!
THOOOM

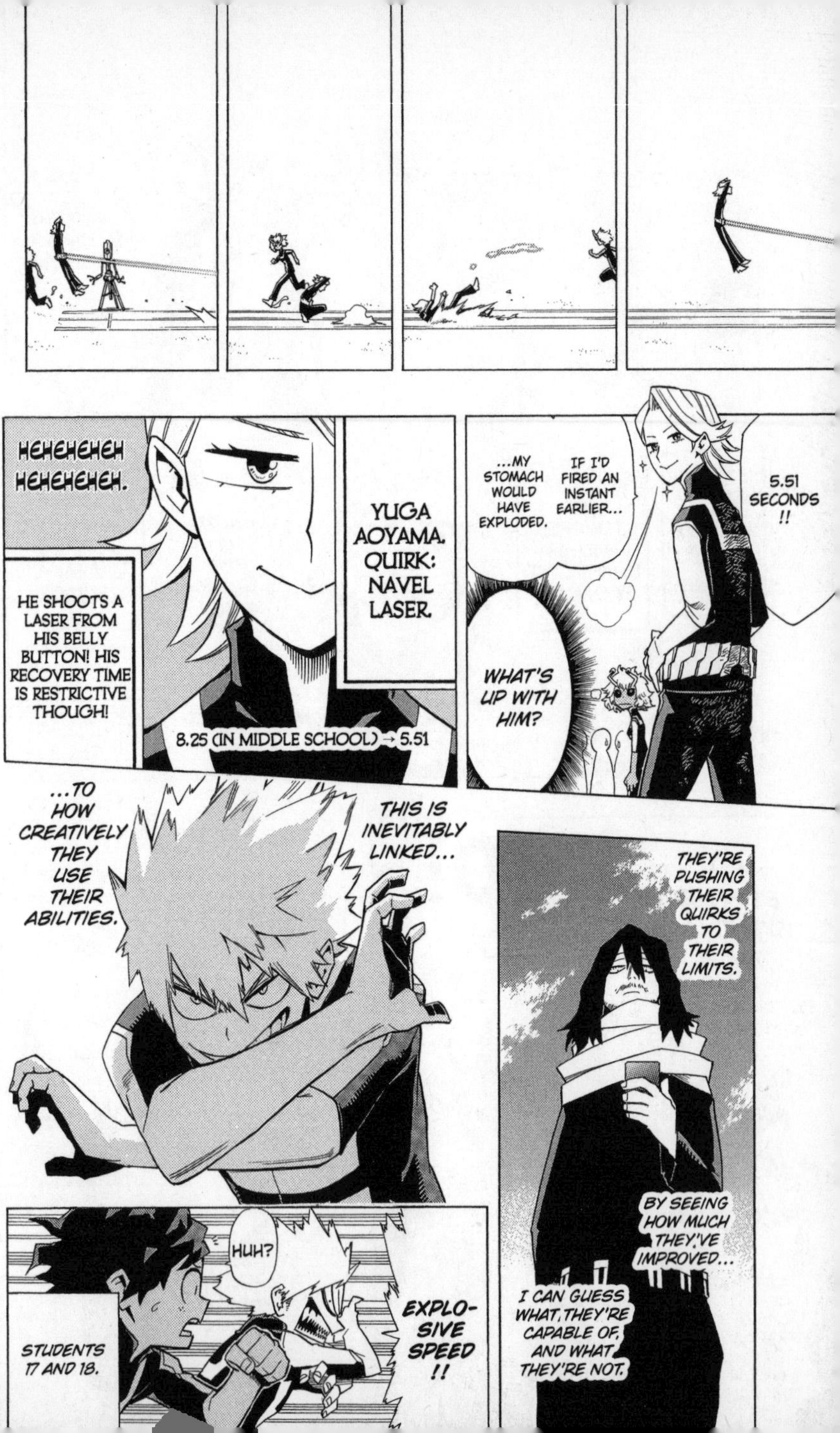
5.51 SECONDS !!
IF I'D FIRED AN INSTANT EARLIER...
...MY STOMACH WOULD HAVE EXPLODED.
WHAT'S UP WITH HIM?
YUGA AOYAMA. QUIRK: NAVEL LASER.
HEHEHEHEH HEHEHEHEH.
HE SHOOTS A LASER FROM HIS BELLY BUTTON! HIS RECOVERY TIME IS RESTRICTIVE THOUGH!
8.25 (IN MIDDLE SCHOOL) → 5.51
THEY'RE PUSHING THEIR QUIRKS TO THEIR LIMITS.
BY SEEING HOW MUCH THEY'VE IMPROVED...
I CAN GUESS WHAT THEY'RE CAPABLE OF, AND WHAT THEY'RE NOT.
THIS IS INEVITABLY LINKED...
...TO HOW CREATIVELY THEY USE THEIR ABILITIES.
HUH?
EXPLOSIVE SPEED !!
STUDENTS 17 AND 18.

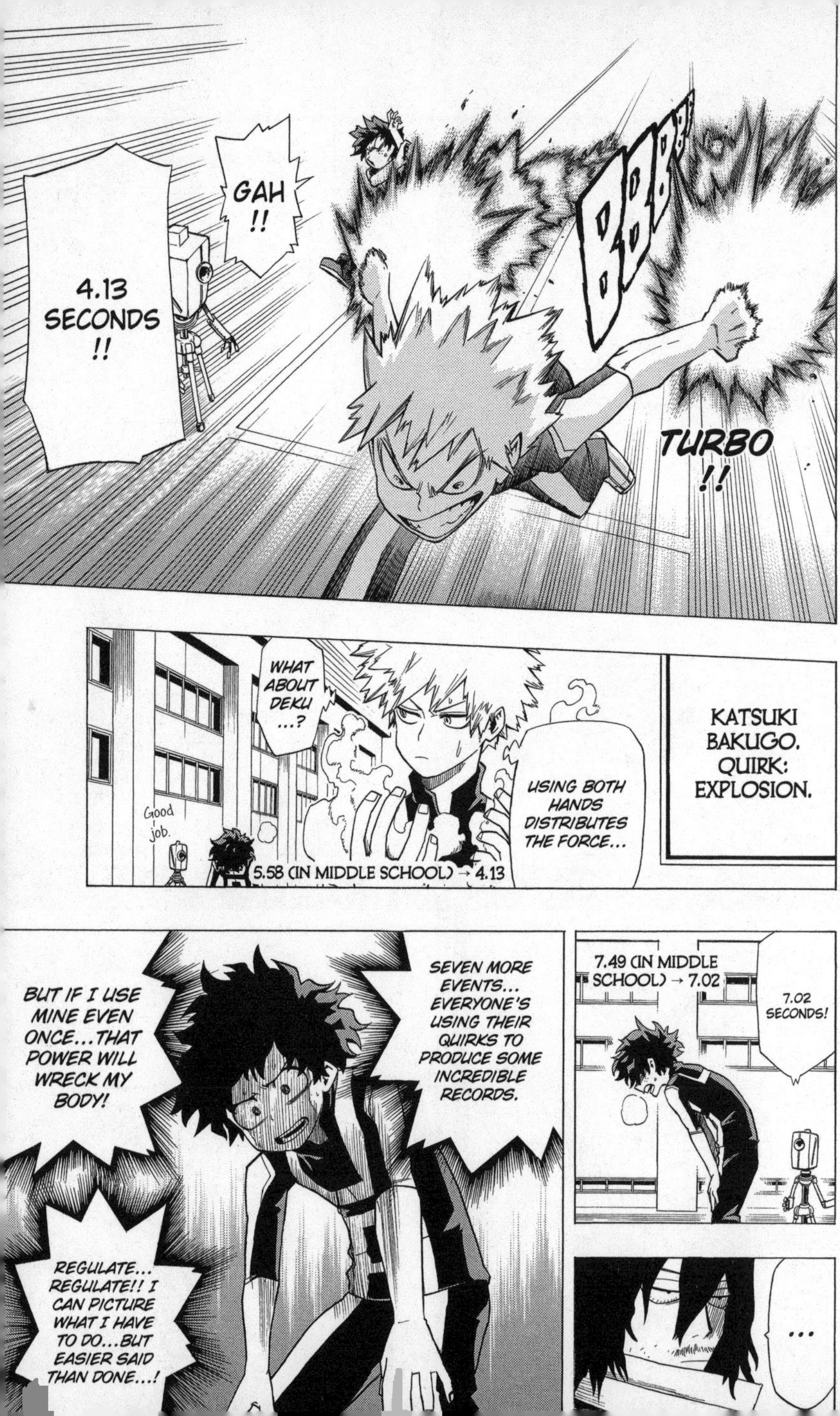
TURBO !!
GAH !!
4.13 SECONDS !!
KATSUKI BAKUGO. QUIRK: EXPLOSION.
USING BOTH HANDS DISTRIBUTES THE FORCE...
WHAT ABOUT DEKU ...?
Good job.
5.58 (IN MIDDLE SCHOOL) → 4.13
7.49 (IN MIDDLE SCHOOL) → 7.02
7.02 SECONDS!
...
SEVEN MORE EVENTS... EVERYONE'S USING THEIR QUIRKS TO PRODUCE SOME INCREDIBLE RECORDS.
BUT IF I USE MINE EVEN ONCE...THAT POWER WILL WRECK MY BODY!
REGULATE... REGULATE!! I CAN PICTURE WHAT I HAVE TO DO...BUT EASIER SAID THAN DONE...!

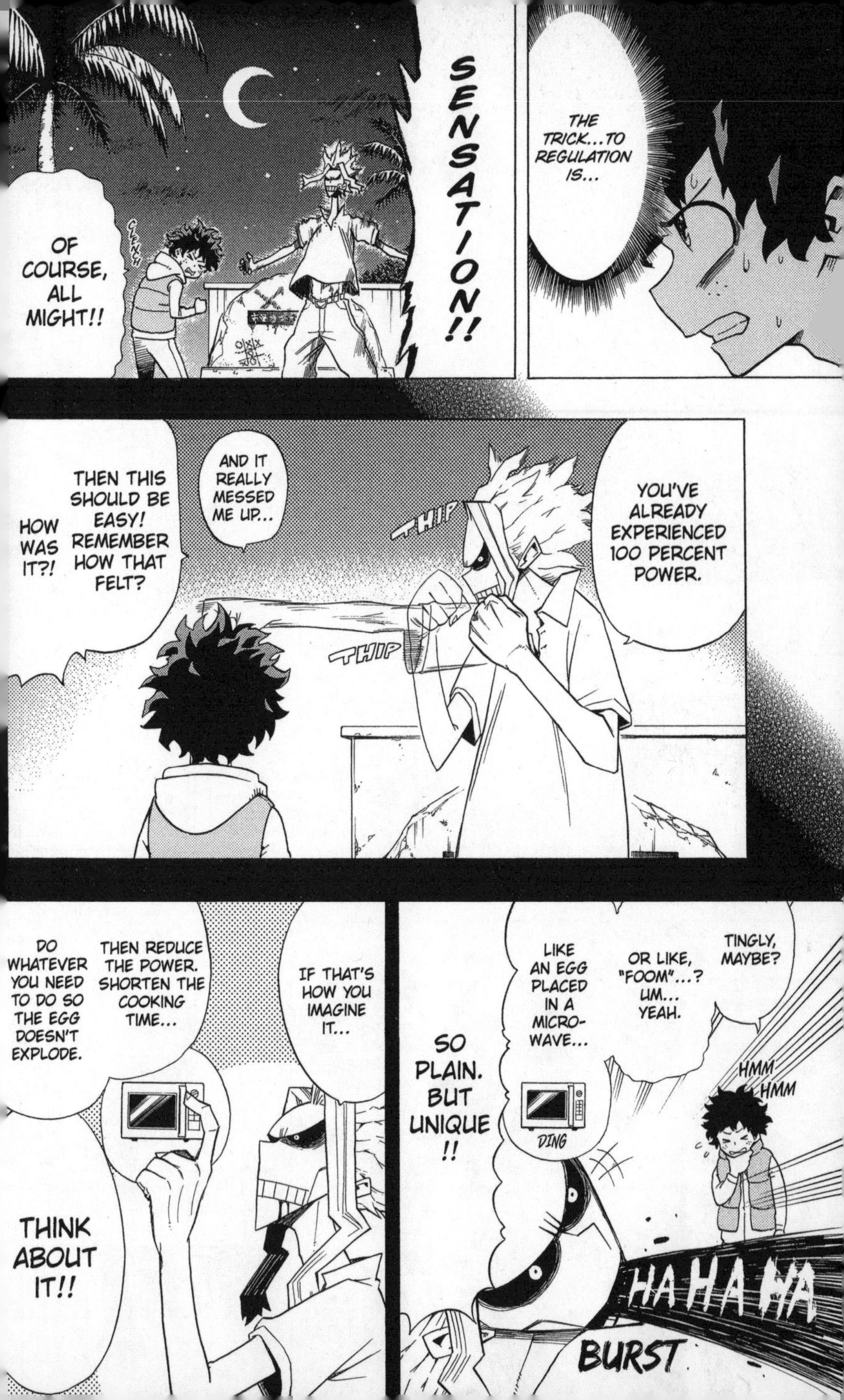
THE TRICK...TO REGULATION IS...
SENSATION!!
OF COURSE, ALL MIGHT!!
CLENCH
YOU'VE ALREADY EXPERIENCED 100 PERCENT POWER.
THIP
THIP
AND IT REALLY MESSED ME UP...
THEN THIS SHOULD BE EASY! REMEMBER HOW THAT FELT?
HOW WAS IT?!
TINGLY, MAYBE?
OR LIKE, "FOOM"...? UM... YEAH.
LIKE AN EGG PLACED IN A MICRO-WAVE...
DING
SO PLAIN. BUT UNIQUE!!
HMM HMM
HA HA HA
BURST
IF THAT'S HOW YOU IMAGINE IT...
THEN REDUCE THE POWER. SHORTEN THE COOKING TIME...
DO WHATEVER YOU NEED TO DO SO THE EGG DOESN'T EXPLODE.
THINK ABOUT IT!!

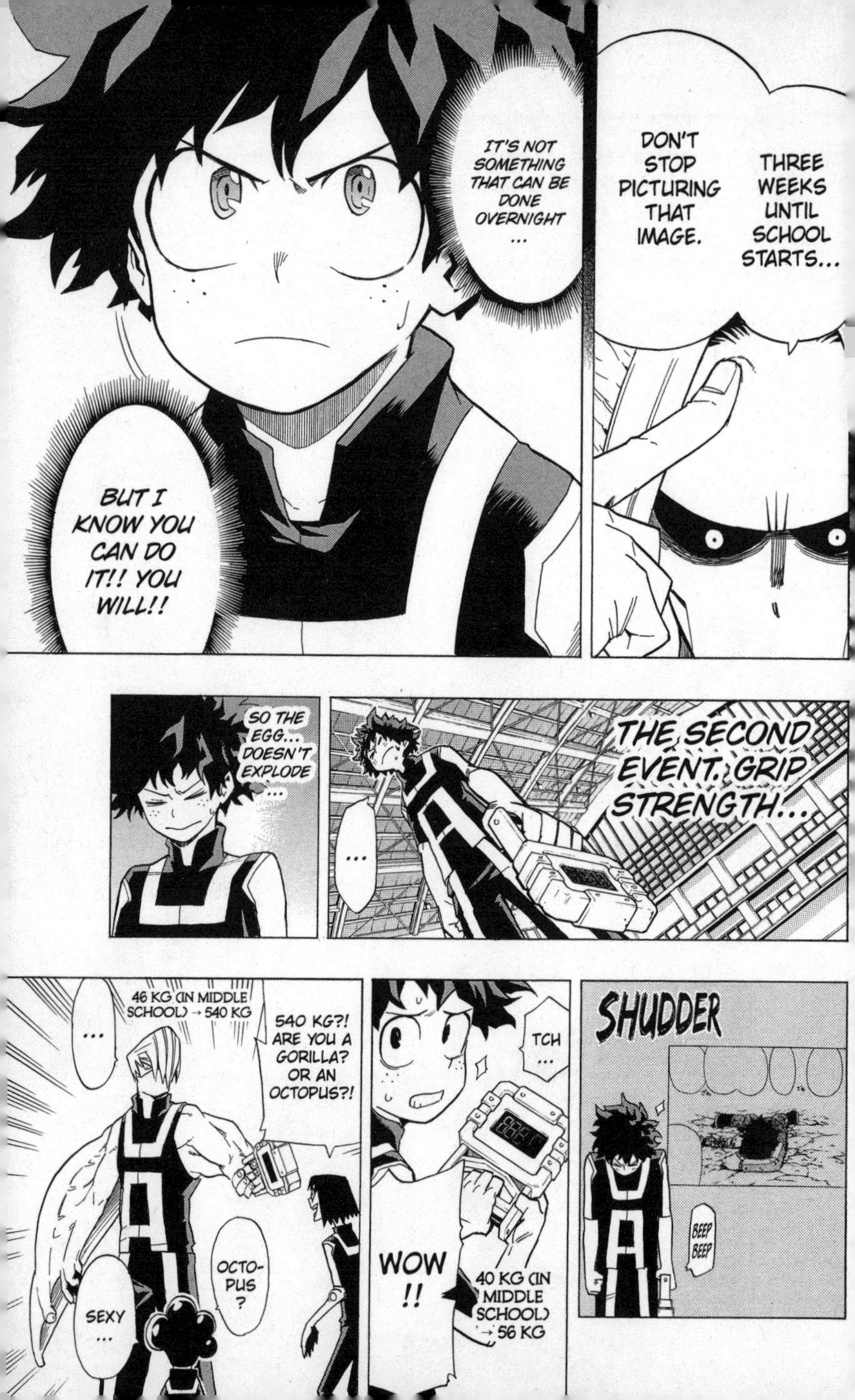
THREE WEEKS UNTIL SCHOOL STARTS...
DON'T STOP PICTURING THAT IMAGE.
IT'S NOT SOMETHING THAT CAN BE DONE OVERNIGHT...
BUT I KNOW YOU CAN DO IT!! YOU WILL!!
THE SECOND EVENT. GRIP STRENGTH...
...
SO THE EGG... DOESN'T EXPLODE...
SHUDDER
BEEP BEEP
TCH...
WOW!!
40 KG (IN MIDDLE SCHOOL) → 56 KG
540 KG?! ARE YOU A GORILLA? OR AN OCTOPUS?!
46 KG (IN MIDDLE SCHOOL) → 540 KG
...
OCTO-PUS?
SEXY...

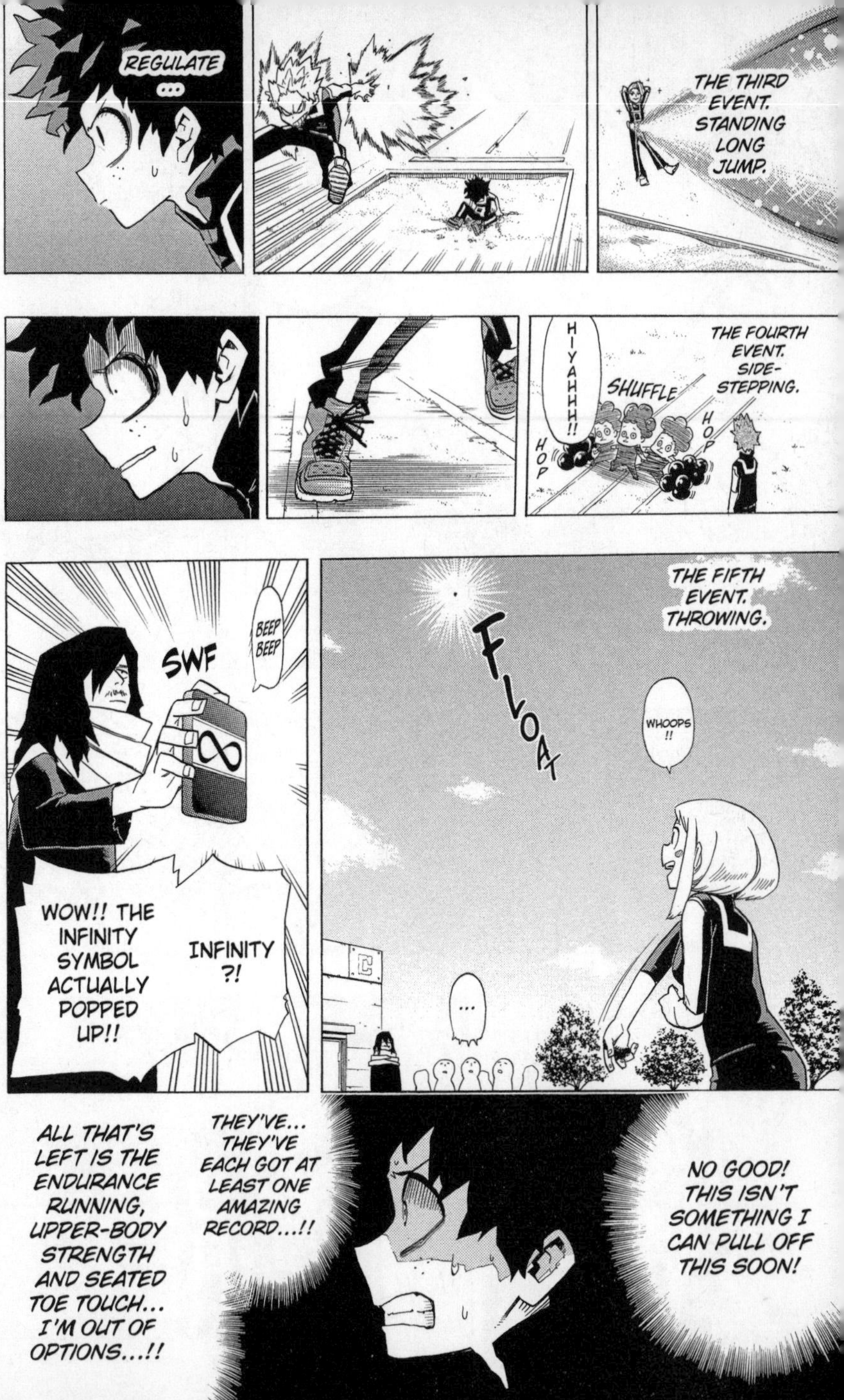
THE THIRD EVENT. STANDING LONG JUMP.
REGULATE ...
THE FOURTH EVENT. SIDE-STEPPING.
HOP
SHUFFLE
HOP
HIYAHHH!!
THE FIFTH EVENT. THROWING.
FLOAT
WHOOPS !!
...
BEEP BEEP
SWF
INFINITY ?!
WOW!! THE INFINITY SYMBOL ACTUALLY POPPED UP!!
NO GOOD! THIS ISN'T SOMETHING I CAN PULL OFF THIS SOON!
THEY'VE... THEY'VE EACH GOT AT LEAST ONE AMAZING RECORD...!!
ALL THAT'S LEFT IS THE ENDURANCE RUNNING, UPPER-BODY STRENGTH AND SEATED TOE TOUCH... I'M OUT OF OPTIONS...!!

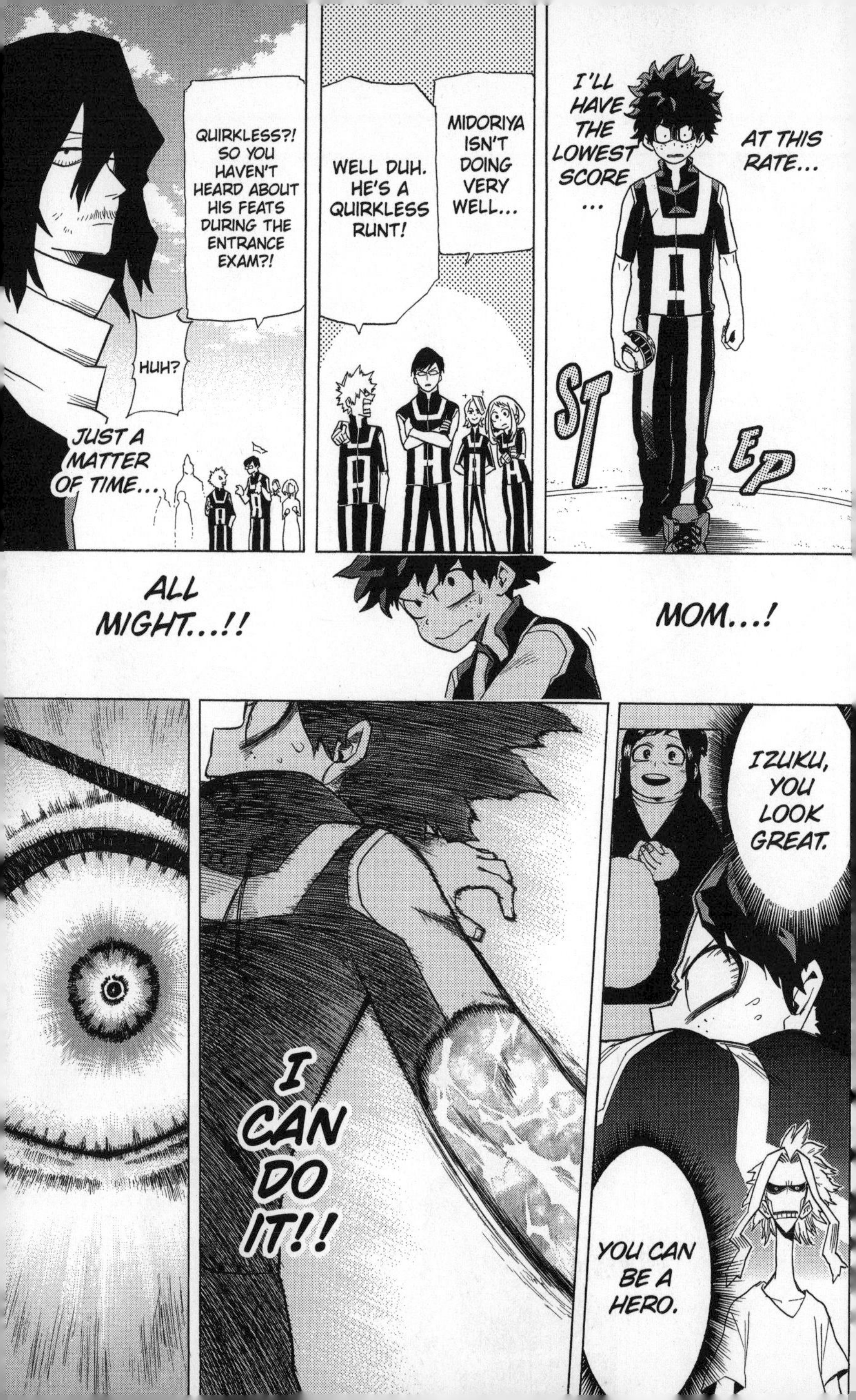
AT THIS RATE...
I'LL HAVE THE LOWEST SCORE...
ST
EP
MIDORIYA ISN'T DOING VERY WELL...
WELL DUH. HE'S A QUIRKLESS RUNT!
QUIRKLESS?! SO YOU HAVEN'T HEARD ABOUT HIS FEATS DURING THE ENTRANCE EXAM?!
HUH?
JUST A MATTER OF TIME...
MOM...!
ALL MIGHT...!!
IZUKU, YOU LOOK GREAT.
YOU CAN BE A HERO.
I CAN DO IT!!

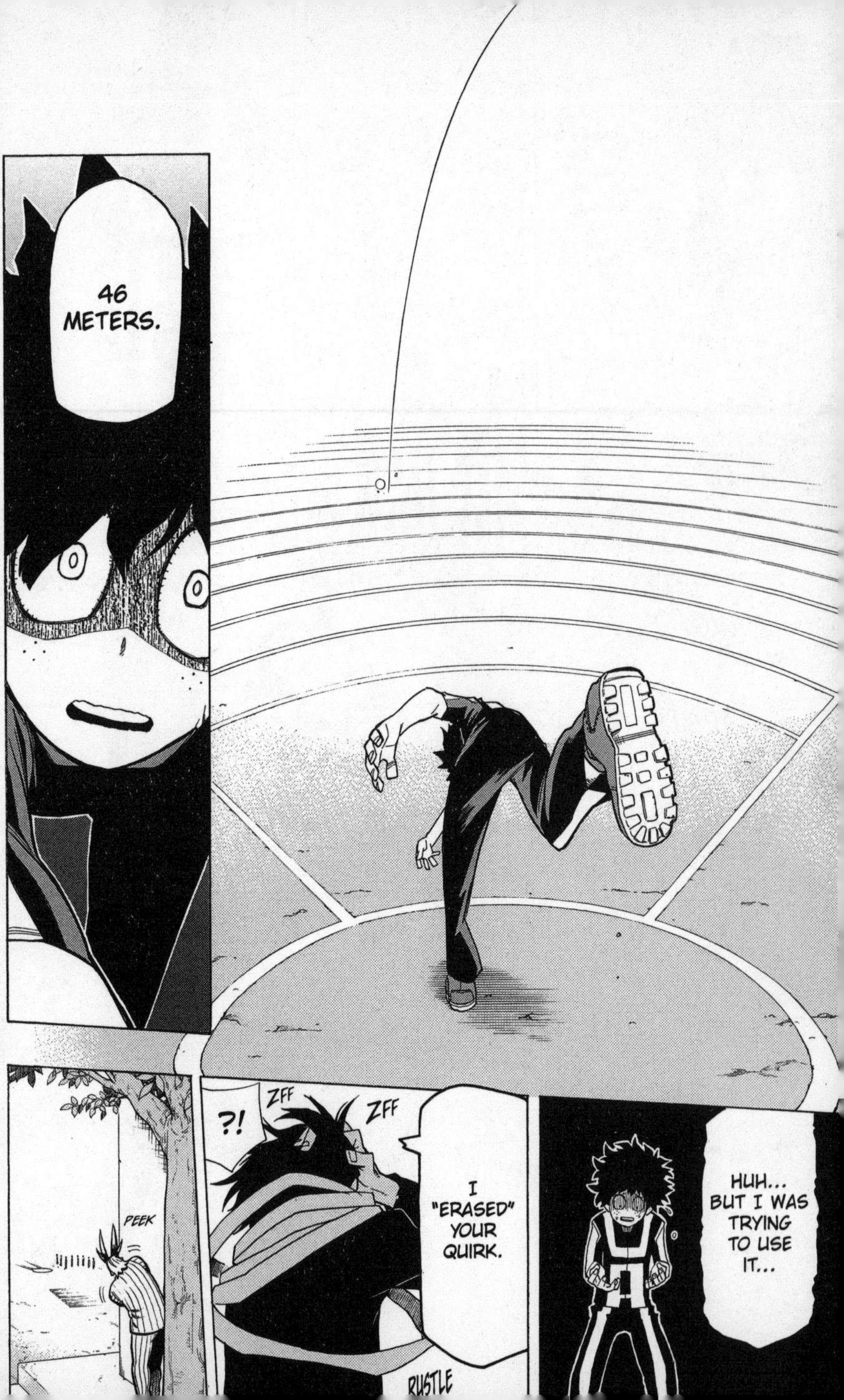
46
METERS.
HUH...
BUT I WAS
TRYING
TO USE
IT...
I
"ERASED"
YOUR
QUIRK.
ZFF
ZFF
?!
RUSTLE
PEEK

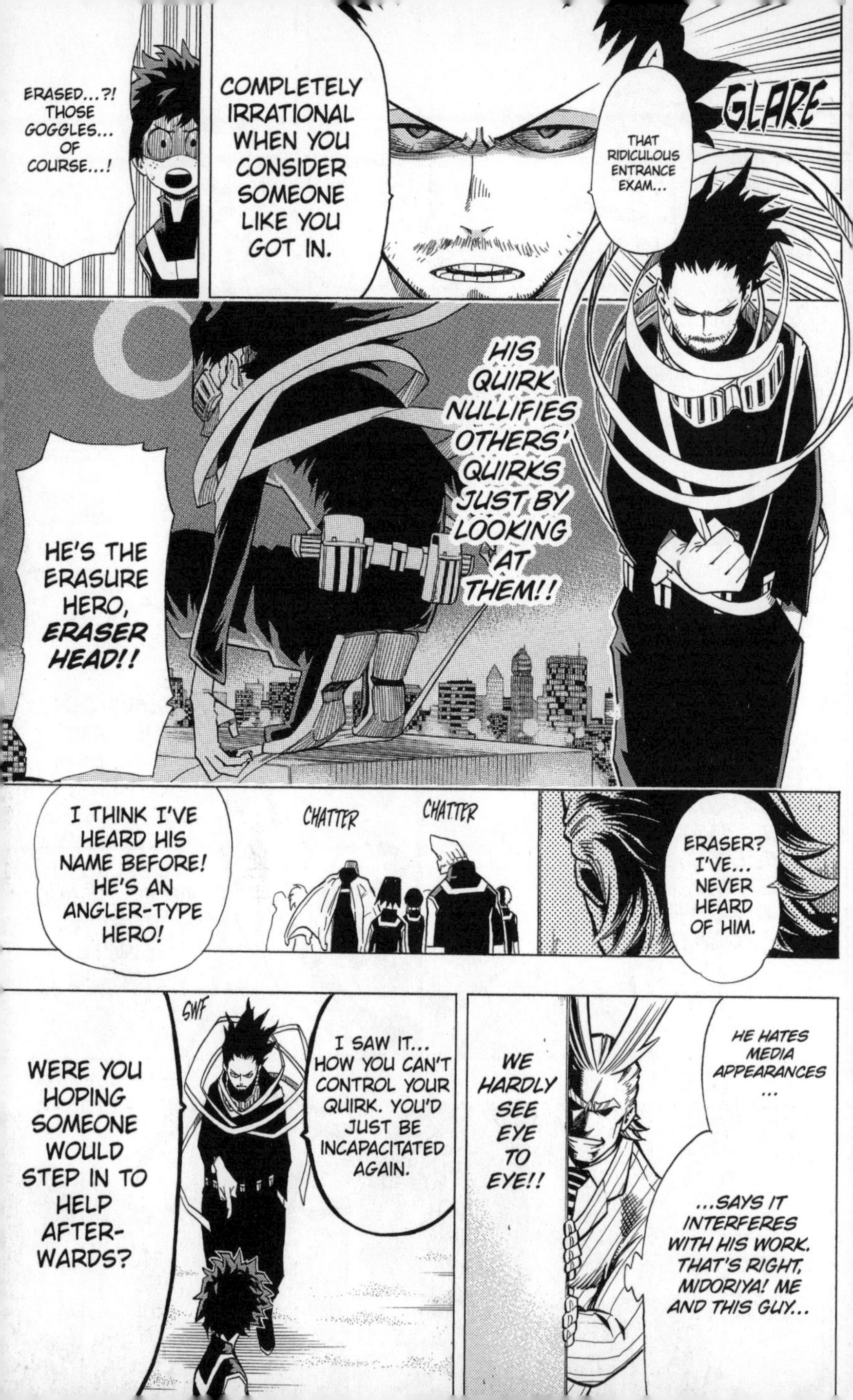
GLARE
THAT RIDICULOUS ENTRANCE EXAM...
COMPLETELY IRRATIONAL WHEN YOU CONSIDER SOMEONE LIKE YOU GOT IN.
ERASED...?! THOSE GOGGLES... OF COURSE...!
HIS QUIRK NULLIFIES OTHERS' QUIRKS JUST BY LOOKING AT THEM!!
HE'S THE ERASURE HERO, ERASER HEAD!!
ERASER? I'VE... NEVER HEARD OF HIM.
CHATTER
CHATTER
I THINK I'VE HEARD HIS NAME BEFORE! HE'S AN ANGLER-TYPE HERO!
HE HATES MEDIA APPEARANCES ...
WE HARDLY SEE EYE TO EYE!!
...SAYS IT INTERFERES WITH HIS WORK. THAT'S RIGHT, MIDORIYA! ME AND THIS GUY...
I SAW IT... HOW YOU CAN'T CONTROL YOUR QUIRK. YOU'D JUST BE INCAPACITATED AGAIN.
SWF
WERE YOU HOPING SOMEONE WOULD STEP IN TO HELP AFTER-WARDS?

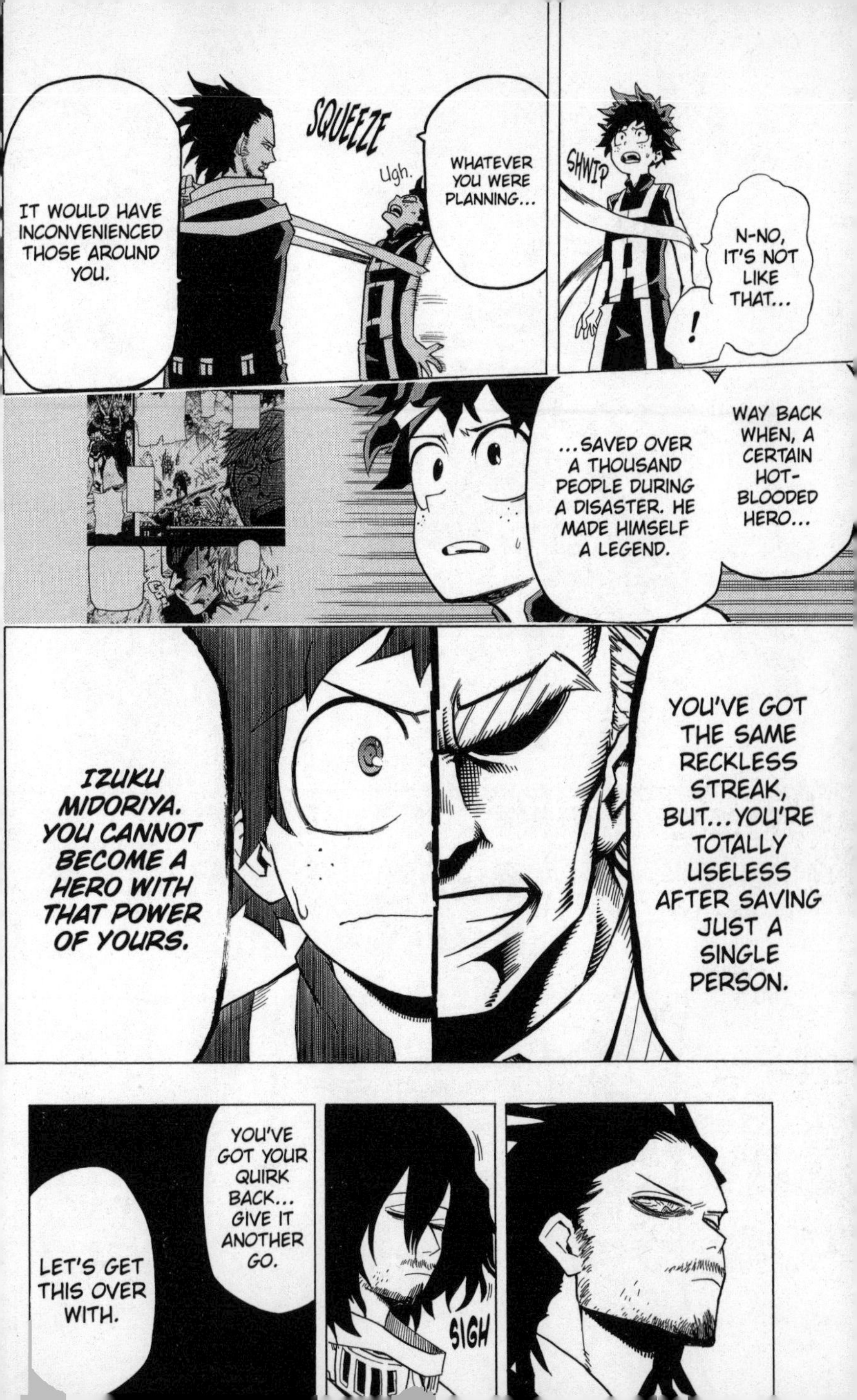
N-NO, IT'S NOT LIKE THAT...
!
SHWIP
WHATEVER YOU WERE PLANNING...
Ugh.
SQUEEZE
IT WOULD HAVE INCONVENIENCED THOSE AROUND YOU.
WAY BACK WHEN, A CERTAIN HOT-BLOODED HERO...
...SAVED OVER A THOUSAND PEOPLE DURING A DISASTER. HE MADE HIMSELF A LEGEND.
YOU'VE GOT THE SAME RECKLESS STREAK, BUT...YOU'RE TOTALLY USELESS AFTER SAVING JUST A SINGLE PERSON.
IZUKU MIDORIYA. YOU CANNOT BECOME A HERO WITH THAT POWER OF YOURS.
SIGH
YOU'VE GOT YOUR QUIRK BACK... GIVE IT ANOTHER GO.
LET'S GET THIS OVER WITH.

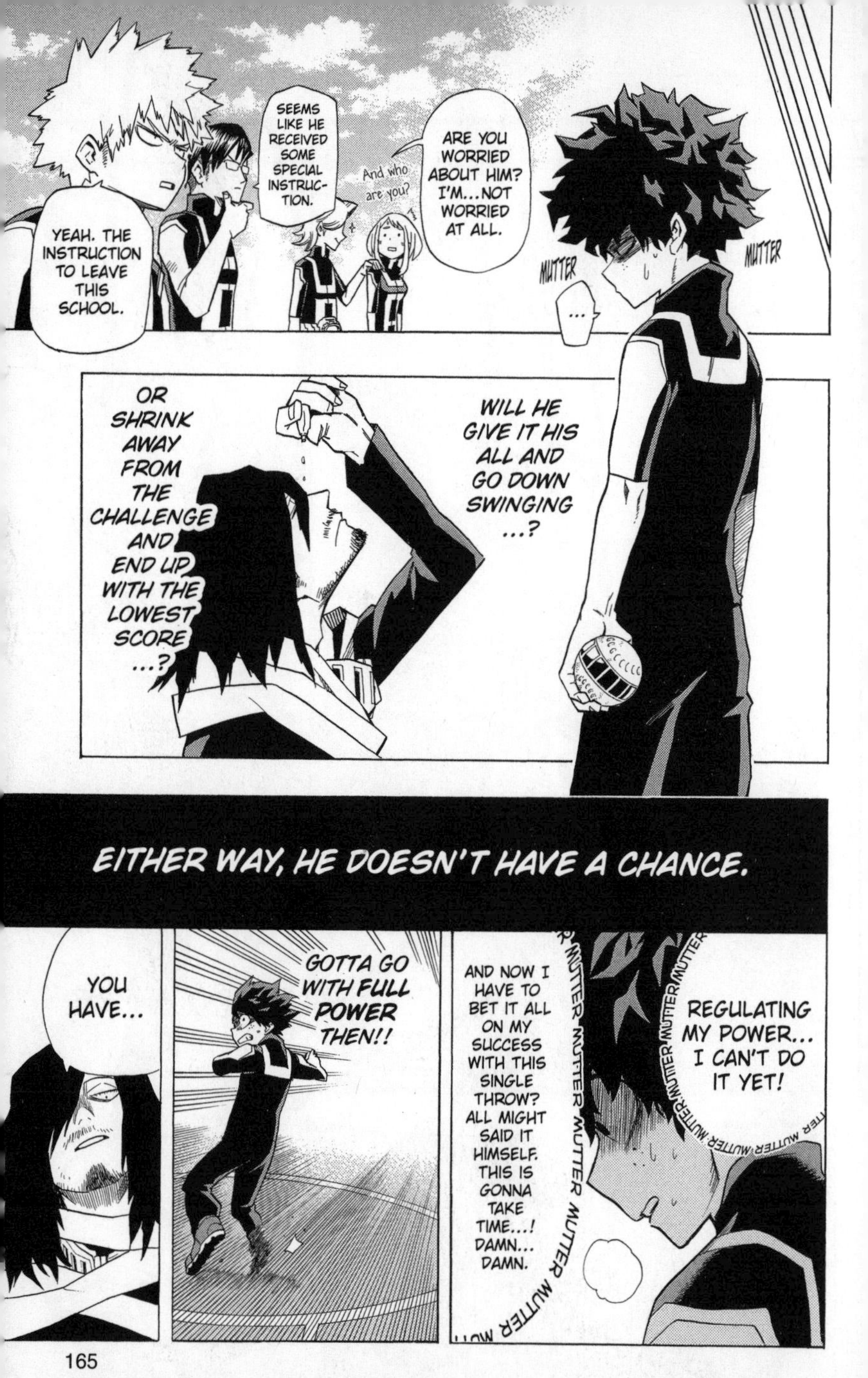
MUTTER
MUTTER
...
ARE YOU WORRIED ABOUT HIM? I'M...NOT WORRIED AT ALL.
And who are you?
SEEMS LIKE HE RECEIVED SOME SPECIAL INSTRUC-TION.
YEAH. THE INSTRUCTION TO LEAVE THIS SCHOOL.
WILL HE GIVE IT HIS ALL AND GO DOWN SWINGING ...?
OR SHRINK AWAY FROM THE CHALLENGE AND END UP WITH THE LOWEST SCORE ...?
EITHER WAY, HE DOESN'T HAVE A CHANCE.
REGULATING MY POWER... I CAN'T DO IT YET!
AND NOW I HAVE TO BET IT ALL ON MY SUCCESS WITH THIS SINGLE THROW? ALL MIGHT SAID IT HIMSELF. THIS IS GONNA TAKE TIME...! DAMN... DAMN.
MUTTER MUTTER MUTTER MUTTER MUTTER MUTTER MUTTER MUTTER
GOTTA GO WITH FULL POWER THEN!!
YOU HAVE...

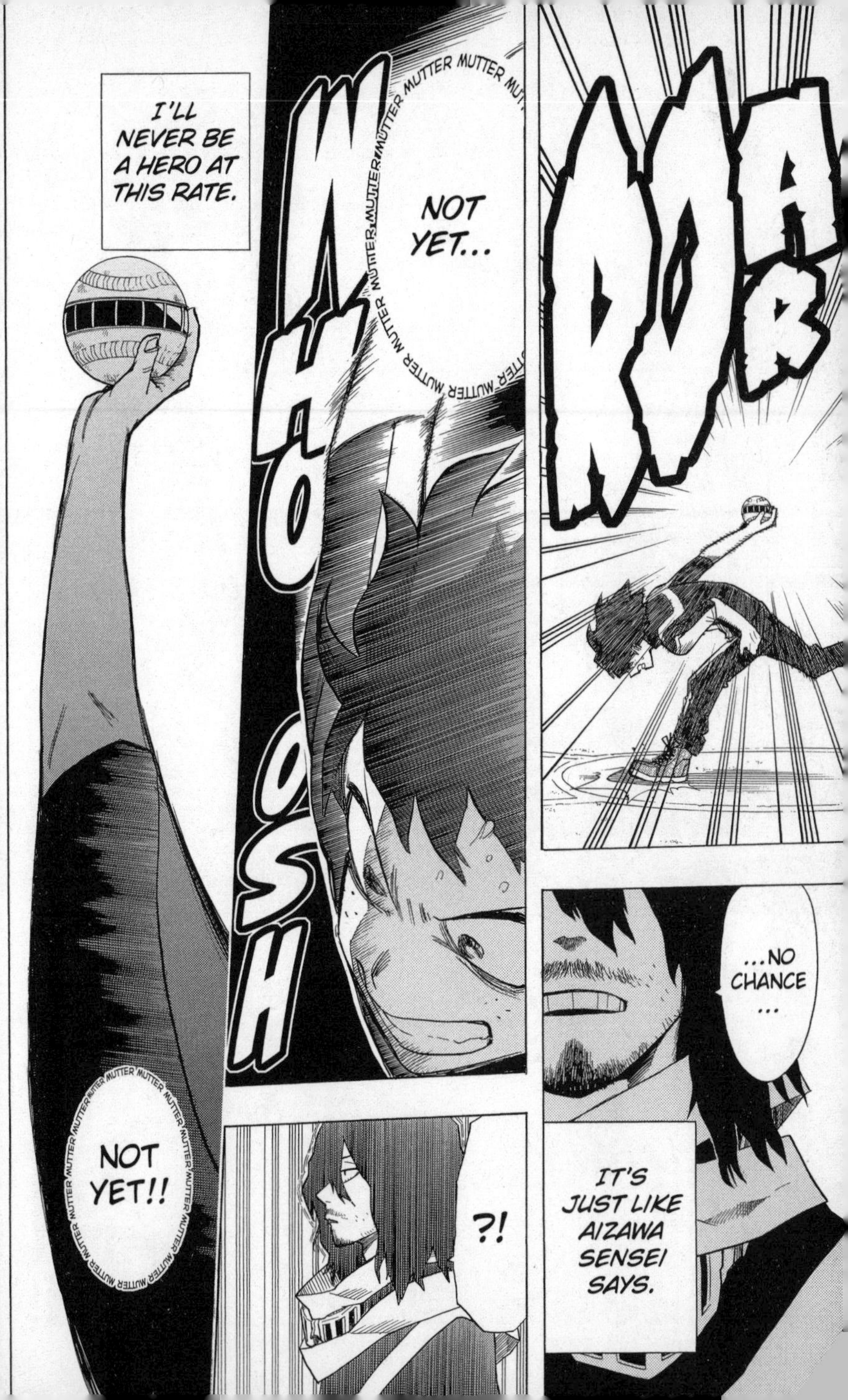
ROAR
...NO CHANCE ...
IT'S JUST LIKE AIZAWA SENSEI SAYS.
WHOOSH
MUTTER MUTTER MUTTER MUTTER MUTTER MUTTER
NOT YET...
?!
I'LL NEVER BE A HERO AT THIS RATE.
MUTTER MUTTER MUTTER MUTTER MUTTER MUTTER
NOT YET!!

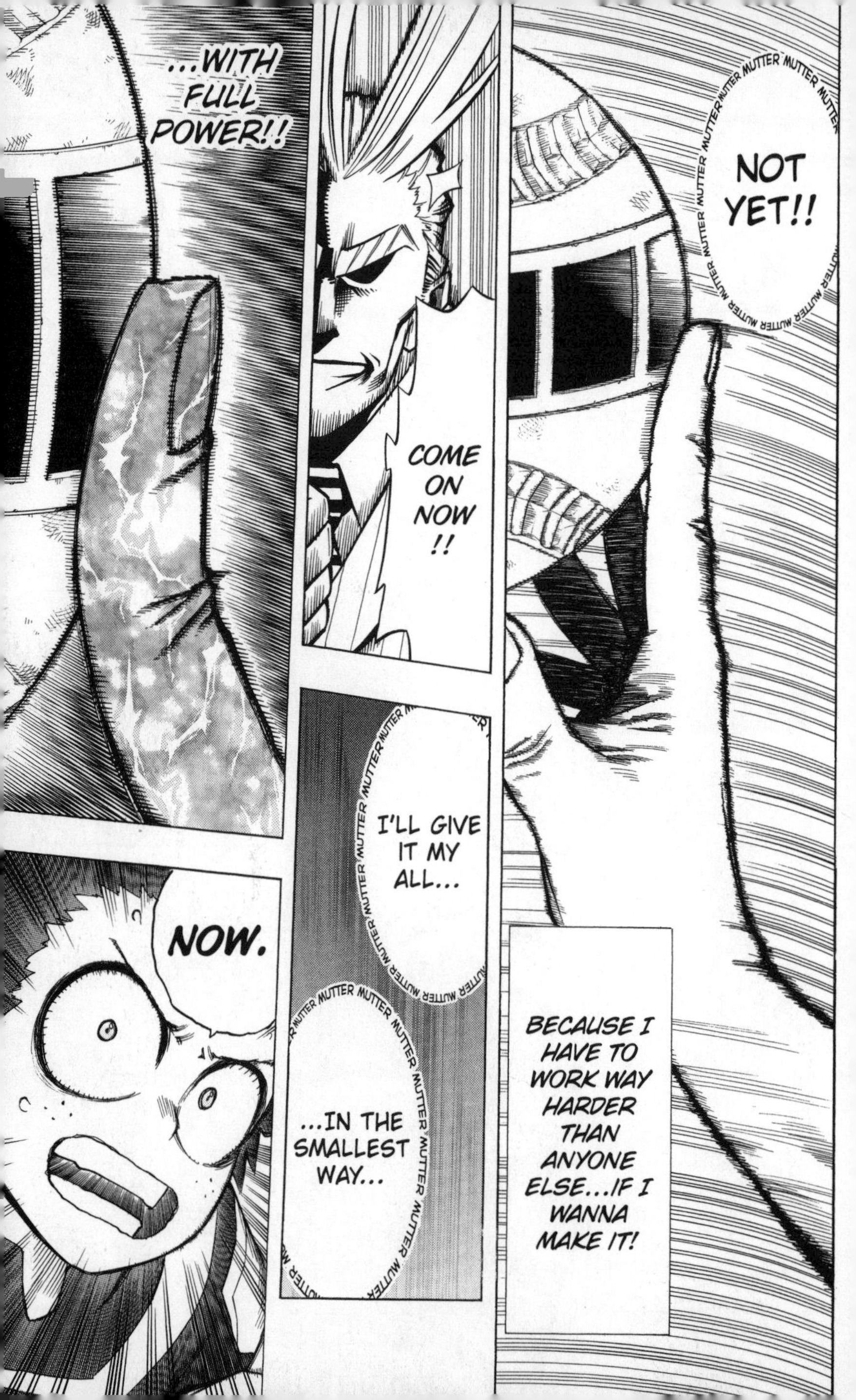
NOT YET!!
BECAUSE I HAVE TO WORK WAY HARDER THAN ANYONE ELSE...IF I WANNA MAKE IT!
COME ON NOW !!
I'LL GIVE IT MY ALL...
...IN THE SMALLEST WAY...
...WITH FULL POWER!!
NOW.

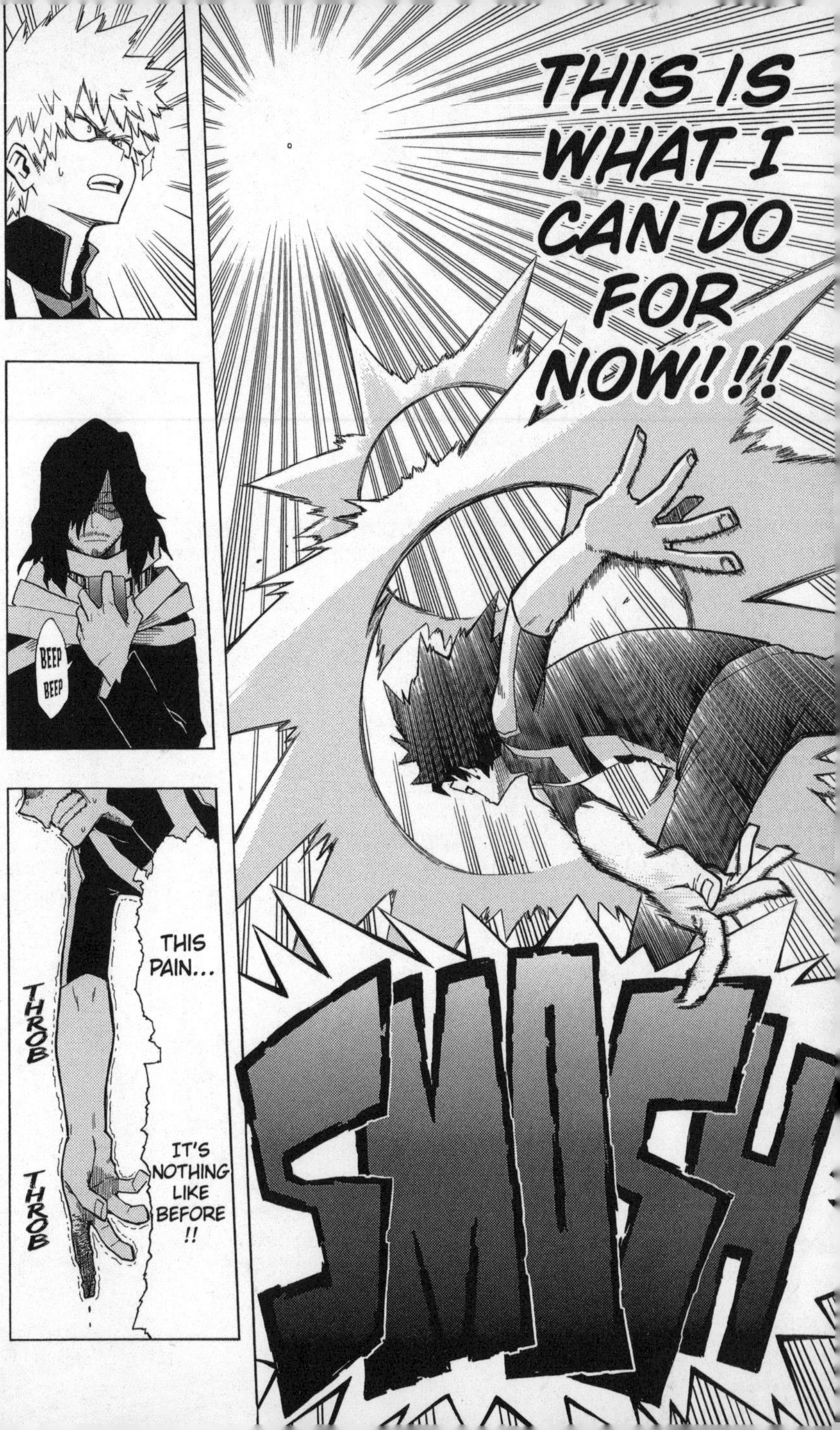
THIS IS WHAT I CAN DO FOR NOW!!!
SMASH
BEEP BEEP
THIS PAIN...
THROB
THROB
IT'S NOTHING LIKE BEFORE!!

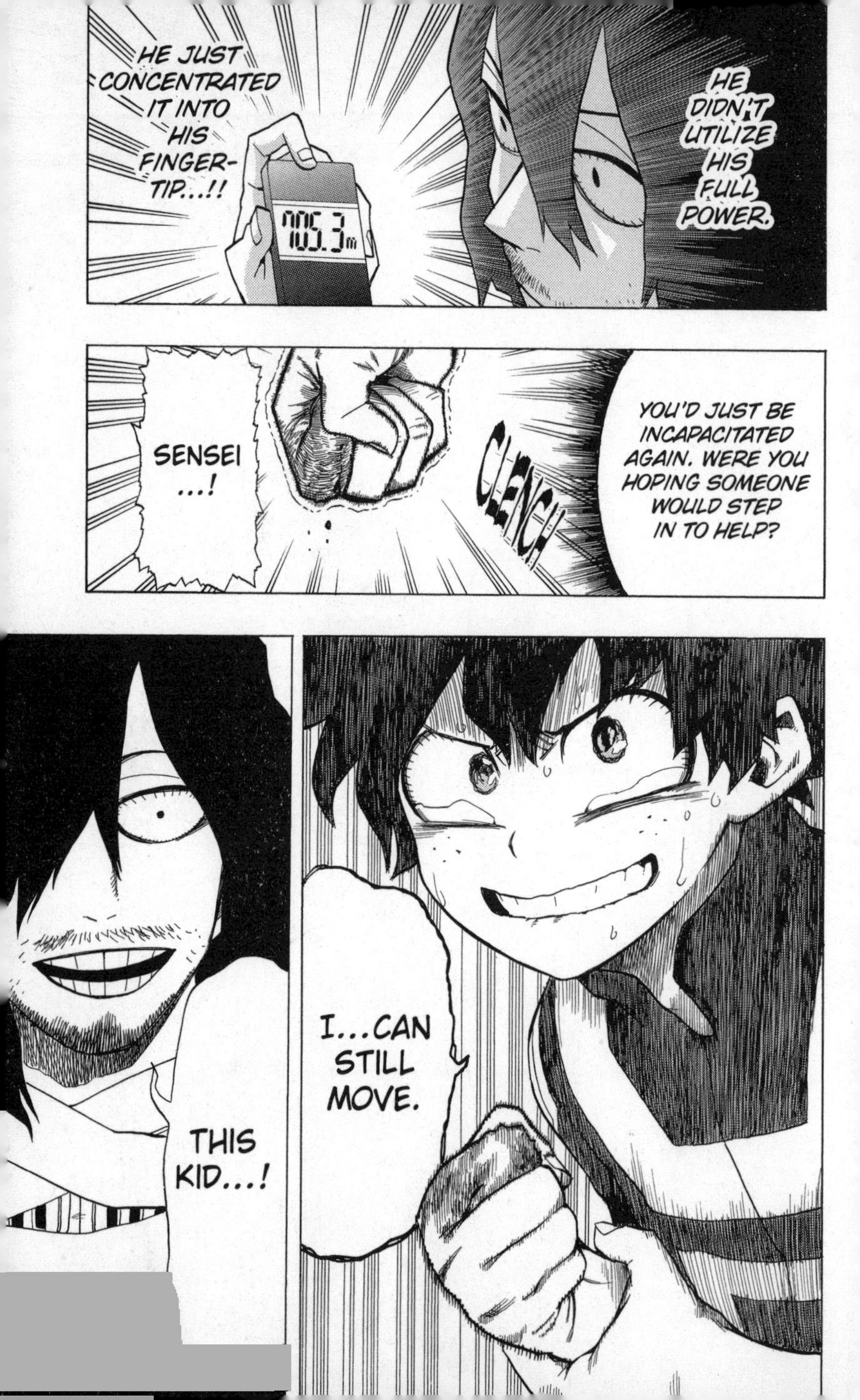
HE DIDN'T UTILIZE HIS FULL POWER.
HE JUST CONCENTRATED IT INTO HIS FINGER-TIP...!!
705.3m
YOU'D JUST BE INCAPACITATED AGAIN. WERE YOU HOPING SOMEONE WOULD STEP IN TO HELP?
CLENCH
SENSEI ...!
I...CAN STILL MOVE.
THIS KID...!

SHOTA AIZAWA [AGE:30]
(ERASER HEAD)

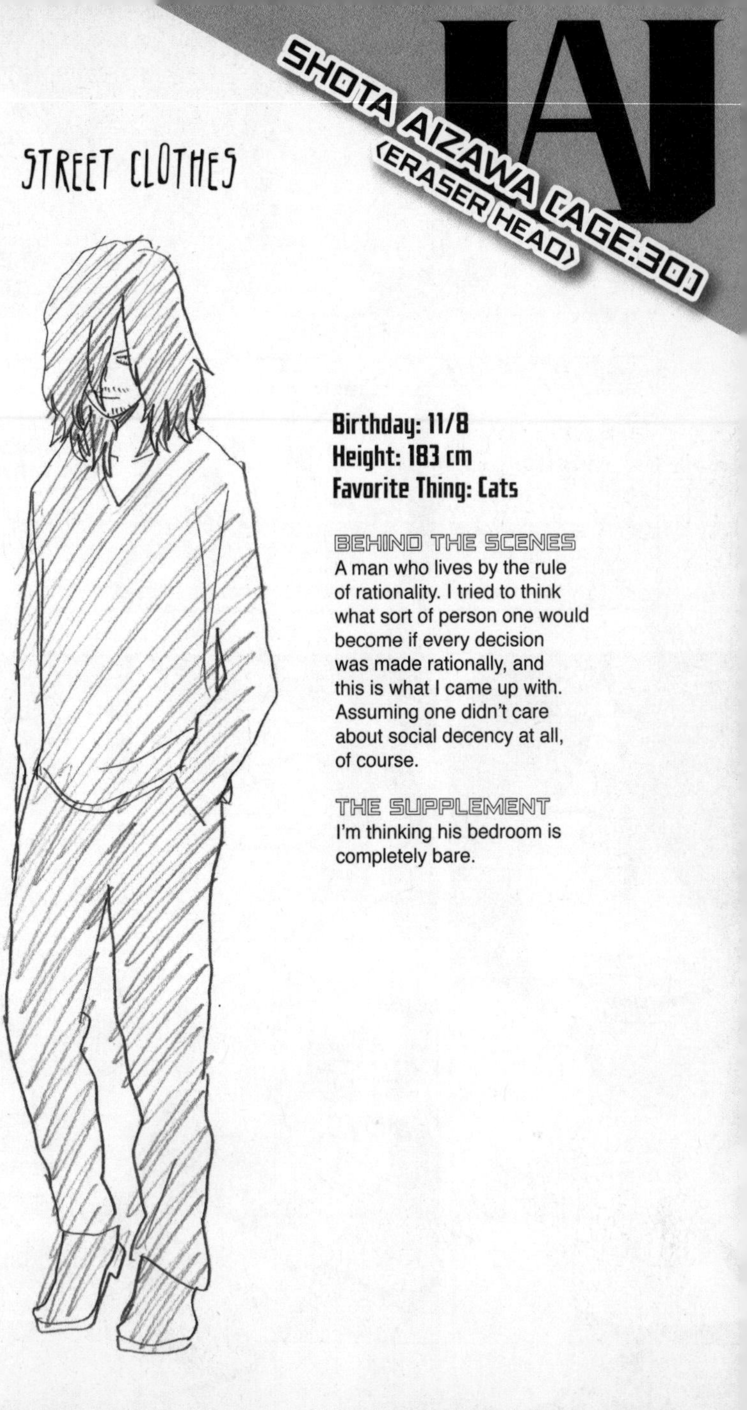
STREET CLOTHES

Birthday: 11/8
Height: 183 cm
Favorite Thing: Cats

BEHIND THE SCENES

A man who lives by the rule of rationality. I tried to think what sort of person one would become if every decision was made rationally, and this is what I came up with. Assuming one didn't care about social decency at all, of course.

THE SUPPLEMENT

I'm thinking his bedroom is completely bare.

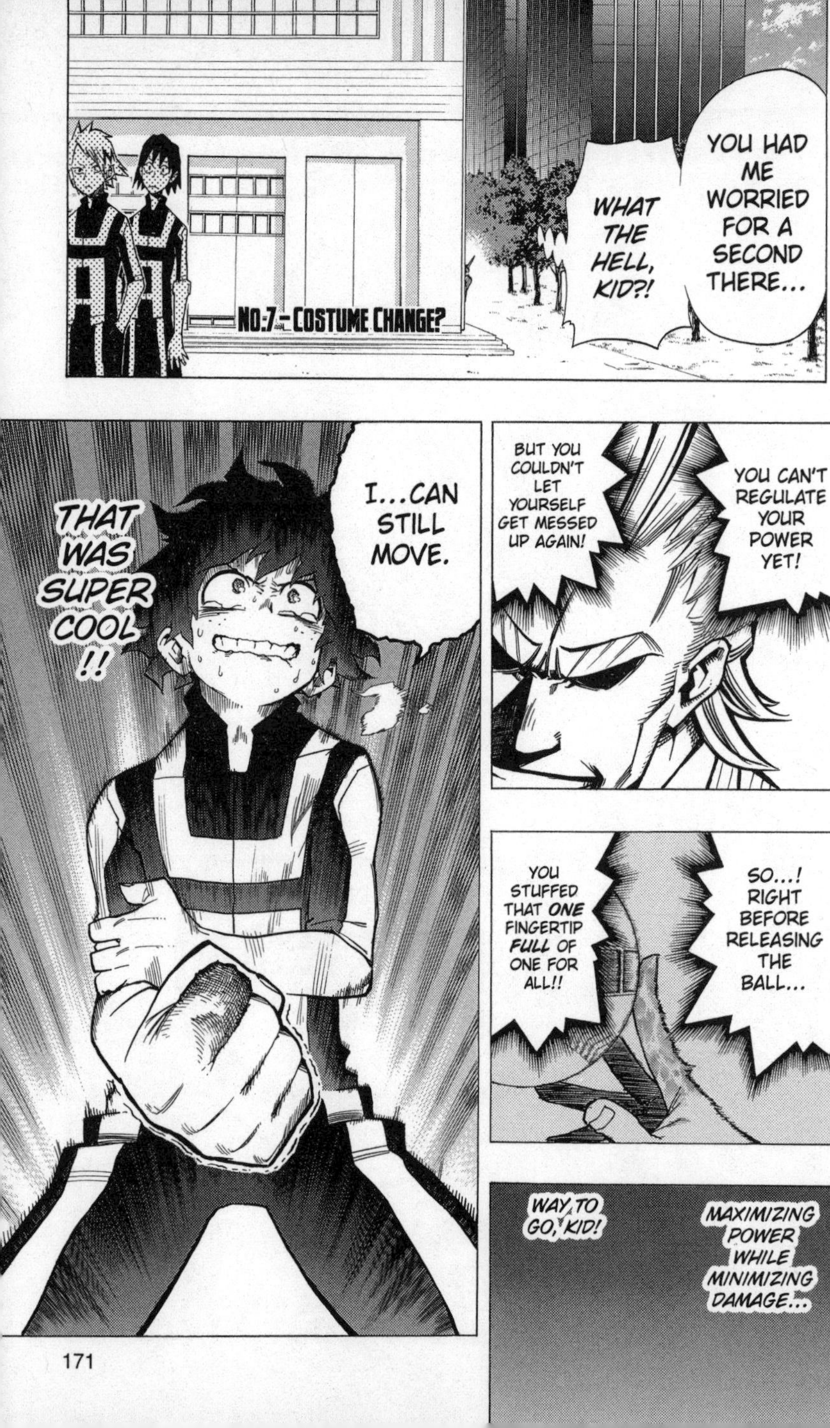
No.7 – Costume Change?
YOU HAD ME WORRIED FOR A SECOND THERE...
WHAT THE HELL, KID?!
YOU CAN'T REGULATE YOUR POWER YET!
BUT YOU COULDN'T LET YOURSELF GET MESSED UP AGAIN!
SO...! RIGHT BEFORE RELEASING THE BALL...
YOU STUFFED THAT ONE FINGERTIP FULL OF ONE FOR ALL!!
MAXIMIZING POWER WHILE MINIMIZING DAMAGE...
WAY, TO GO, KID!
I...CAN STILL MOVE.
THAT WAS SUPER COOL!!

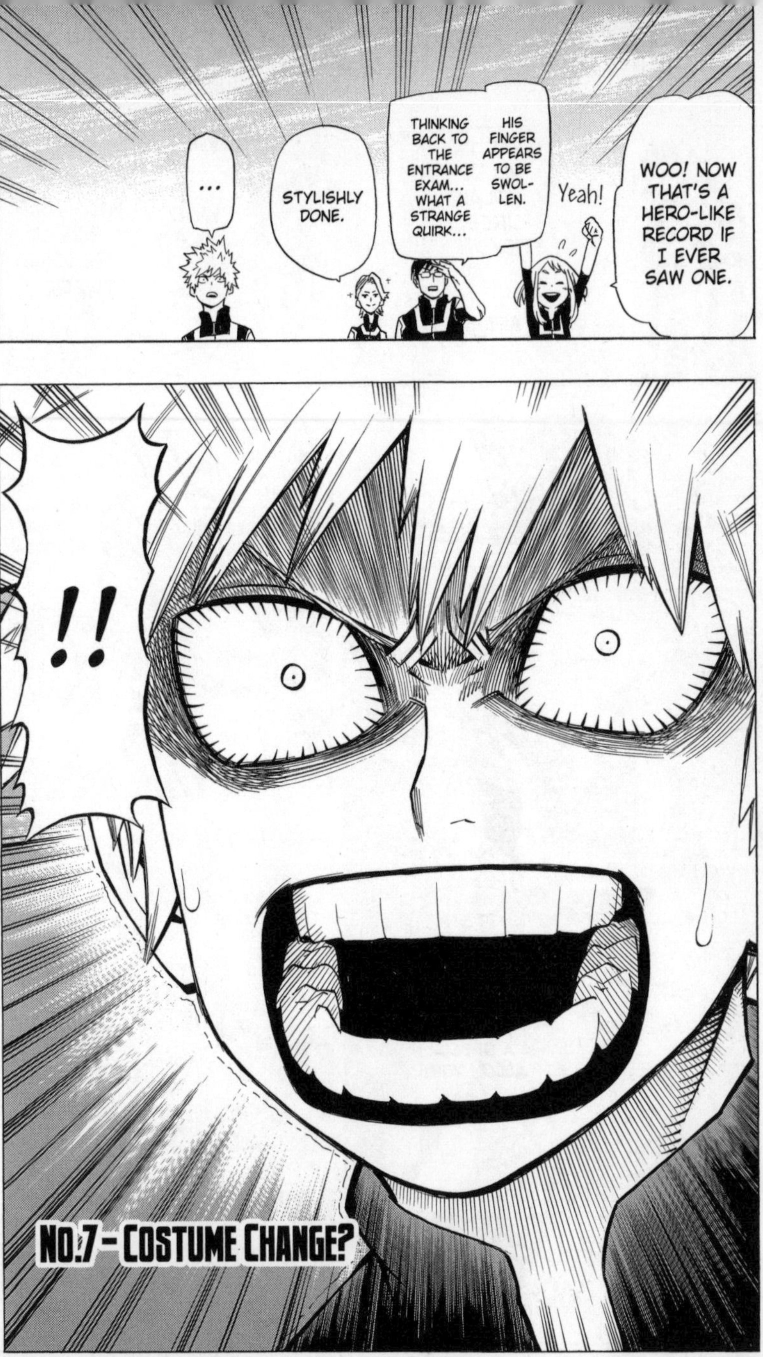
WOO! NOW THAT'S A HERO-LIKE RECORD IF I EVER SAW ONE.
Yeah!
HIS FINGER APPEARS TO BE SWOL-LEN.
THINKING BACK TO THE ENTRANCE EXAM... WHAT A STRANGE QUIRK...
STYLISHLY DONE.
...
!!
NO.7 - COSTUME CHANGE?

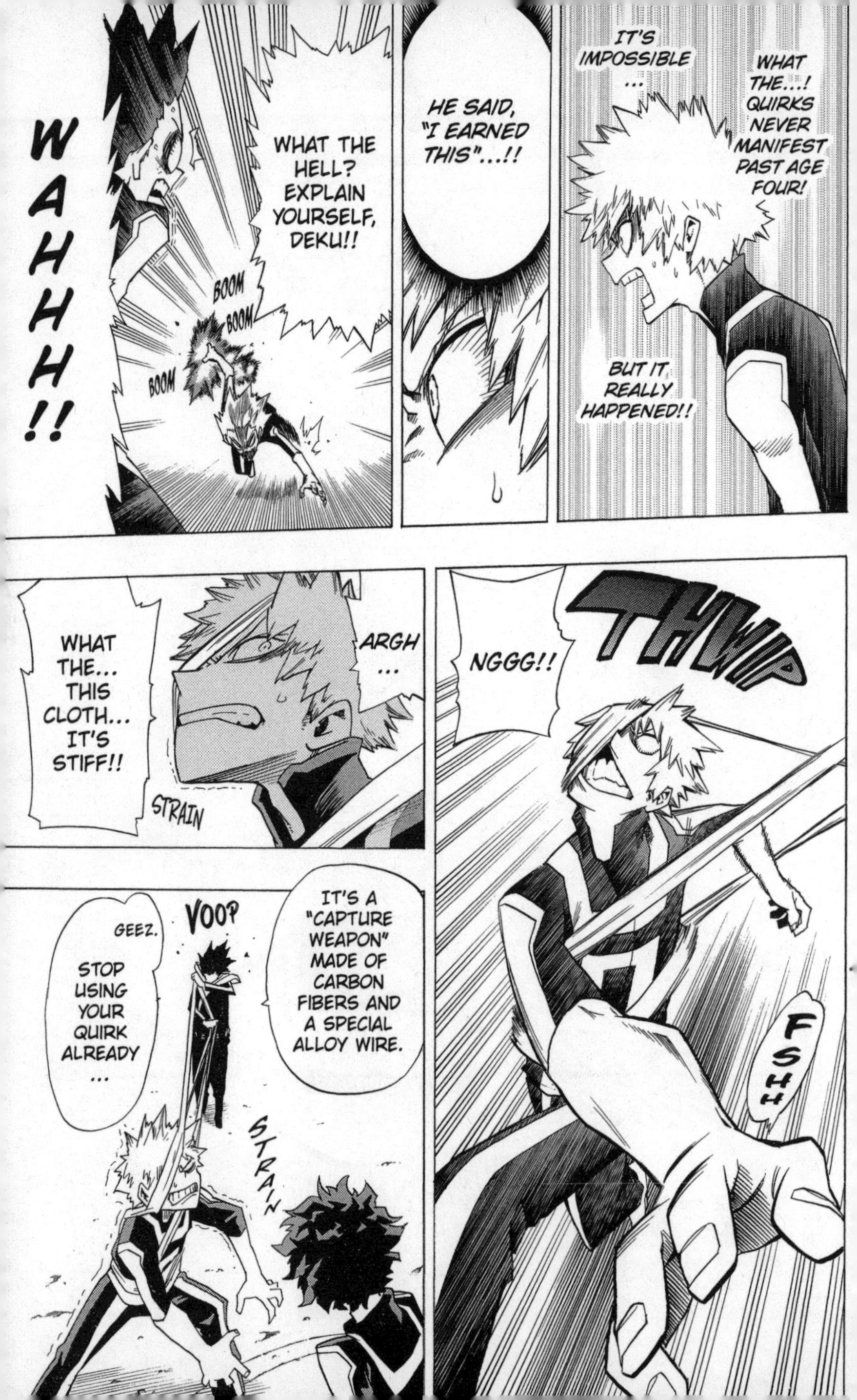
WHAT THE...! QUIRKS NEVER MANIFEST PAST AGE FOUR!
IT'S IMPOSSIBLE ...
BUT IT REALLY HAPPENED!!
HE SAID, "I EARNED THIS"...!!
WHAT THE HELL? EXPLAIN YOURSELF, DEKU!!
BOOM
BOOM
BOOM
WAHHHH!!
THWIP
NGGG!!
FSHH
ARGH ...
WHAT THE... THIS CLOTH... IT'S STIFF!!
STRAIN
IT'S A "CAPTURE WEAPON" MADE OF CARBON FIBERS AND A SPECIAL ALLOY WIRE.
VOOP
GEEZ.
STOP USING YOUR QUIRK ALREADY ...
STRAIN

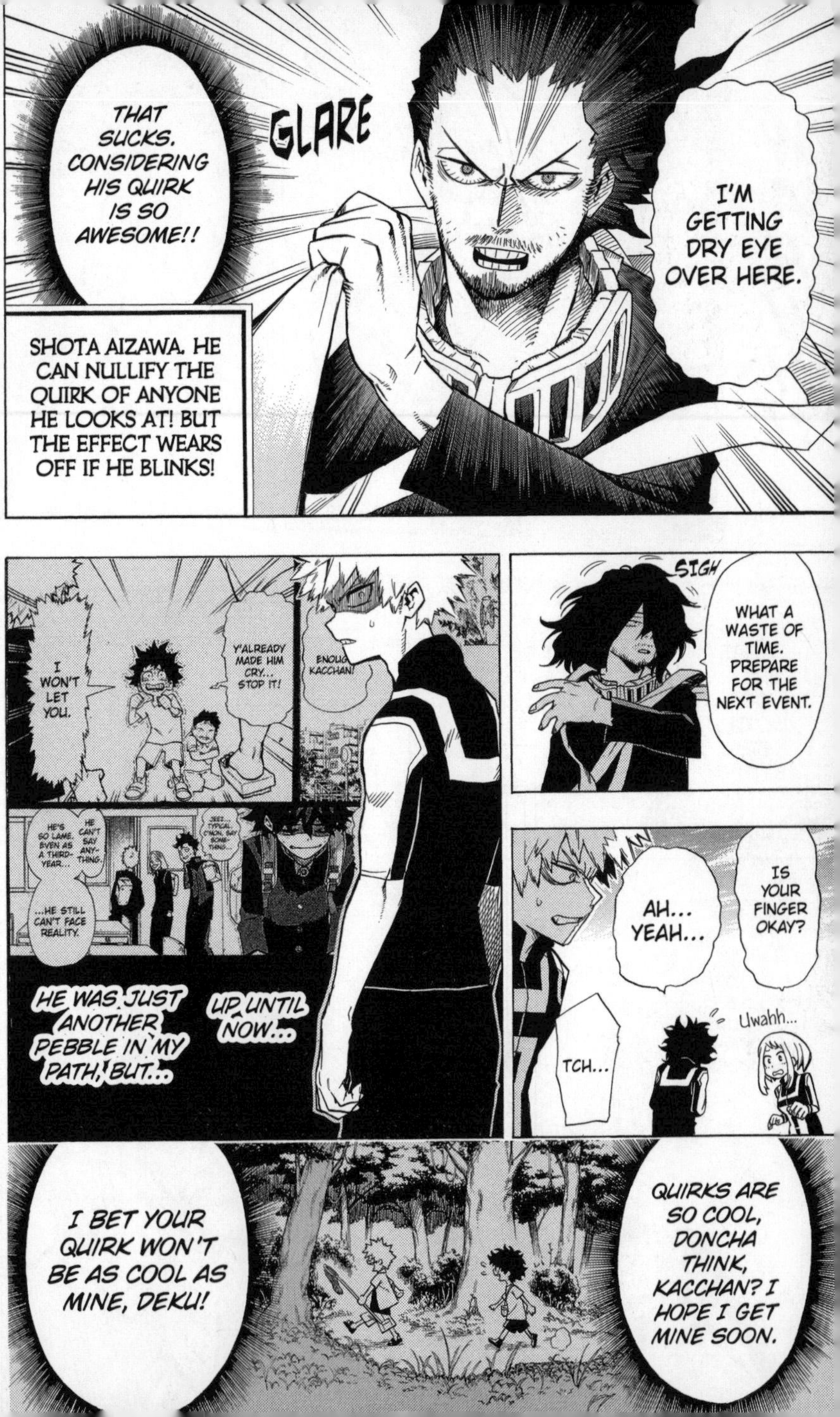
I'M GETTING DRY EYE OVER HERE.
GLARE
THAT SUCKS. CONSIDERING HIS QUIRK IS SO AWESOME!!
SHOTA AIZAWA. HE CAN NULLIFY THE QUIRK OF ANYONE HE LOOKS AT! BUT THE EFFECT WEARS OFF IF HE BLINKS!
SIGH
WHAT A WASTE OF TIME. PREPARE FOR THE NEXT EVENT.
IS YOUR FINGER OKAY?
AH... YEAH...
Uwahh...
TCH...
ENOUG KACCHAN!
Y'ALREADY MADE HIM CRY... STOP IT!
I WON'T LET YOU.
JEEZ... TYPICAL. C'MON, SAY SOME-THING.
HE CAN'T SAY ANY-THING.
HE'S SO LAME. EVEN AS A THIRD-YEAR...
...HE STILL CAN'T FACE REALITY.
HE WAS JUST ANOTHER PEBBLE IN MY PATH, BUT...
UP UNTIL NOW...
QUIRKS ARE SO COOL, DONCHA THINK, KACCHAN? I HOPE I GET MINE SOON.
I BET YOUR QUIRK WON'T BE AS COOL AS MINE, DEKU!

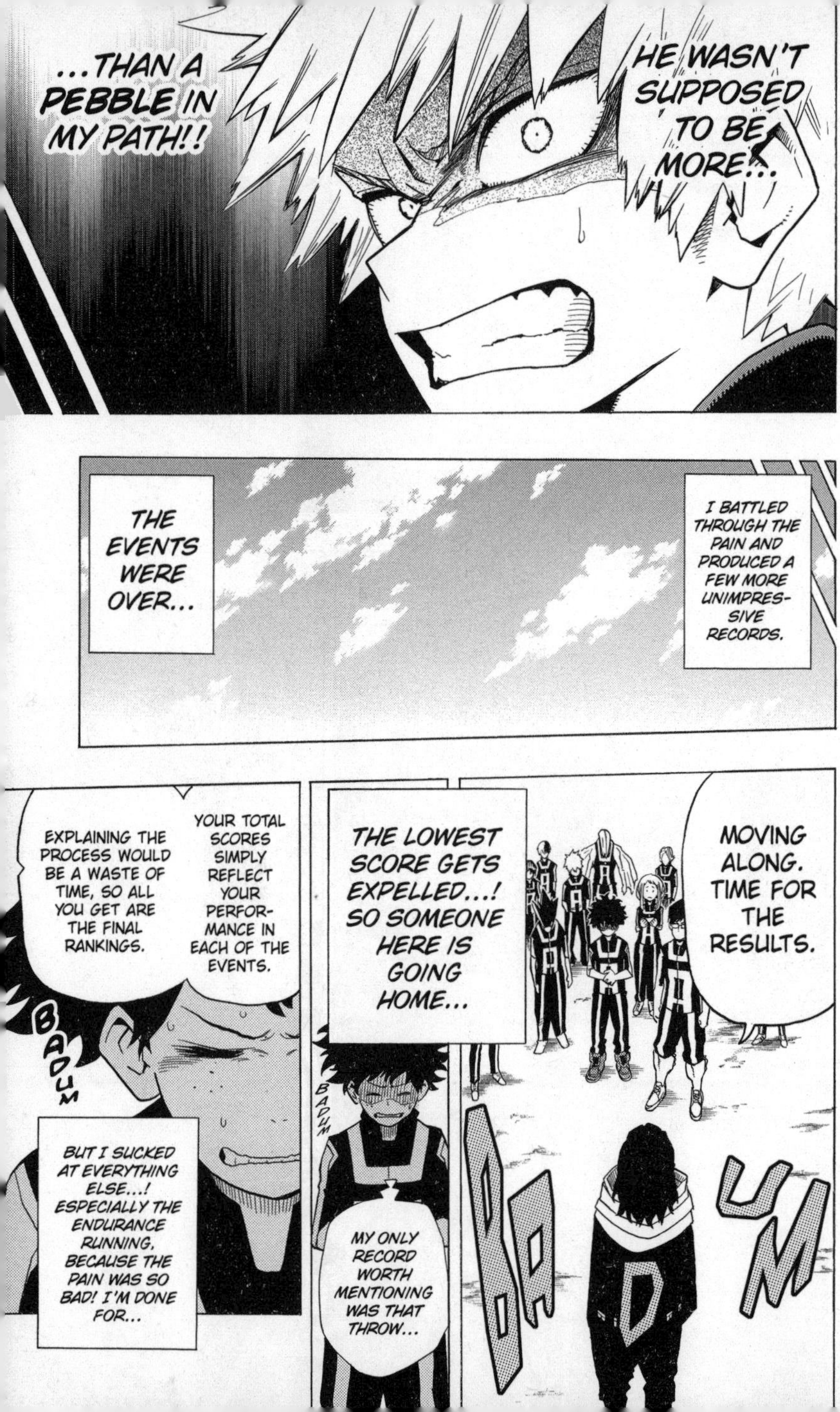
HE WASN'T SUPPOSED TO BE MORE...
...THAN A PEBBLE IN MY PATH!!
I BATTLED THROUGH THE PAIN AND PRODUCED A FEW MORE UNIMPRES-SIVE RECORDS.
THE EVENTS WERE OVER...
MOVING ALONG. TIME FOR THE RESULTS.
THE LOWEST SCORE GETS EXPELLED...! SO SOMEONE HERE IS GOING HOME...
BADUM
MY ONLY RECORD WORTH MENTIONING WAS THAT THROW...
BADUM
YOUR TOTAL SCORES SIMPLY REFLECT YOUR PERFOR-MANCE IN EACH OF THE EVENTS.
EXPLAINING THE PROCESS WOULD BE A WASTE OF TIME, SO ALL YOU GET ARE THE FINAL RANKINGS.
BADUM
BUT I SUCKED AT EVERYTHING ELSE...! ESPECIALLY THE ENDURANCE RUNNING, BECAUSE THE PAIN WAS SO BAD! I'M DONE FOR...

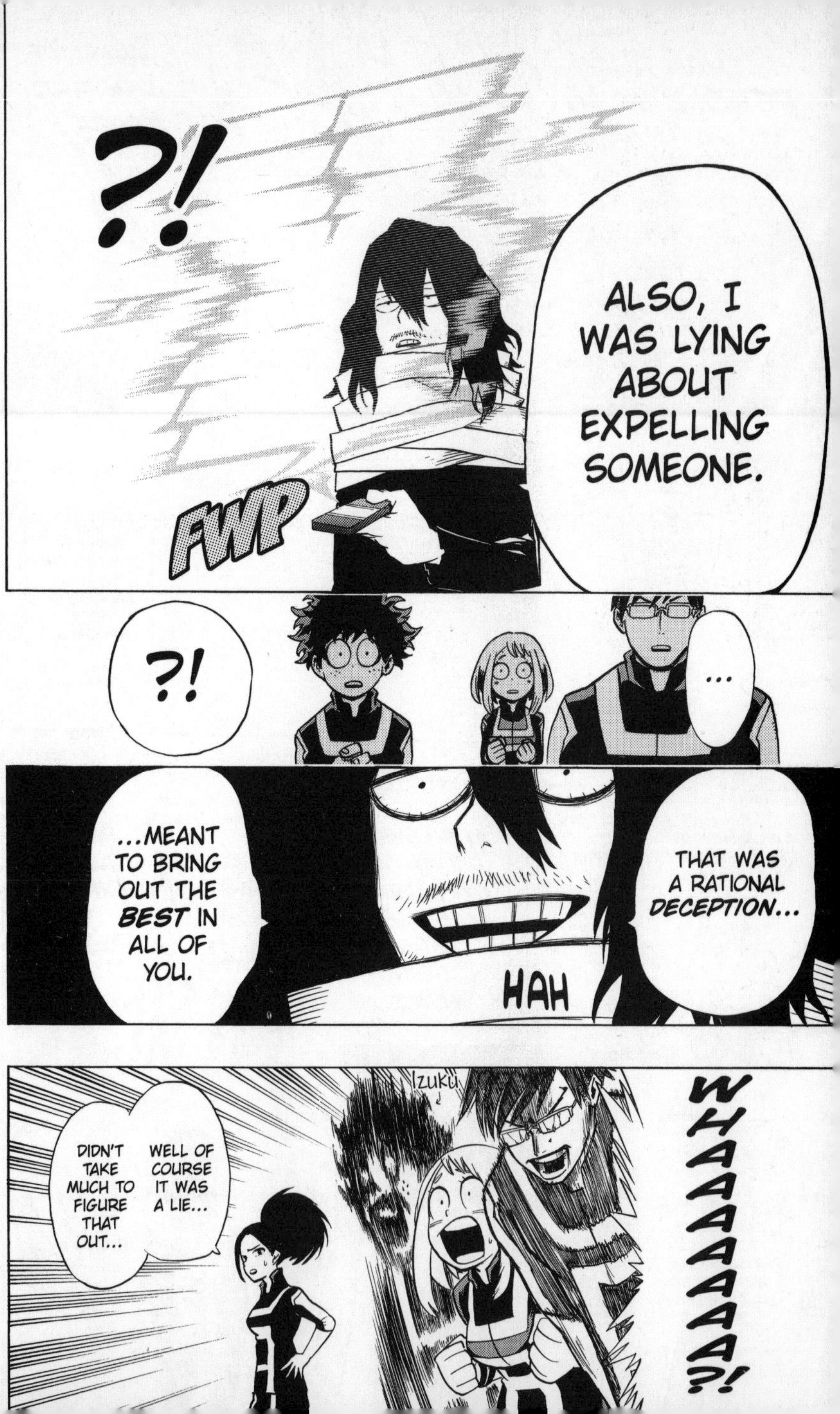
ALSO, I WAS LYING ABOUT EXPELLING SOMEONE.
?!
FWP
...
?!
THAT WAS A RATIONAL DECEPTION...
...MEANT TO BRING OUT THE BEST IN ALL OF YOU.
HAH
WHAAAAAAAAA?!
IZUKU
WELL OF COURSE IT WAS A LIE...
DIDN'T TAKE MUCH TO FIGURE THAT OUT...

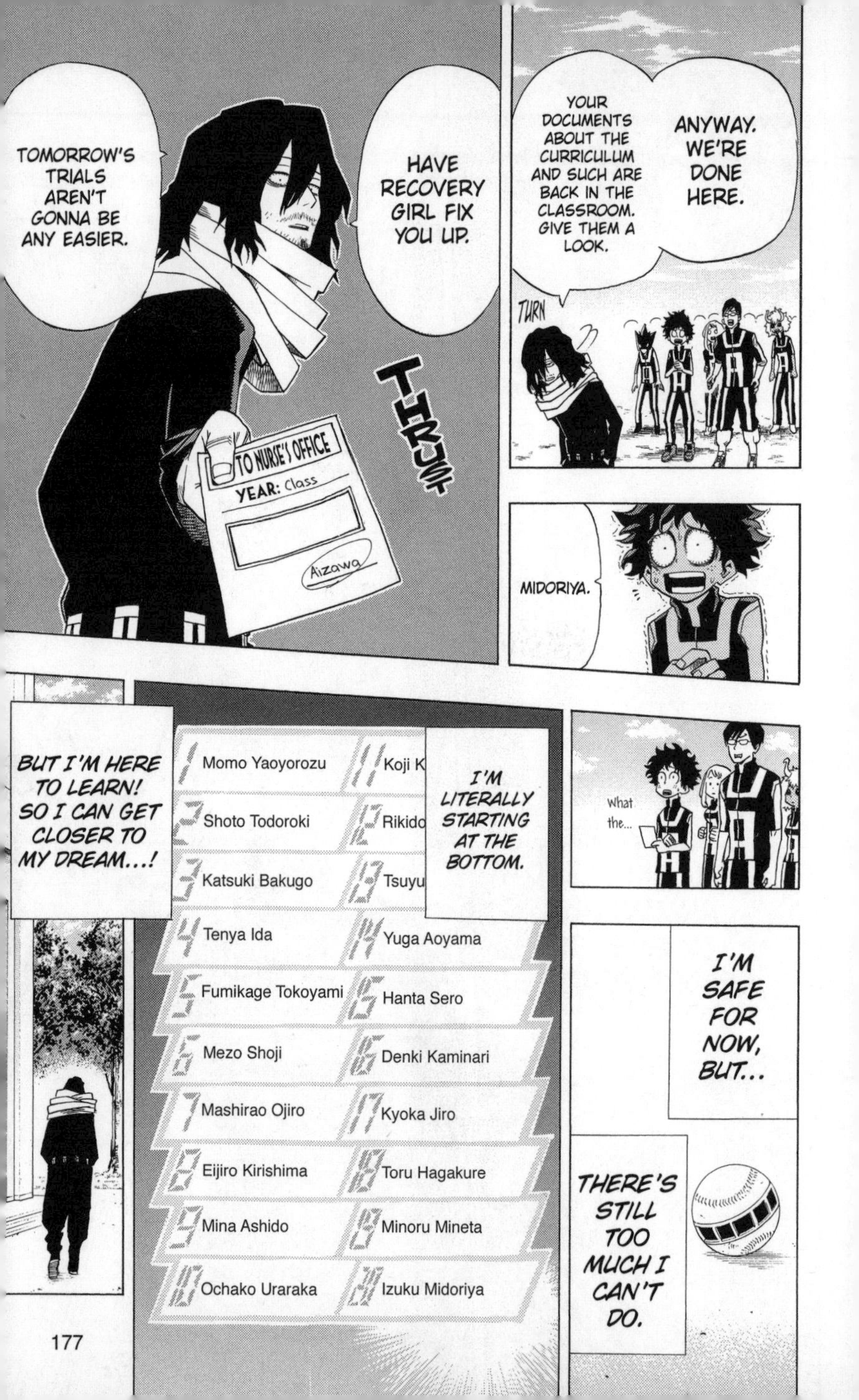
ANYWAY. WE'RE DONE HERE.
YOUR DOCUMENTS ABOUT THE CURRICULUM AND SUCH ARE BACK IN THE CLASSROOM. GIVE THEM A LOOK.
TURN
MIDORIYA.
HAVE RECOVERY GIRL FIX YOU UP.
TOMORROW'S TRIALS AREN'T GONNA BE ANY EASIER.
THRUST
TO NURSE'S OFFICE
YEAR: Class
Aizawa
What the...
I'M SAFE FOR NOW, BUT...
THERE'S STILL TOO MUCH I CAN'T DO.
I'M LITERALLY STARTING AT THE BOTTOM.
1 Momo Yaoyorozu
2 Shoto Todoroki
3 Katsuki Bakugo
4 Tenya Ida
5 Fumikage Tokoyami
6 Mezo Shoji
7 Mashirao Ojiro
8 Eijiro Kirishima
9 Mina Ashido
10 Ochako Uraraka
11 Koji K
12 Rikido
13 Tsuyu
14 Yuga Aoyama
15 Hanta Sero
16 Denki Kaminari
17 Kyoka Jiro
18 Toru Hagakure
19 Minoru Mineta
20 Izuku Midoriya
BUT I'M HERE TO LEARN! SO I CAN GET CLOSER TO MY DREAM...!

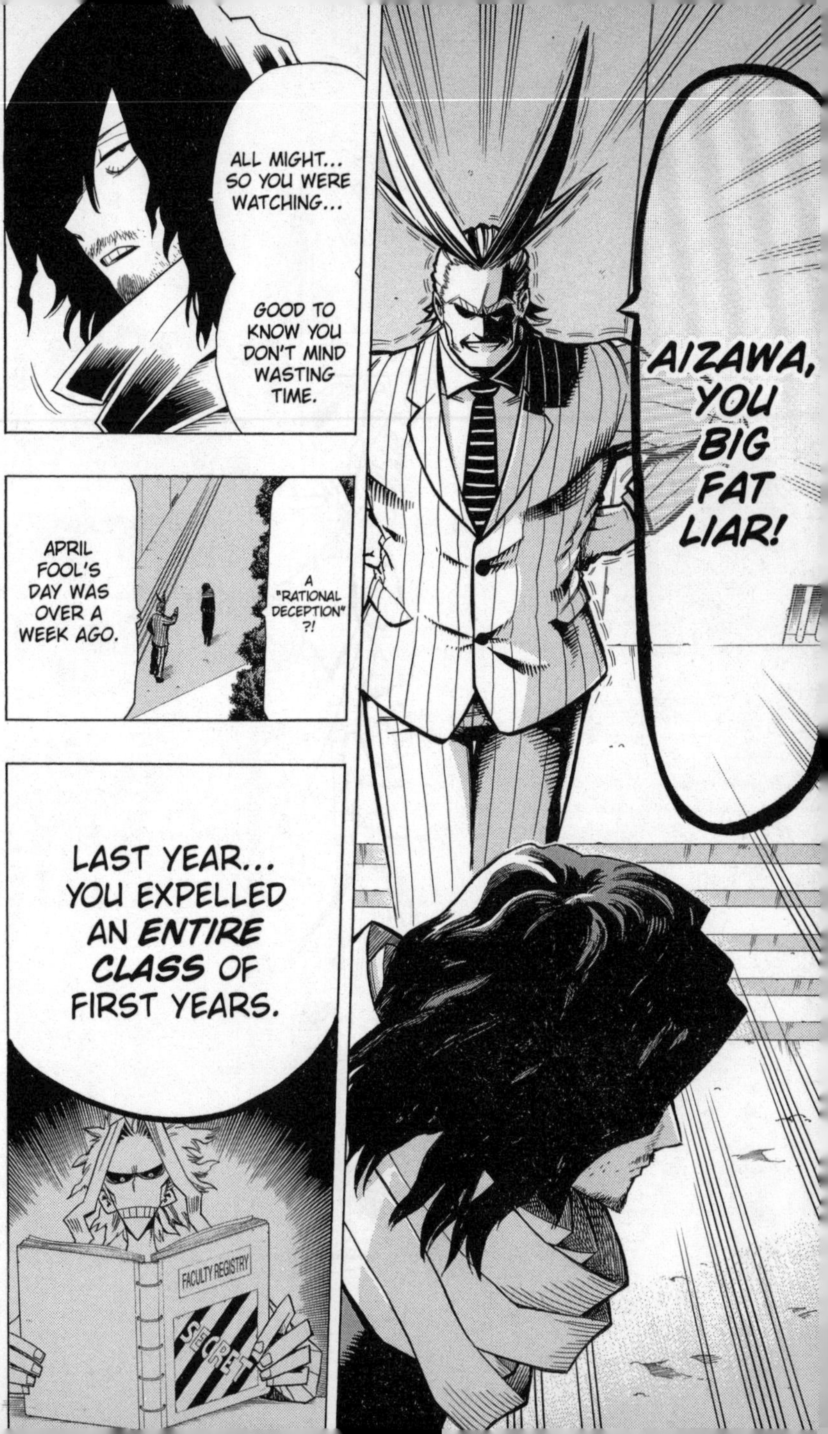
AIZAWA, YOU BIG FAT LIAR!
ALL MIGHT... SO YOU WERE WATCHING...
GOOD TO KNOW YOU DON'T MIND WASTING TIME.
APRIL FOOL'S DAY WAS OVER A WEEK AGO.
A "RATIONAL DECEPTION" ?!
LAST YEAR... YOU EXPELLED AN ENTIRE CLASS OF FIRST YEARS.
FACULTY REGISTRY
SECRET

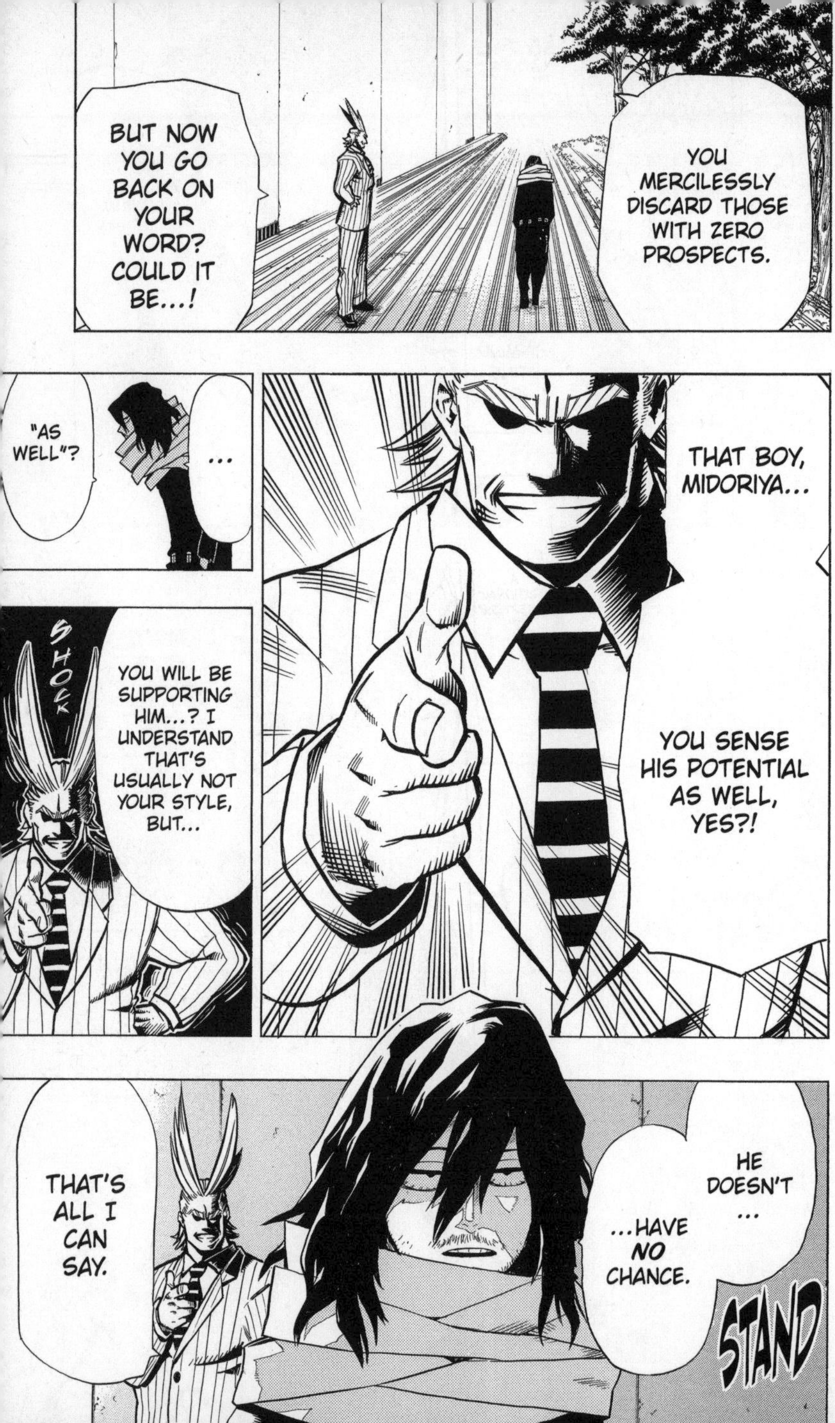
YOU MERCILESSLY DISCARD THOSE WITH ZERO PROSPECTS.
BUT NOW YOU GO BACK ON YOUR WORD? COULD IT BE...!
THAT BOY, MIDORIYA...
YOU SENSE HIS POTENTIAL AS WELL, YES?!
...
"AS WELL"?
SHOCK
YOU WILL BE SUPPORTING HIM...? I UNDERSTAND THAT'S USUALLY NOT YOUR STYLE, BUT...
HE DOESN'T ...
...HAVE NO CHANCE.
STAND
THAT'S ALL I CAN SAY.

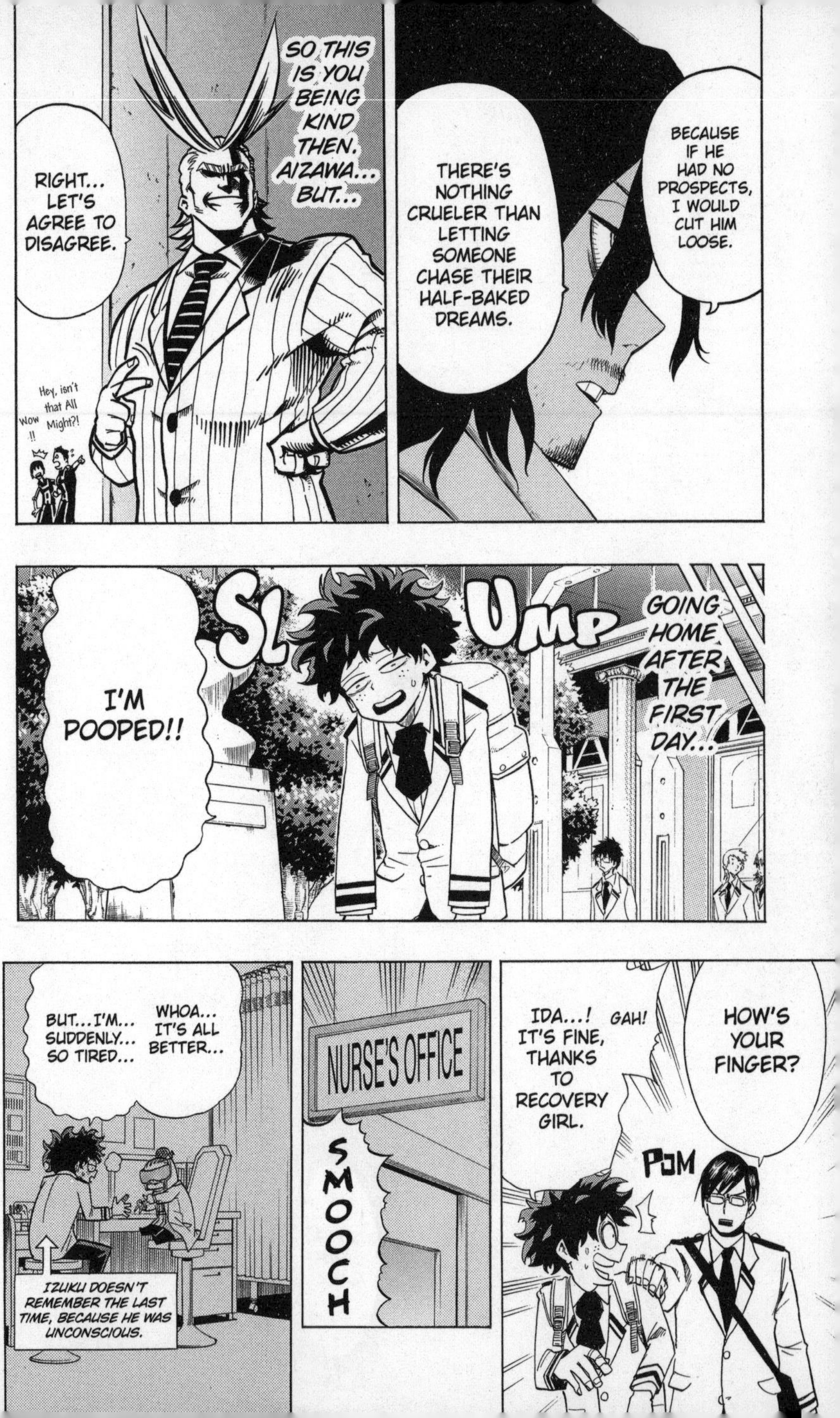
BECAUSE IF HE HAD NO PROSPECTS, I WOULD CUT HIM LOOSE.
THERE'S NOTHING CRUELER THAN LETTING SOMEONE CHASE THEIR HALF-BAKED DREAMS.
SO THIS IS YOU BEING KIND THEN. AIZAWA... BUT...
RIGHT... LET'S AGREE TO DISAGREE.
Hey, isn't that All Might?!
Wow !!
GOING HOME AFTER THE FIRST DAY...
SLUMP
I'M POOPED!!
HOW'S YOUR FINGER?
GAH!
IDA...! IT'S FINE, THANKS TO RECOVERY GIRL.
PJM
NURSE'S OFFICE
SMOOCH
WHOA... IT'S ALL BETTER...
BUT...I'M... SUDDENLY... SO TIRED...
IZUKU DOESN'T REMEMBER THE LAST TIME, BECAUSE HE WAS UNCONSCIOUS.

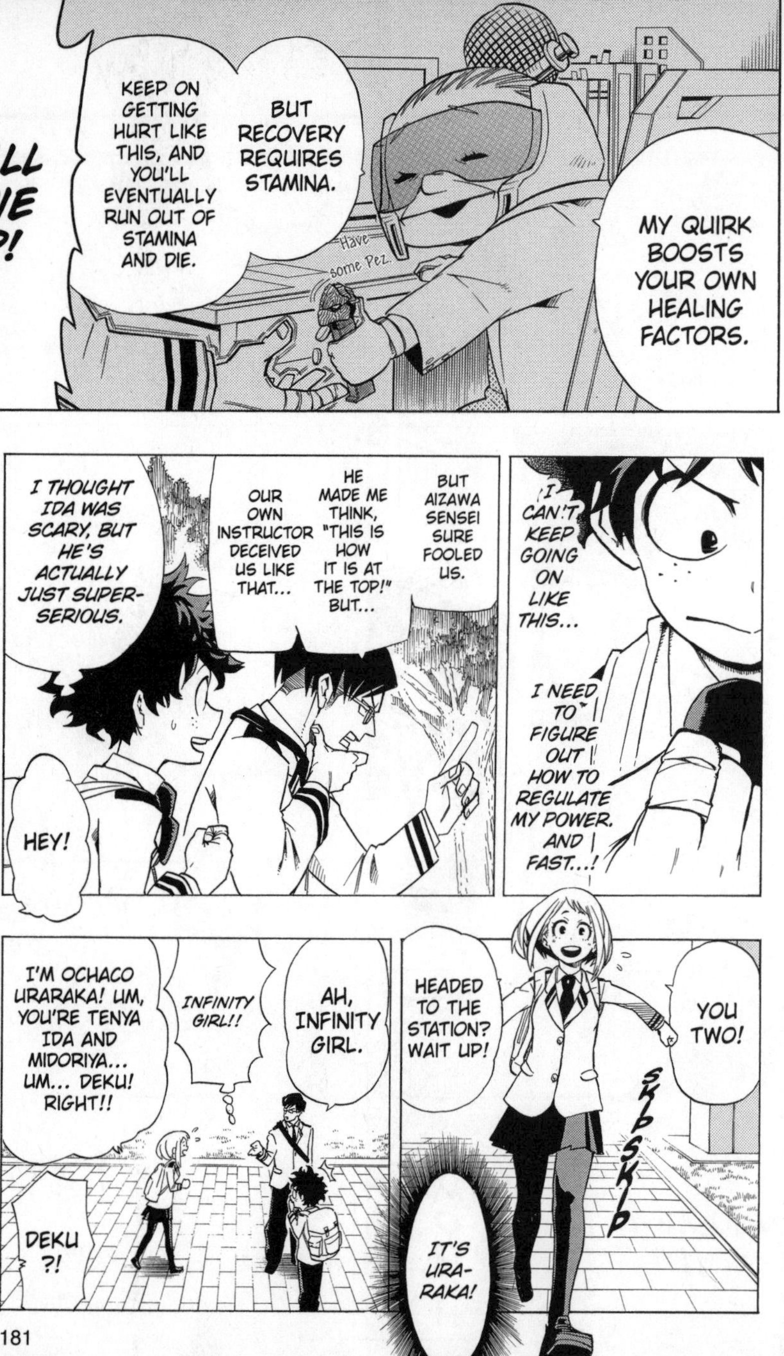
MY QUIRK BOOSTS YOUR OWN HEALING FACTORS.
BUT RECOVERY REQUIRES STAMINA.
KEEP ON GETTING HURT LIKE THIS, AND YOU'LL EVENTUALLY RUN OUT OF STAMINA AND DIE.
Have some Pez.
I'LL DIE ?!
I CAN'T KEEP GOING ON LIKE THIS...
I NEED TO FIGURE OUT HOW TO REGULATE MY POWER. AND FAST...!
BUT AIZAWA SENSEI SURE FOOLED US.
HE MADE ME THINK, "THIS IS HOW IT IS AT THE TOP!" BUT...
OUR OWN INSTRUCTOR DECEIVED US LIKE THAT...
I THOUGHT IDA WAS SCARY, BUT HE'S ACTUALLY JUST SUPER-SERIOUS.
HEY!
YOU TWO!
SKIPSKIP
HEADED TO THE STATION? WAIT UP!
IT'S URA-RAKA!
AH, INFINITY GIRL.
INFINITY GIRL!!
I'M OCHACO URARAKA! UM, YOU'RE TENYA IDA AND MIDORIYA... UM... DEKU! RIGHT!!
DEKU ?!

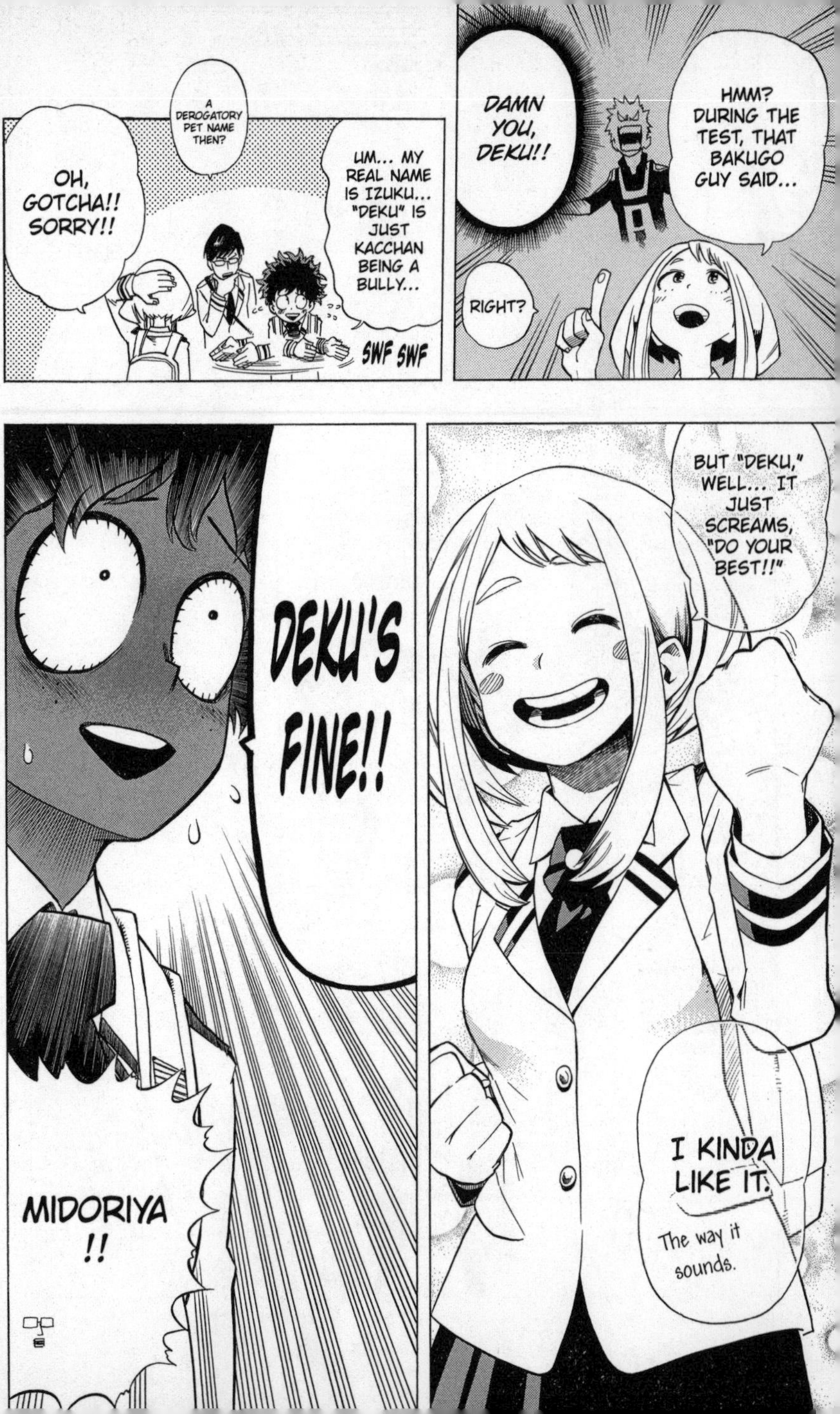
HMM? DURING THE TEST, THAT BAKUGO GUY SAID...
DAMN YOU, DEKU!!
RIGHT?
UM... MY REAL NAME IS IZUKU... "DEKU" IS JUST KACCHAN BEING A BULLY...
SWF SWF
A DEROGATORY PET NAME THEN?
OH, GOTCHA!! SORRY!!
BUT "DEKU," WELL... IT JUST SCREAMS, "DO YOUR BEST!!"
I KINDA LIKE IT.
The way it sounds.
DEKU'S FINE!!
MIDORIYA !!

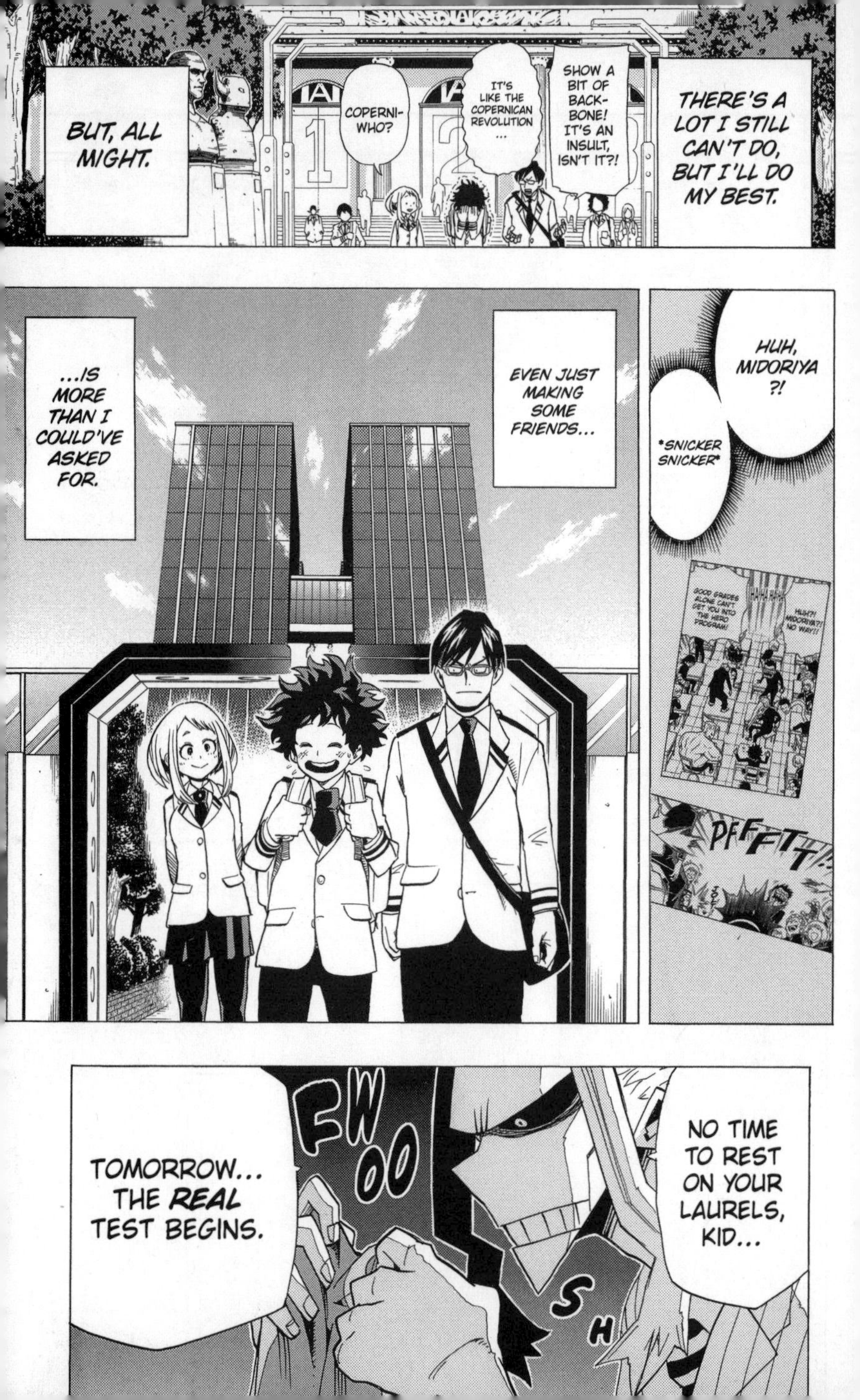
THERE'S A LOT I STILL CAN'T DO, BUT I'LL DO MY BEST.
SHOW A BIT OF BACK-BONE! IT'S AN INSULT, ISN'T IT?!
IT'S LIKE THE COPERNICAN REVOLUTION...
COPERNI-WHO?
BUT, ALL MIGHT.
HUH, MIDORIYA ?!
SNICKER SNICKER
HUH?! MIDORIYA?! NO WAY!!
GOOD GRADES ALONE CAN'T GET YOU INTO THE HERO PROGRAM!
HAHAHA
PFFFTT
EVEN JUST MAKING SOME FRIENDS...
...IS MORE THAN I COULD'VE ASKED FOR.
NO TIME TO REST ON YOUR LAURELS, KID...
TOMORROW... THE REAL TEST BEGINS.
FWOOSH

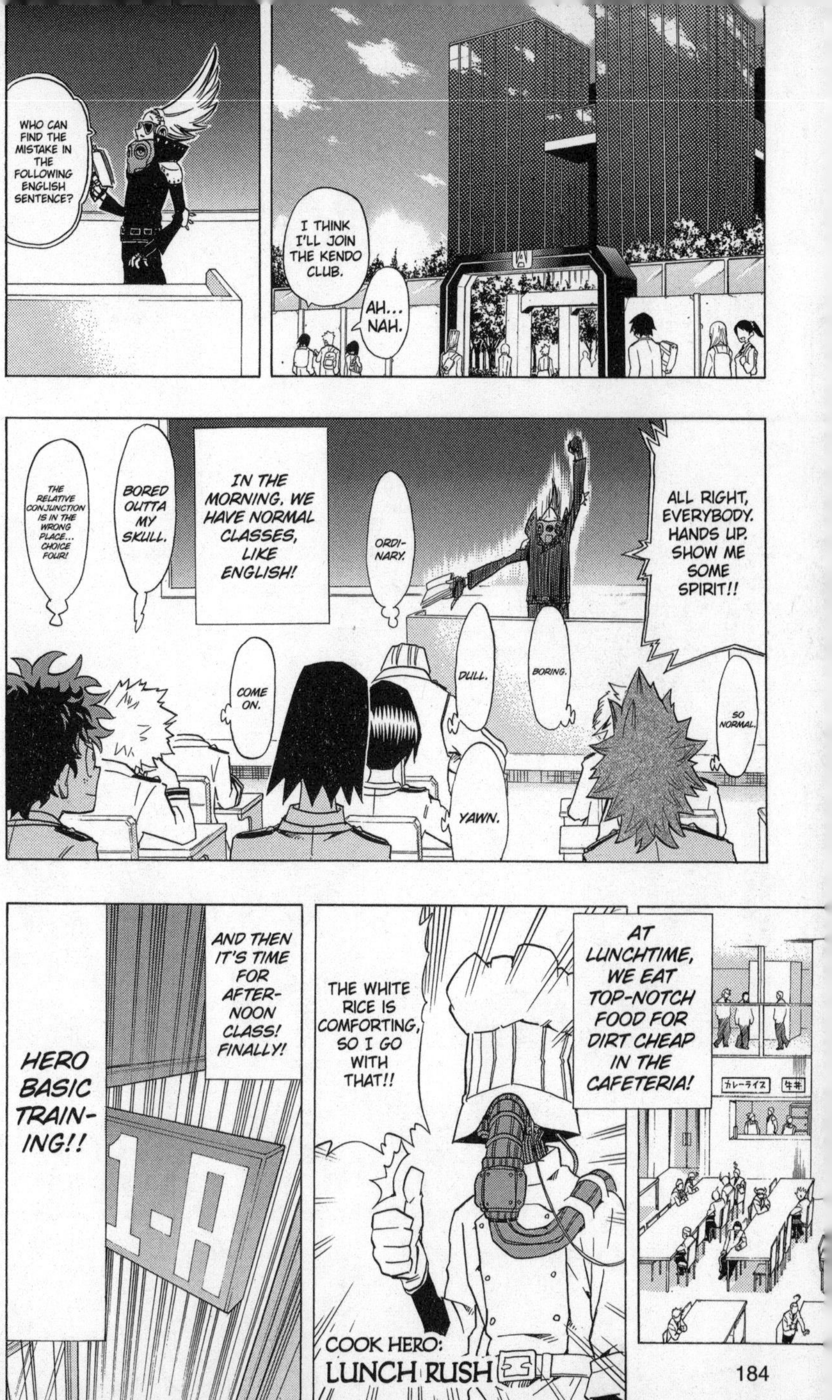
I THINK I'LL JOIN THE KENDO CLUB.
AH... NAH.
WHO CAN FIND THE MISTAKE IN THE FOLLOWING ENGLISH SENTENCE?
ALL RIGHT, EVERYBODY. HANDS UP. SHOW ME SOME SPIRIT!!
SO NORMAL.
BORING.
DULL.
YAWN.
ORDI-NARY.
COME ON.
IN THE MORNING, WE HAVE NORMAL CLASSES, LIKE ENGLISH!
BORED OUTTA MY SKULL.
THE RELATIVE CONJUNCTION IS IN THE WRONG PLACE... CHOICE FOUR!
AT LUNCHTIME, WE EAT TOP-NOTCH FOOD FOR DIRT CHEAP IN THE CAFETERIA!
カレーライス
牛丼
THE WHITE RICE IS COMFORTING, SO I GO WITH THAT!!
COOK HERO: LUNCH RUSH
AND THEN IT'S TIME FOR AFTER-NOON CLASS! FINALLY!
HERO BASIC TRAIN-ING!!
1-A

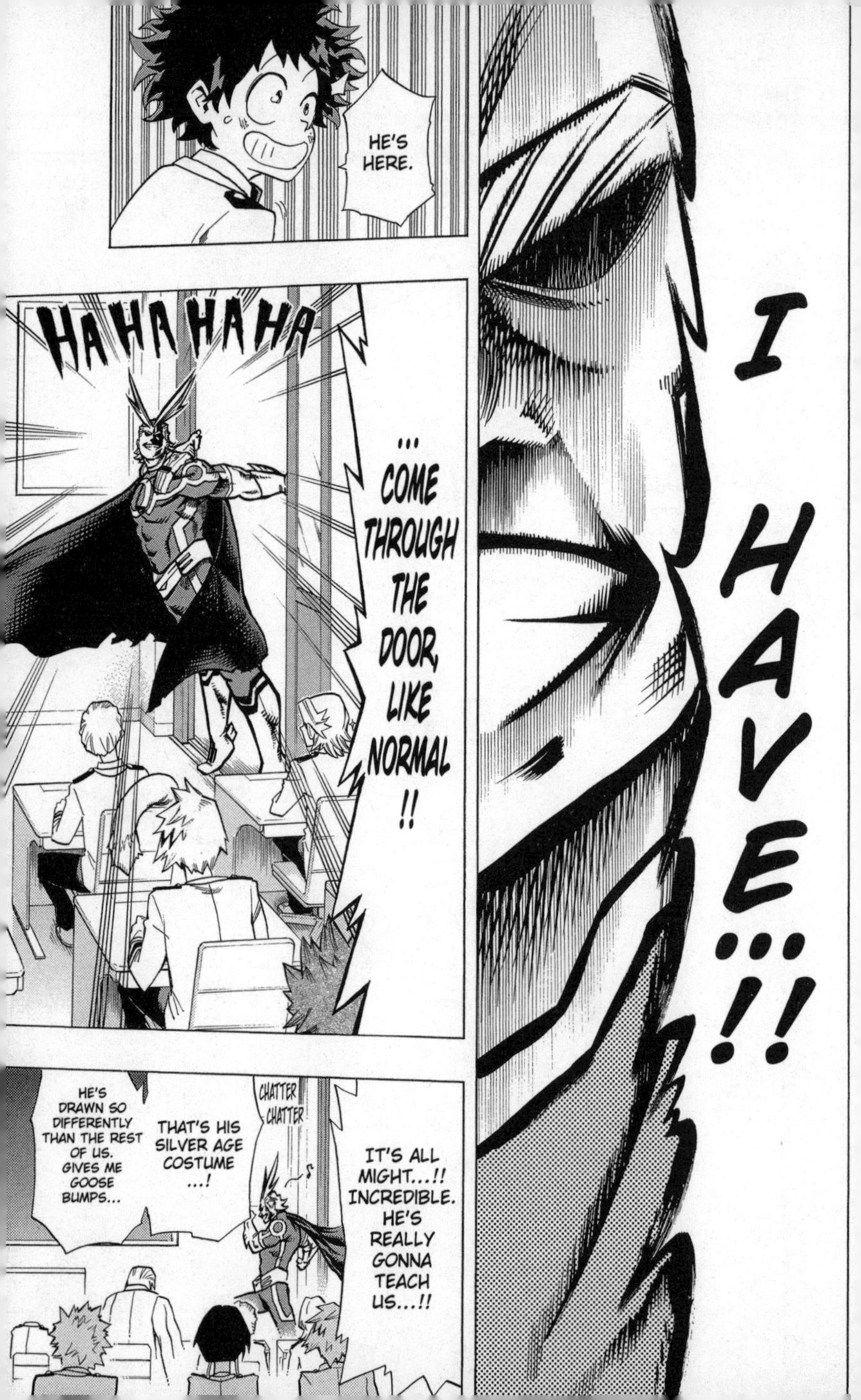
I HAVE...!!
HE'S HERE.
HAHAHAHAHA
...COME THROUGH THE DOOR, LIKE NORMAL!!
IT'S ALL MIGHT...!! INCREDIBLE. HE'S REALLY GONNA TEACH US...!!
CHATTER CHATTER
THAT'S HIS SILVER AGE COSTUME...!
HE'S DRAWN SO DIFFERENTLY THAN THE REST OF US. GIVES ME GOOSE BUMPS...

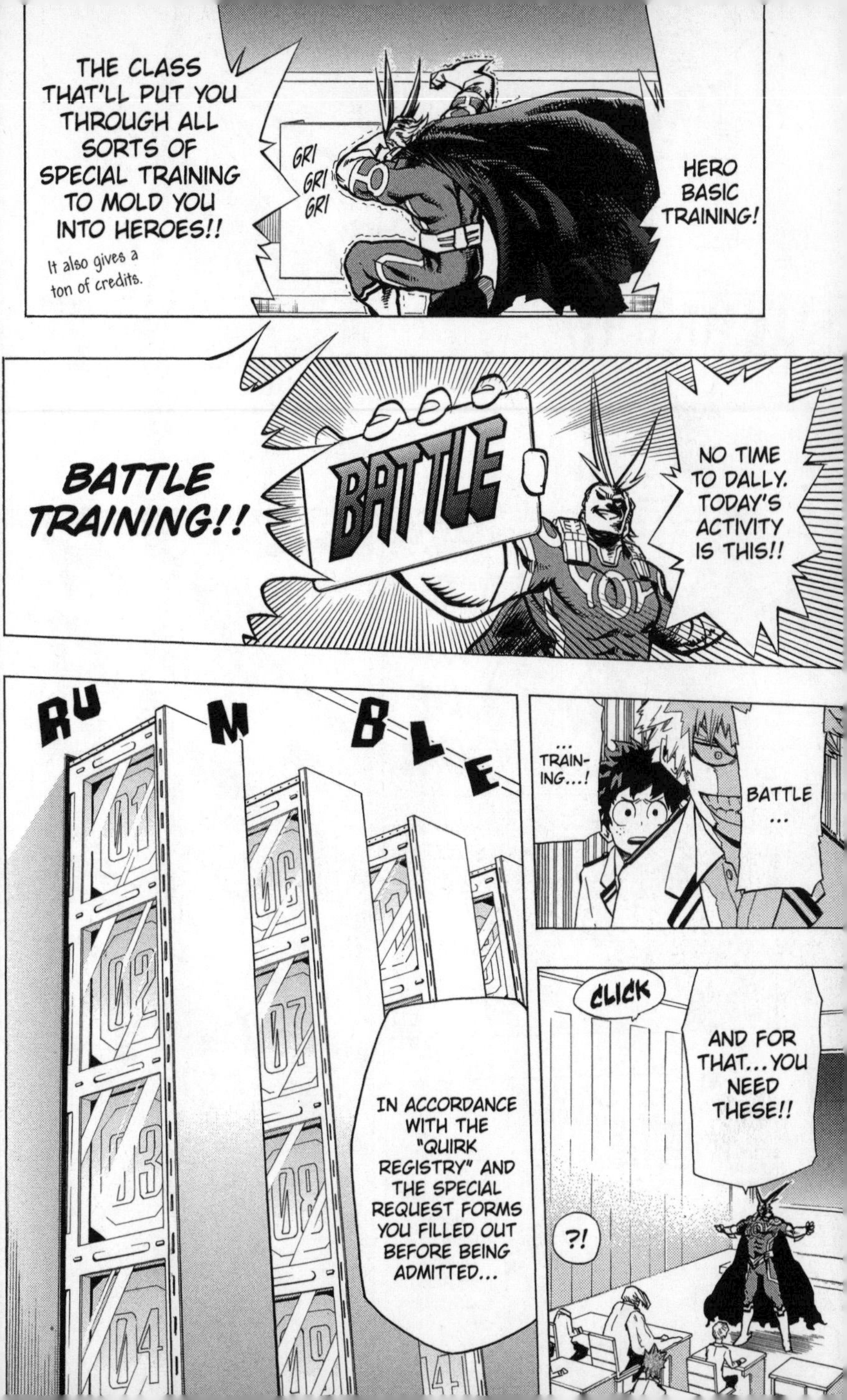
HERO BASIC TRAINING!
THE CLASS THAT'LL PUT YOU THROUGH ALL SORTS OF SPECIAL TRAINING TO MOLD YOU INTO HEROES!!
GRI GRI GRI
It also gives a ton of credits.
NO TIME TO DALLY. TODAY'S ACTIVITY IS THIS!!
BATTLE
BATTLE TRAINING!!
BATTLE ...
...TRAIN-ING...!
CLICK
AND FOR THAT...YOU NEED THESE!!
?!
RUMBLE
IN ACCORDANCE WITH THE "QUIRK REGISTRY" AND THE SPECIAL REQUEST FORMS YOU FILLED OUT BEFORE BEING ADMITTED...

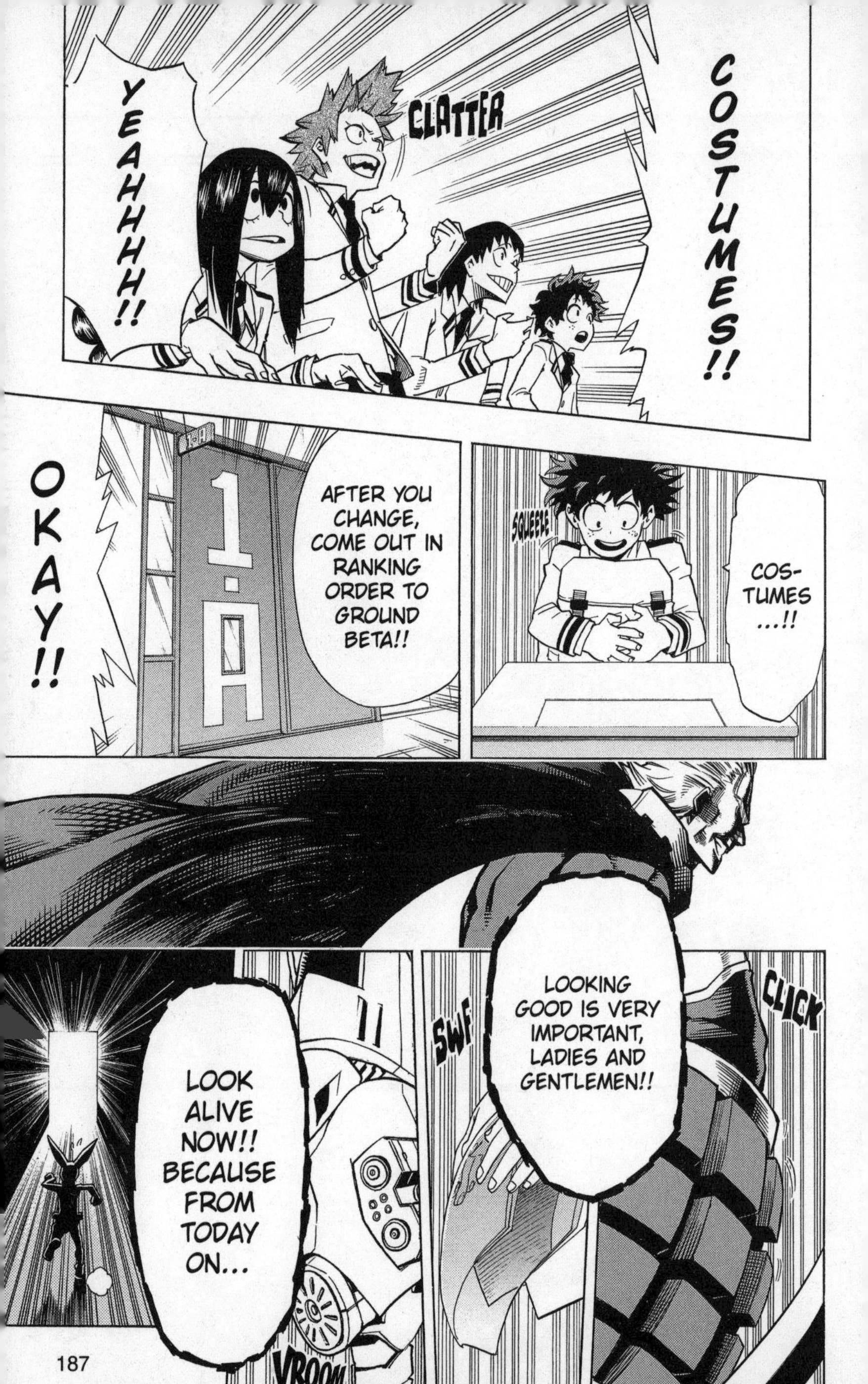
COSTUMES!!
CLATTER
YEAHHHHH!!
COS-
TUMES
...!!
SQUEEZE
AFTER YOU CHANGE, COME OUT IN RANKING ORDER TO GROUND BETA!!
OKAY!!
CLICK
LOOKING GOOD IS VERY IMPORTANT, LADIES AND GENTLEMEN!!
SWF
LOOK ALIVE NOW!! BECAUSE FROM TODAY ON...
VROOM

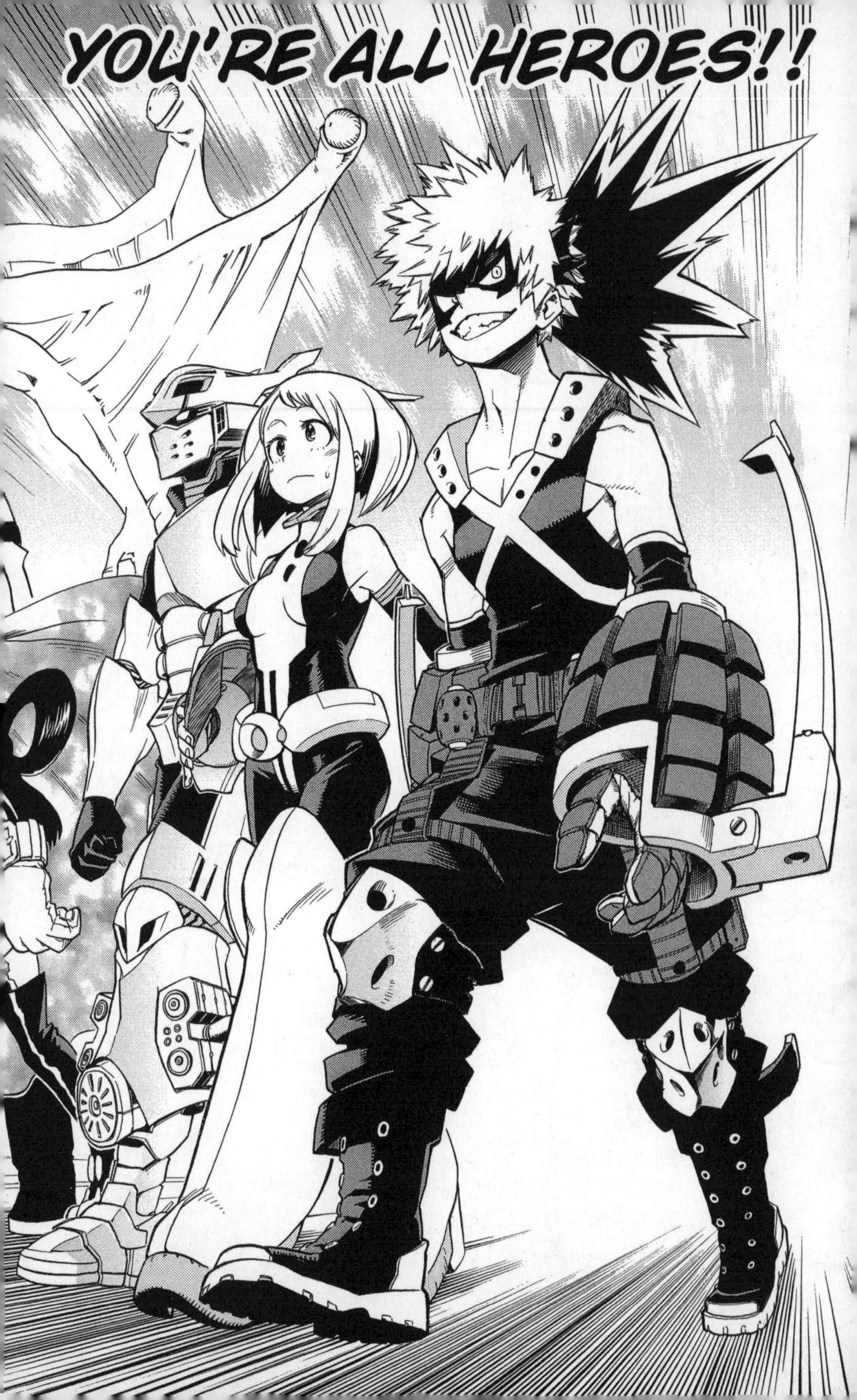
YOU'RE ALL HEROES!!

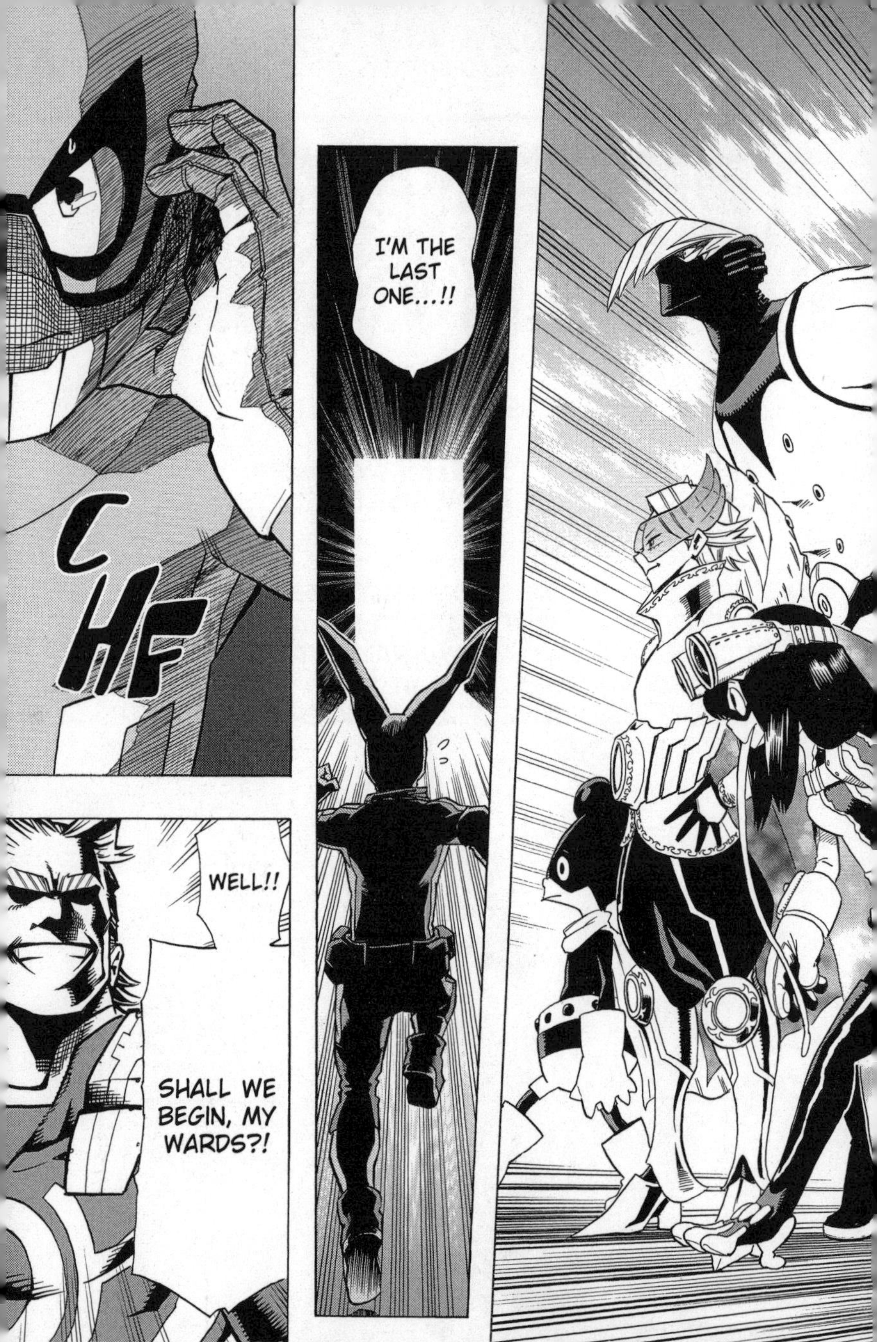
I'M THE LAST ONE...!!
CHF
WELL!!
SHALL WE BEGIN, MY WARDS?!

VOLUME 1 – IZUKU MIDORIYA: ORIGIN (END)

AFTERWORD

THANK YOU FOR READING VOLUME 1.

THIS IS A STORY I'VE BEEN WANTING TO DO FOR A WHILE, SO I'M REALLY GLAD IT GOT SERIALIZED.

THE NEXT VOLUME IS GOING TO SEE AN EXPLOSION OF NEW CHARACTERS, AND I'LL KEEP WRACKING MY BRAIN AND ABUSING MY RIGHT HAND AT FULL THROTTLE TO MAKE IT A FUN EXPERIENCE FOR EVERYONE.

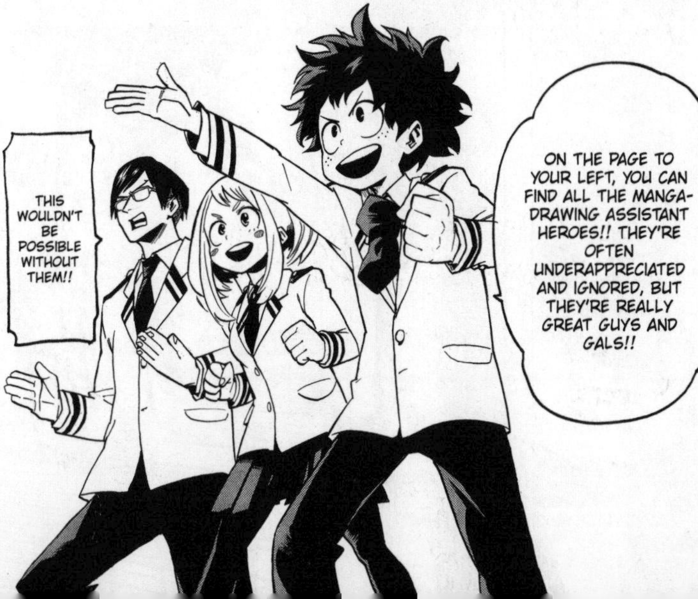
ON THE PAGE TO YOUR LEFT, YOU CAN FIND ALL THE MANGA-DRAWING ASSISTANT HEROES!! THEY'RE OFTEN UNDERAPPRECIATED AND IGNORED, BUT THEY'RE REALLY GREAT GUYS AND GALS!!
THIS WOULDN'T BE POSSIBLE WITHOUT THEM!!

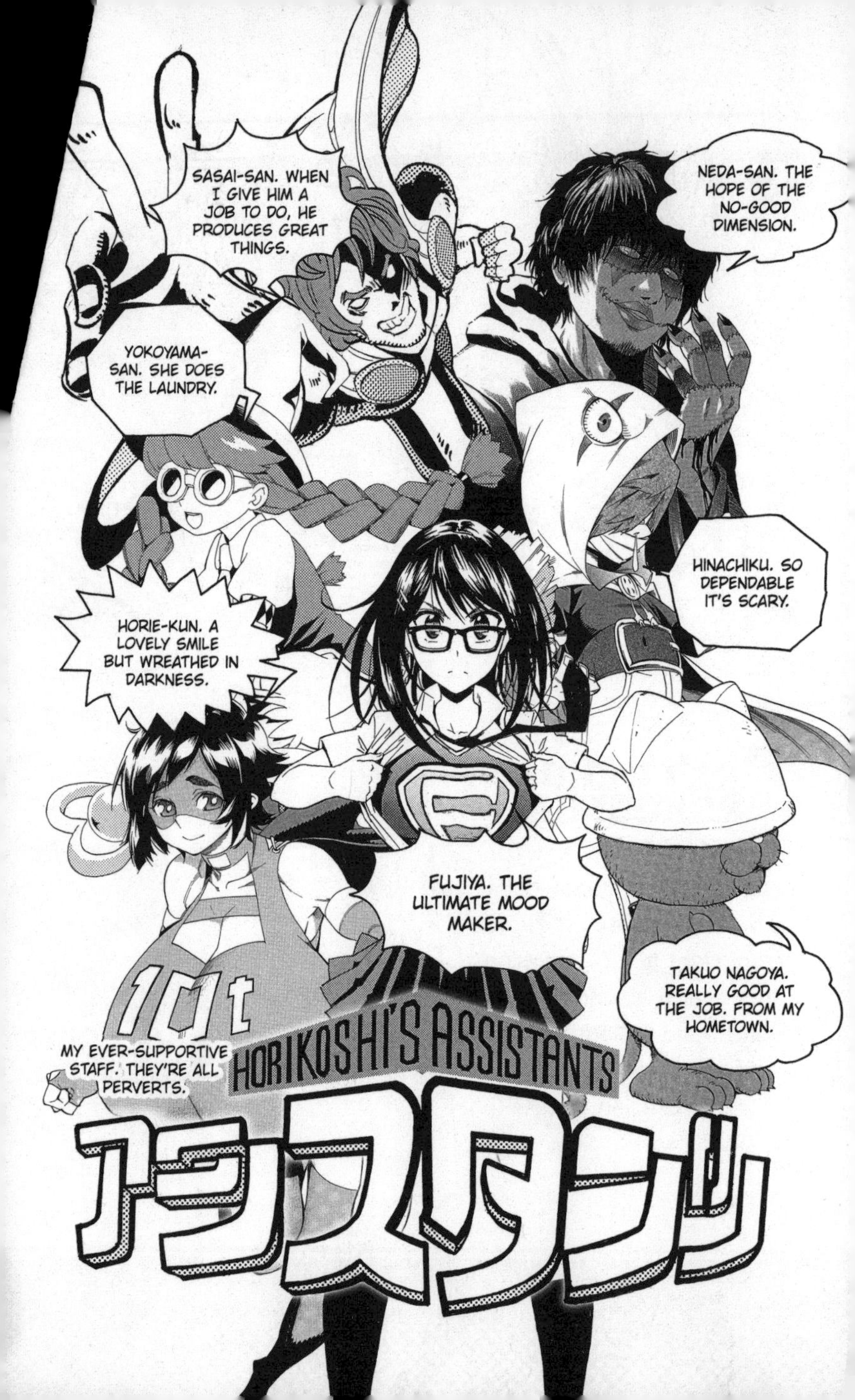
NEDA-SAN. THE HOPE OF THE NO-GOOD DIMENSION.
SASAI-SAN. WHEN I GIVE HIM A JOB TO DO, HE PRODUCES GREAT THINGS.
YOKOYAMA-SAN. SHE DOES THE LAUNDRY.
HINACHIKU. SO DEPENDABLE IT'S SCARY.
HORIE-KUN. A LOVELY SMILE BUT WREATHED IN DARKNESS.
FUJIYA. THE ULTIMATE MOOD MAKER.
TAKUO NAGOYA. REALLY GOOD AT THE JOB. FROM MY HOMETOWN.
10t
MY EVER-SUPPORTIVE STAFF. THEY'RE ALL PERVERTS.
HORIKOSHI'S ASSISTANTS
アシスタンツ

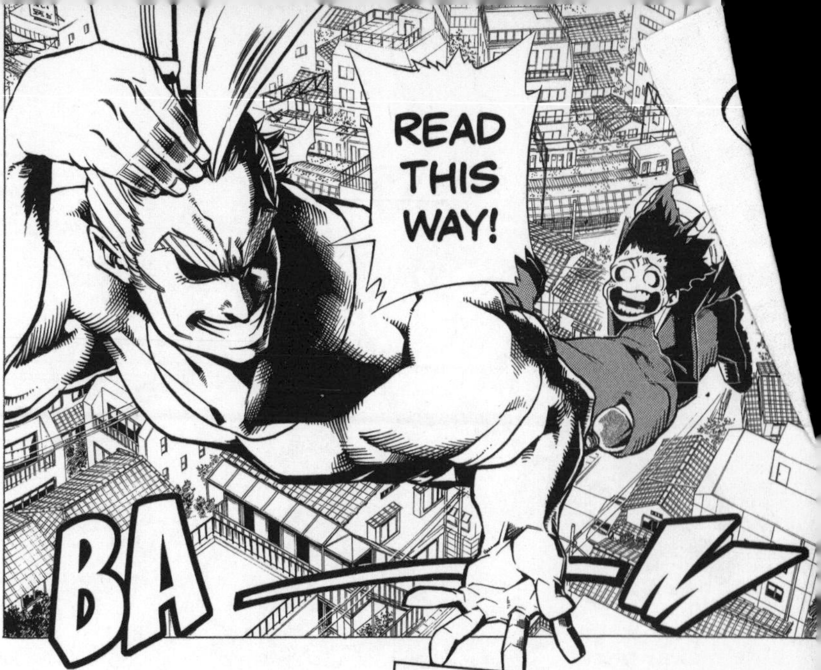
READ THIS WAY!
BA-M

MY HERO ACADEMIA

reads from right to left, starting in the upper-right corner. Japanese is read from right to left, meaning that action, sound effects and word-balloon order are completely reversed from English order.

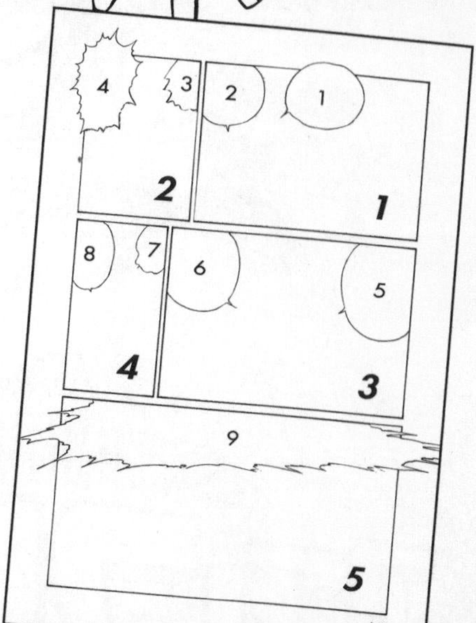
1
2
3
4
5
1
2
3
4
5
6
7
8
9
142